D0325043

Volume 3

Story by Emily Rodda

Illustrated by Makoto Niwano

Translated by Mayumi Kobayashi

Lettered by Wilson Ramos Jr.

KC
KODANSHA
COMICS

ST. JOHN THE BAPTIST PARISH LIBRARY
2020 NEW HIGHWAY 51
LAPLACE, LOUISIANA 70068

Deltora Quest volume 3, is a work of fiction. Names, characters, places, and incidents are the products of the author's imagination or are used fictitiously. Any resemblance to actual events, locales, or persons, living or dead, is entirely coincidental.

Original story by Emily Rodda

A Kodansha Comics Trade Paperback Original

Deltora Quest volume 3 copyright © 2006 Makoto Niwano © 2006 DELTORA QUEST PARTNERS
English translation copyright © 2011 Makoto Niwano © 2011 DELTORA QUEST PARTNERS

All rights reserved.

Published in the United States by Kodansha Comics, an imprint of Kodansha USA Publishing, LLC, New York.

Publication rights for this English edition arranged through Kodansha Ltd., Tokyo.

First published in Japan in 2006 by Kodansha Ltd., Tokyo.

ISBN 978-1-935429-30-2

Printed in the United States of America

www.kodanshacomics.com

9 8 7 6 5 4 3 2 1

Translator: Alethea Nibley and Athena Nibley
Lettering: Wilson Ramos Jr.

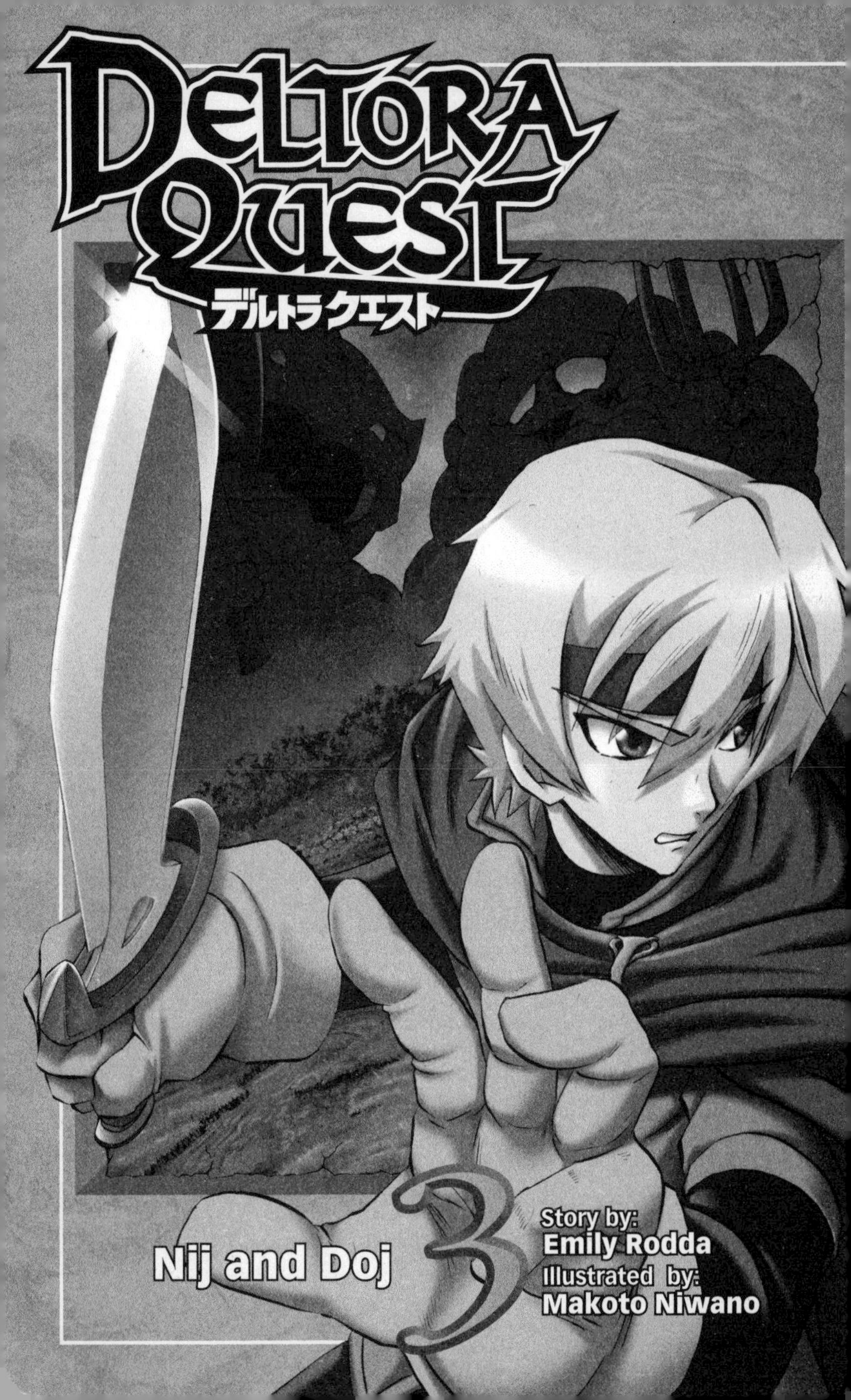
Deltora Quest
デルトラクエスト
3
Nij and Doj
Story by:
Emily Rodda
Illustrated by:
Makoto Niwano

DELTORA QUEST
デルトラクエスト

Volume 3: Character Introduction

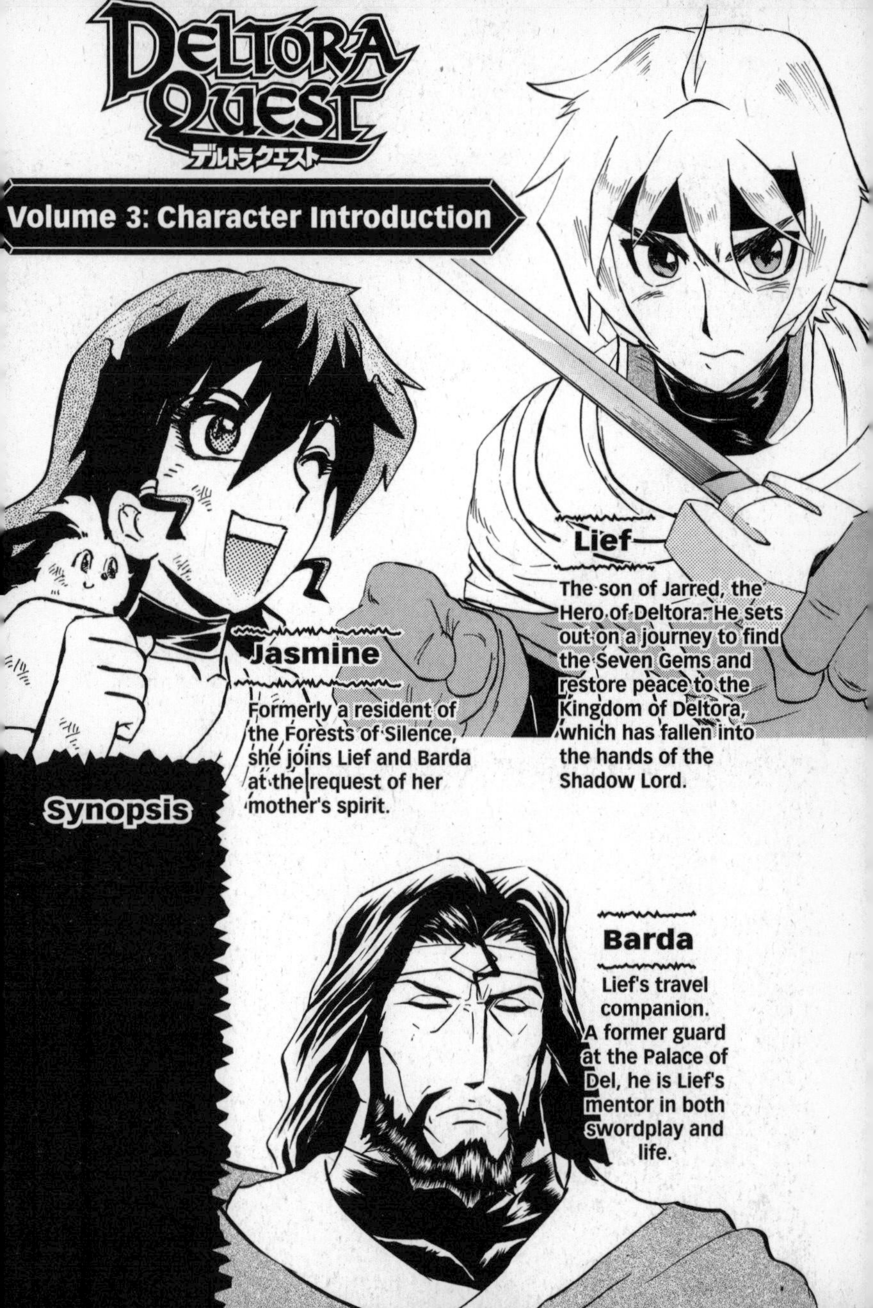

Lief

The son of Jarred, the Hero of Deltora. He sets out on a journey to find the Seven Gems and restore peace to the Kingdom of Deltora, which has fallen into the hands of the Shadow Lord.

Jasmine

Formerly a resident of the Forests of Silence, she joins Lief and Barda at the request of her mother's spirit.

Synopsis

Barda

Lief's travel companion. A former guard at the Palace of Del, he is Lief's mentor in both swordplay and life.

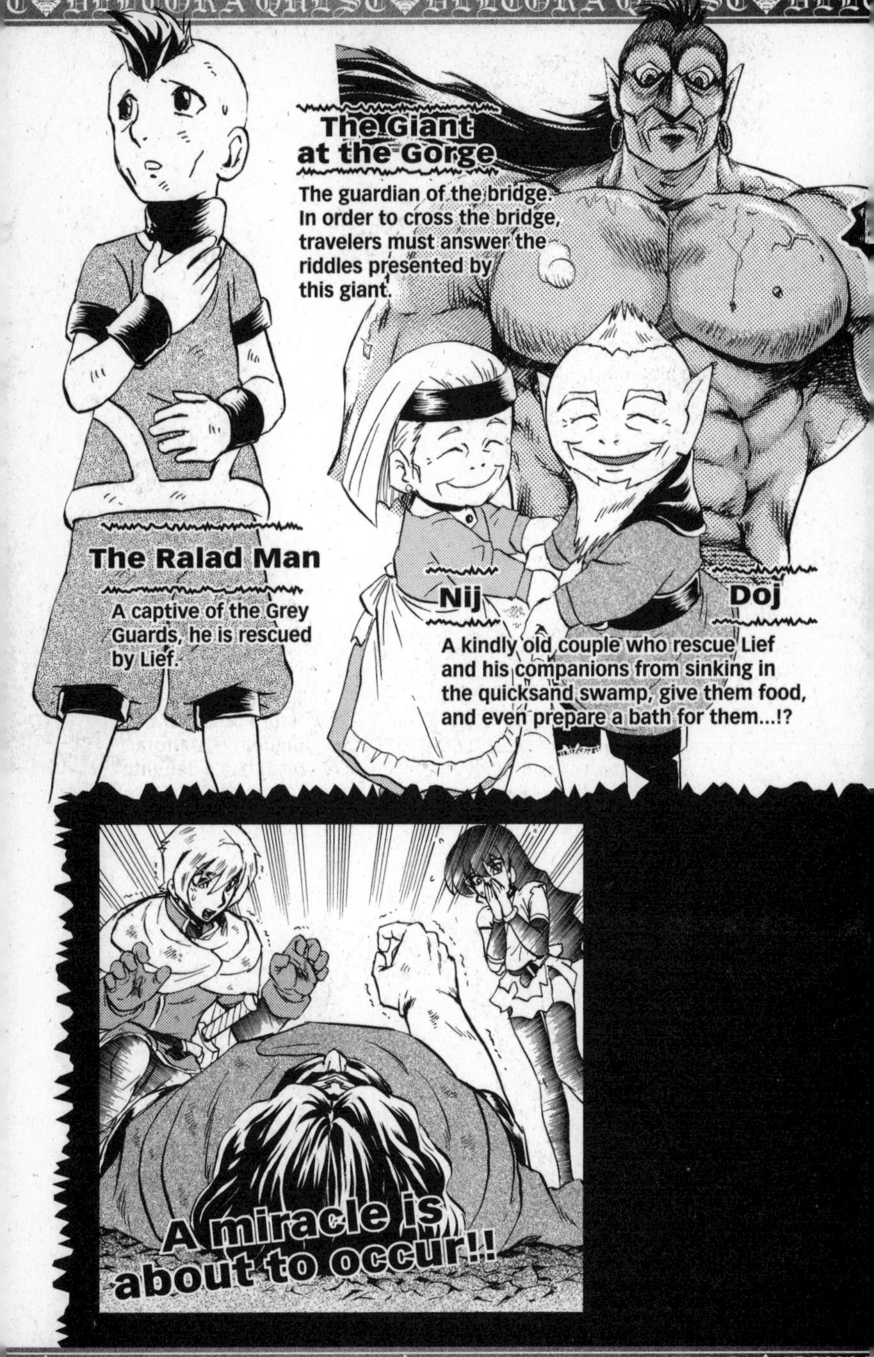
The Giant at the Gorge
The guardian of the bridge. In order to cross the bridge, travelers must answer the riddles presented by this giant.
The Ralad Man
A captive of the Grey Guards, he is rescued by Lief.
Doj
Nij
A kindly old couple who rescue Lief and his companions from sinking in the quicksand swamp, give them food, and even prepare a bath for them...!?
A miracle is about to occur!!

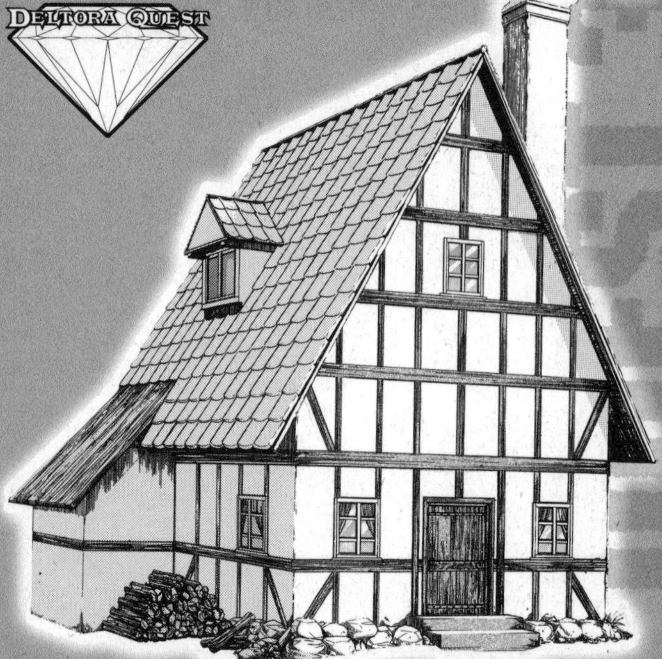
DELTORA QUEST

Volume 3: Table Of Contents

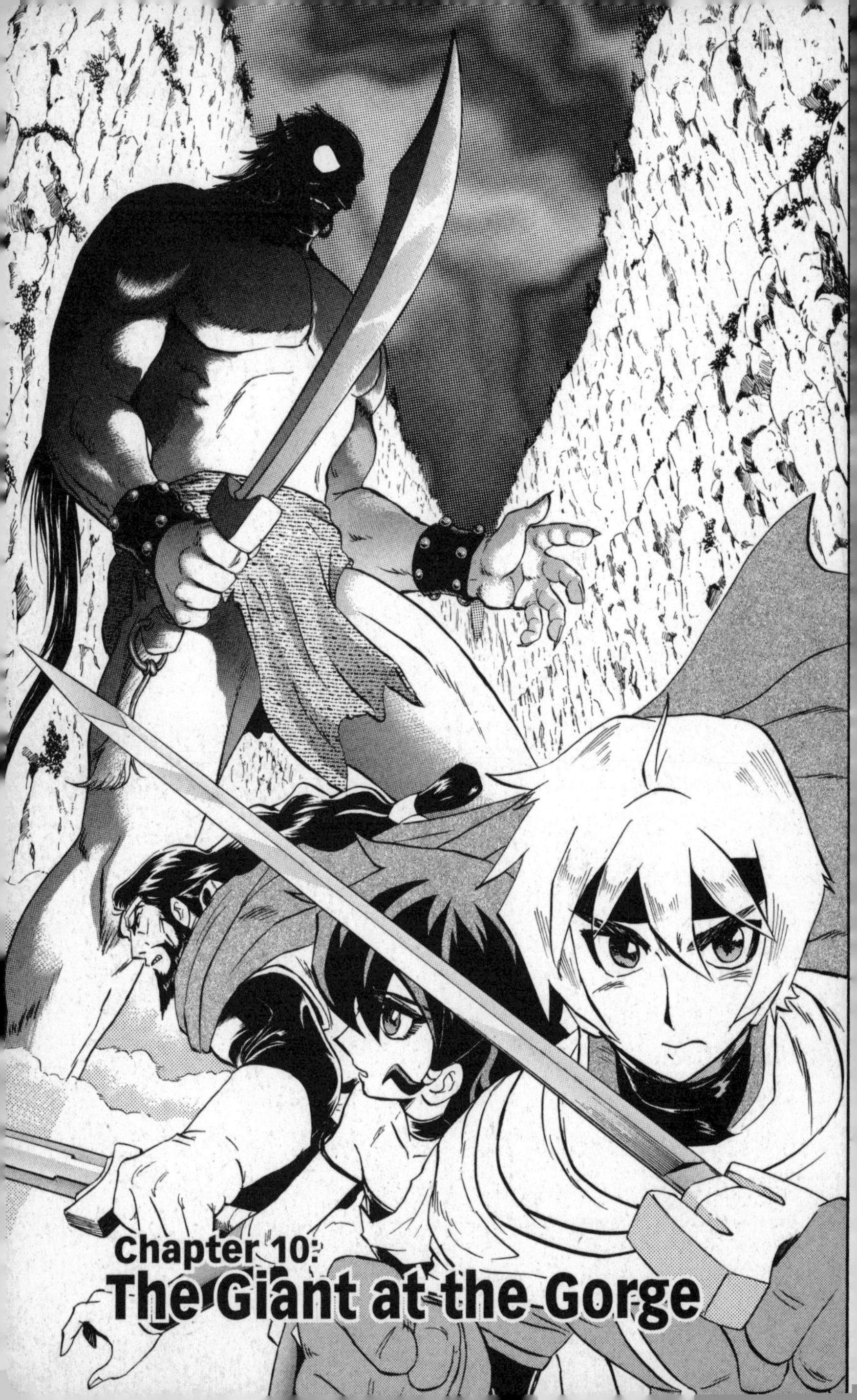
Chapter 10:
The Giant at the Gorge

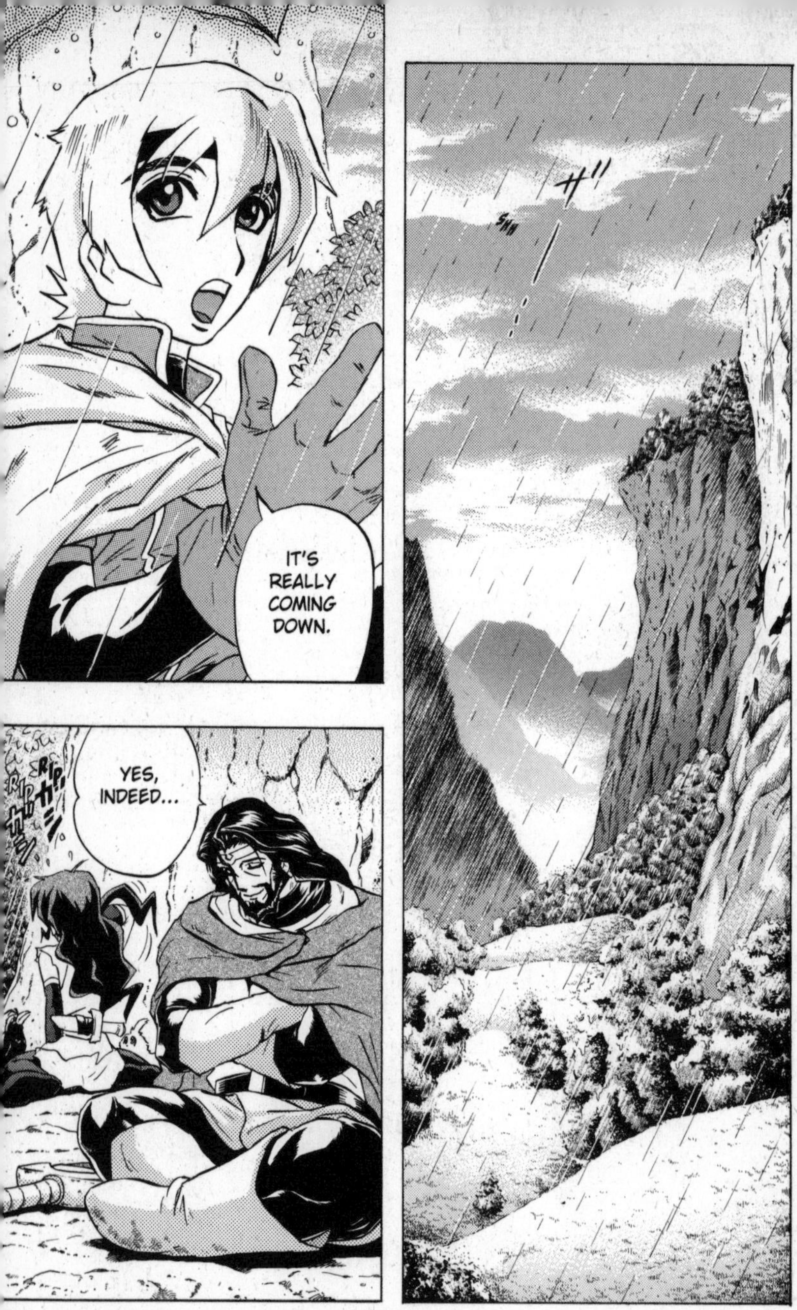
SHH
IT'S REALLY COMING DOWN.
YES, INDEED...
RIP!
RIP!

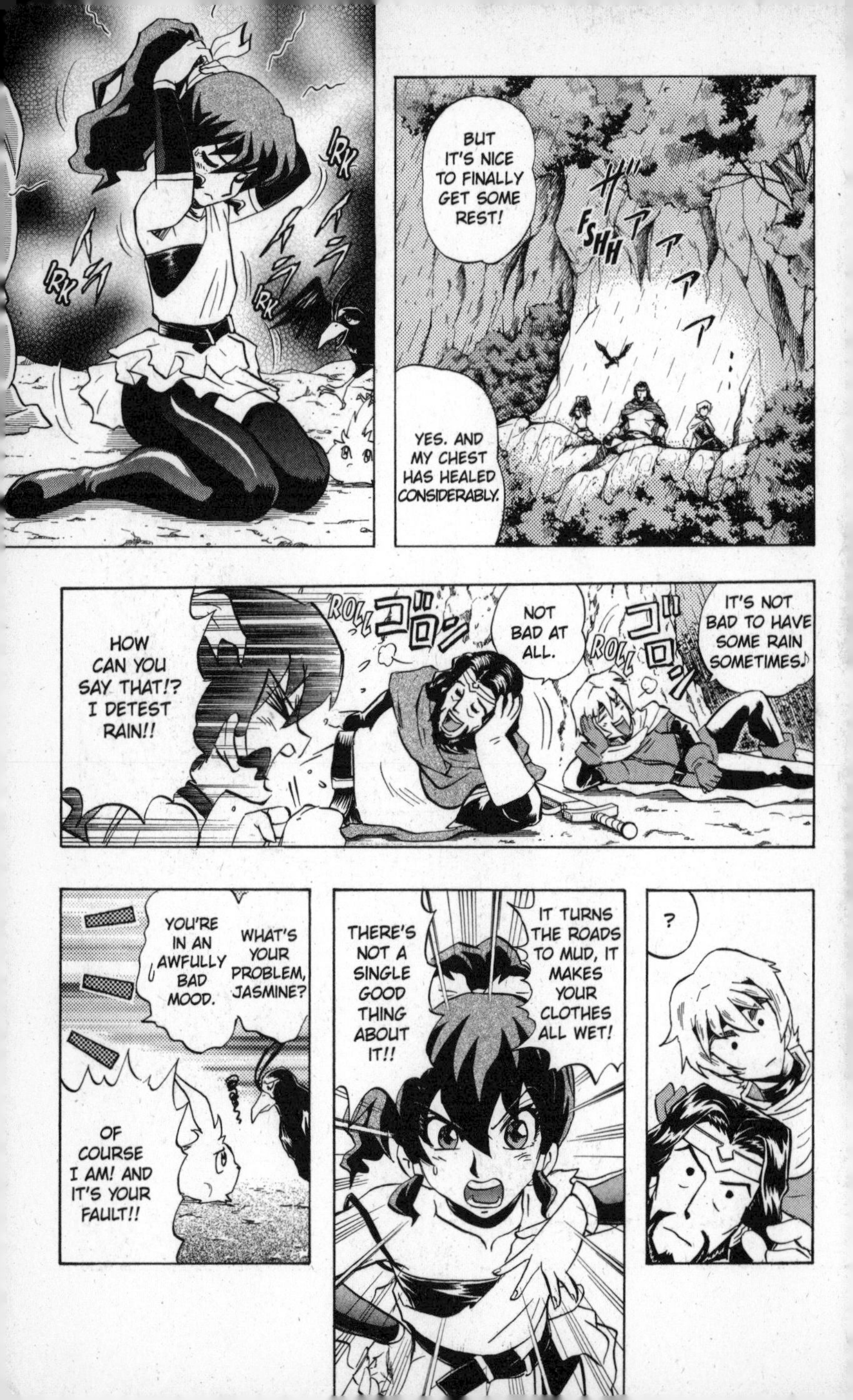
BUT IT'S NICE TO FINALLY GET SOME REST!
FSHH
YES. AND MY CHEST HAS HEALED CONSIDERABLY.
IRK
IRK
IRK
IT'S NOT BAD TO HAVE SOME RAIN SOMETIMES♪
ROLL
NOT BAD AT ALL.
ROLL
HOW CAN YOU SAY THAT!? I DETEST RAIN!!
?
IT TURNS THE ROADS TO MUD, IT MAKES YOUR CLOTHES ALL WET!
THERE'S NOT A SINGLE GOOD THING ABOUT IT!!
WHAT'S YOUR PROBLEM, JASMINE?
YOU'RE IN AN AWFULLY BAD MOOD.
OF COURSE I AM! AND IT'S YOUR FAULT!!

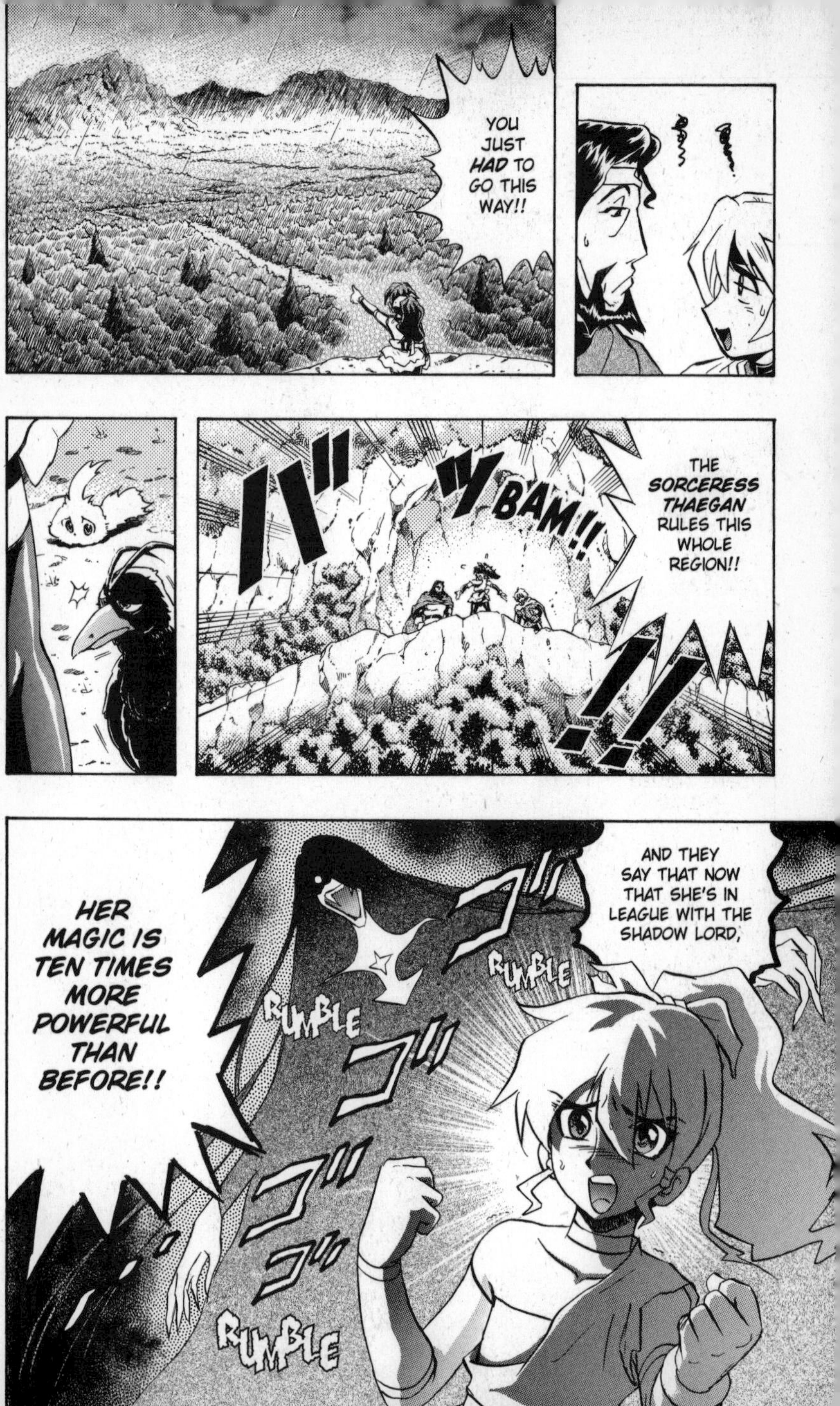
YOU JUST HAD TO GO THIS WAY!!
BAM!!
THE SORCERESS THAEGAN RULES THIS WHOLE REGION!!
AND THEY SAY THAT NOW THAT SHE'S IN LEAGUE WITH THE SHADOW LORD,
HER MAGIC IS TEN TIMES MORE POWERFUL THAN BEFORE!!
RUMBLE
RUMBLE
RUMBLE

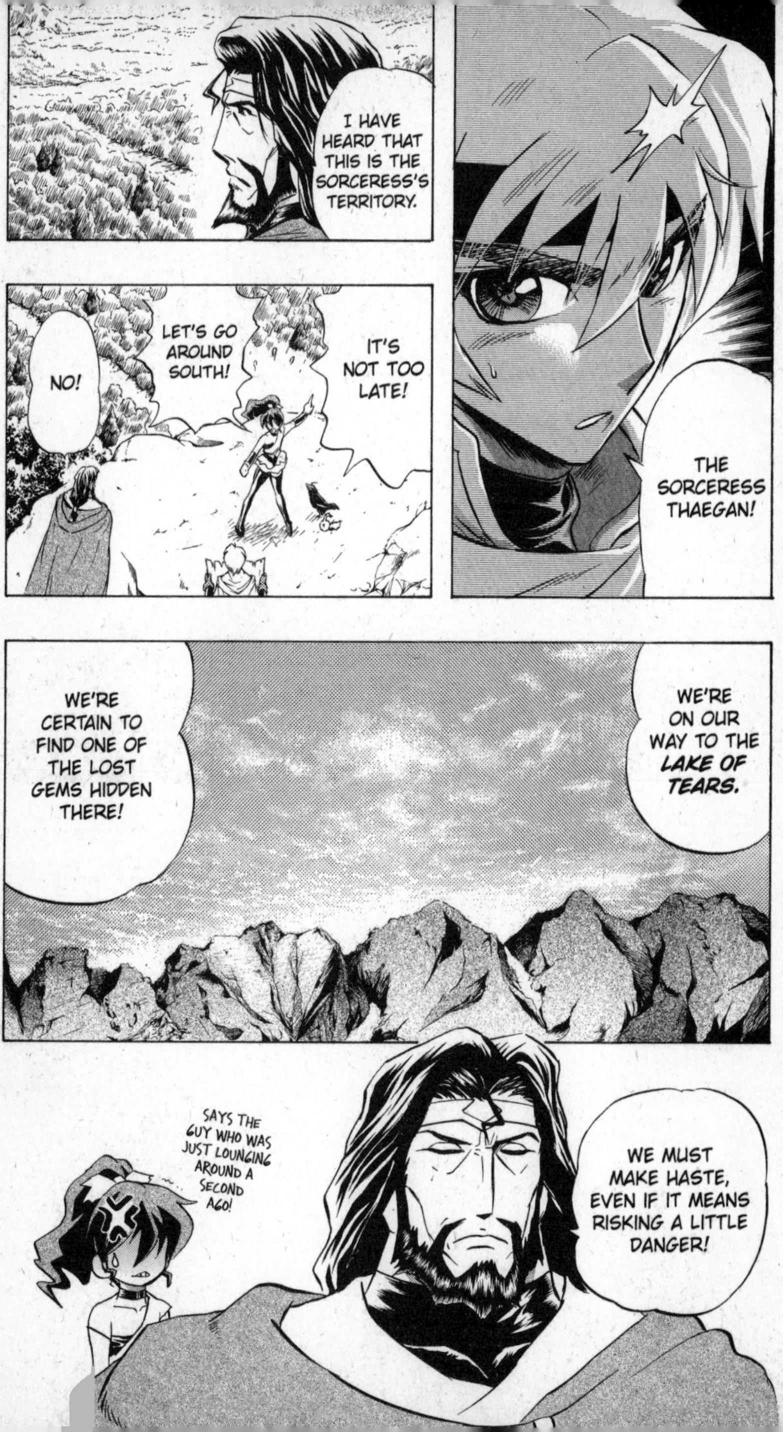
THE SORCERESS THAEGAN!
I HAVE HEARD THAT THIS IS THE SORCERESS'S TERRITORY.
IT'S NOT TOO LATE!
LET'S GO AROUND SOUTH!
NO!
WE'RE ON OUR WAY TO THE *LAKE OF TEARS.*
WE'RE CERTAIN TO FIND ONE OF THE LOST GEMS HIDDEN THERE!
WE MUST MAKE HASTE, EVEN IF IT MEANS RISKING A LITTLE DANGER!
SAYS THE GUY WHO WAS JUST LOUNGING AROUND A SECOND AGO!

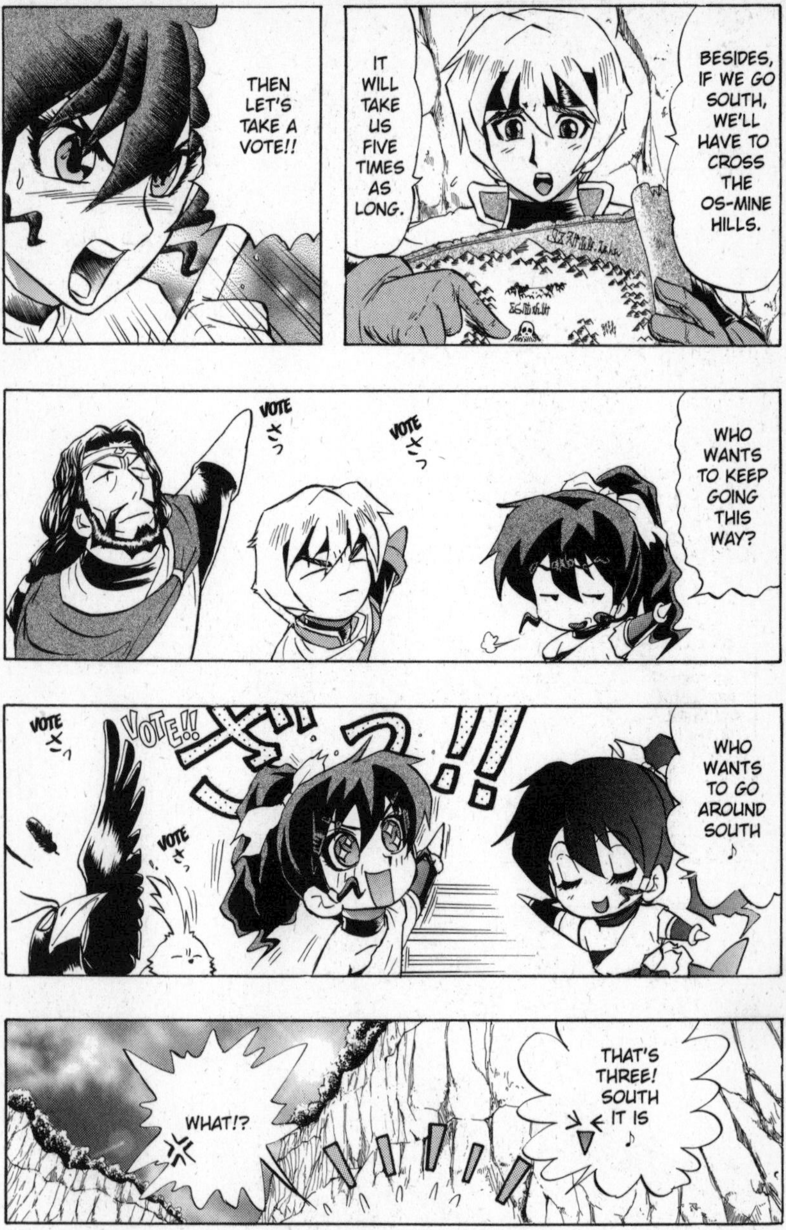
BESIDES, IF WE GO SOUTH, WE'LL HAVE TO CROSS THE OS-MINE HILLS.
IT WILL TAKE US FIVE TIMES AS LONG.
THEN LET'S TAKE A VOTE!!
WHO WANTS TO KEEP GOING THIS WAY?
VOTE さっ
VOTE さっ
WHO WANTS TO GO AROUND SOUTH ♪
VOTE!!
VOTE さっ
VOTE さっ
THAT'S THREE! SOUTH IT IS ♪
WHAT!?

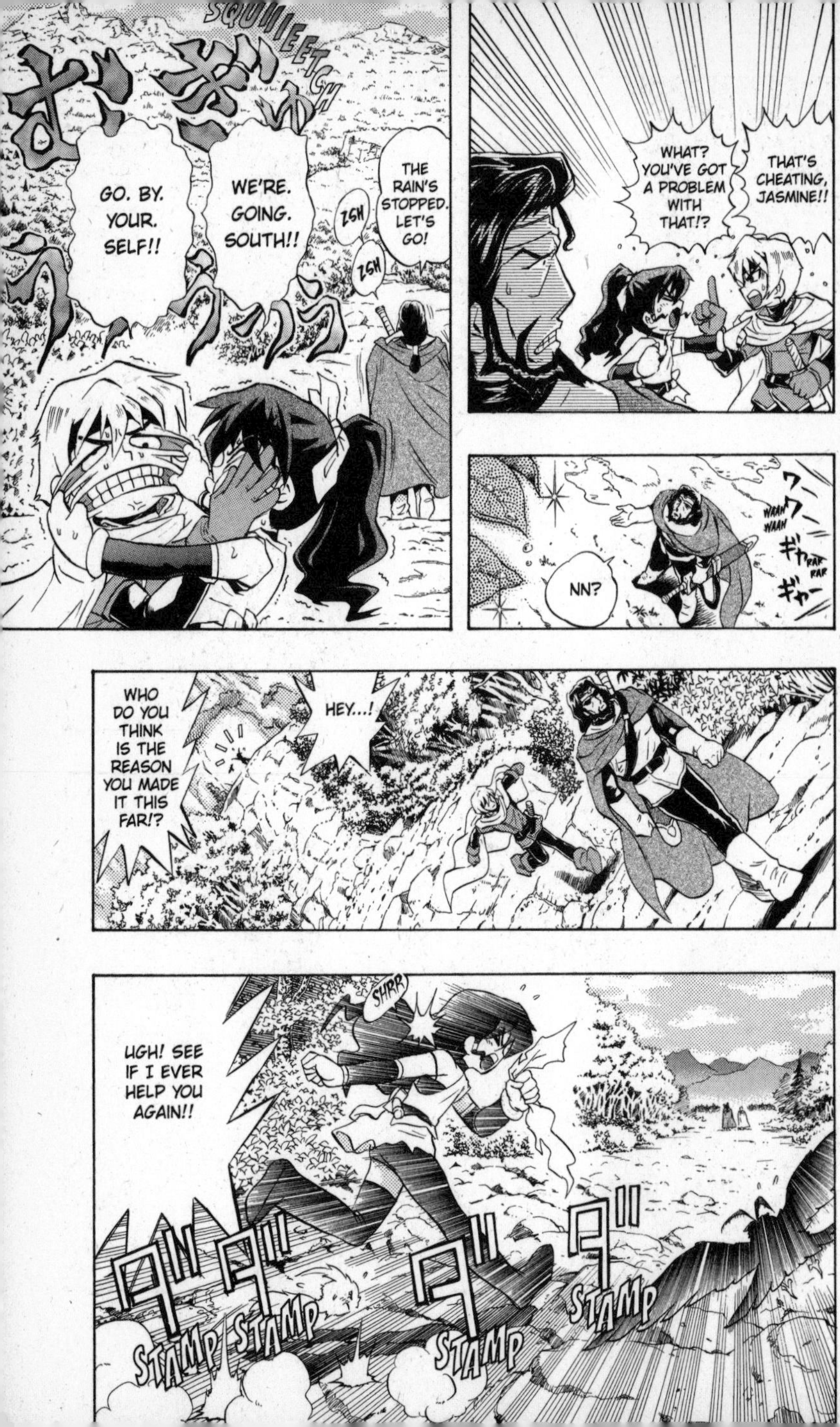
THAT'S CHEATING, JASMINE!!
WHAT? YOU'VE GOT A PROBLEM WITH THAT!?
WAAN WAAN
RAR RAR
NN?
SQUIIEETCH
THE RAIN'S STOPPED. LET'S GO!
ZSH
ZSH
WE'RE. GOING. SOUTH!!
GO. BY. YOUR. SELF!!
HEY...!
WHO DO YOU THINK IS THE REASON YOU MADE IT THIS FAR!?
SHRR
UGH! SEE IF I EVER HELP YOU AGAIN!!
STAMP
STAMP
STAMP
STAMP

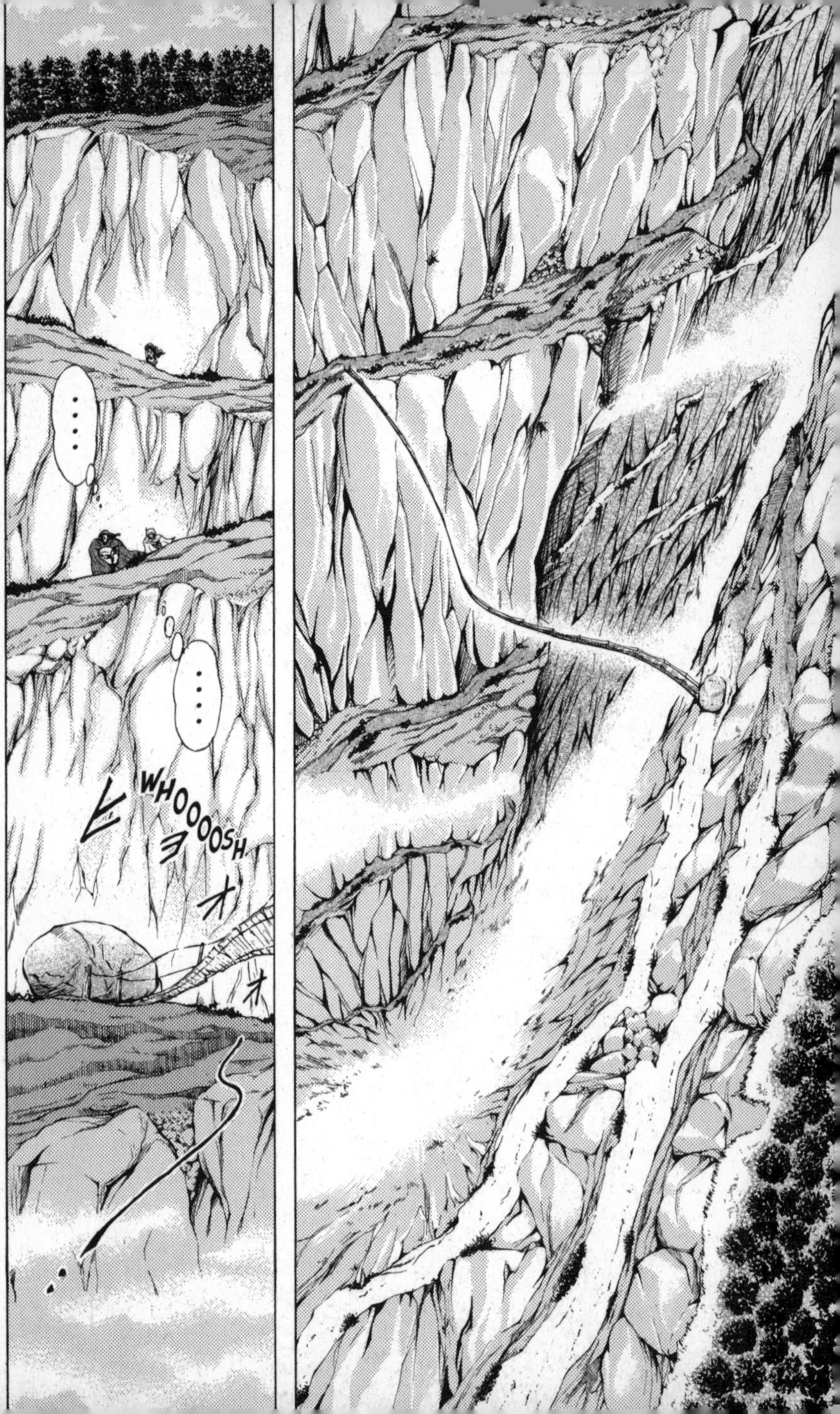

....
.....
WHOOOOSH

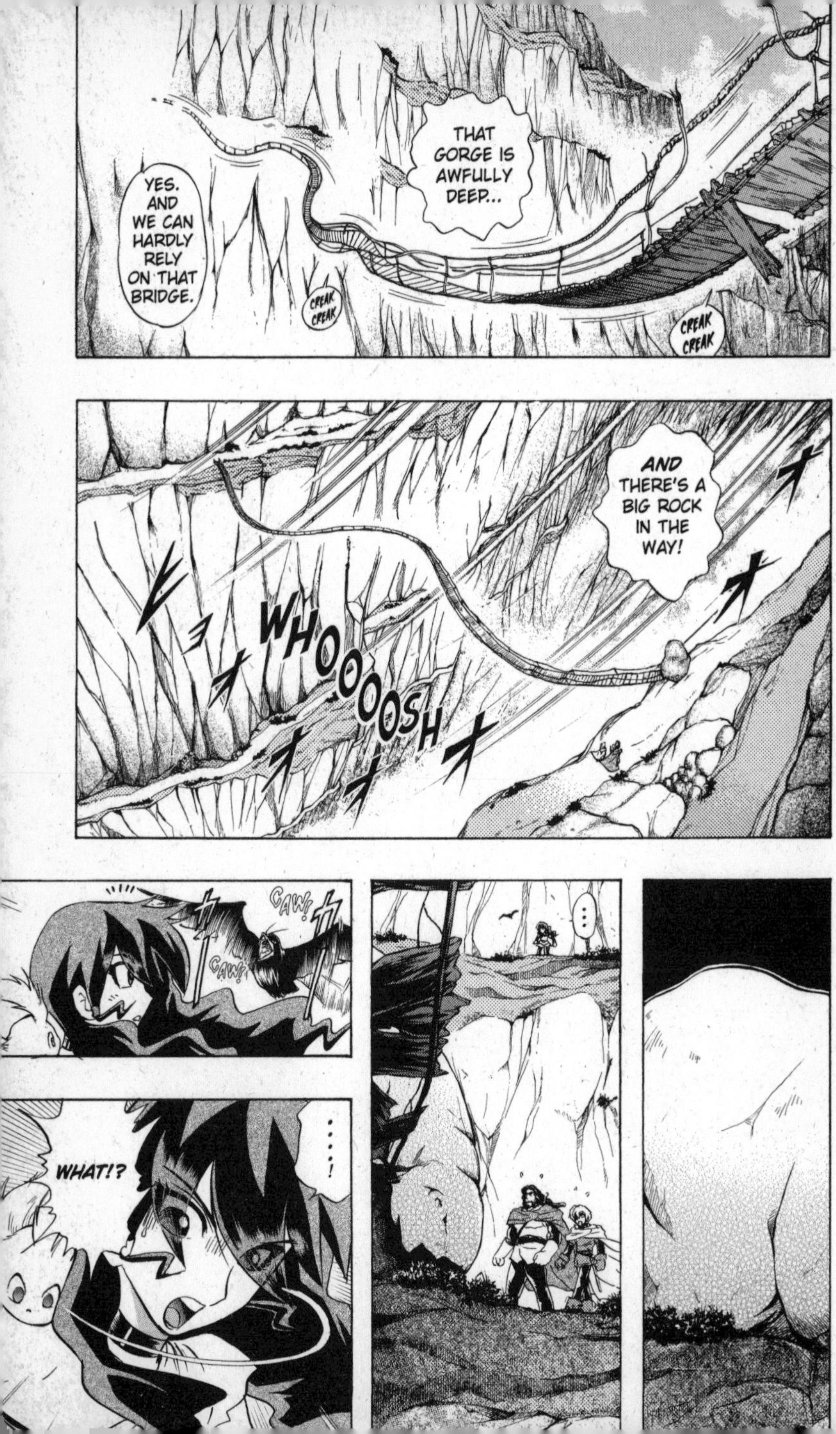
THAT GORGE IS AWFULLY DEEP...
YES. AND WE CAN HARDLY RELY ON THAT BRIDGE.
CREAK CREAK
CREAK CREAK
AND THERE'S A BIG ROCK IN THE WAY!
WHOOOOSH
...
CAW!
CAW!
....!
WHAT!?

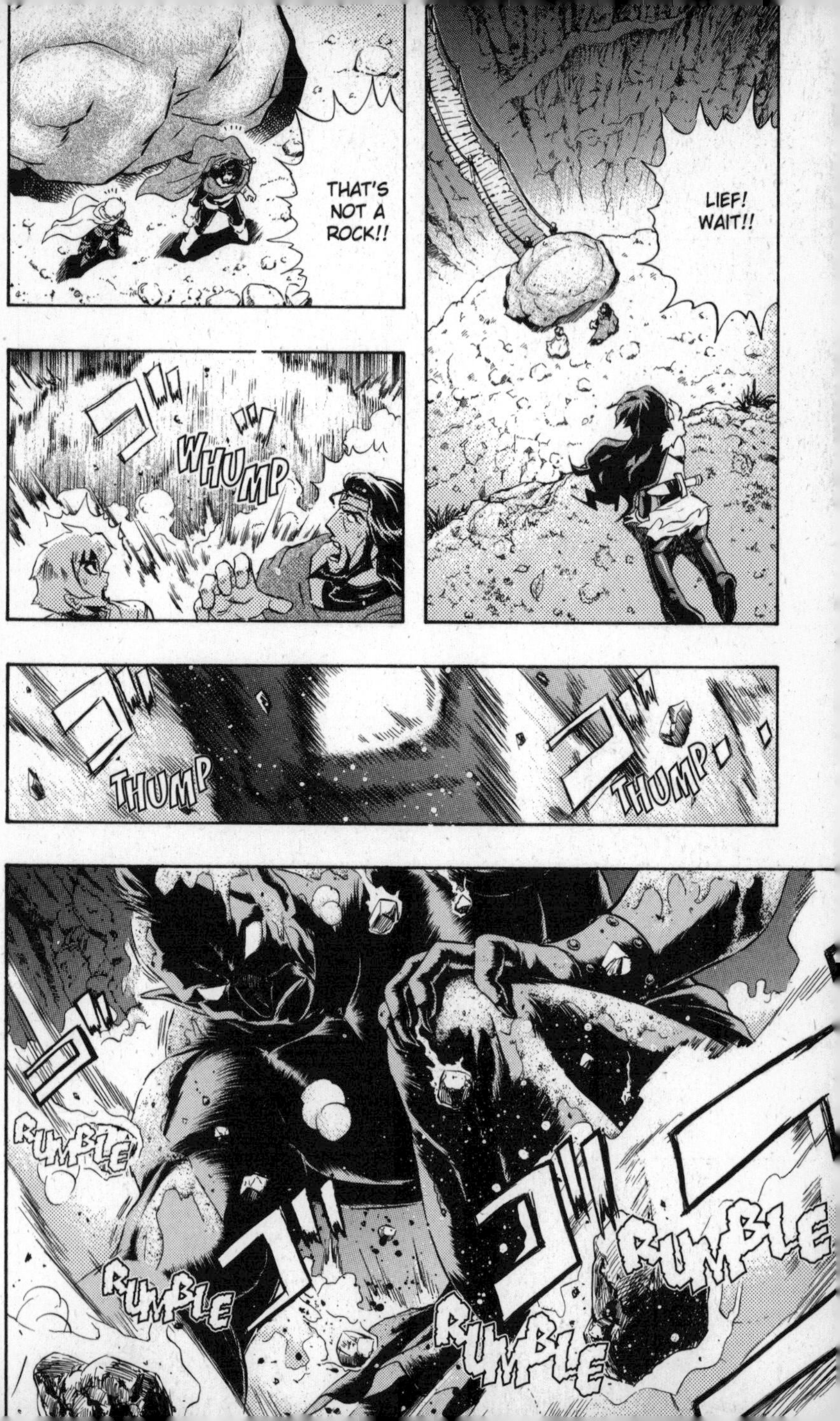
LIEF! WAIT!!
THAT'S NOT A ROCK!!
WHUMP
THUMP..
THUMP
RUMBLE
RUMBLE
RUMBLE
RUMBLE

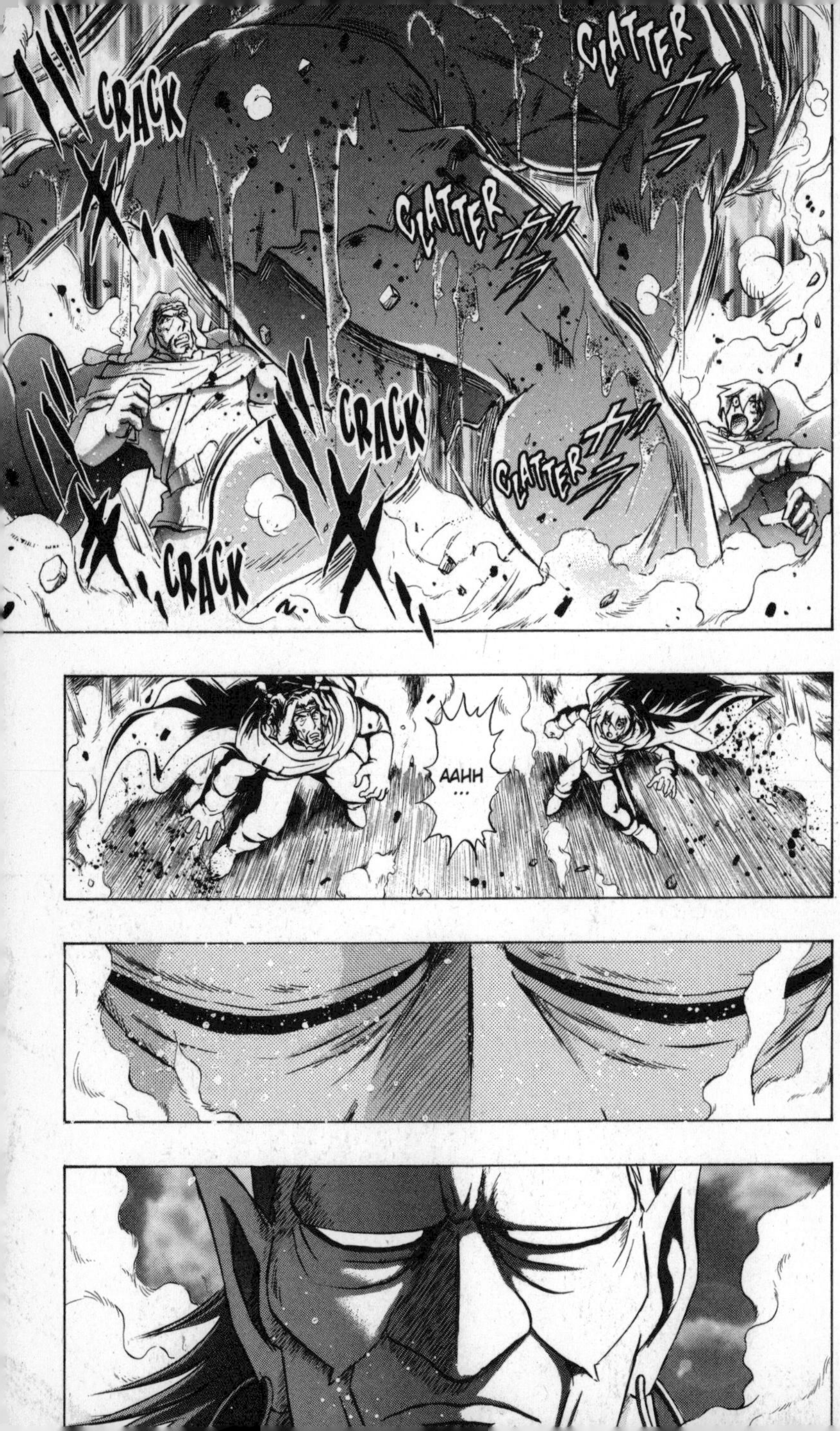
CLATTER
CLATTER
CRACK
CLATTER
CRACK
CRACK
AAHH…

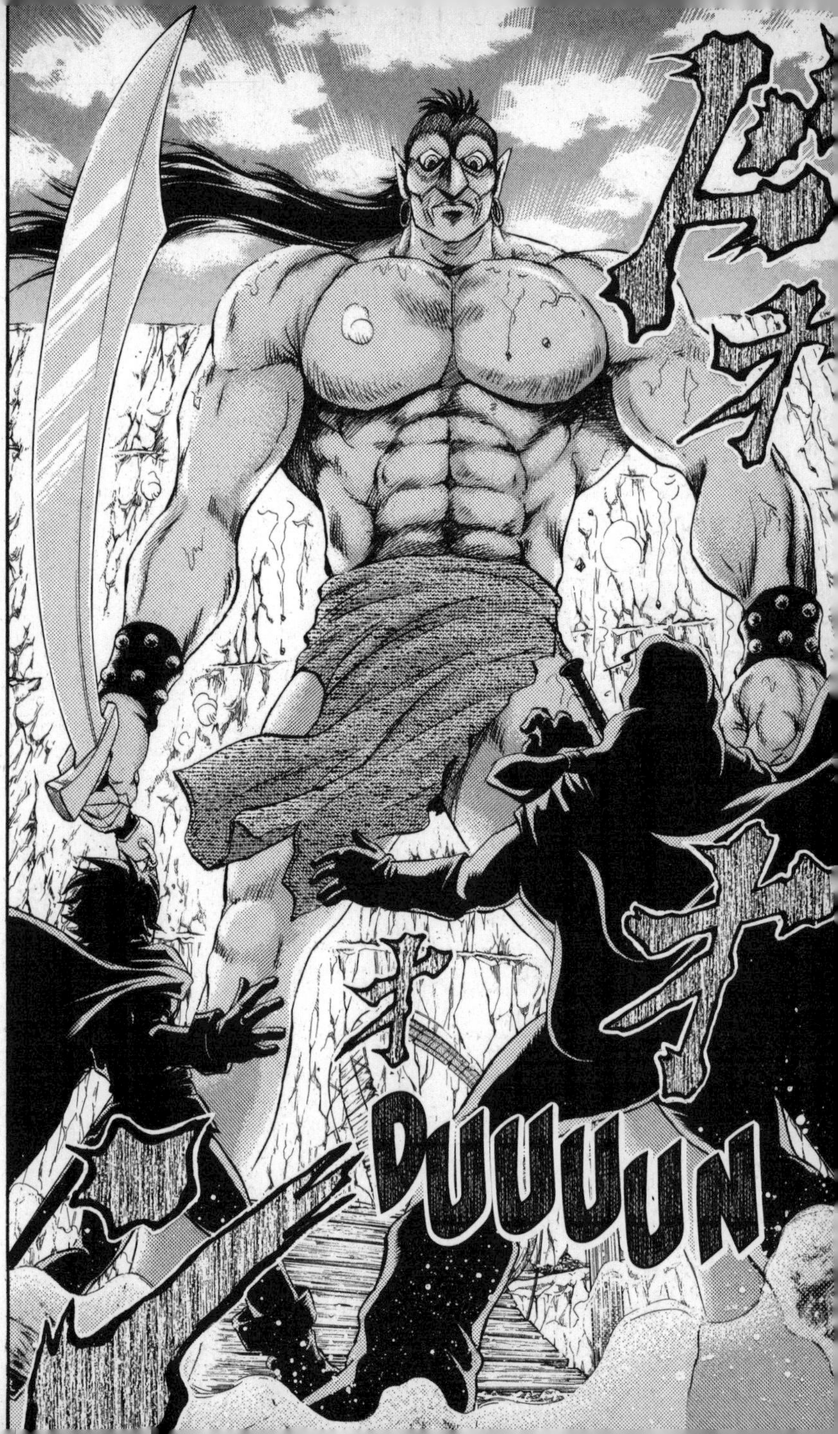
DUUUUN

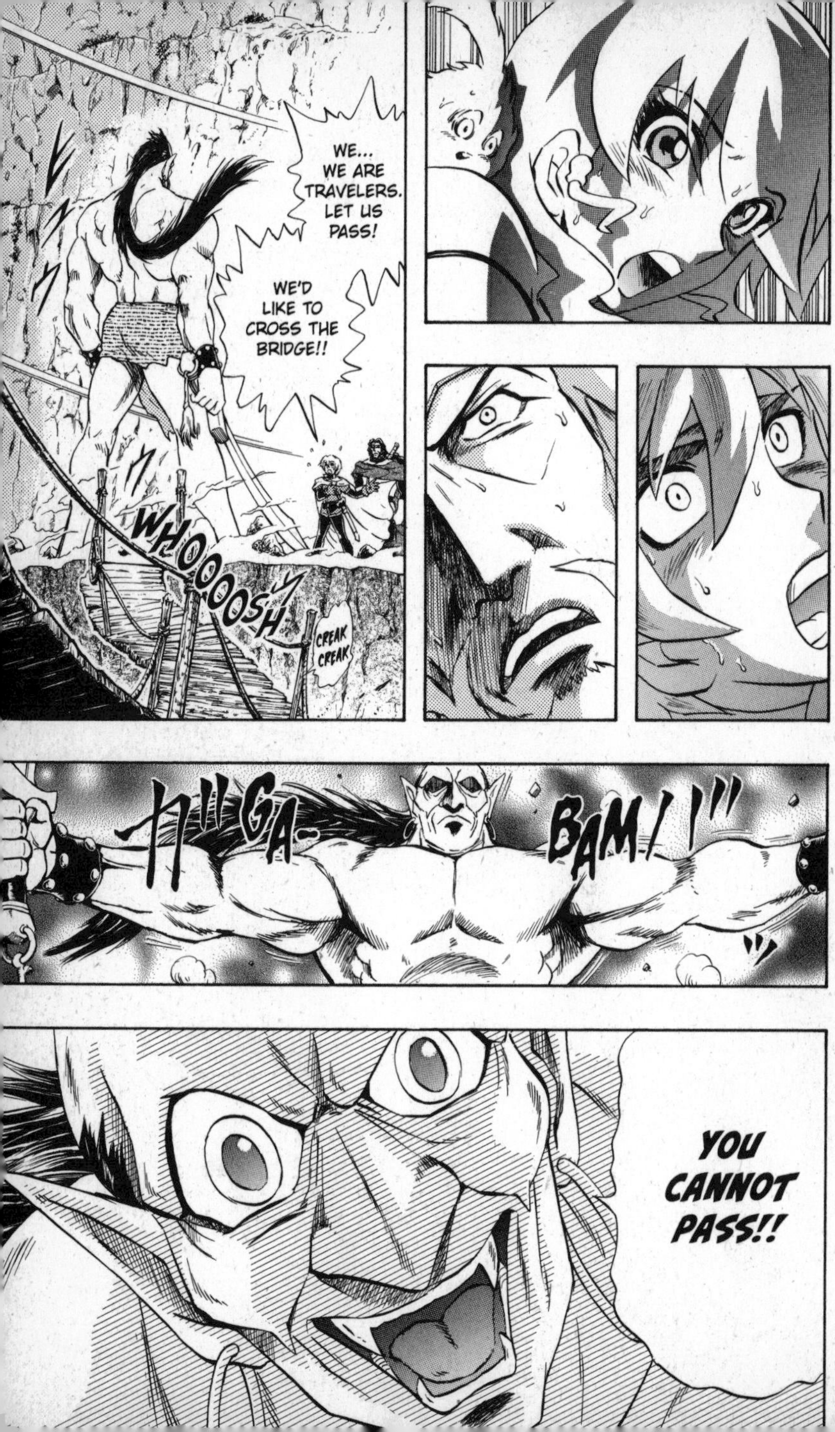
WE... WE ARE TRAVELERS. LET US PASS!
WE'D LIKE TO CROSS THE BRIDGE!!
WHOOOOOSH
CREAK CREAK
GA-
BAM!!
YOU CANNOT PASS!!

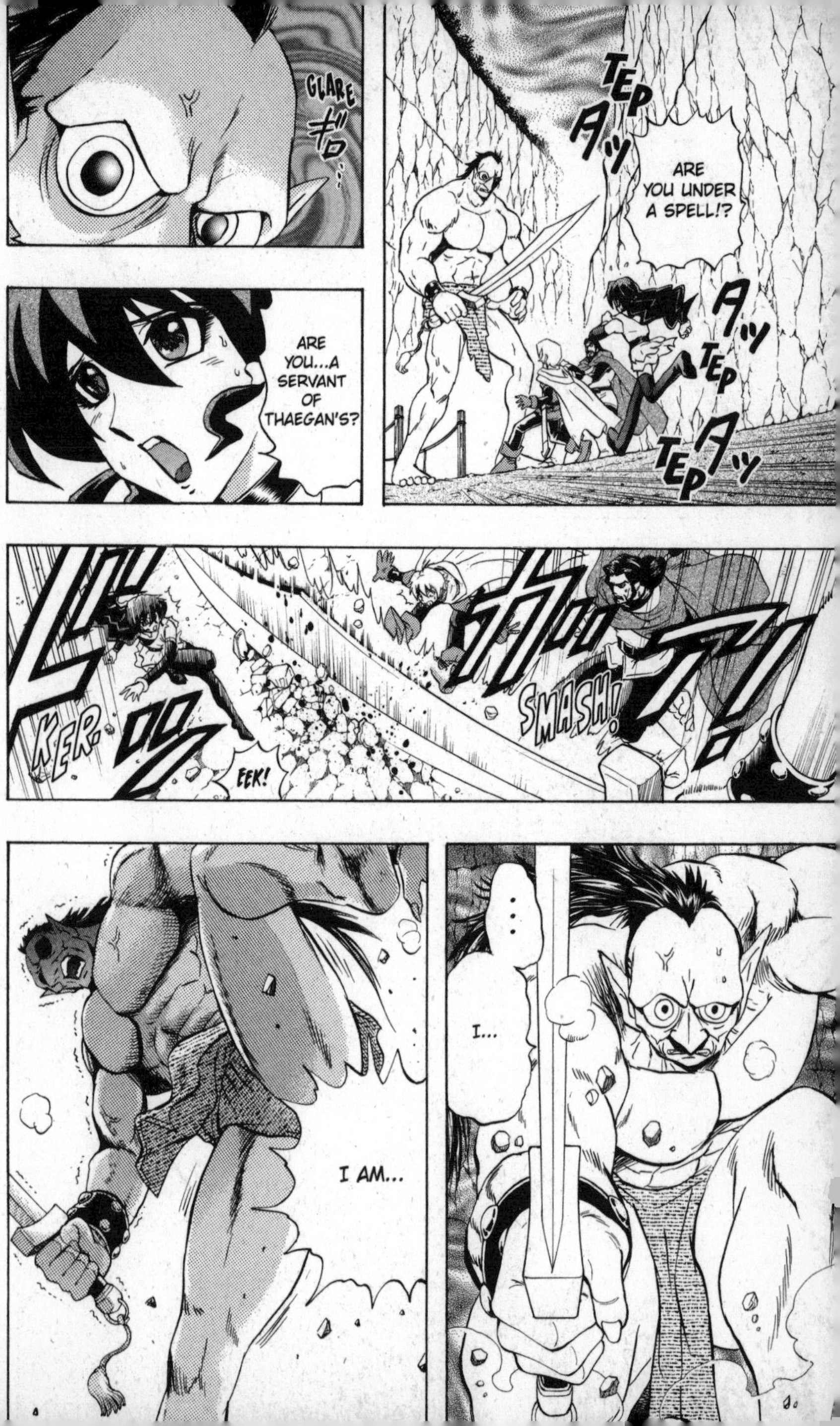
TEP
タッ
ARE YOU UNDER A SPELL!?
タッ
TEP
TEP
GLARE
ギロ…
ARE YOU...A SERVANT OF THAEGAN'S?
SMASH!
KER-
EEK!
...
I...
I AM...

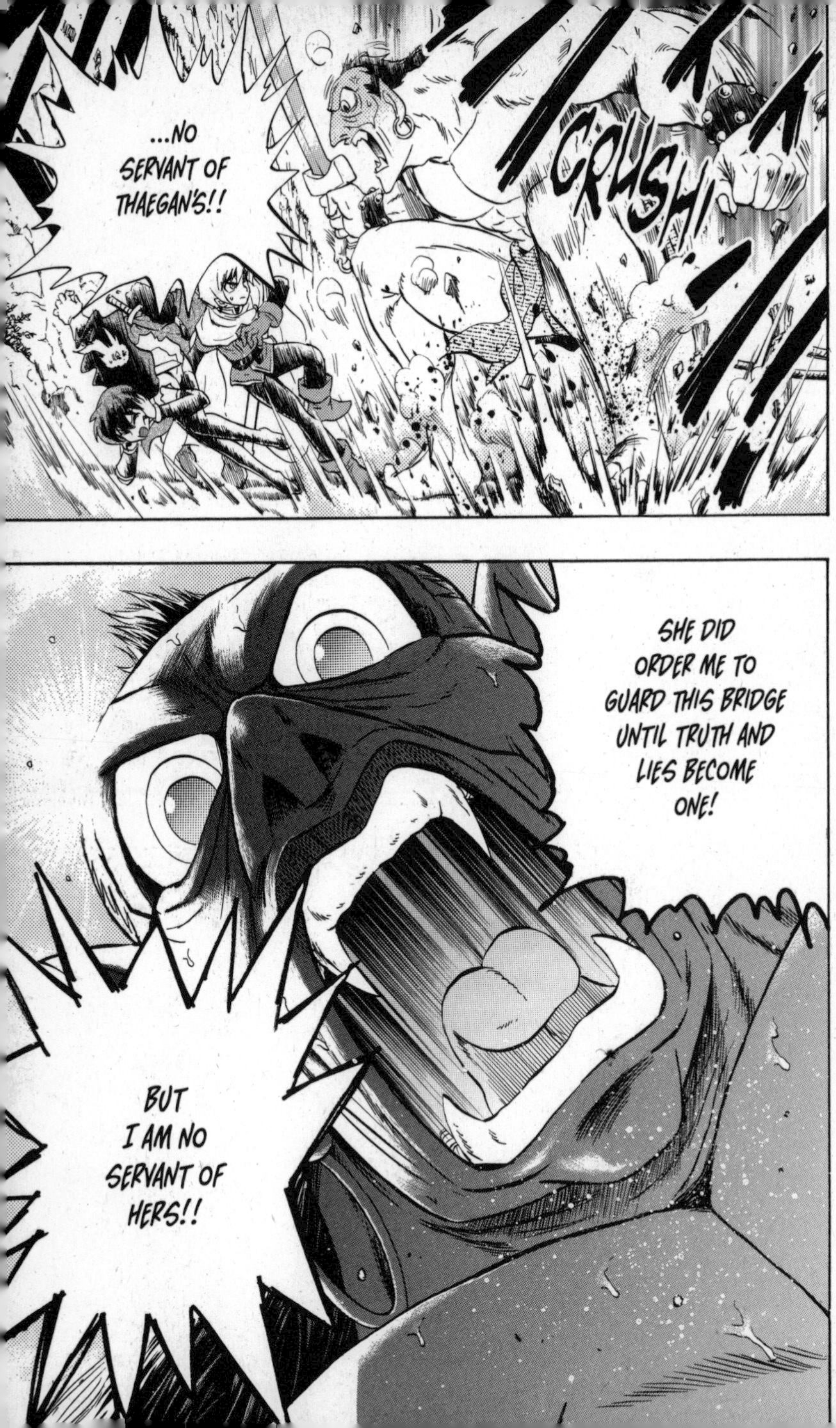
CRUSH!
...NO SERVANT OF THAEGAN'S!!
SHE DID ORDER ME TO GUARD THIS BRIDGE UNTIL TRUTH AND LIES BECOME ONE!
BUT I AM NO SERVANT OF HERS!!

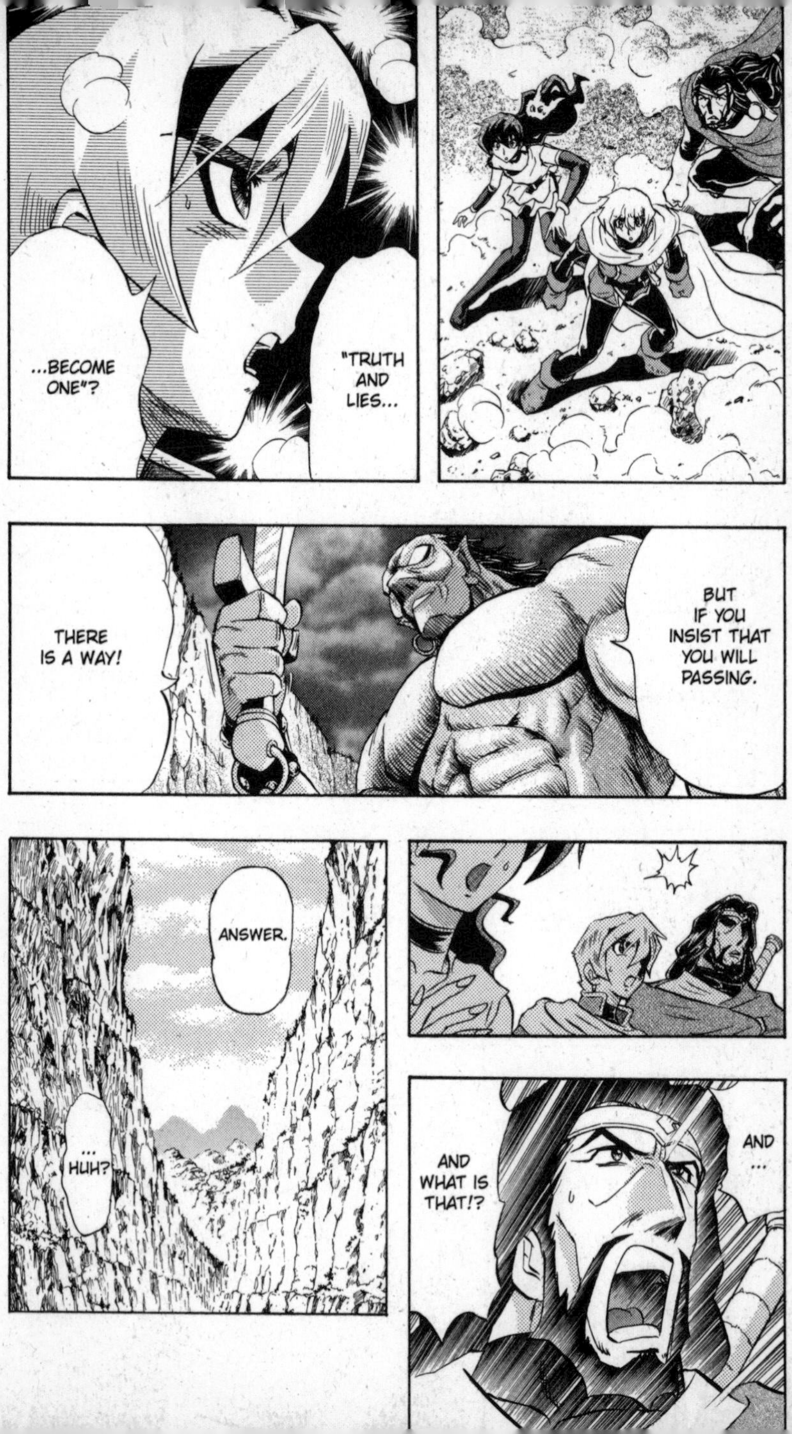
"TRUTH AND LIES...
...BECOME ONE"?
BUT IF YOU INSIST THAT YOU WILL PASSING.
THERE IS A WAY!
AND ...
AND WHAT IS THAT!?
ANSWER.
... HUH?

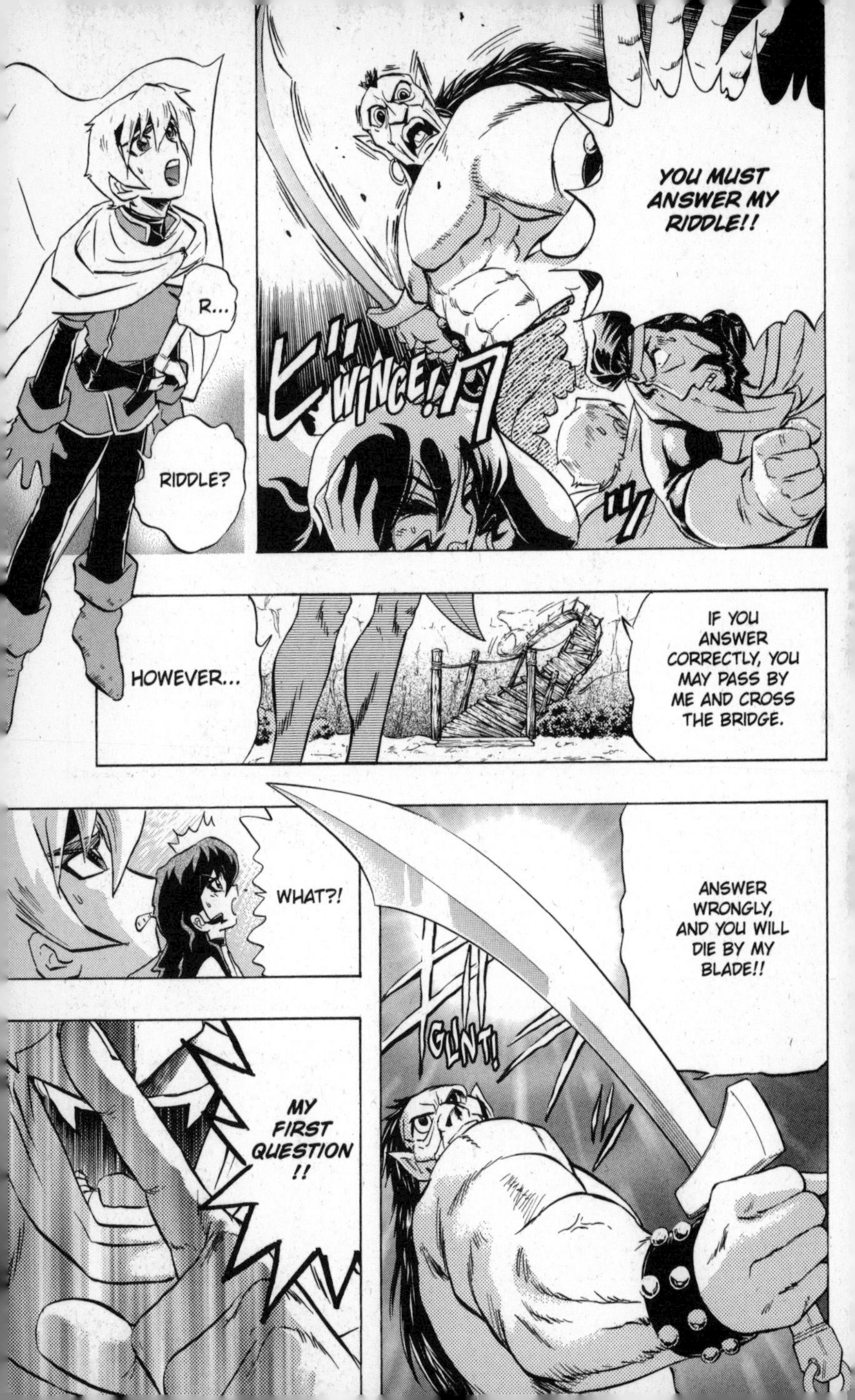
YOU MUST ANSWER MY RIDDLE!!
ヒッ WINCE!!
R...
RIDDLE?
IF YOU ANSWER CORRECTLY, YOU MAY PASS BY ME AND CROSS THE BRIDGE.
HOWEVER...
ANSWER WRONGLY, AND YOU WILL DIE BY MY BLADE!!
GLINT!
WHAT?!
MY FIRST QUESTION !!

MAKE THESE STICKS INTO THREE WITHOUT REMOVING ONE!!

GA-TTER カラン...
GA-TTER カラン...

?

INTO THREE?

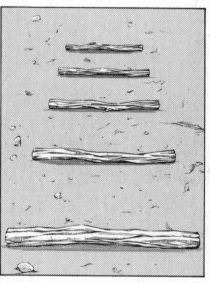

THREE!

YES.

SMIRK

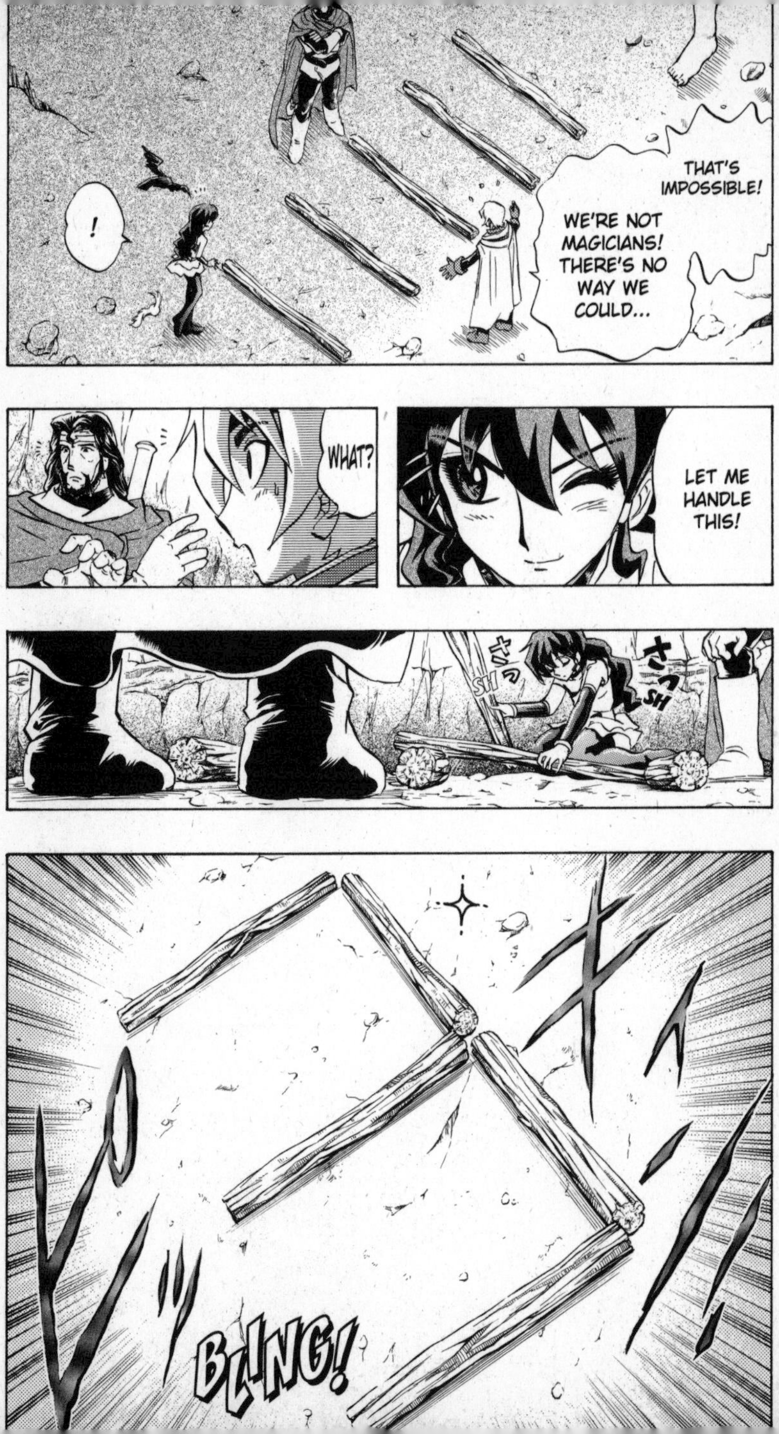
THAT'S IMPOSSIBLE!
WE'RE NOT MAGICIANS! THERE'S NO WAY WE COULD...
!
LET ME HANDLE THIS!
WHAT?
さっ SH
さっ SH
BLING!

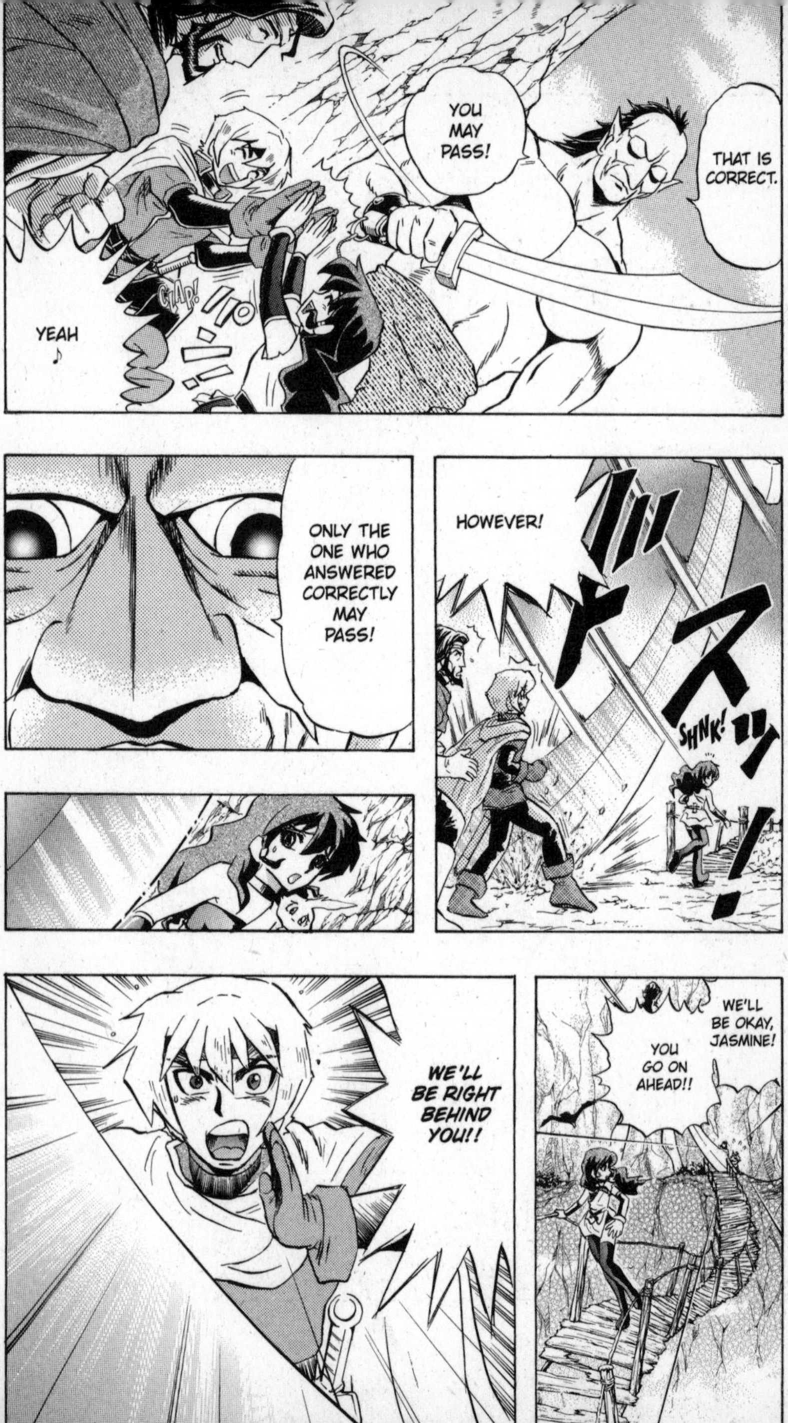
THAT IS CORRECT.
YOU MAY PASS!
CLAP!
YEAH ♪
HOWEVER!
SHNK!
ONLY THE ONE WHO ANSWERED CORRECTLY MAY PASS!
WE'LL BE OKAY, JASMINE!
YOU GO ON AHEAD!!
WE'LL BE RIGHT BEHIND YOU!!

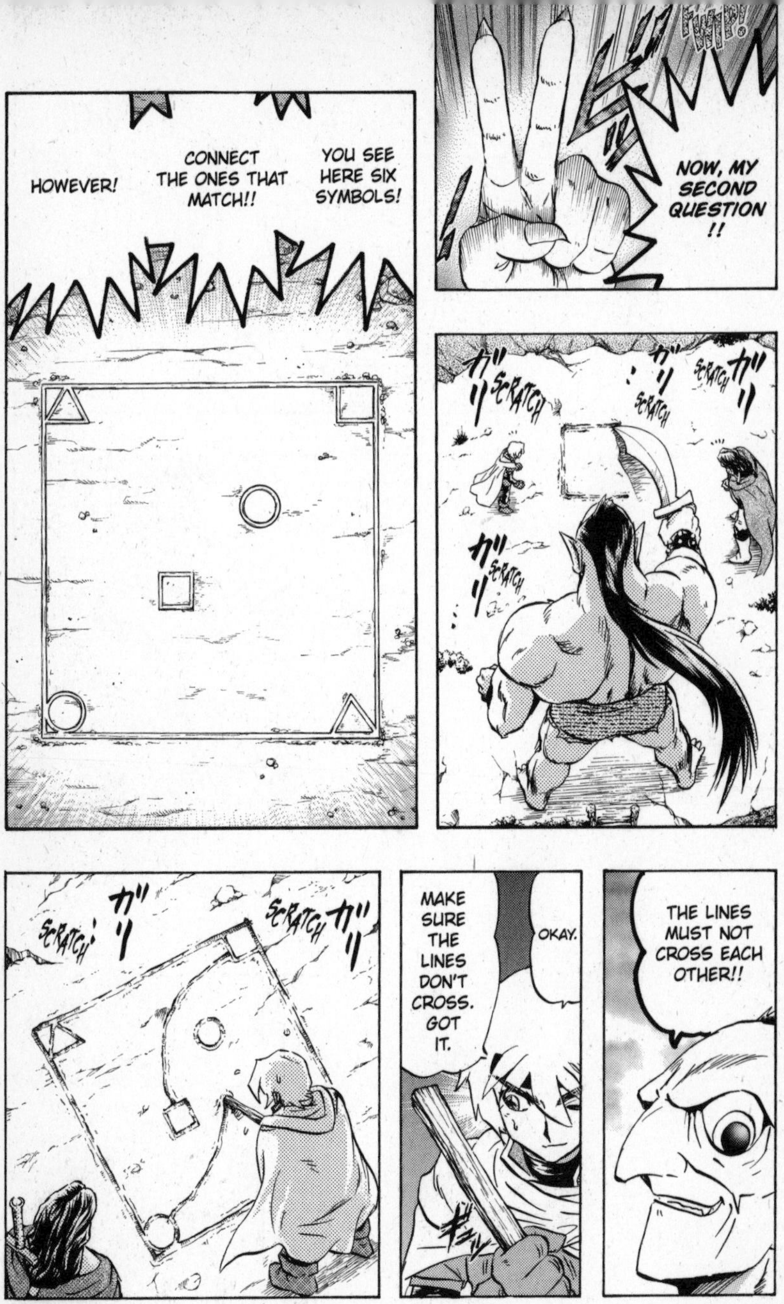
FWIP!
NOW, MY SECOND QUESTION !!
SCRATCH
SCRATCH
SCRATCH
SCRATCH
YOU SEE HERE SIX SYMBOLS!
CONNECT THE ONES THAT MATCH!!
HOWEVER!
THE LINES MUST NOT CROSS EACH OTHER!!
OKAY.
MAKE SURE THE LINES DON'T CROSS. GOT IT.
SCRATCH
SCRATCH

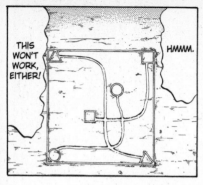

LIKE THIS?
NO, THAT'S NOT RIGHT ...
HMMM.
THIS WON'T WORK, EITHER!
MM. I'VE GOT IT.
WHAT!?
ドーン!!
DUN!
HOW IS THIS?
THAT IS CORRECT!!
I'M GOING ON!
I TRUST YOU'LL BE ALRIGHT, LIEF!?
Y... YEAH, OF COURSE!

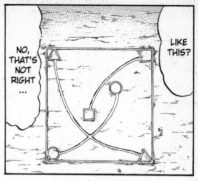

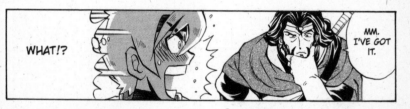

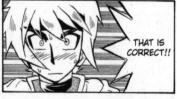

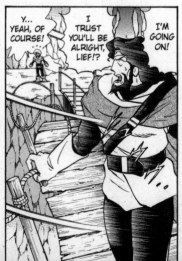

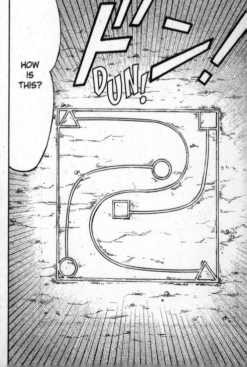

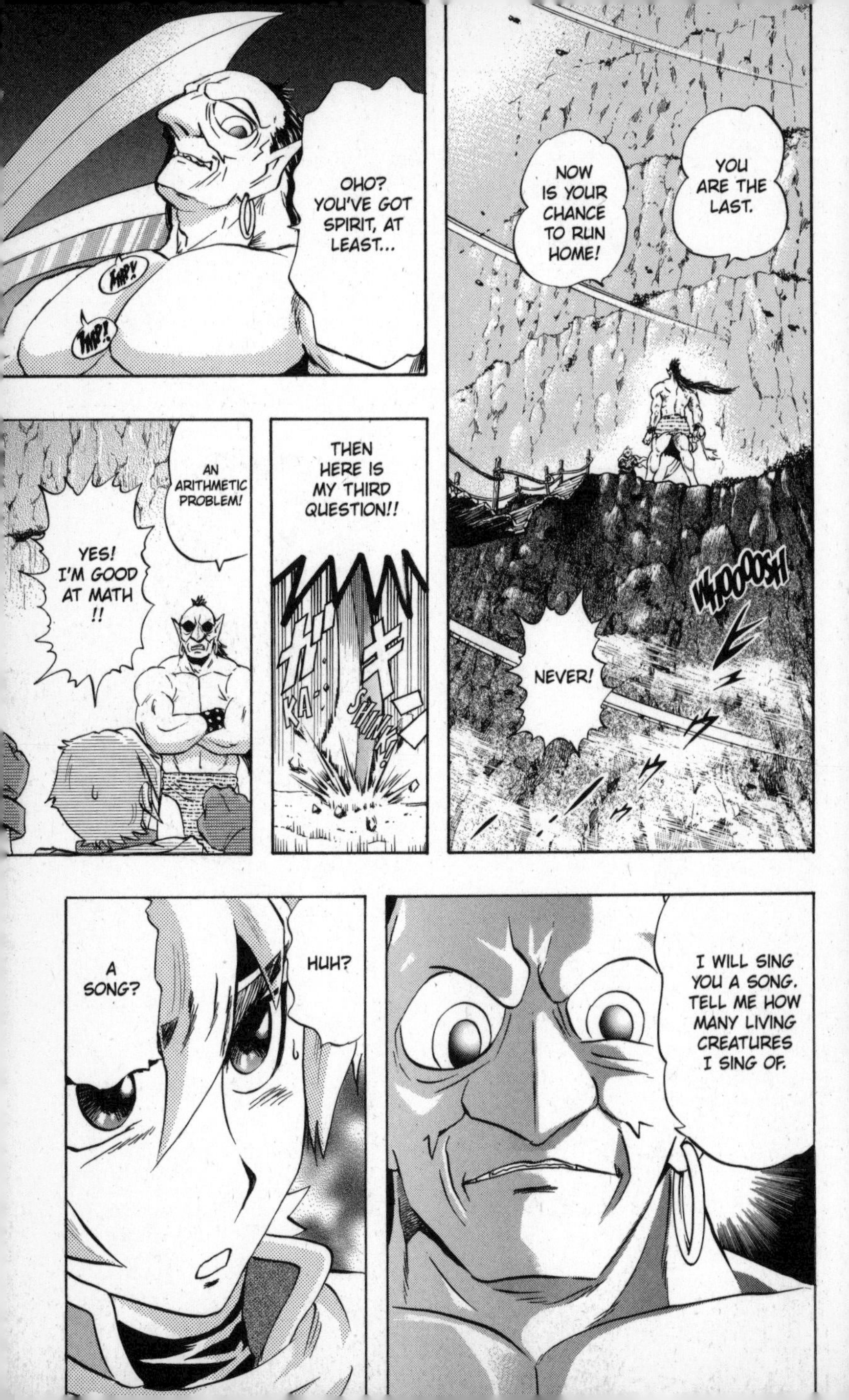

YOU ARE THE LAST.
NOW IS YOUR CHANCE TO RUN HOME!
WHOOOOSH
NEVER!
OHO? YOU'VE GOT SPIRIT, AT LEAST...
THMP!
THMP!
THEN HERE IS MY THIRD QUESTION!!
KA-SHINK!
AN ARITHMETIC PROBLEM!
YES! I'M GOOD AT MATH !!
I WILL SING YOU A SONG. TELL ME HOW MANY LIVING CREATURES I SING OF.
HUH?
A SONG?

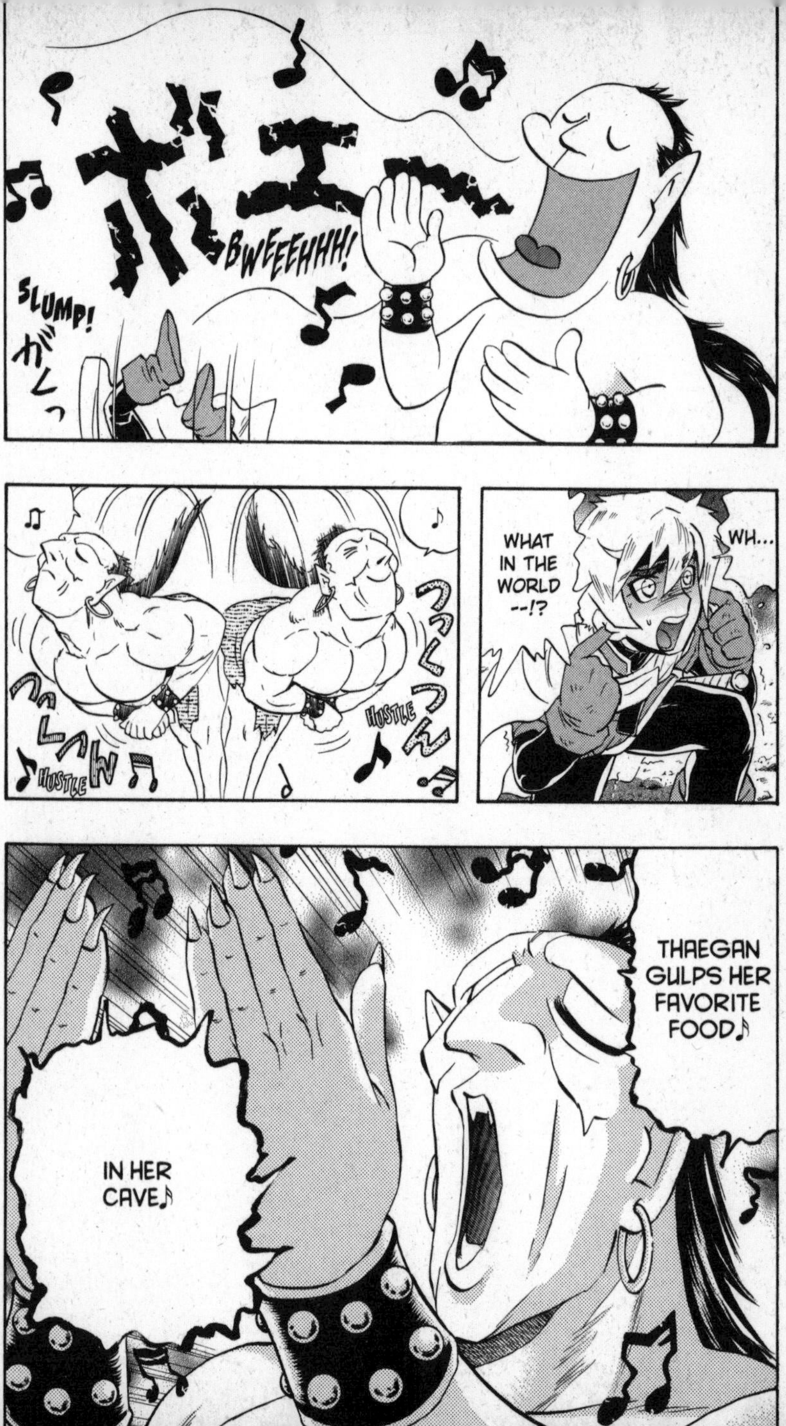
ボエ～
BWEEEHHH!
SLUMP!
がくっ
WH...
WHAT IN THE WORLD --!?
つっくつん
HUSTLE
つっくつん
HUSTLE
THAEGAN GULPS HER FAVORITE FOOD♪
IN HER CAVE♪

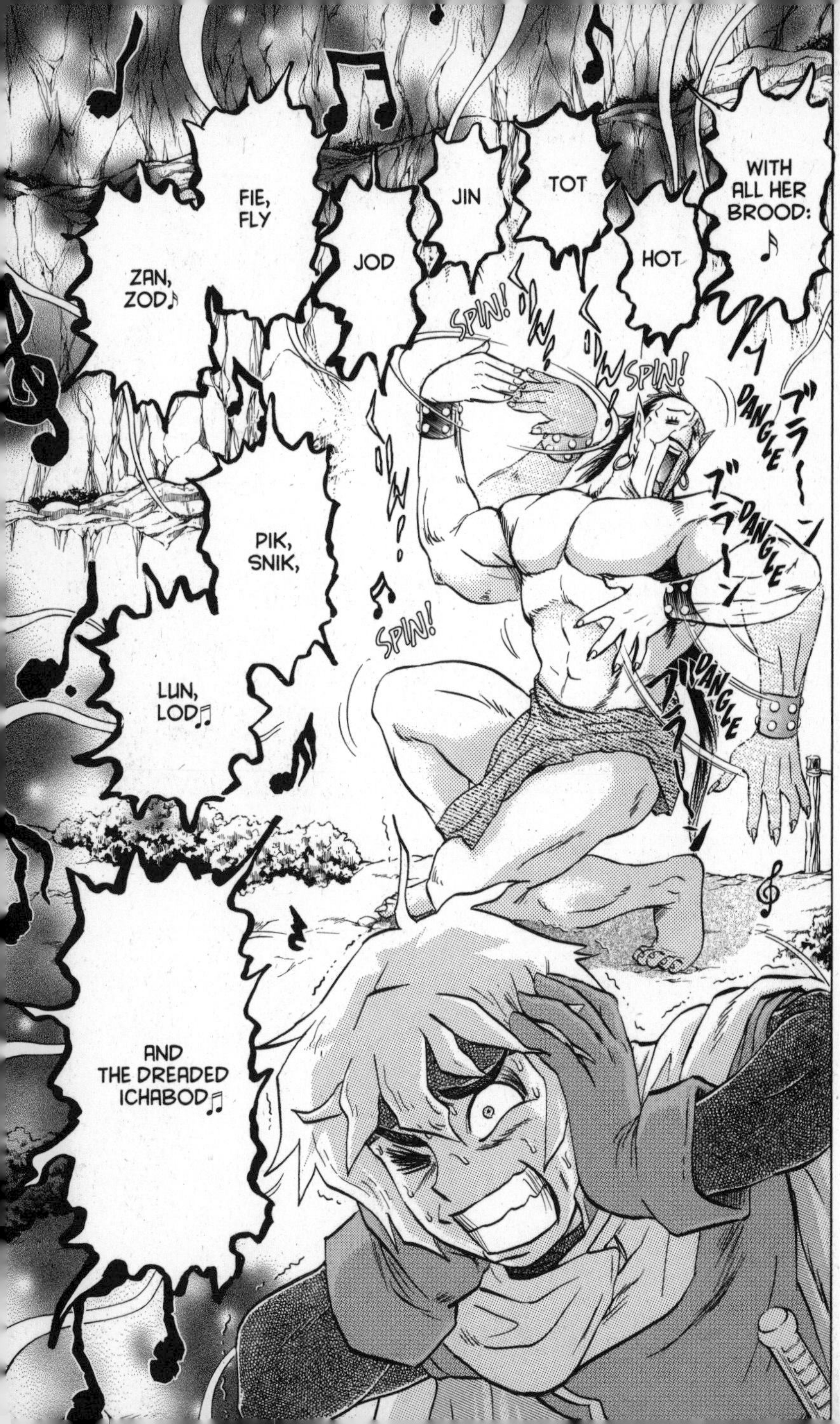
WITH ALL HER BROOD: ♪
TOT
HOT
JIN
JOD
FIE, FLY
ZAN, ZOD♪
SPIN!
SPIN!
DANGLE
DANGLE
DANGLE
SPIN!
PIK, SNIK,
LUN, LOD♫
AND THE DREADED ICHABOD♫

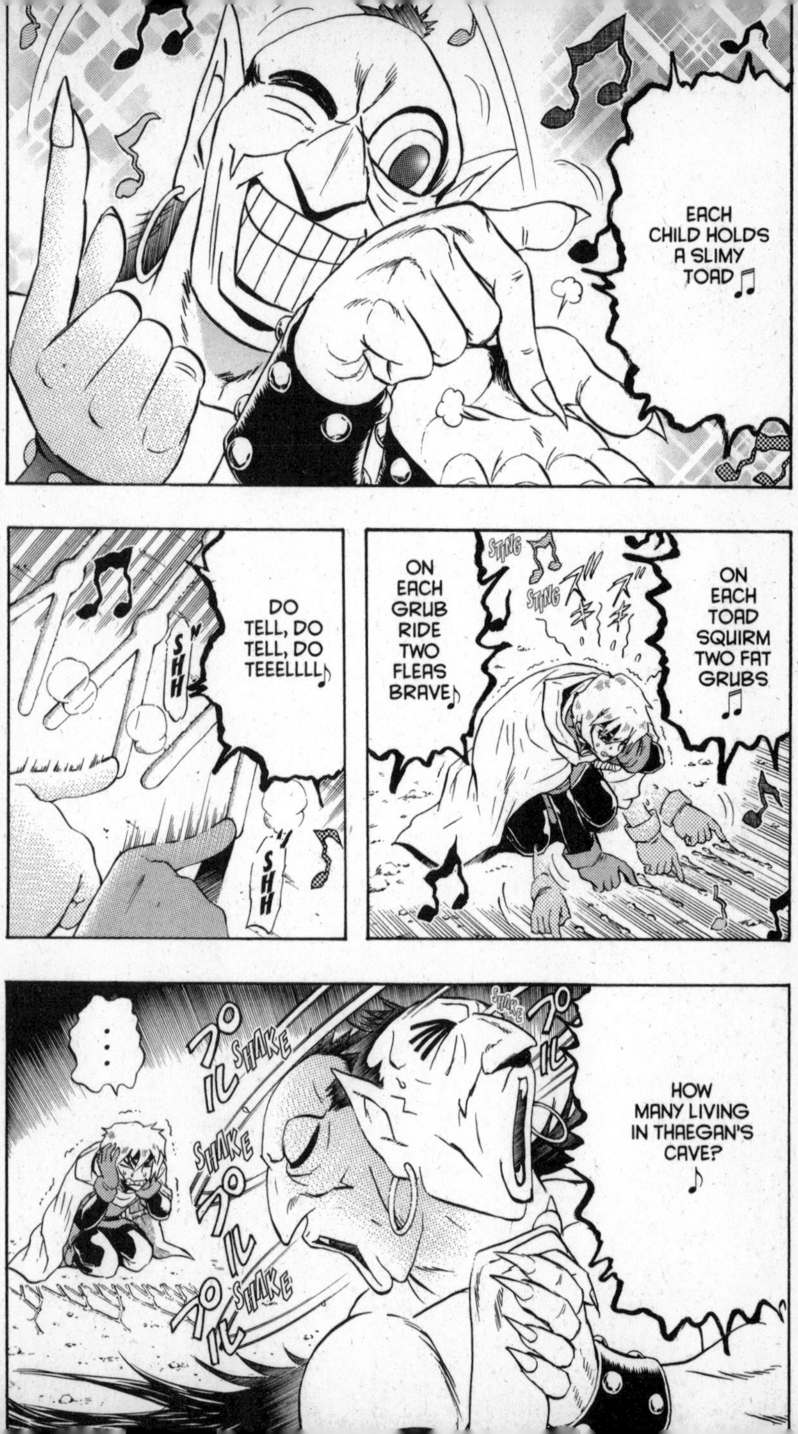
EACH CHILD HOLDS A SLIMY TOAD ♫
STING
ズキ
STING
ズキ
ON EACH TOAD SQUIRM TWO FAT GRUBS ♫
ON EACH GRUB RIDE TWO FLEAS BRAVE ♪
DO TELL, DO TELL, DO TEEELLLL ♪
SHH
SHH
SHAKE
プル
HOW MANY LIVING IN THAEGAN'S CAVE? ♪
プル
SHAKE
SHAKE
プル
SHAKE
プル
...

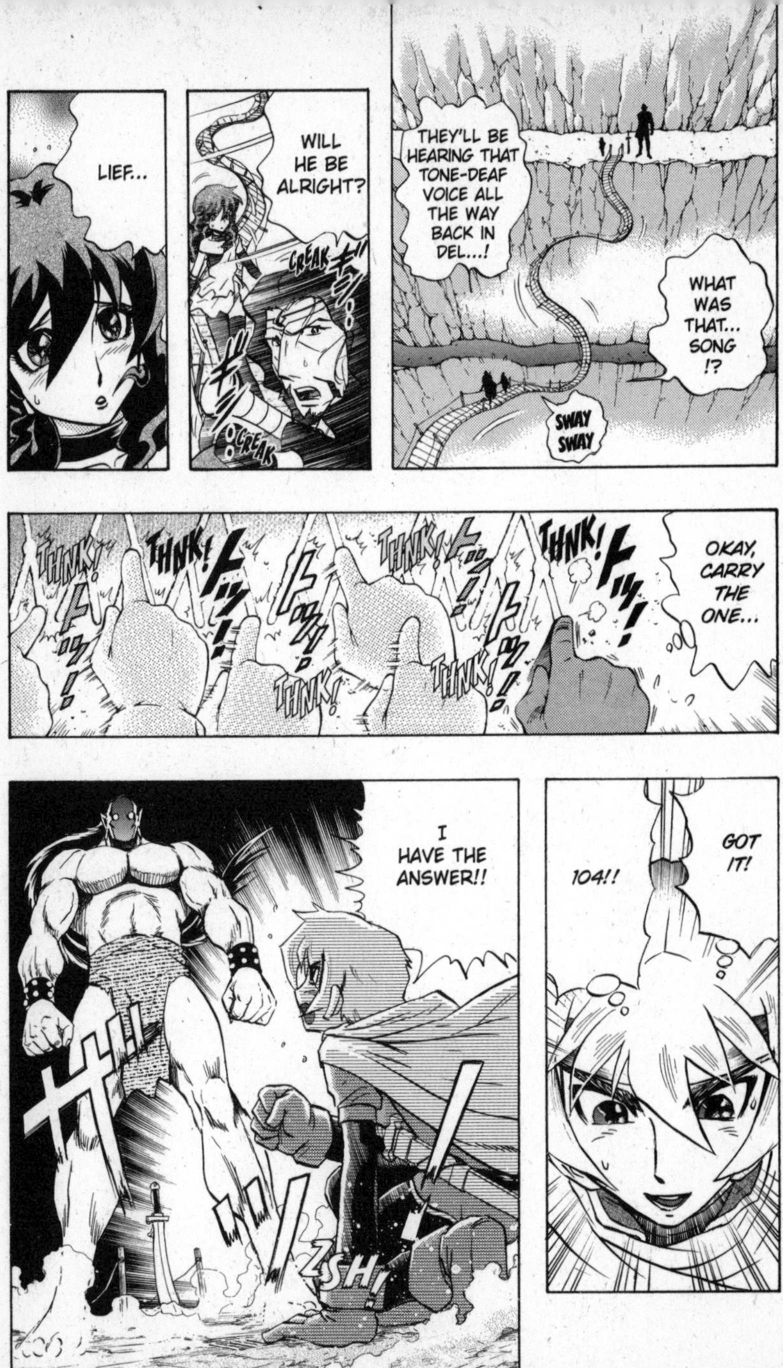

WHAT WAS THAT... SONG !?
THEY'LL BE HEARING THAT TONE-DEAF VOICE ALL THE WAY BACK IN DEL...!
SWAY SWAY
WILL HE BE ALRIGHT?
CREAK
CREAK
LIEF...
OKAY, CARRY THE ONE...
THNK!
THNK!
THNK!
THNK!
THNK!
THNK!
GOT IT!
104!!
I HAVE THE ANSWER!!
ZSH!

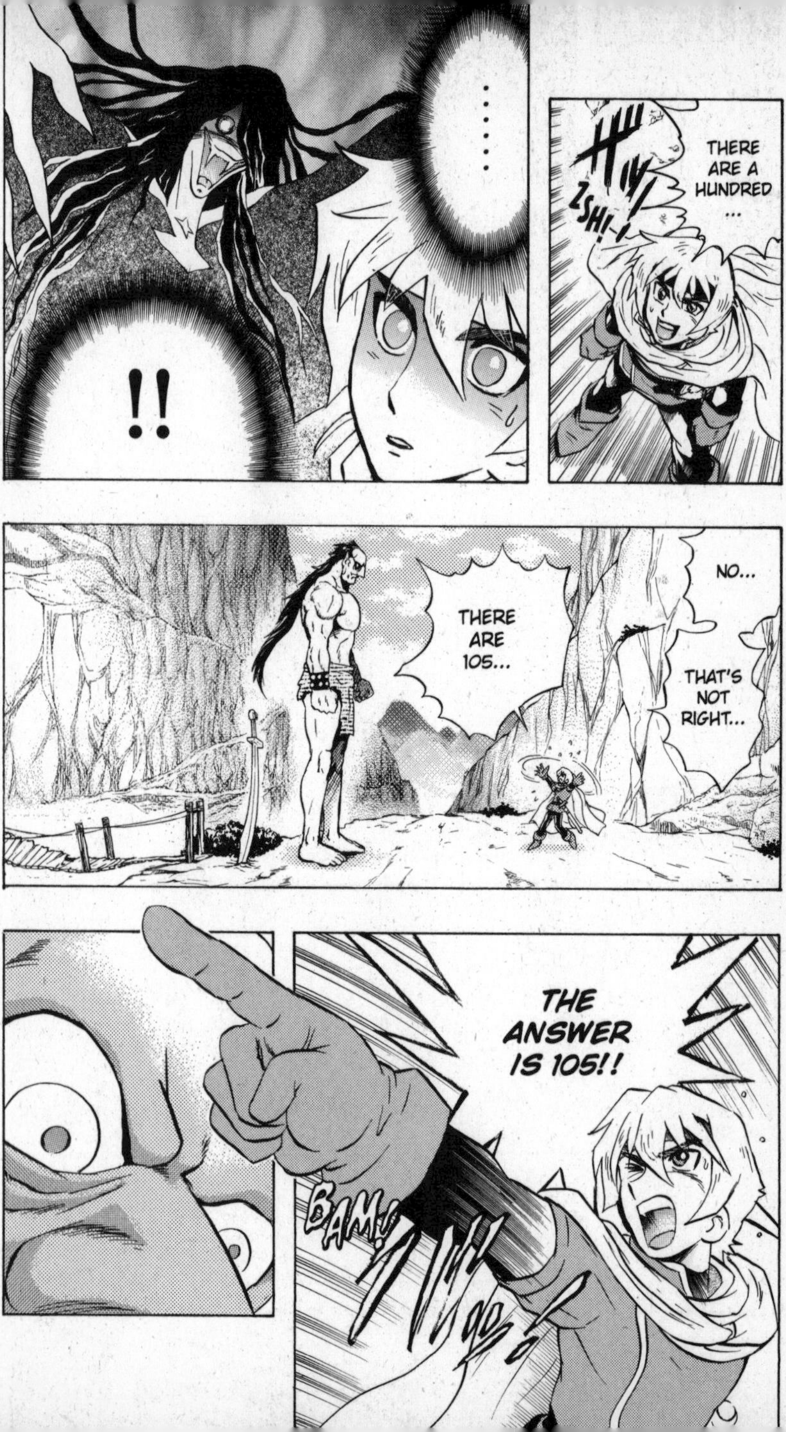
THERE ARE A HUNDRED ...
ZSHI!
…
!!
NO...
THAT'S NOT RIGHT...
THERE ARE 105...
THE ANSWER IS 105!!
BAM!

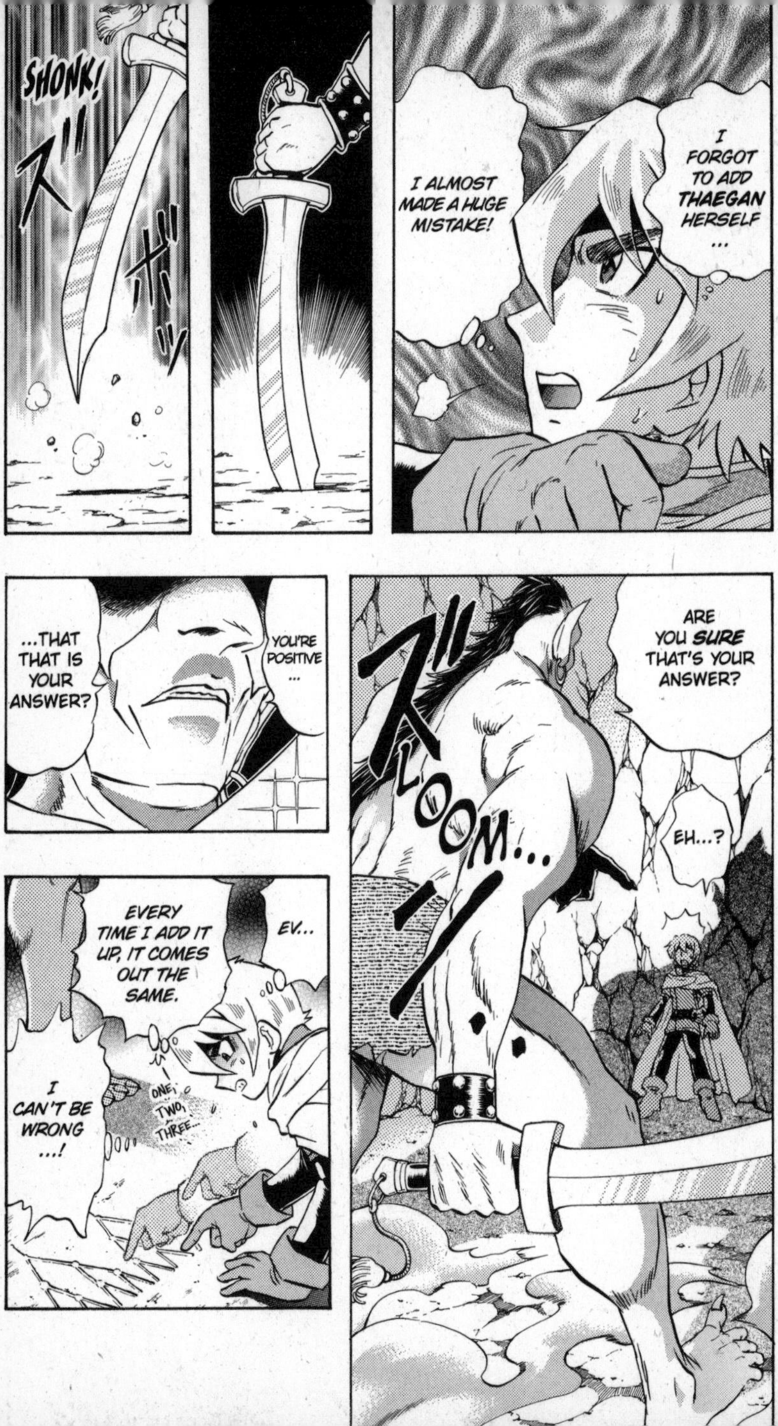
I FORGOT TO ADD THAEGAN HERSELF ...
I ALMOST MADE A HUGE MISTAKE!
SHONK!
ARE YOU SURE THAT'S YOUR ANSWER?
LOOM...!
EH...?
YOU'RE POSITIVE ...
...THAT THAT IS YOUR ANSWER?
EV...
EVERY TIME I ADD IT UP, IT COMES OUT THE SAME.
ONE, TWO, THREE...
I CAN'T BE WRONG ...!

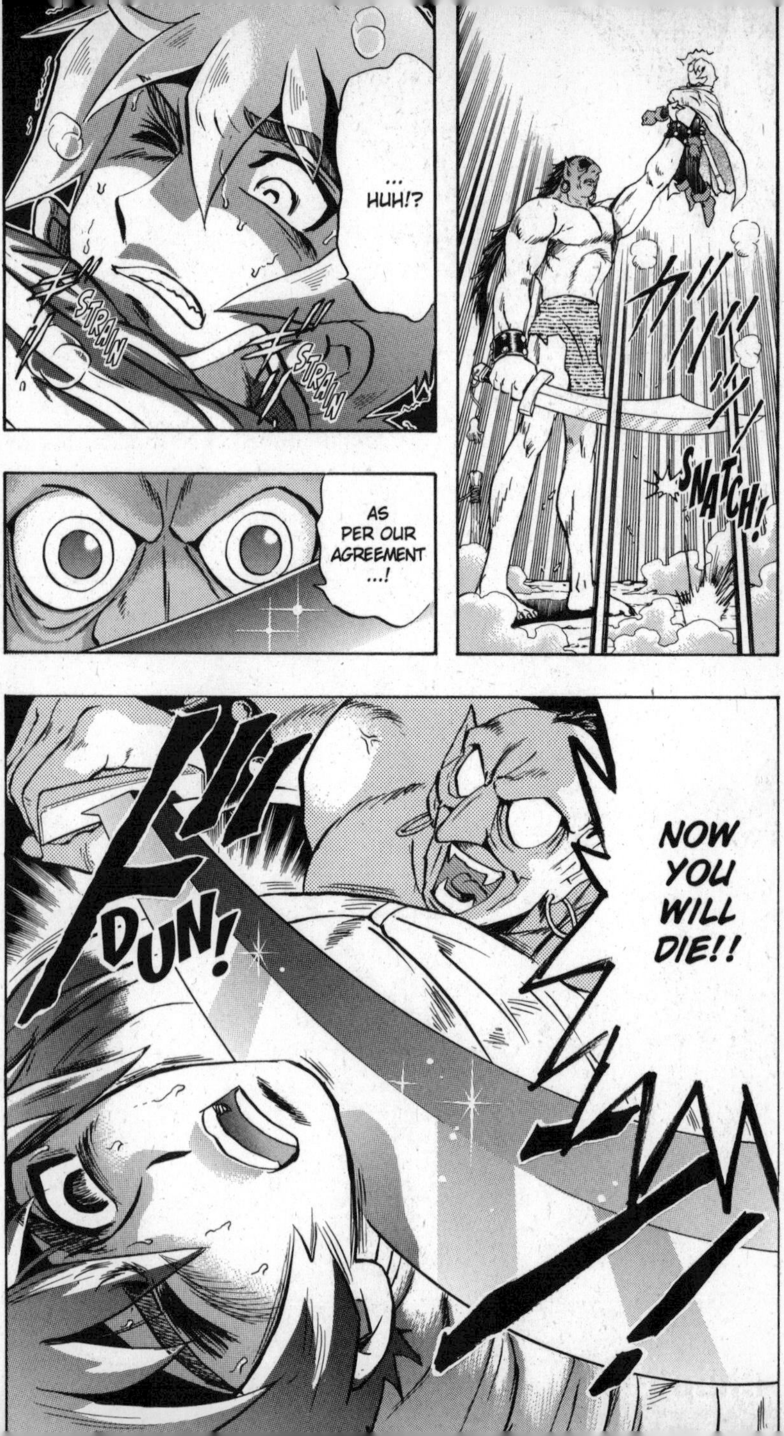
SNATCH!
... HUH!?
STRAIN
STRAIN
AS PER OUR AGREEMENT ...!
NOW YOU WILL DIE!!
DUN!

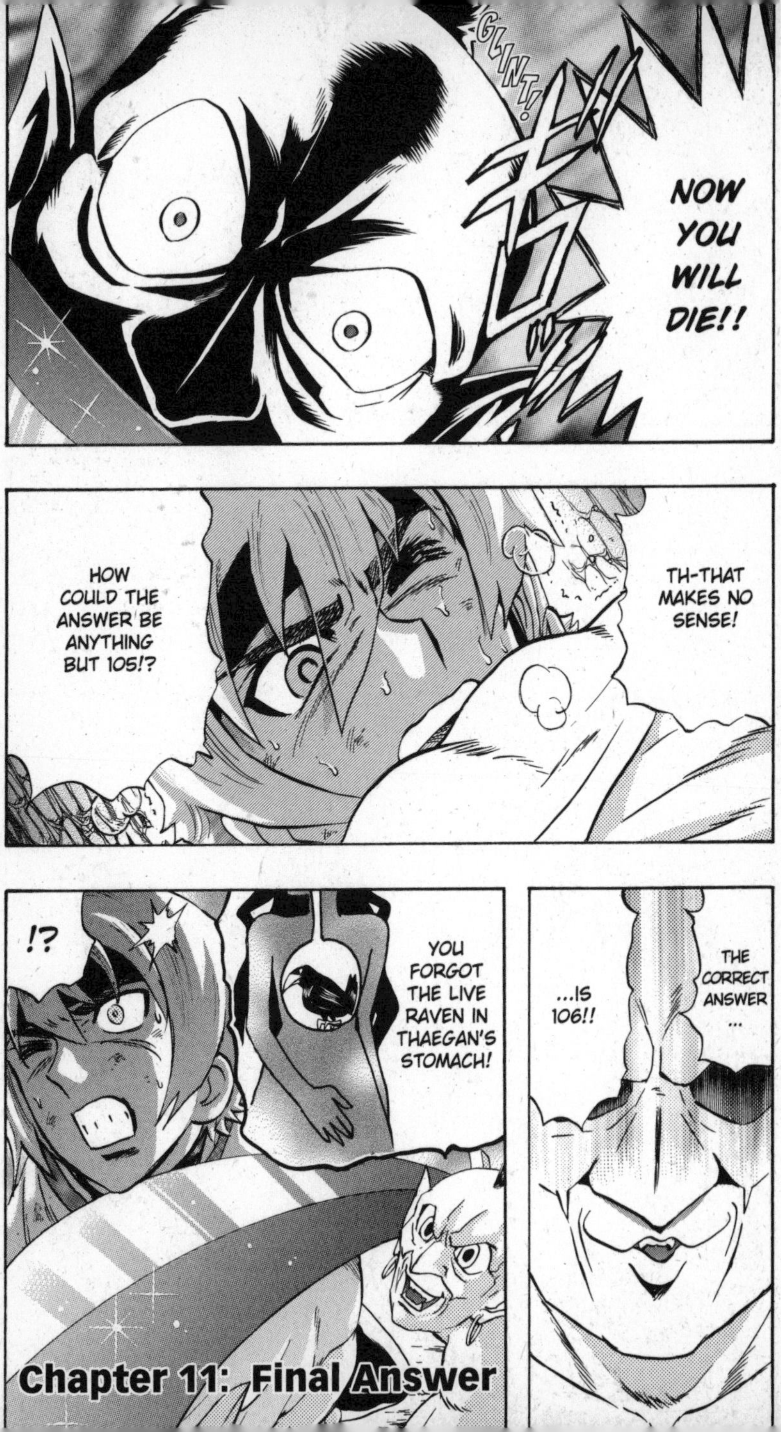
GLINT!
NOW YOU WILL DIE!!
TH-THAT MAKES NO SENSE!
HOW COULD THE ANSWER BE ANYTHING BUT 105!?
THE CORRECT ANSWER ...
...IS 106!!
YOU FORGOT THE LIVE RAVEN IN THAEGAN'S STOMACH!
!?

Chapter 11: Final Answer

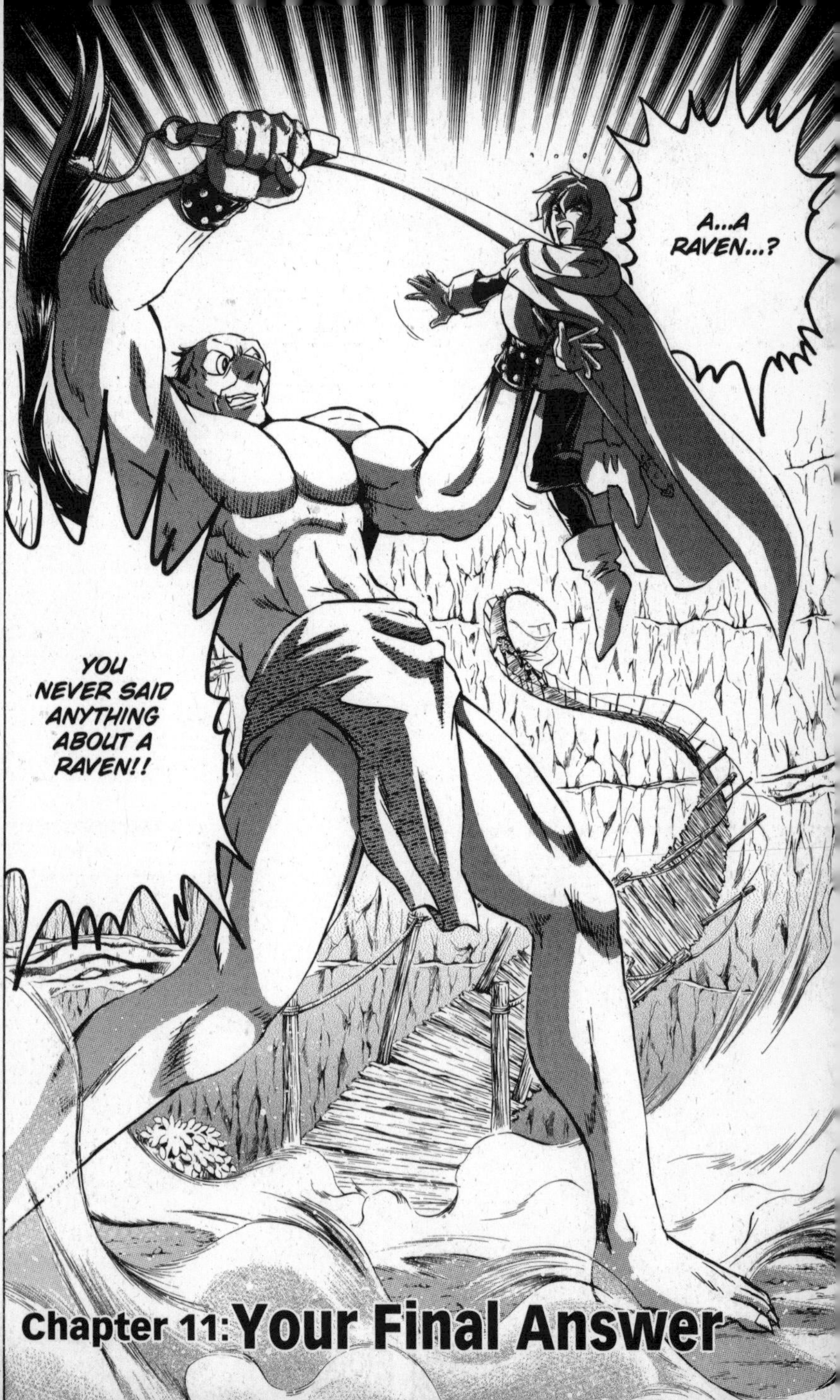
A...A RAVEN...?
YOU NEVER SAID ANYTHING ABOUT A RAVEN!!

Chapter 11: Your Final Answer

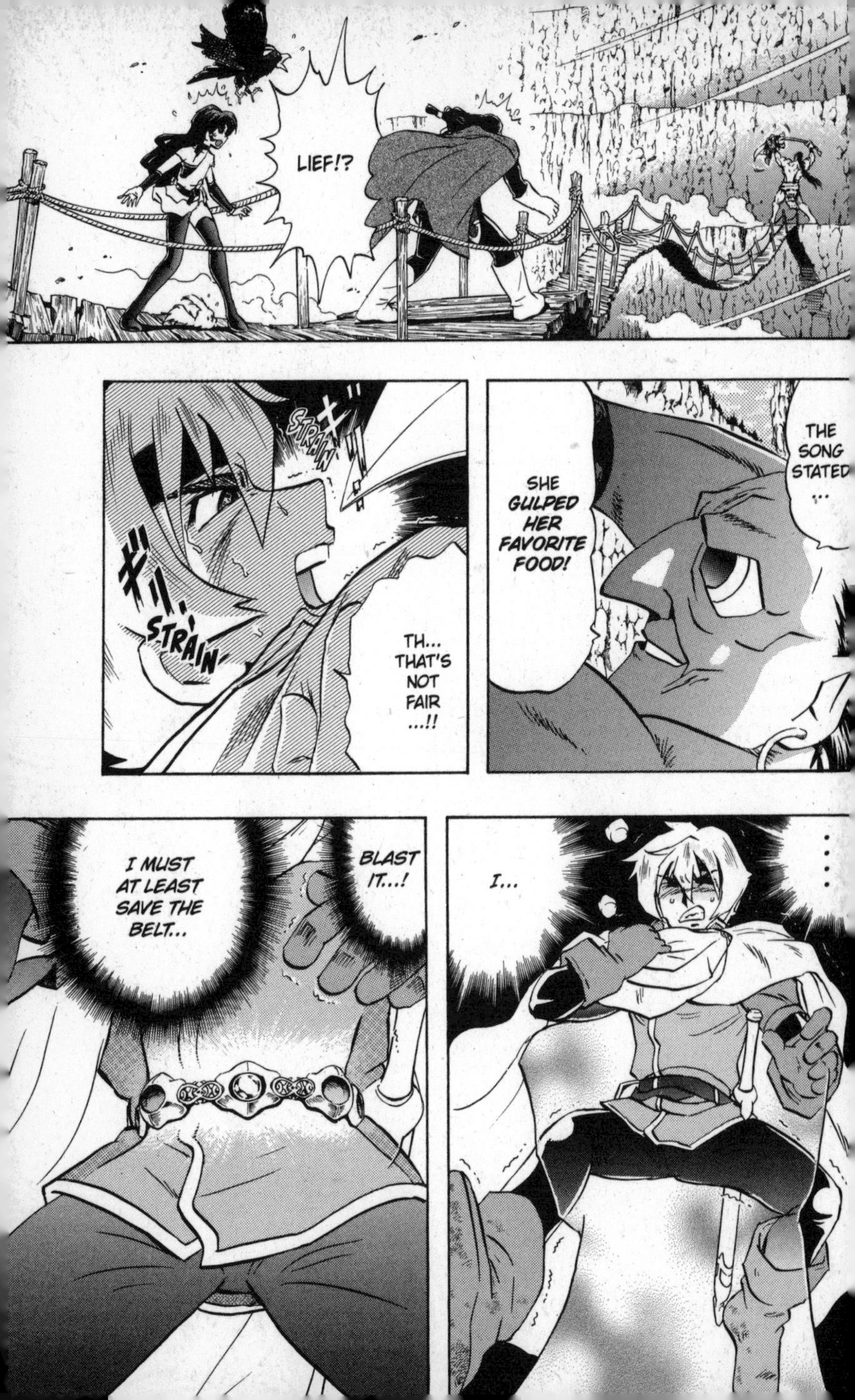
LIEF!?
THE SONG STATED ...
SHE GULPED HER FAVORITE FOOD!
STRAIN
TH... THAT'S NOT FAIR ...!!
STRAIN
....
I...
BLAST IT...!
I MUST AT LEAST SAVE THE BELT...

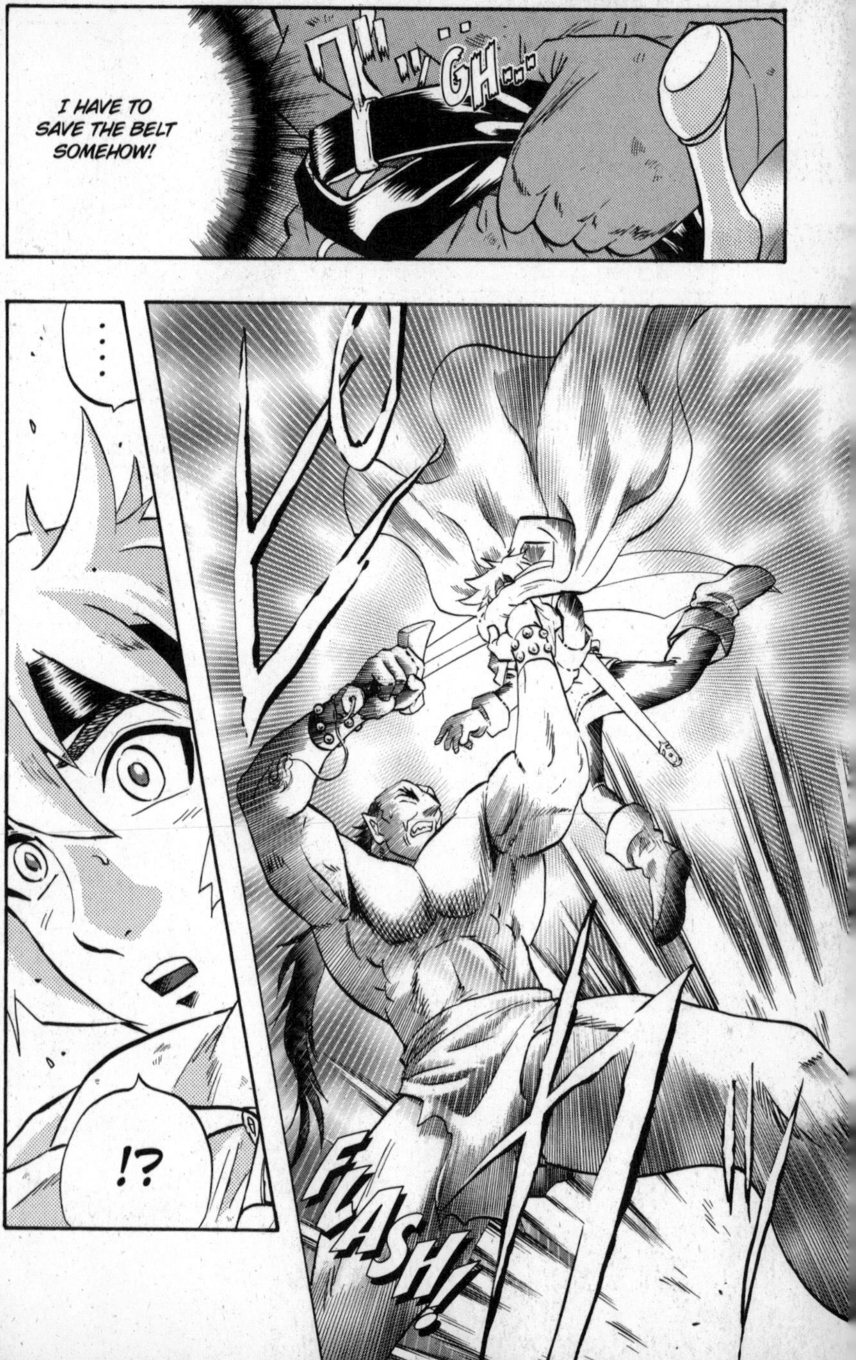
GH...
I HAVE TO SAVE THE BELT SOMEHOW!
FLASH!
....
!?

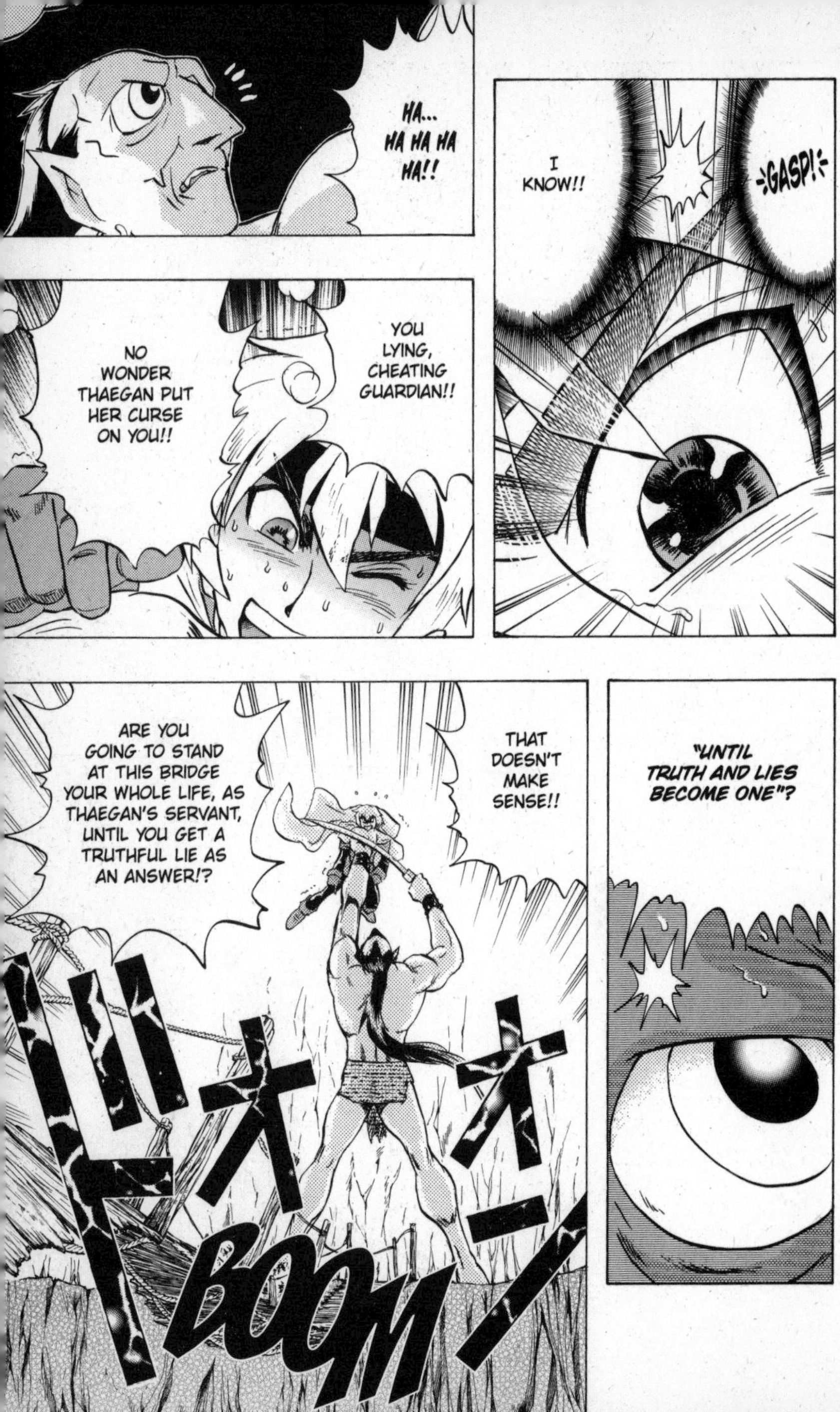
-GASP!-
I KNOW!!
HA... HA HA HA HA!!
YOU LYING, CHEATING GUARDIAN!!
NO WONDER THAEGAN PUT HER CURSE ON YOU!!
"UNTIL TRUTH AND LIES BECOME ONE"?
THAT DOESN'T MAKE SENSE!!
ARE YOU GOING TO STAND AT THIS BRIDGE YOUR WHOLE LIFE, AS THAEGAN'S SERVANT, UNTIL YOU GET A TRUTHFUL LIE AS AN ANSWER!?
BOOM!

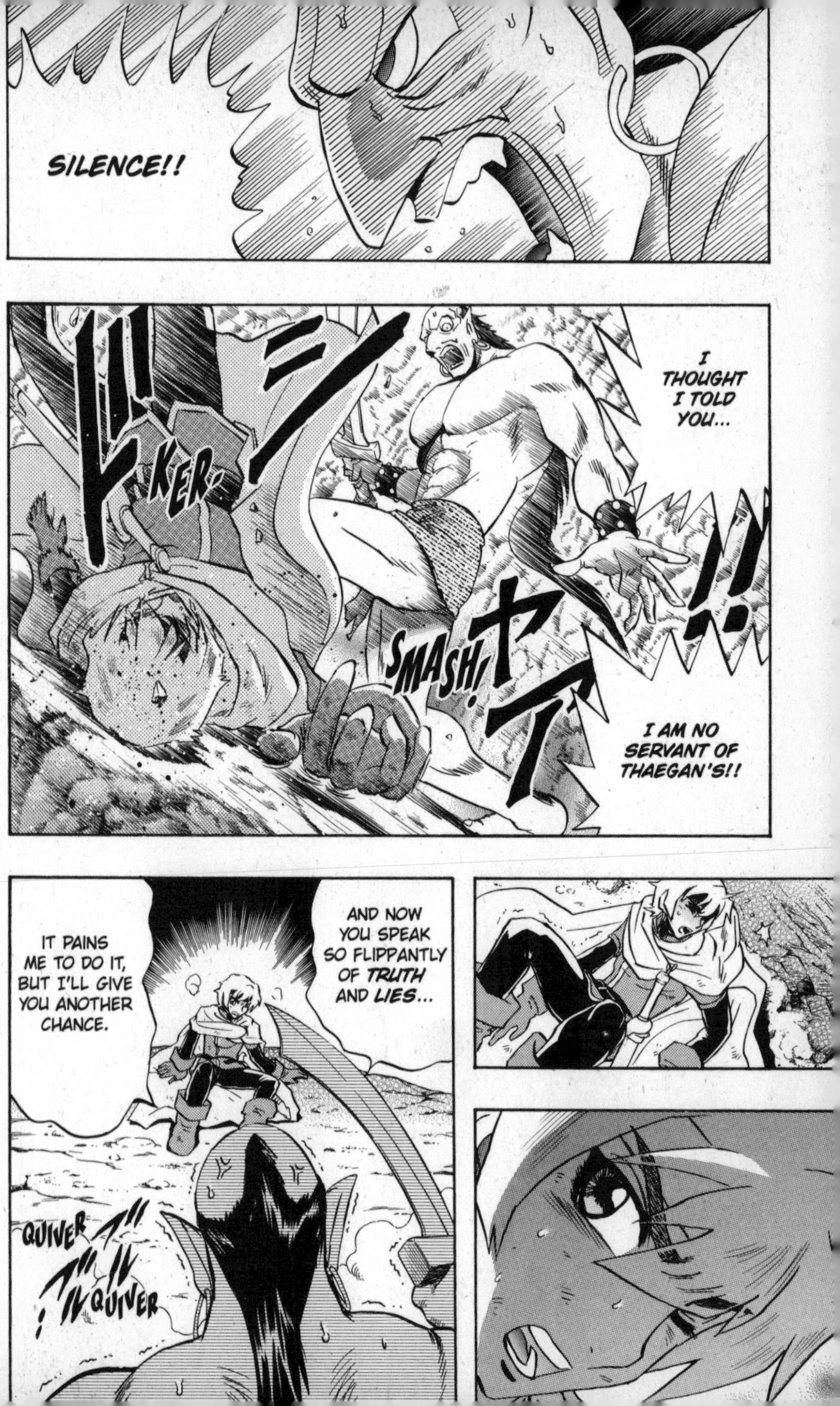
SILENCE!!
I THOUGHT I TOLD YOU...
KER-
I AM NO SERVANT OF THAEGAN'S!!
SMASH!
AND NOW YOU SPEAK SO FLIPPANTLY OF TRUTH AND LIES...
IT PAINS ME TO DO IT, BUT I'LL GIVE YOU ANOTHER CHANCE.
QUIVER
QUIVER

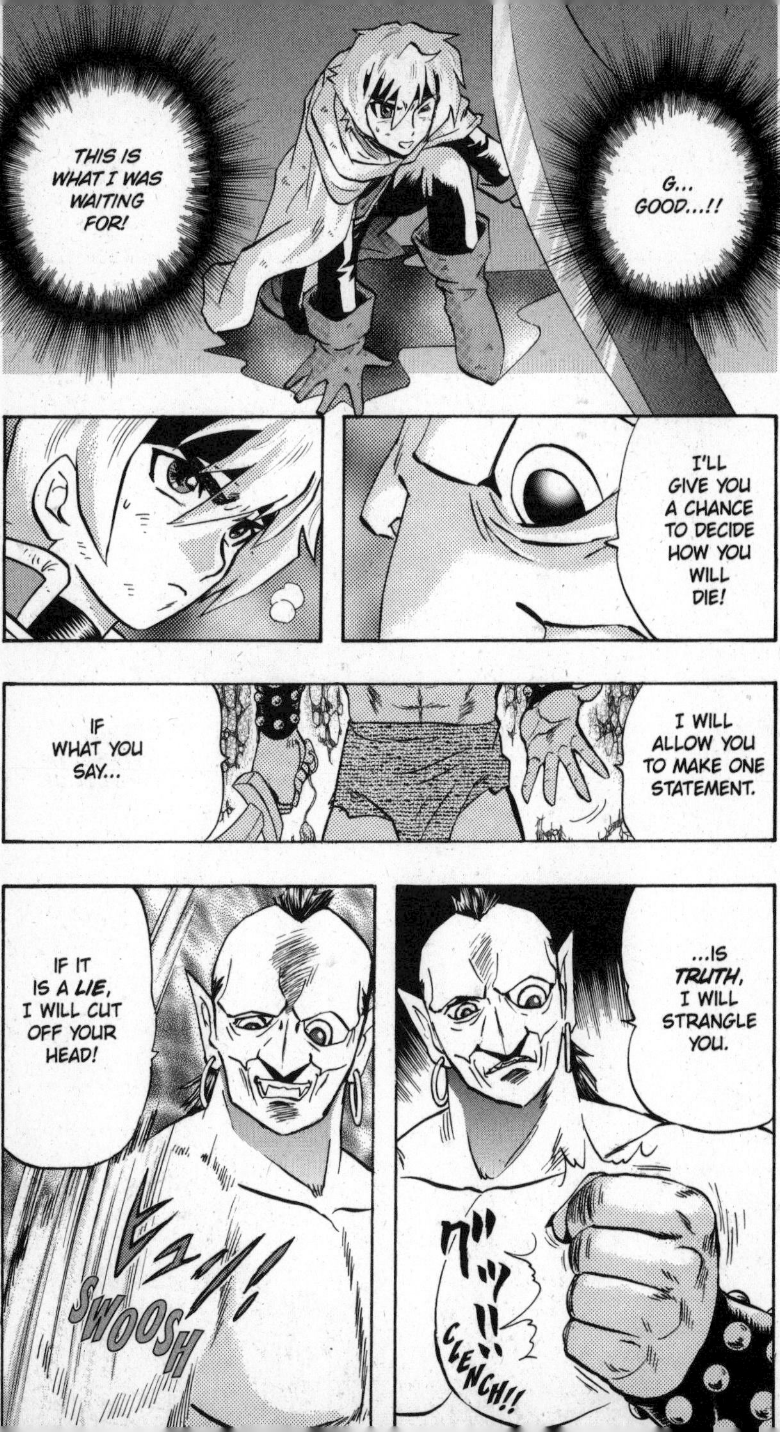
G... GOOD...!!
THIS IS WHAT I WAS WAITING FOR!
I'LL GIVE YOU A CHANCE TO DECIDE HOW YOU WILL DIE!
I WILL ALLOW YOU TO MAKE ONE STATEMENT.
IF WHAT YOU SAY...
...IS *TRUTH*, I WILL STRANGLE YOU.
CLENCH!!
IF IT IS A *LIE*, I WILL CUT OFF YOUR HEAD!
SWOOSH

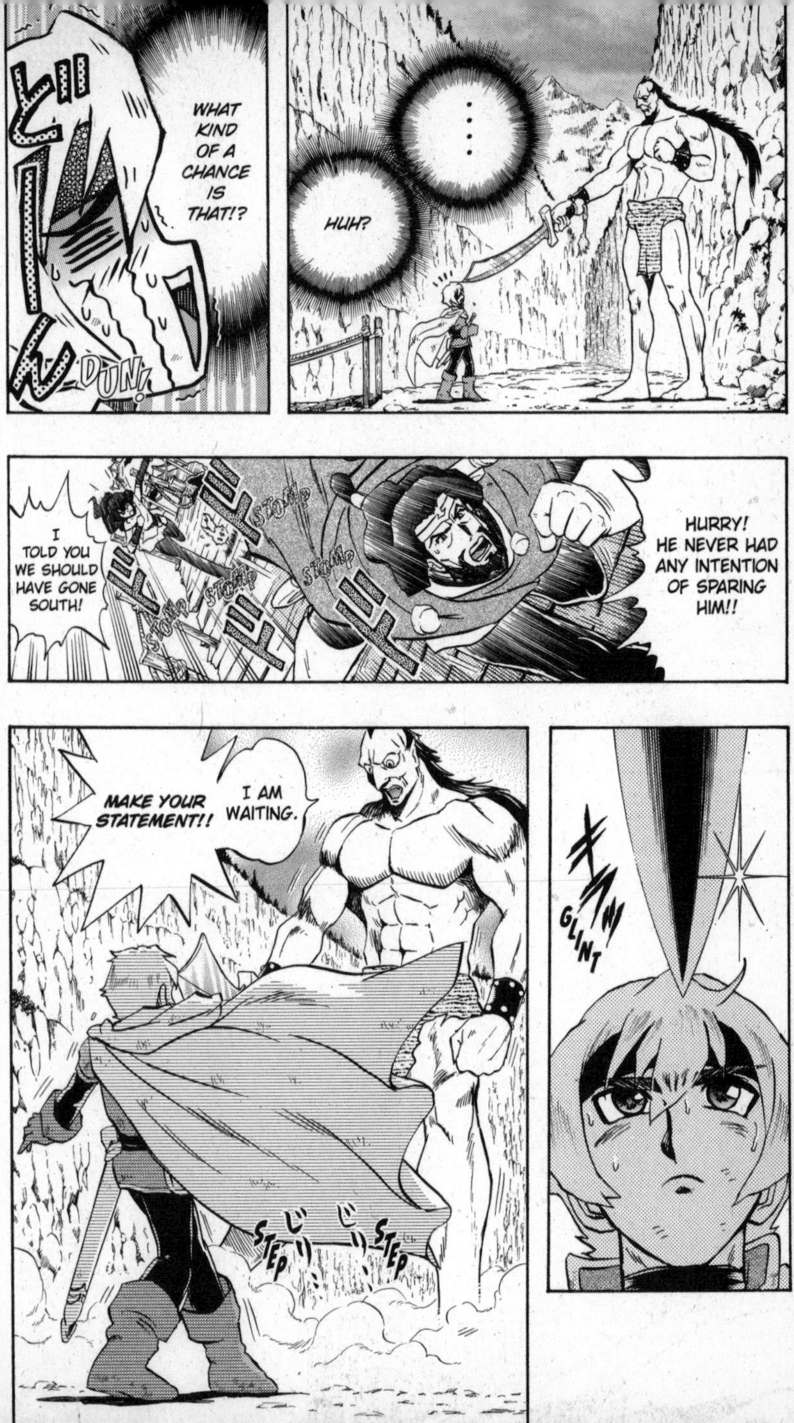
....
HUH?
WHAT KIND OF A CHANCE IS THAT!?
DUN!
HURRY! HE NEVER HAD ANY INTENTION OF SPARING HIM!!
STOMP
STOMP
STOMP
STOMP
I TOLD YOU WE SHOULD HAVE GONE SOUTH!
GLINT
I AM WAITING.
MAKE YOUR STATEMENT!!
STEP
STEP

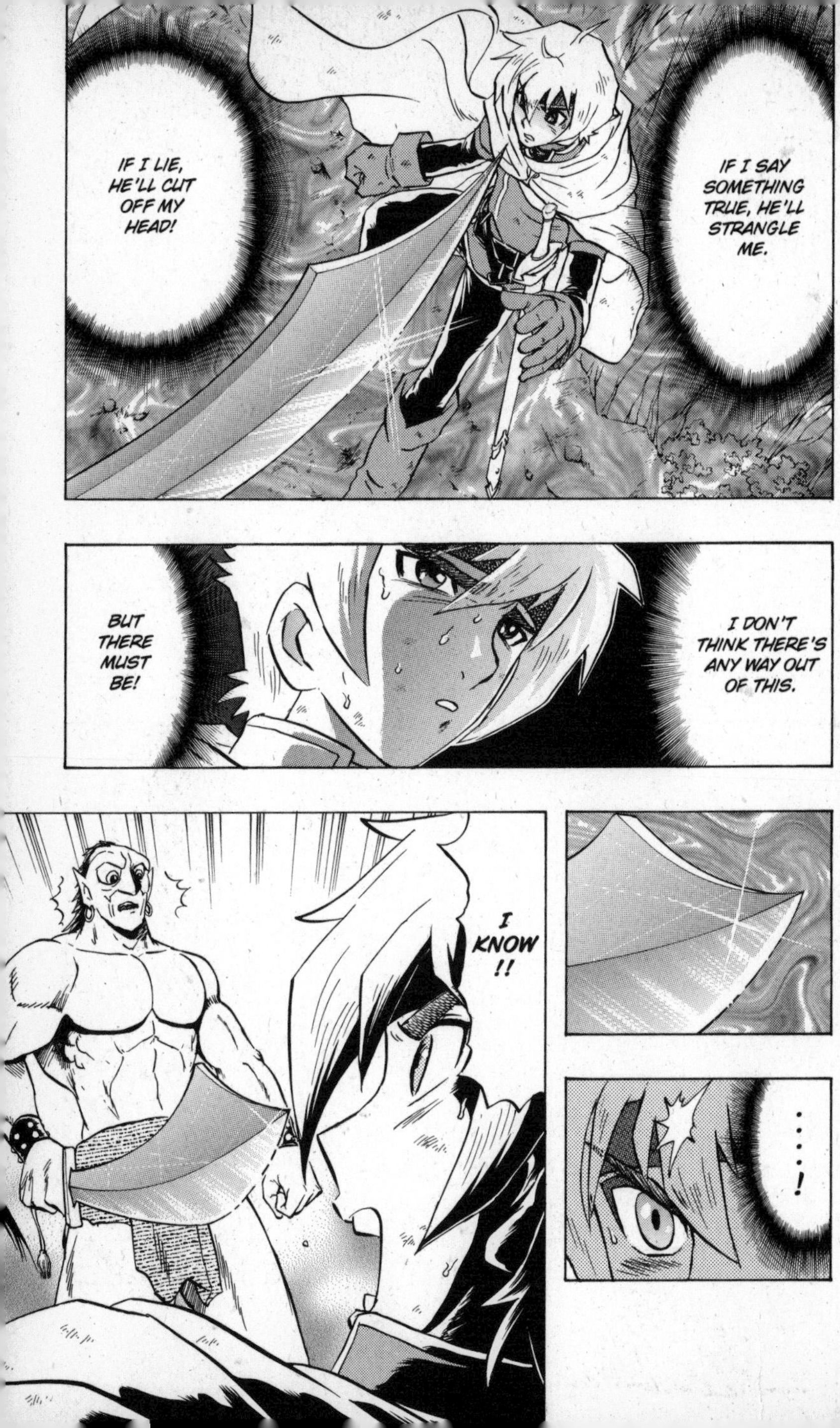
IF I SAY SOMETHING TRUE, HE'LL STRANGLE ME.
IF I LIE, HE'LL CUT OFF MY HEAD!
I DON'T THINK THERE'S ANY WAY OUT OF THIS.
BUT THERE MUST BE!
....!
I KNOW !!

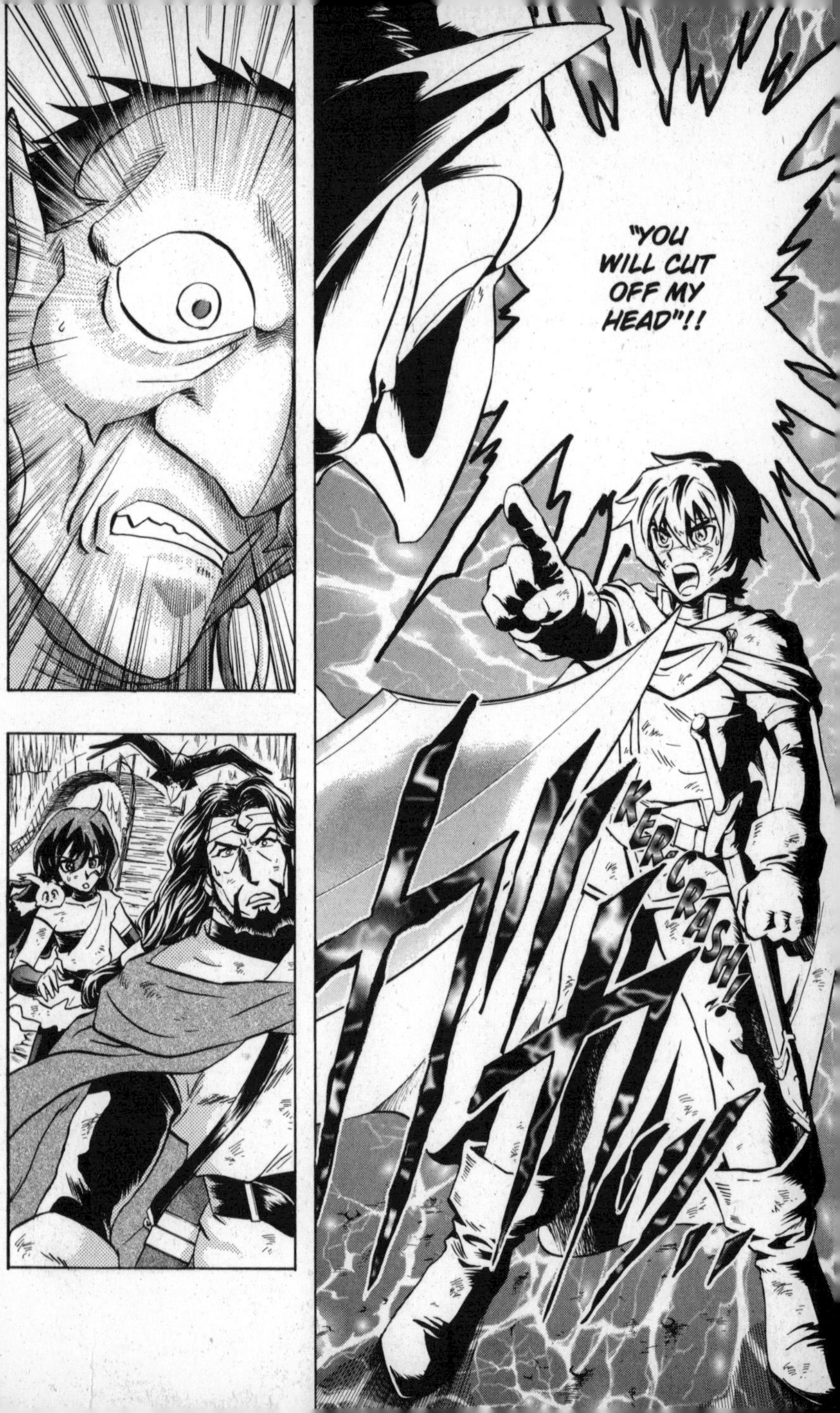
"YOU WILL CUT OFF MY HEAD"!!
KER-CRASH!

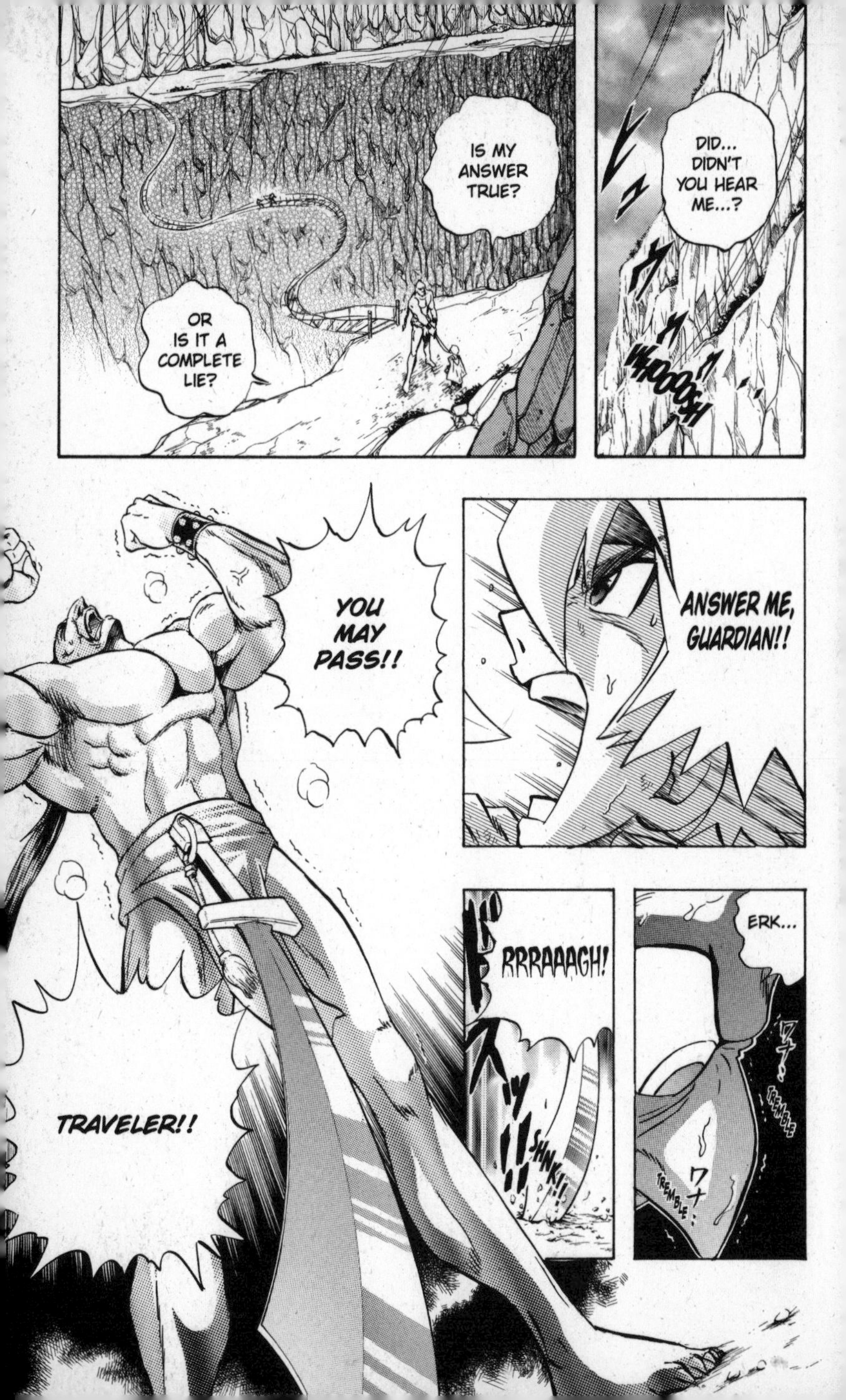
DID... DIDN'T YOU HEAR ME...?
WHOOOSH
IS MY ANSWER TRUE?
OR IS IT A COMPLETE LIE?
ANSWER ME, GUARDIAN!!
ERK...
TREMBLE
TREMBLE
RRRAAAGH!
SHNK!!
YOU MAY PASS!!
TRAVELER!!

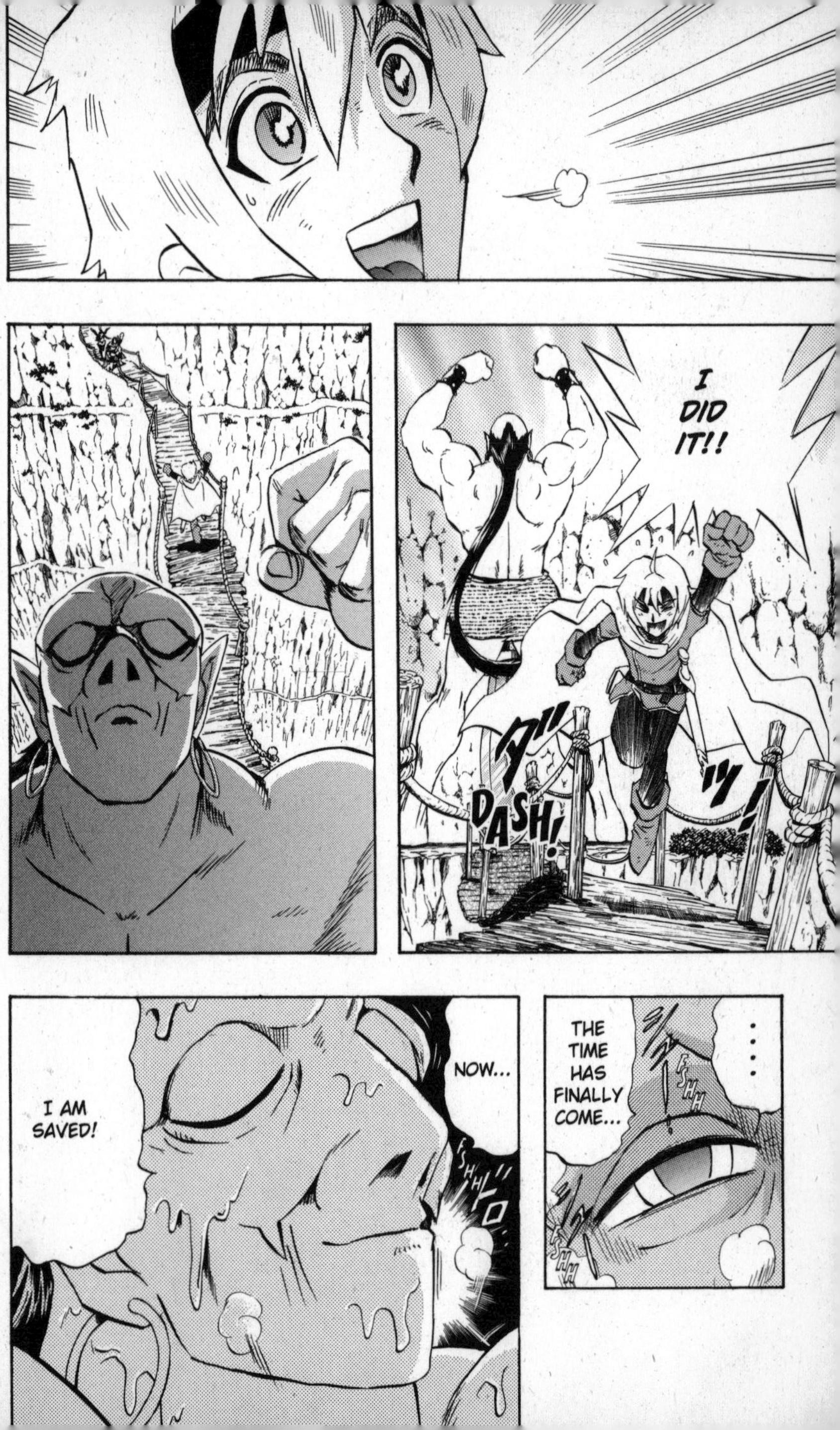
I DID IT!!
DASH!
....
THE TIME HAS FINALLY COME...
NOW...
I AM SAVED!

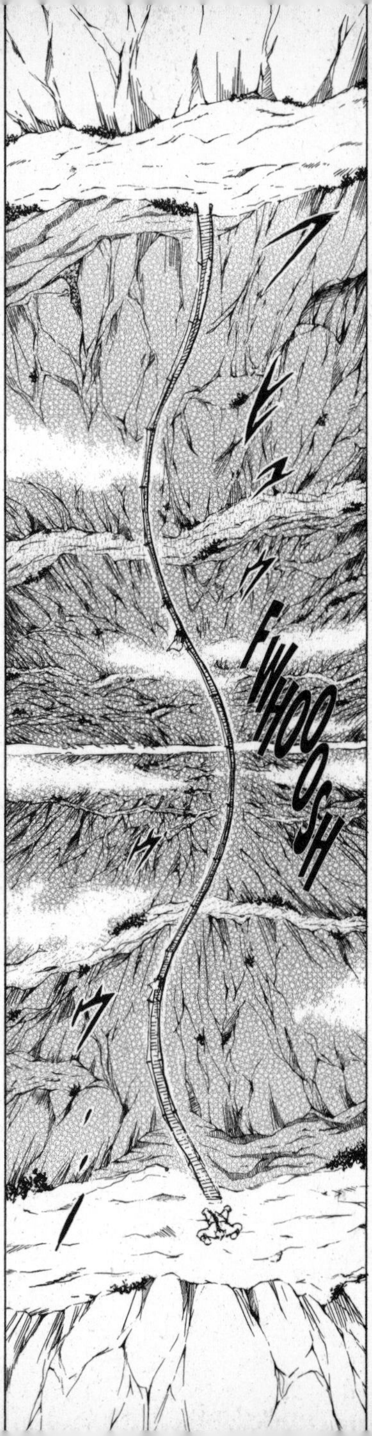
FWHOOOSH

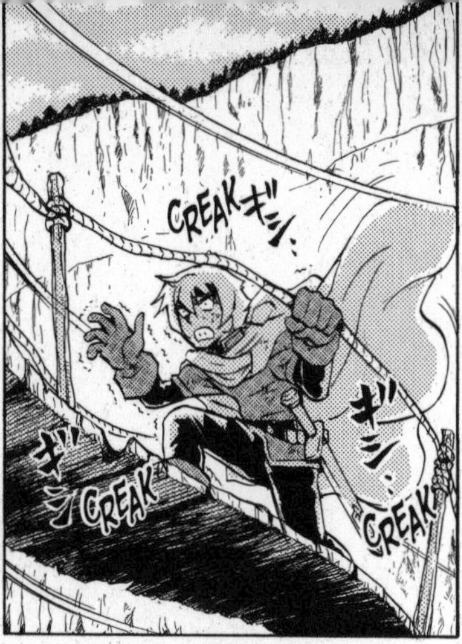
CREAK
CREAK
CREAK

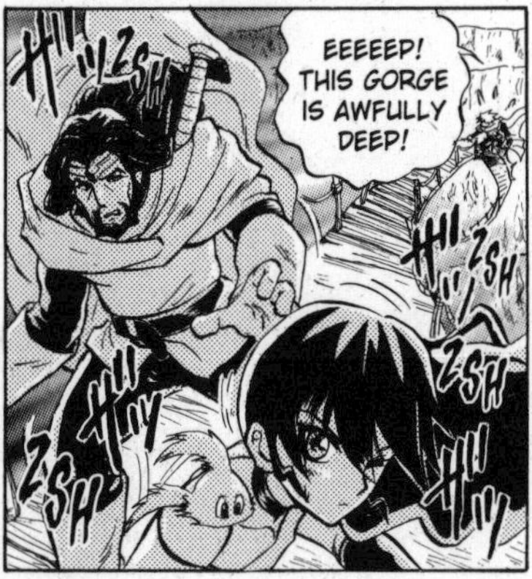
EEEEEP! THIS GORGE IS AWFULLY DEEP!
ZSH
ZSH
ZSH
ZSH

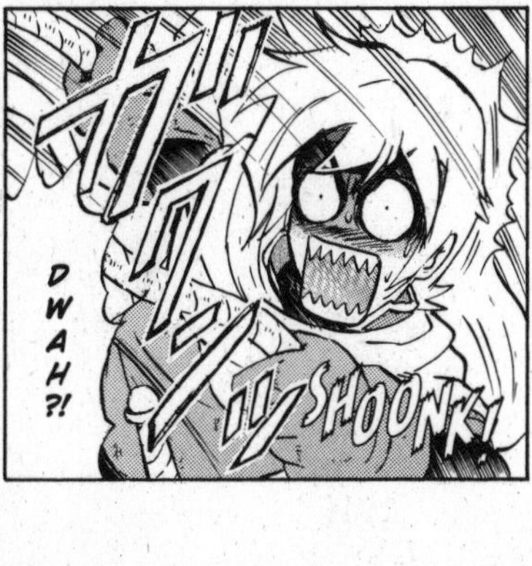
DWAH?!
SHOONK!

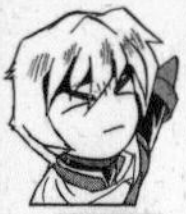

WHY DIDN'T LIEF DIE?

IF LIEF'S ANSWER, "YOU WILL CUT OFF MY HEAD," WERE TRUE, THEN THE GIANT WOULD STRANGLE HIM, MAKING HIS ANSWER A LIE, AND SO HE COULDN'T KILL HIM THAT WAY. IF LIEF'S ANSWER WERE A LIE, THEN THE GIANT WOULD HAVE CUT OFF HIS HEAD, MAKING THE ANSWER TRUE, AND SO HE COULDN'T KILL LIEF THAT WAY, EITHER.

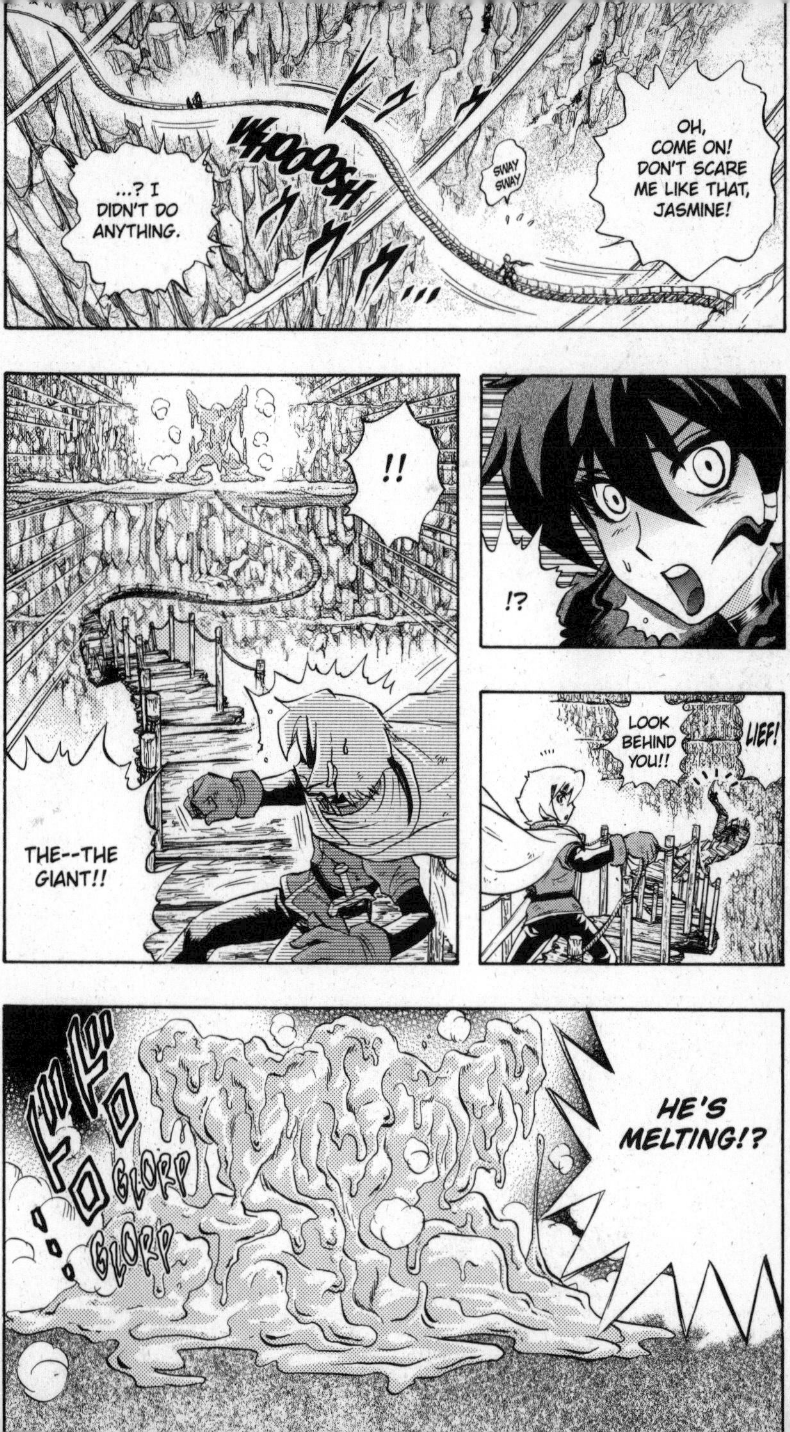
OH, COME ON! DON'T SCARE ME LIKE THAT, JASMINE!
SWAY SWAY
WHOOOOSH
...? I DIDN'T DO ANYTHING.
!?
LIEF!
LOOK BEHIND YOU!!
!!
THE--THE GIANT!!
HE'S MELTING!?
GLORP
GLORP

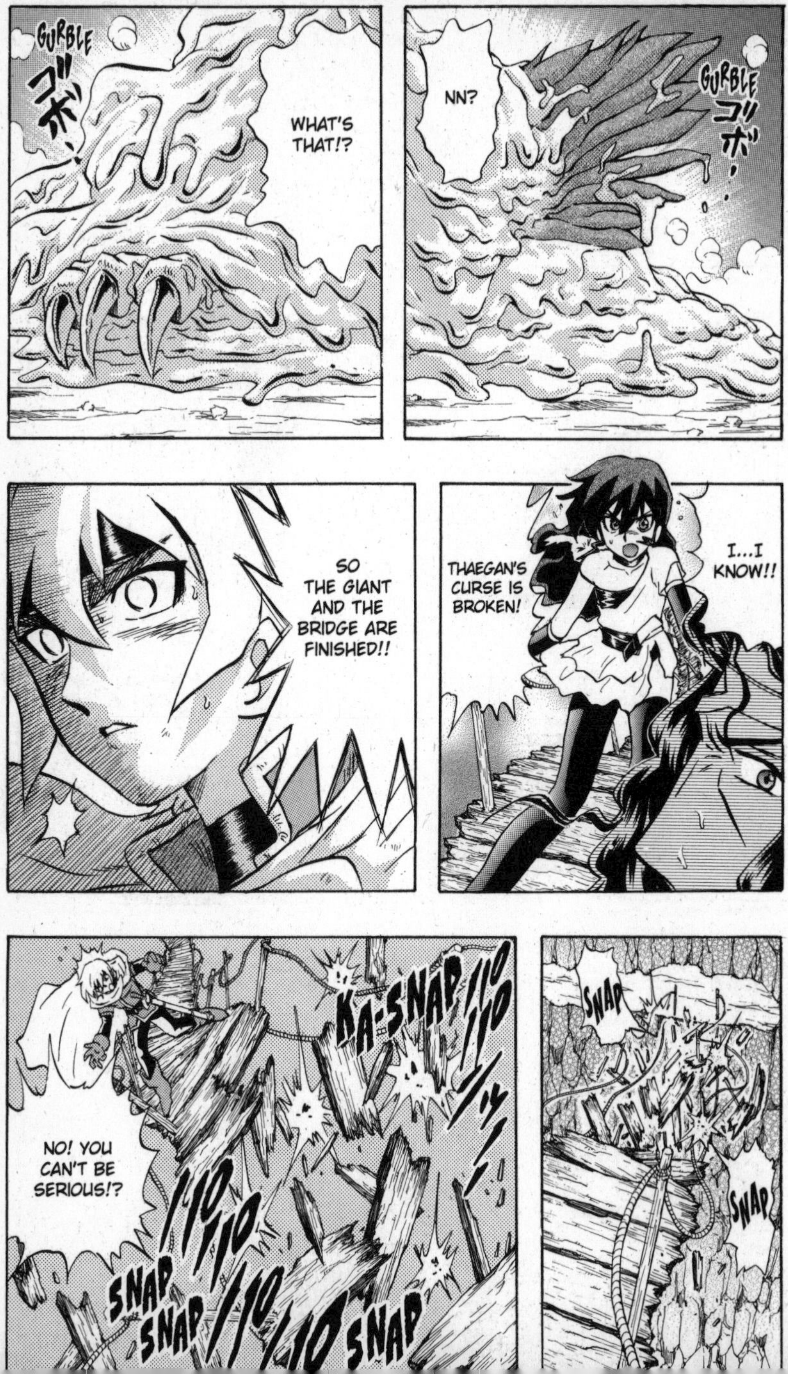
GURBLE
ゴボ
NN?
GURBLE
ゴボ
WHAT'S THAT!?
I...I KNOW!!
THAEGAN'S CURSE IS BROKEN!
SO THE GIANT AND THE BRIDGE ARE FINISHED!!
SNAP
SNAP
KA-SNAP
NO! YOU CAN'T BE SERIOUS!?
SNAP
SNAP
SNAP

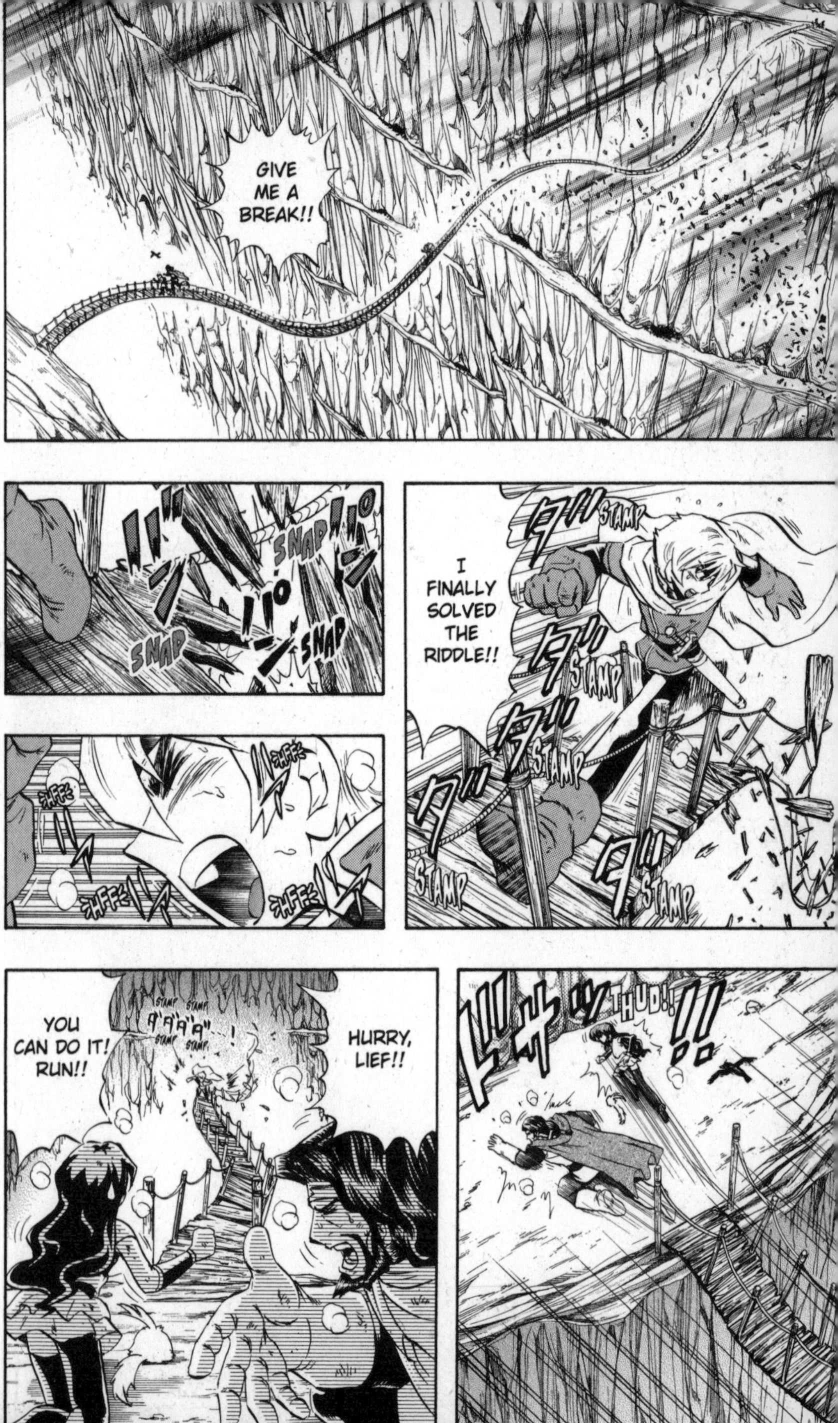
GIVE ME A BREAK!!
STAMP
I FINALLY SOLVED THE RIDDLE!!
STAMP
STAMP
STAMP
STAMP
SNAP
SNAP
SNAP
HUFF
HUFF
HUFF
HUFF
THUD!!
STAMP STAMP
STAMP STAMP
HURRY, LIEF!!
YOU CAN DO IT! RUN!!

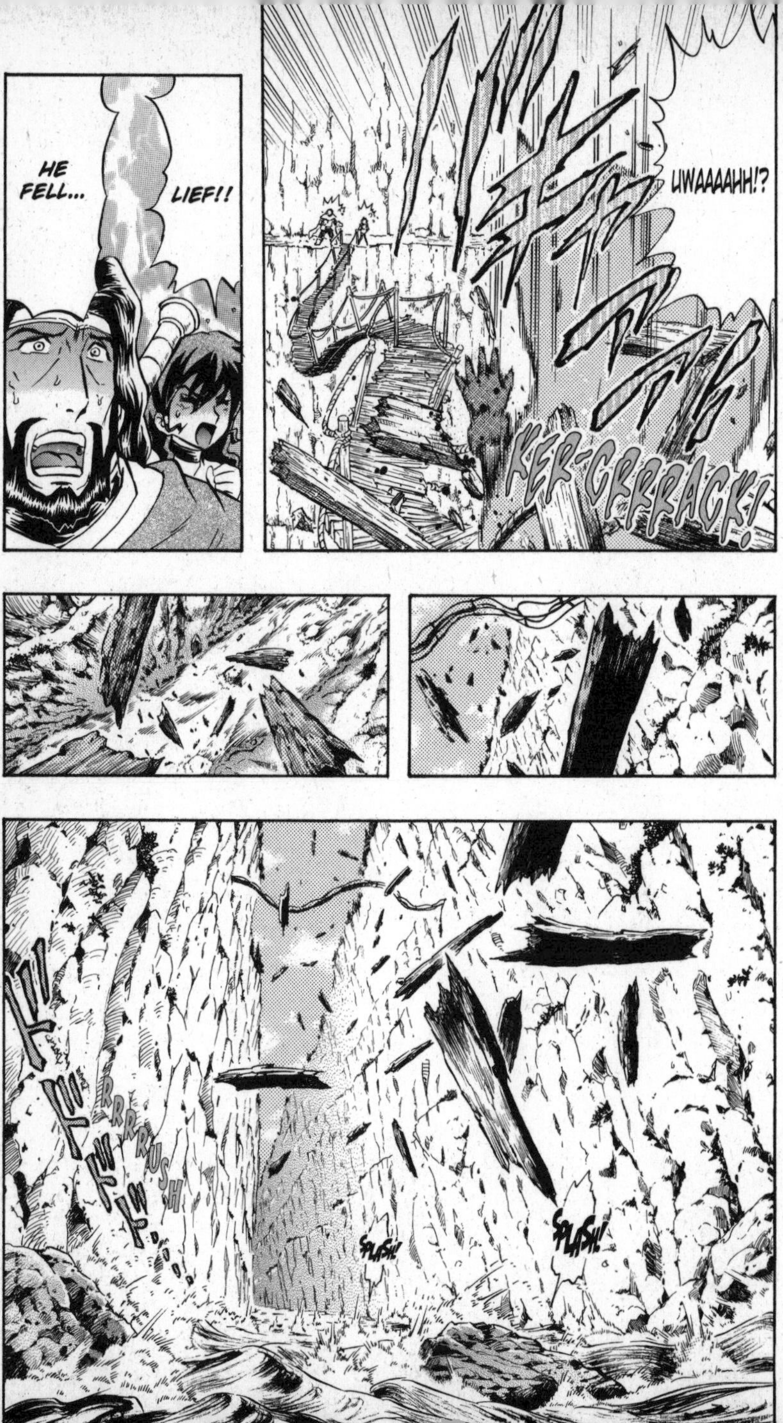
UWAAAAAH!?
KER-CRRRACK!
LIEF!!
HE FELL...
RRRRRUSH
SPLASH!
SPLASH!

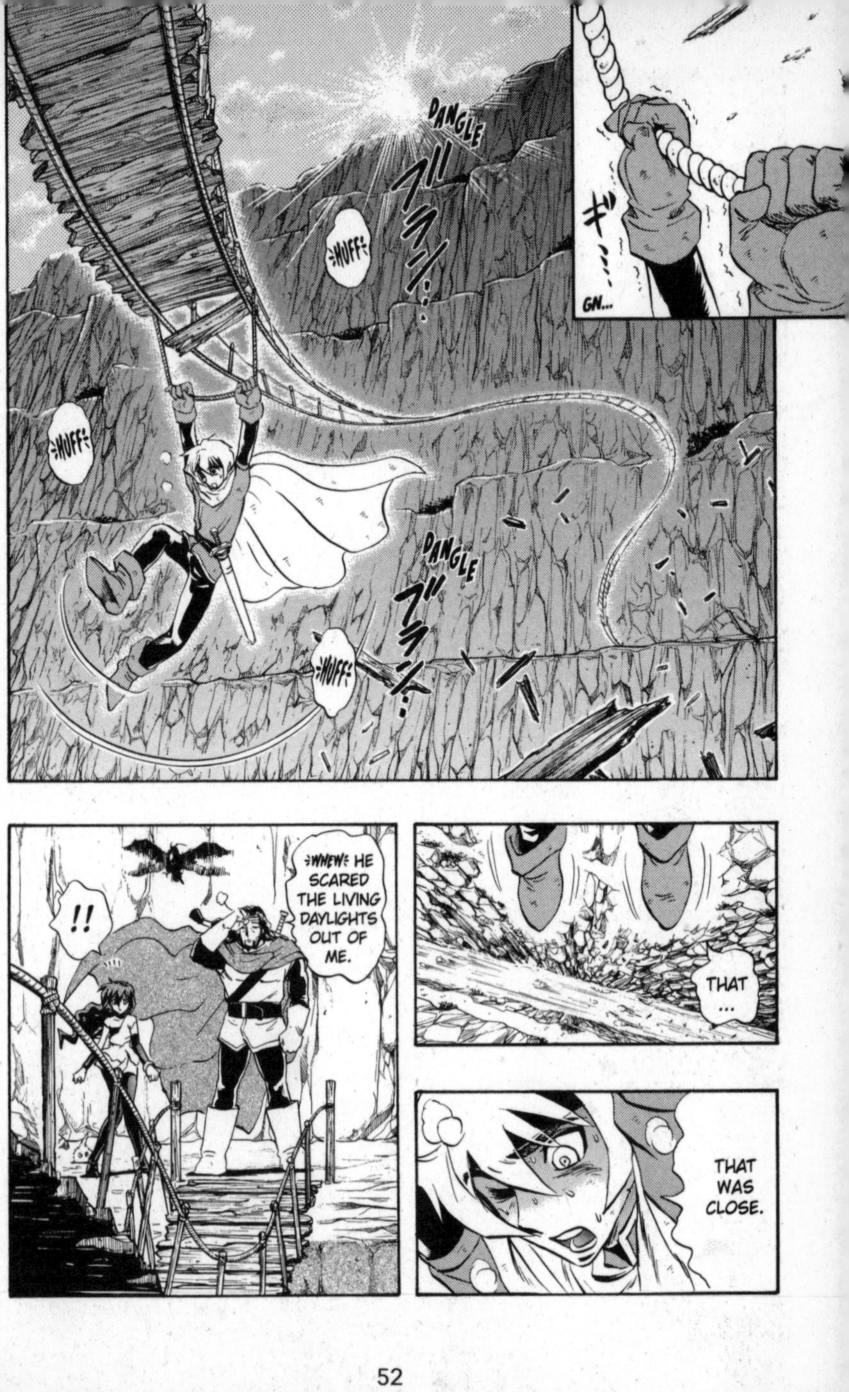
GN...
DANGLE
HUFF
HUFF
DANGLE
HUFF
THAT ...
THAT WAS CLOSE.
WHEW HE SCARED THE LIVING DAYLIGHTS OUT OF ME.
!!

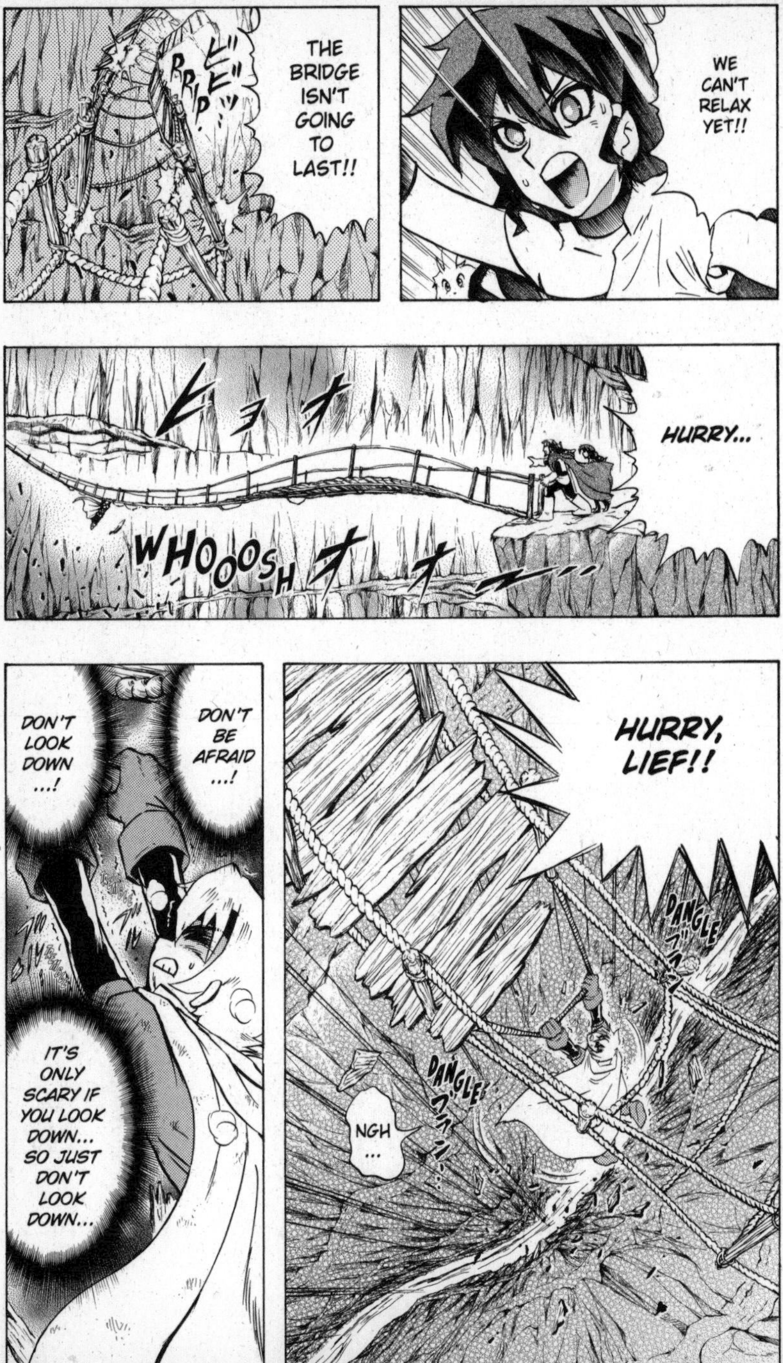
WE CAN'T RELAX YET!!
RRIP
THE BRIDGE ISN'T GOING TO LAST!!
HURRY...
WHOOOSH
HURRY, LIEF!!
DANGLE
DANGLE
NGH ...
DON'T BE AFRAID ...!
DON'T LOOK DOWN ...!
IT'S ONLY SCARY IF YOU LOOK DOWN... SO JUST DON'T LOOK DOWN...

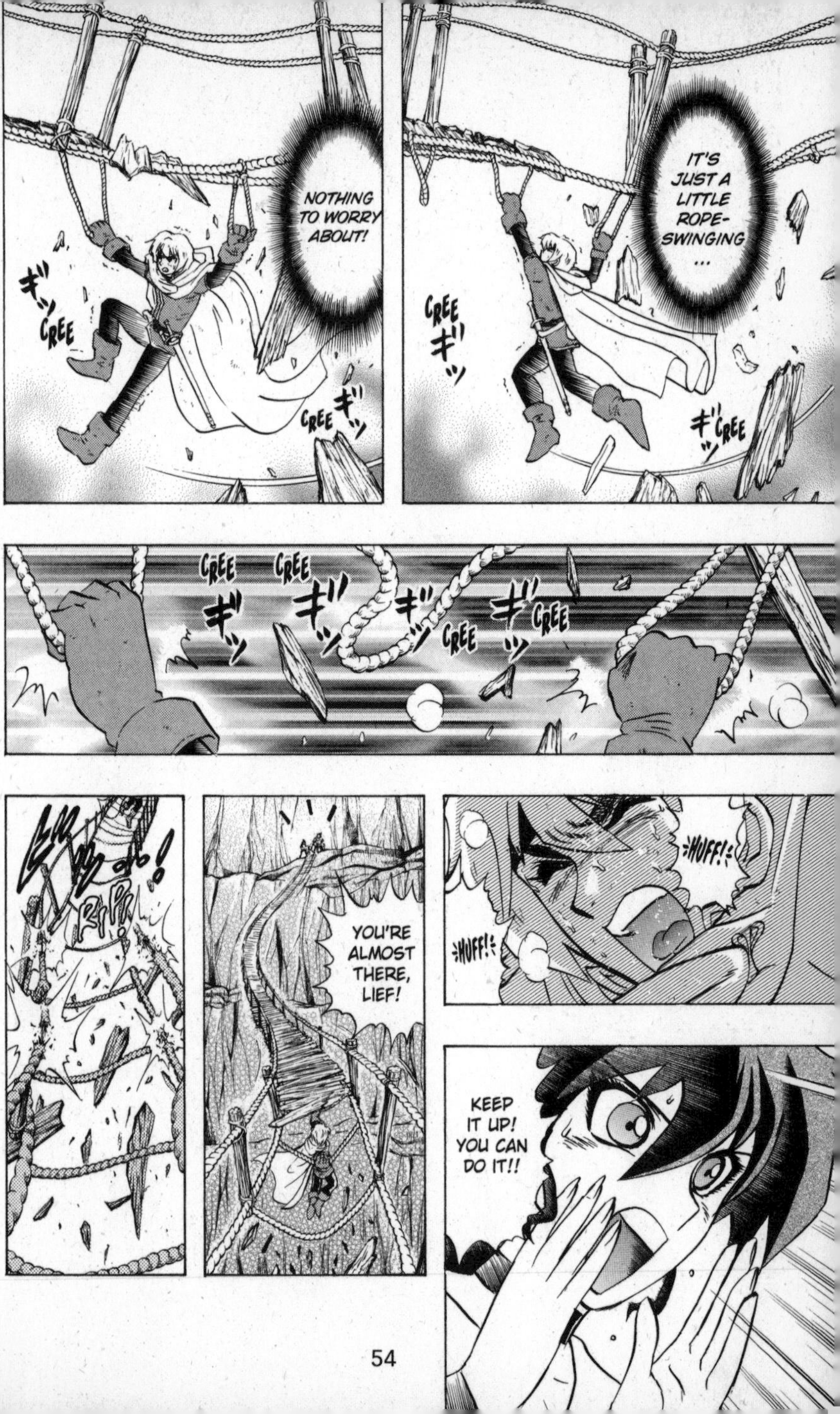

IT'S JUST A LITTLE ROPE-SWINGING...
CREE
ギッ
ギッ CREE
NOTHING TO WORRY ABOUT!
ギッ CREE
CREE ギッ
CREE ギッ
CREE ギッ
CREE ギッ
CREE ギッ
!HUFF!
!HUFF!
KEEP IT UP! YOU CAN DO IT!!
YOU'RE ALMOST THERE, LIEF!
RIP!

SNAP!!

SHOONK!!

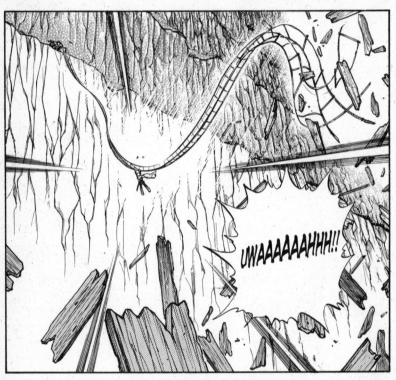

UWAAAAAAHHH!!

LIEF!!

BAM!!

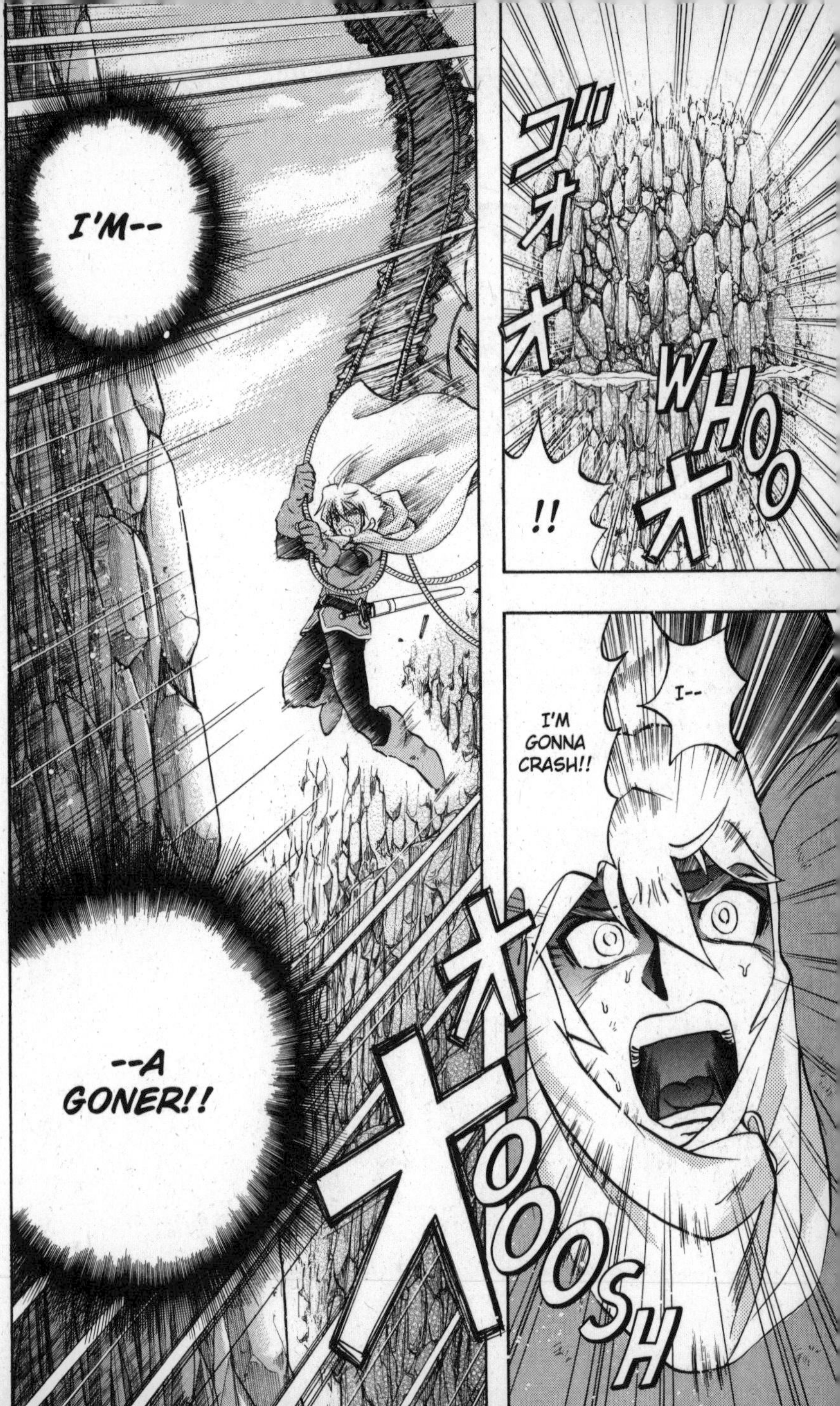
ゴオオ
WHOO
オ
!!
I--
I'M GONNA CRASH!!
オ
オ
OOOSH
I'M--
--A GONER!!

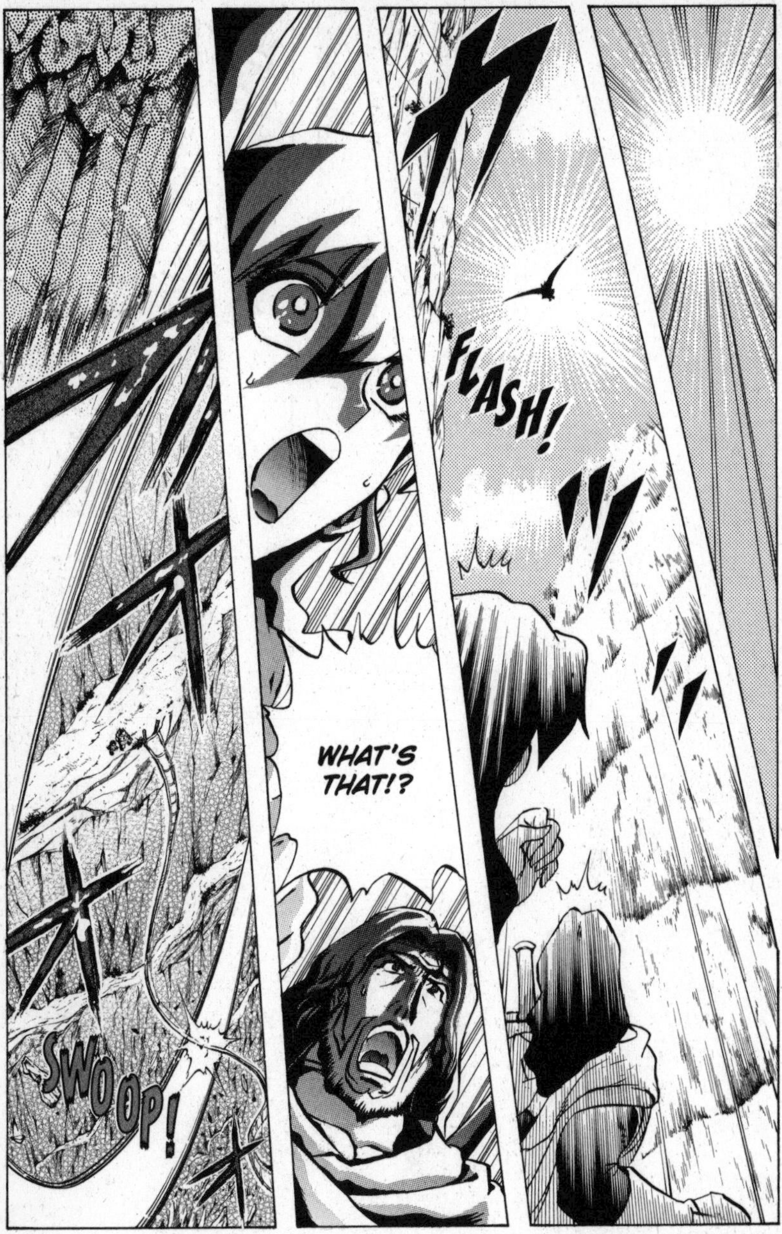
FLASH!
WHAT'S THAT!?
SWOOP!

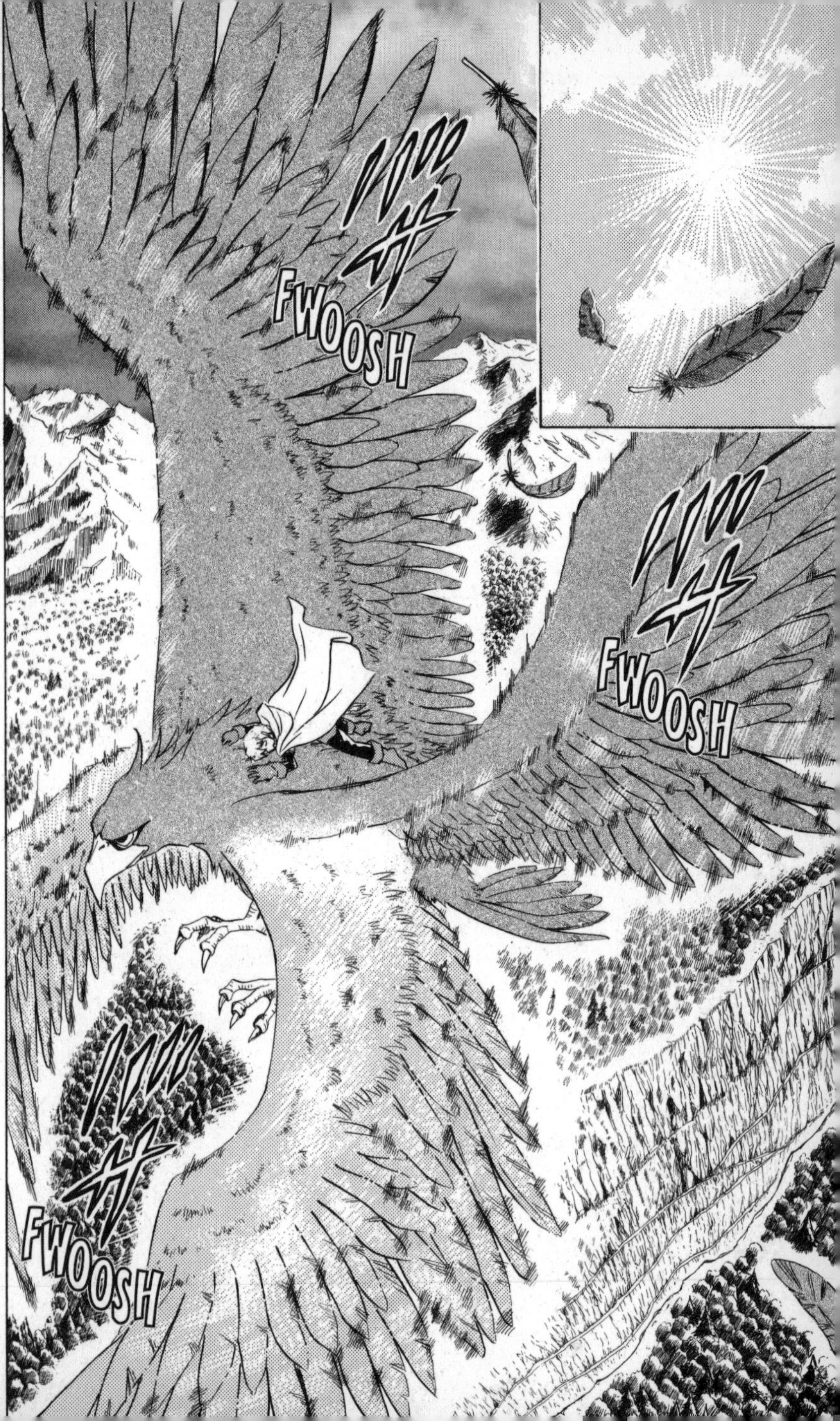
FWOOSH
FWOOSH
FWOOSH

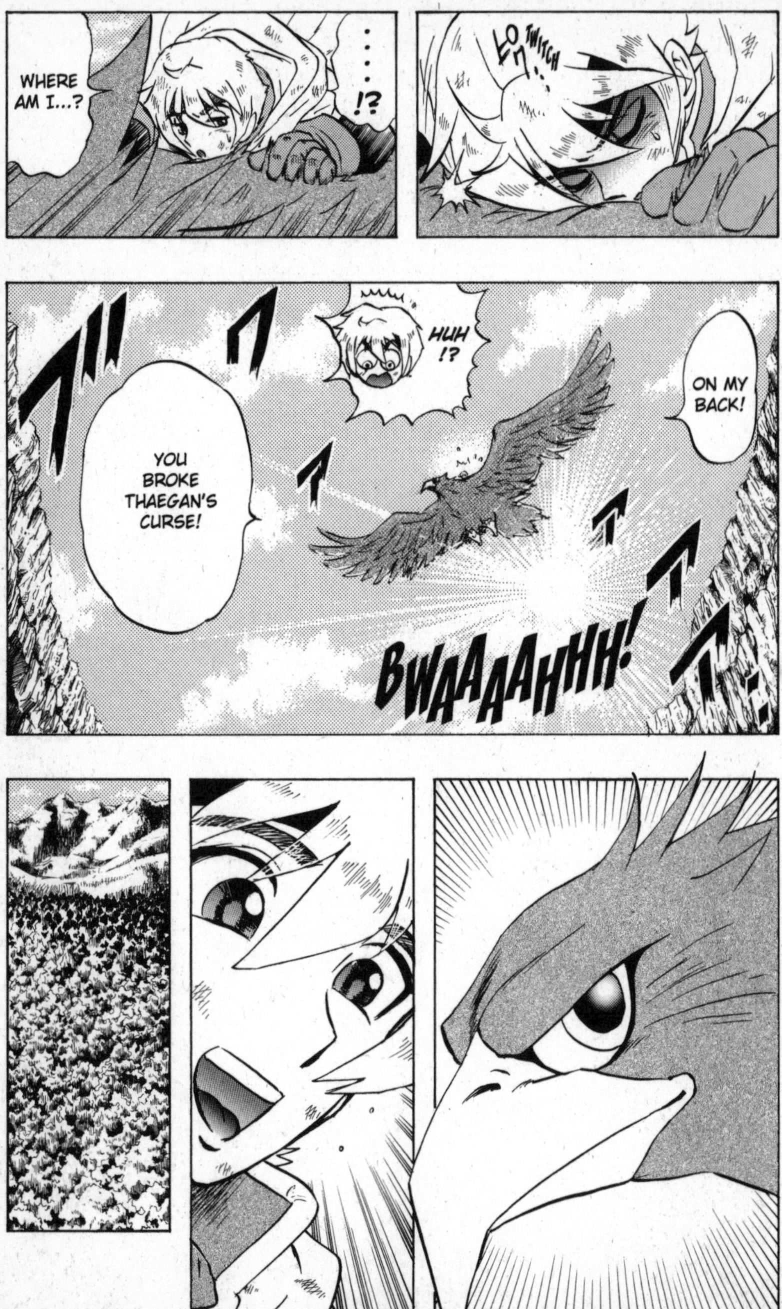
TWITCH
. . . . .
!?
WHERE AM I...?
ON MY BACK!
HUH !?
YOU BROKE THAEGAN'S CURSE!
BWAAAAHHH!

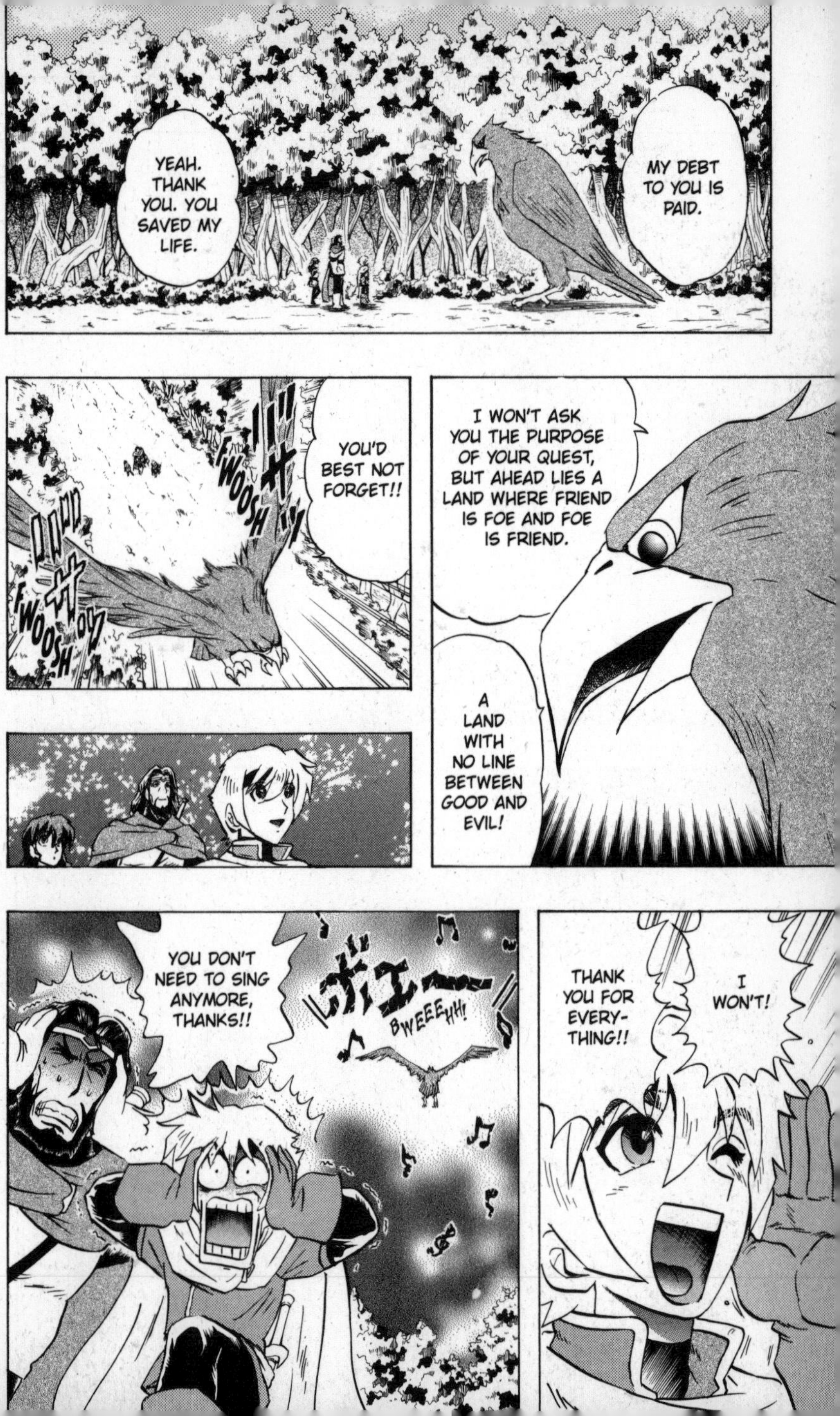
MY DEBT TO YOU IS PAID.
YEAH. THANK YOU. YOU SAVED MY LIFE.
I WON'T ASK YOU THE PURPOSE OF YOUR QUEST, BUT AHEAD LIES A LAND WHERE FRIEND IS FOE AND FOE IS FRIEND.
A LAND WITH NO LINE BETWEEN GOOD AND EVIL!
YOU'D BEST NOT FORGET!!
FWOOSH
FWOOSH
I WON'T!
THANK YOU FOR EVERY-THING!!
BWEEEHH!
YOU DON'T NEED TO SING ANYMORE, THANKS!!

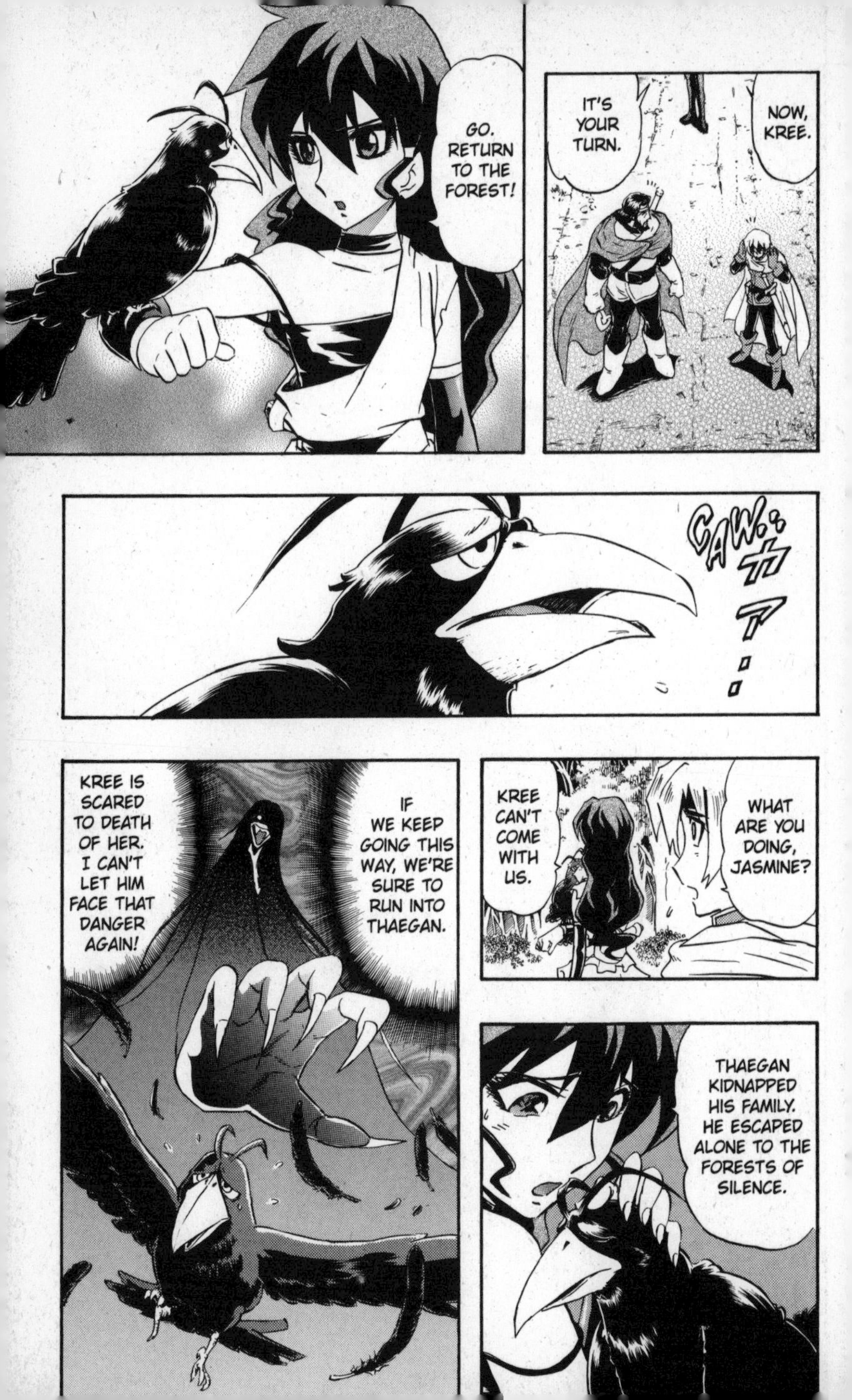
NOW, KREE.
IT'S YOUR TURN.
GO. RETURN TO THE FOREST!
CAW
WHAT ARE YOU DOING, JASMINE?
KREE CAN'T COME WITH US.
THAEGAN KIDNAPPED HIS FAMILY. HE ESCAPED ALONE TO THE FORESTS OF SILENCE.
IF WE KEEP GOING THIS WAY, WE'RE SURE TO RUN INTO THAEGAN.
KREE IS SCARED TO DEATH OF HER. I CAN'T LET HIM FACE THAT DANGER AGAIN!

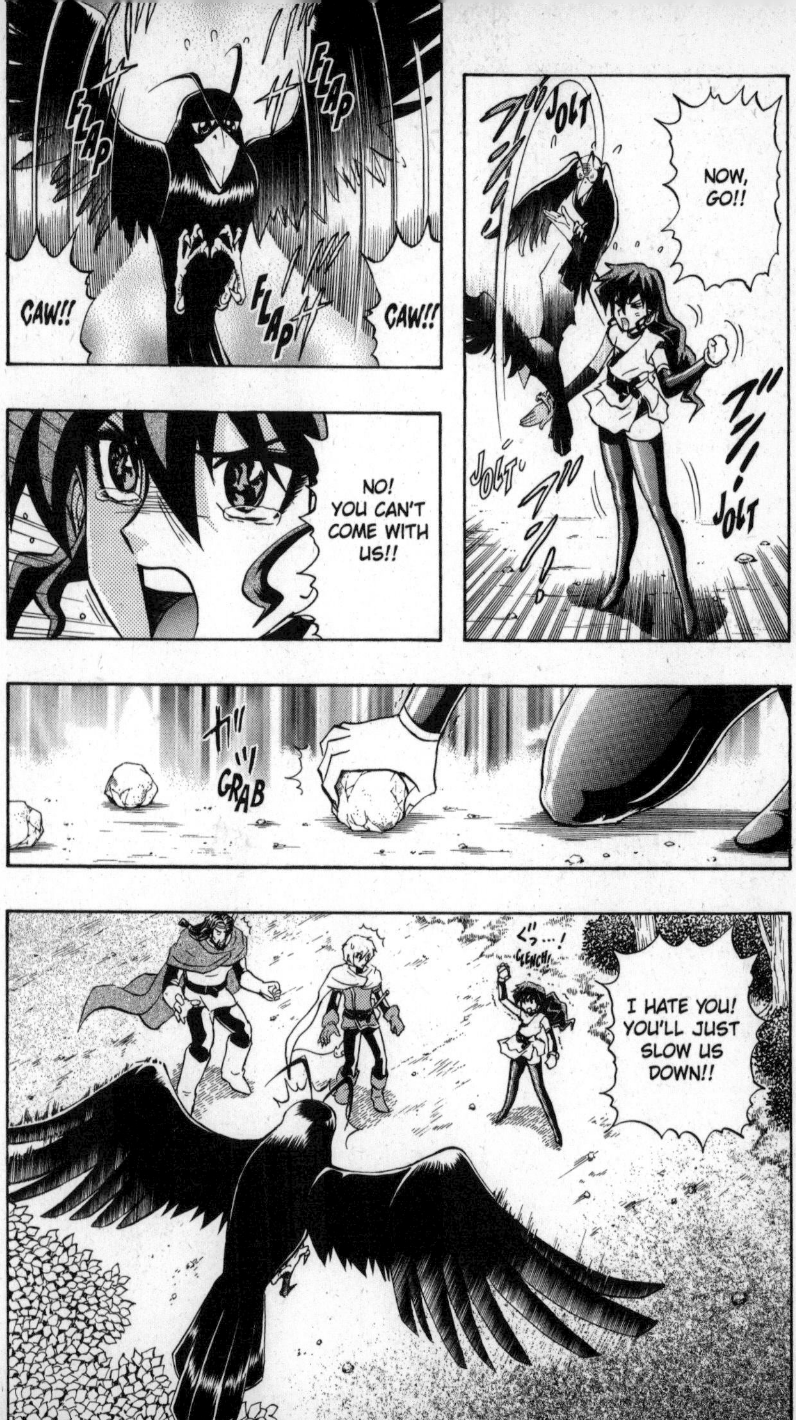
JOLT
NOW, GO!!
JOLT
JOLT
FLAP
FLAP
CAW!!
FLAP
CAW!!
NO! YOU CAN'T COME WITH US!!
GRAB
ぐっ…!
CLENCH!
I HATE YOU! YOU'LL JUST SLOW US DOWN!!

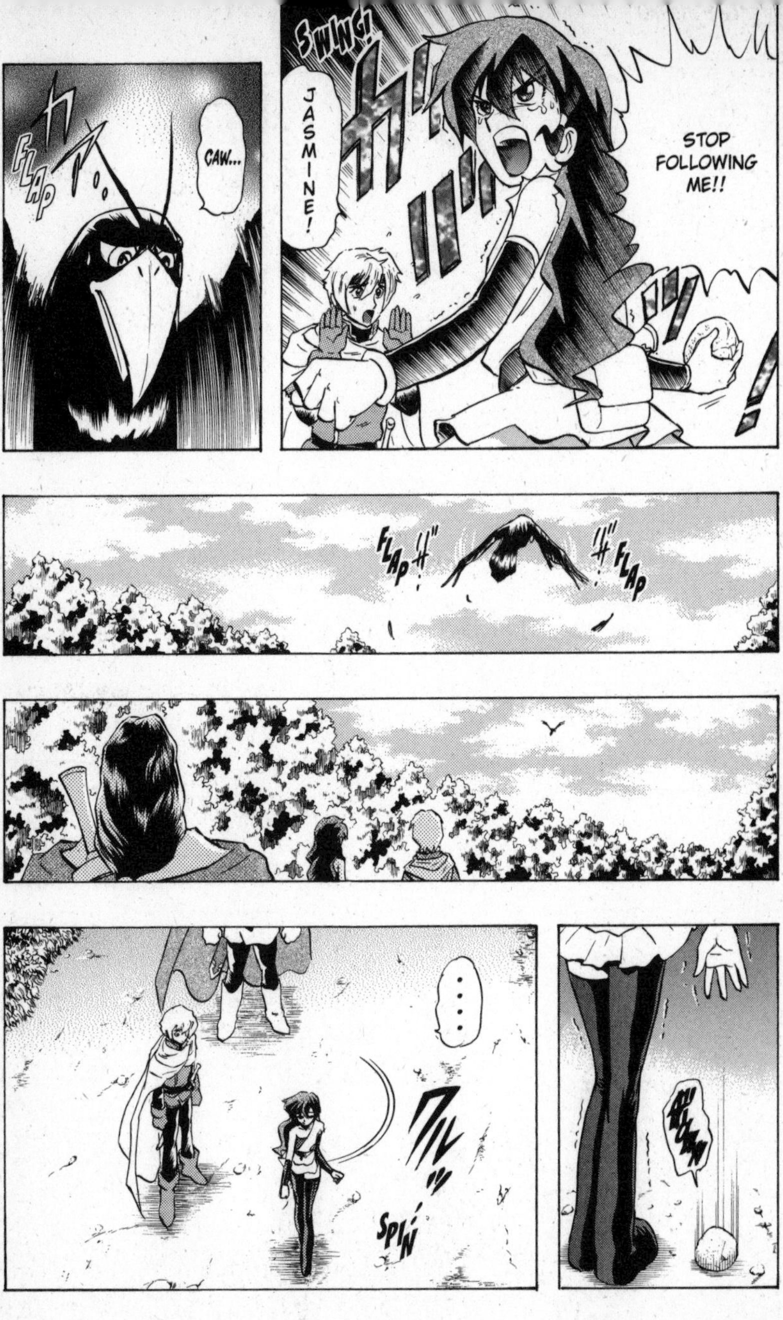
SWING!
STOP FOLLOWING ME!!
JASMINE!
CAW...
FLAP
FLAP
FLAP
....
SPIN

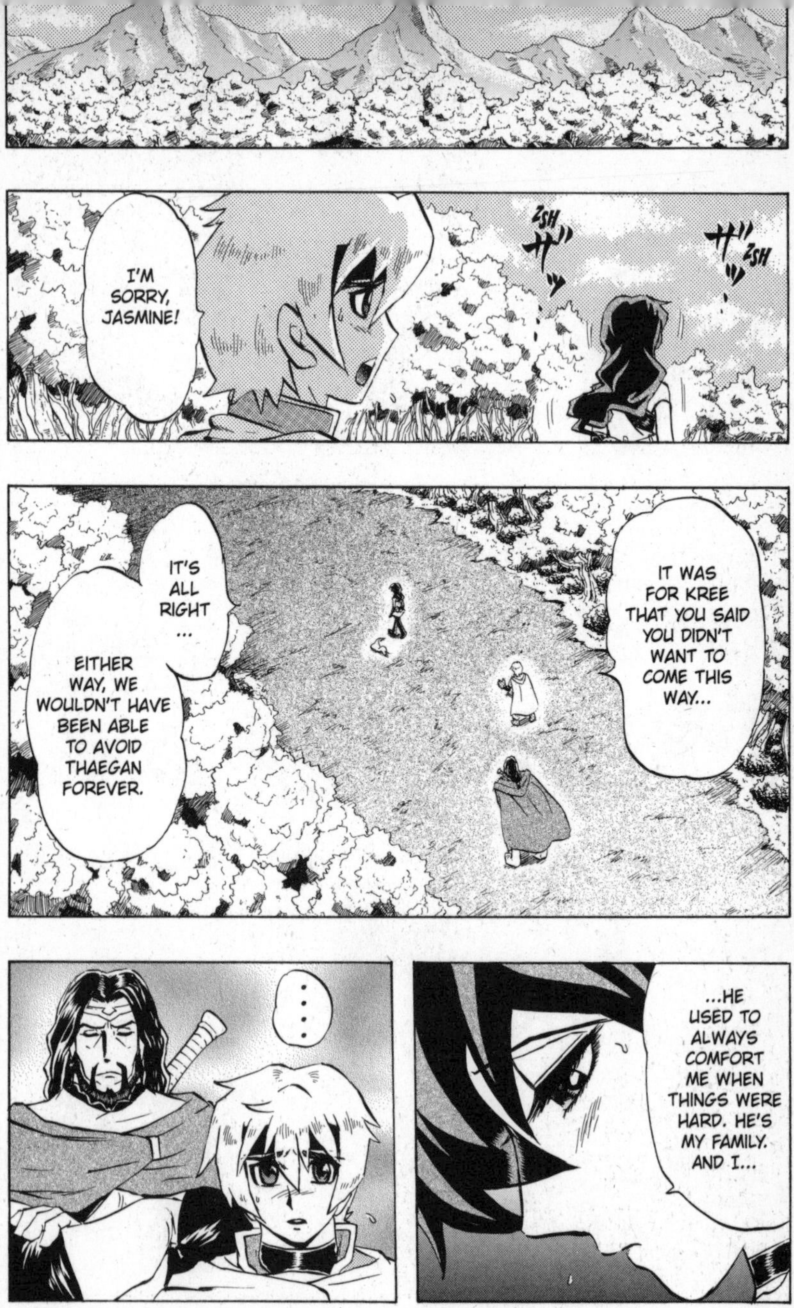
ZSH
ZSH
I'M SORRY, JASMINE!
IT WAS FOR KREE THAT YOU SAID YOU DIDN'T WANT TO COME THIS WAY...
IT'S ALL RIGHT ...
EITHER WAY, WE WOULDN'T HAVE BEEN ABLE TO AVOID THAEGAN FOREVER.
...HE USED TO ALWAYS COMFORT ME WHEN THINGS WERE HARD. HE'S MY FAMILY. AND I...
....

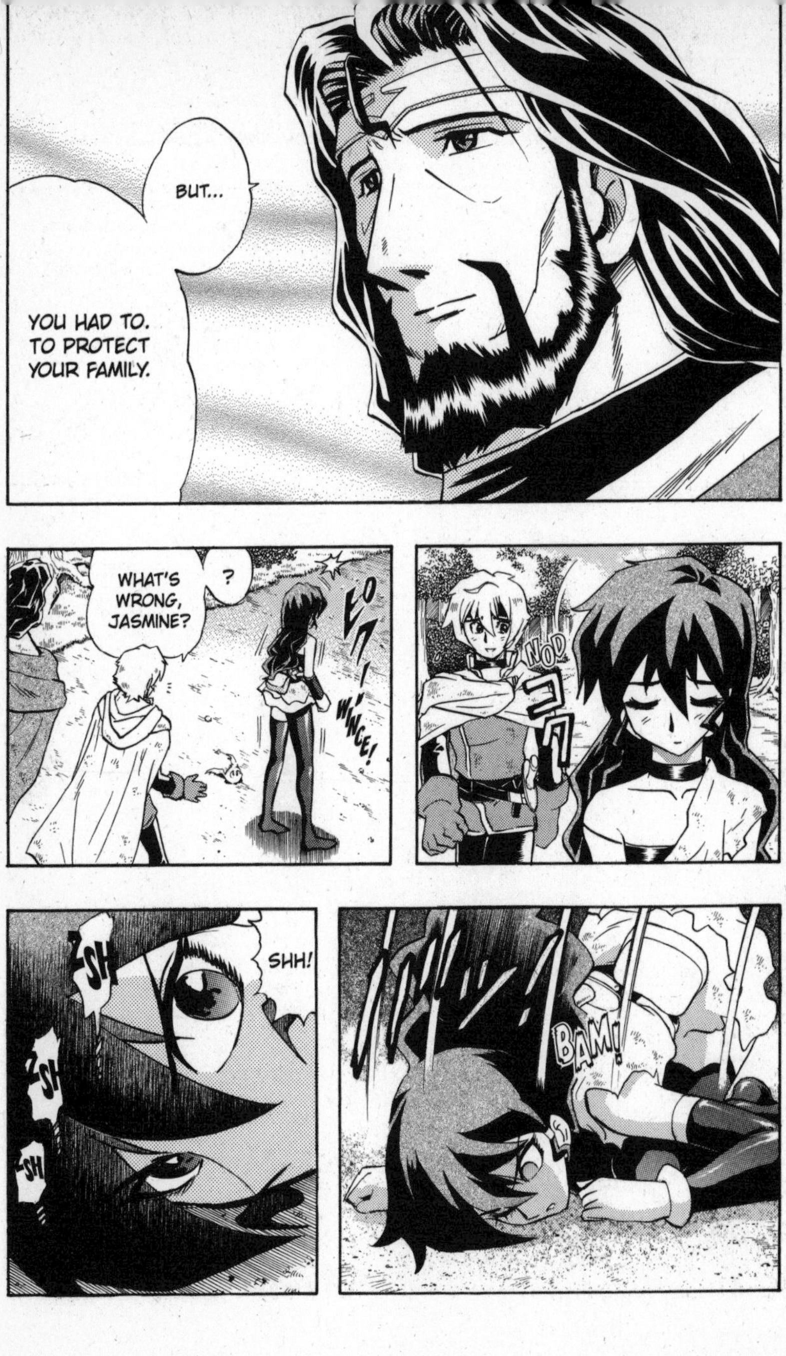
BUT...
YOU HAD TO. TO PROTECT YOUR FAMILY.
NOD
?
WHAT'S WRONG, JASMINE?
WINCE!
BAM!
SHH!
ZSH
ZSH
ZSH

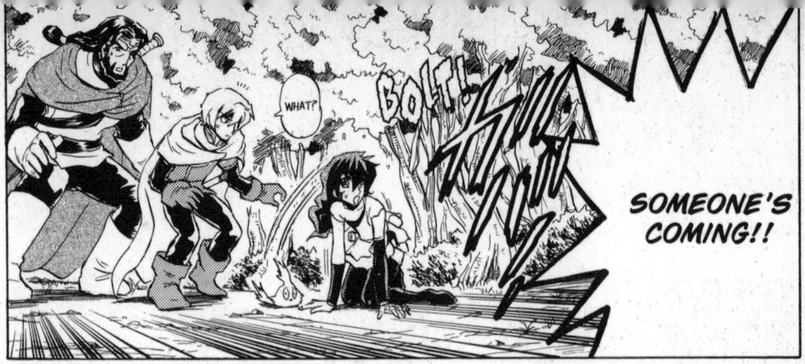
BOLT!
WHAT?
SOMEONE'S COMING!!

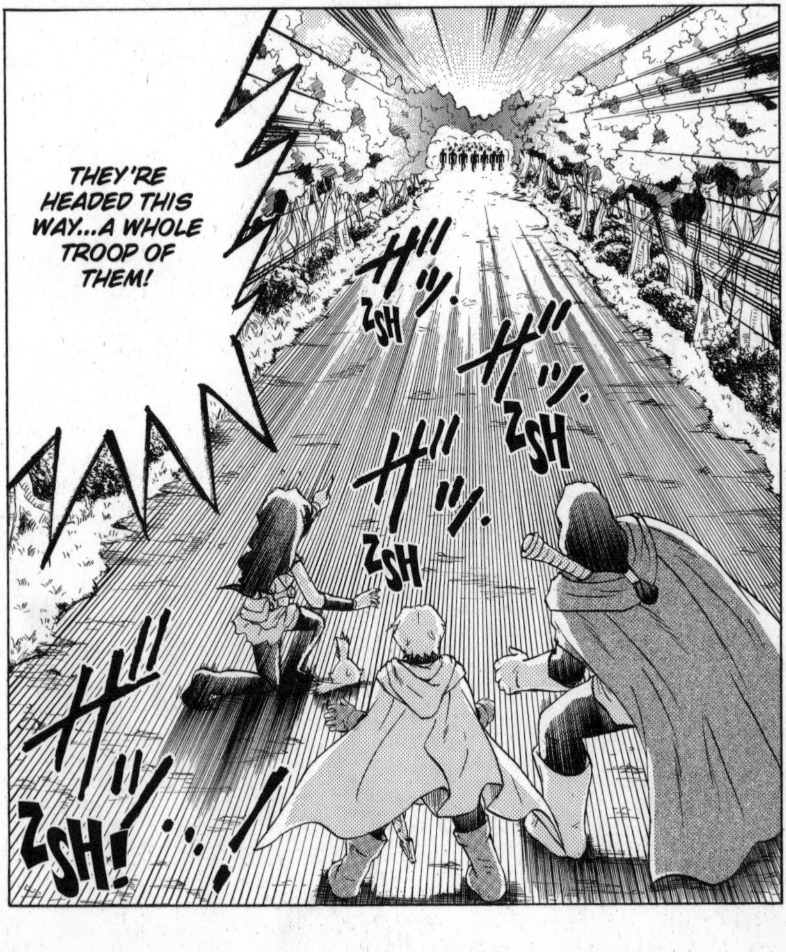
THEY'RE HEADED THIS WAY...A WHOLE TROOP OF THEM!
ZSH
ZSH
ZSH
ZSH!

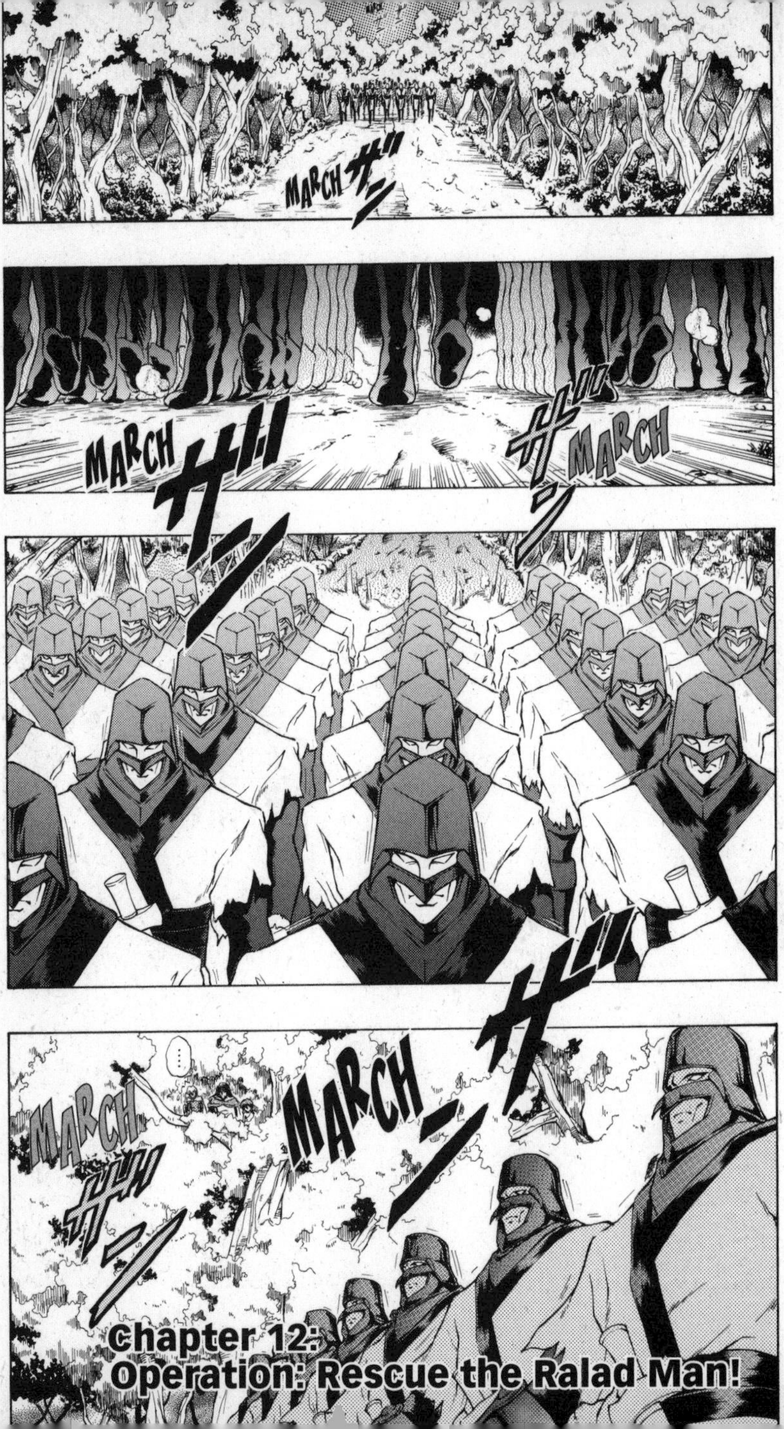
MARCH
MARCH
MARCH
MARCH
.....
MARCH
Chapter 12:
Operation: Rescue the Ralad Man!

Chapter 12: Operation: Rescue the Ralad Man!

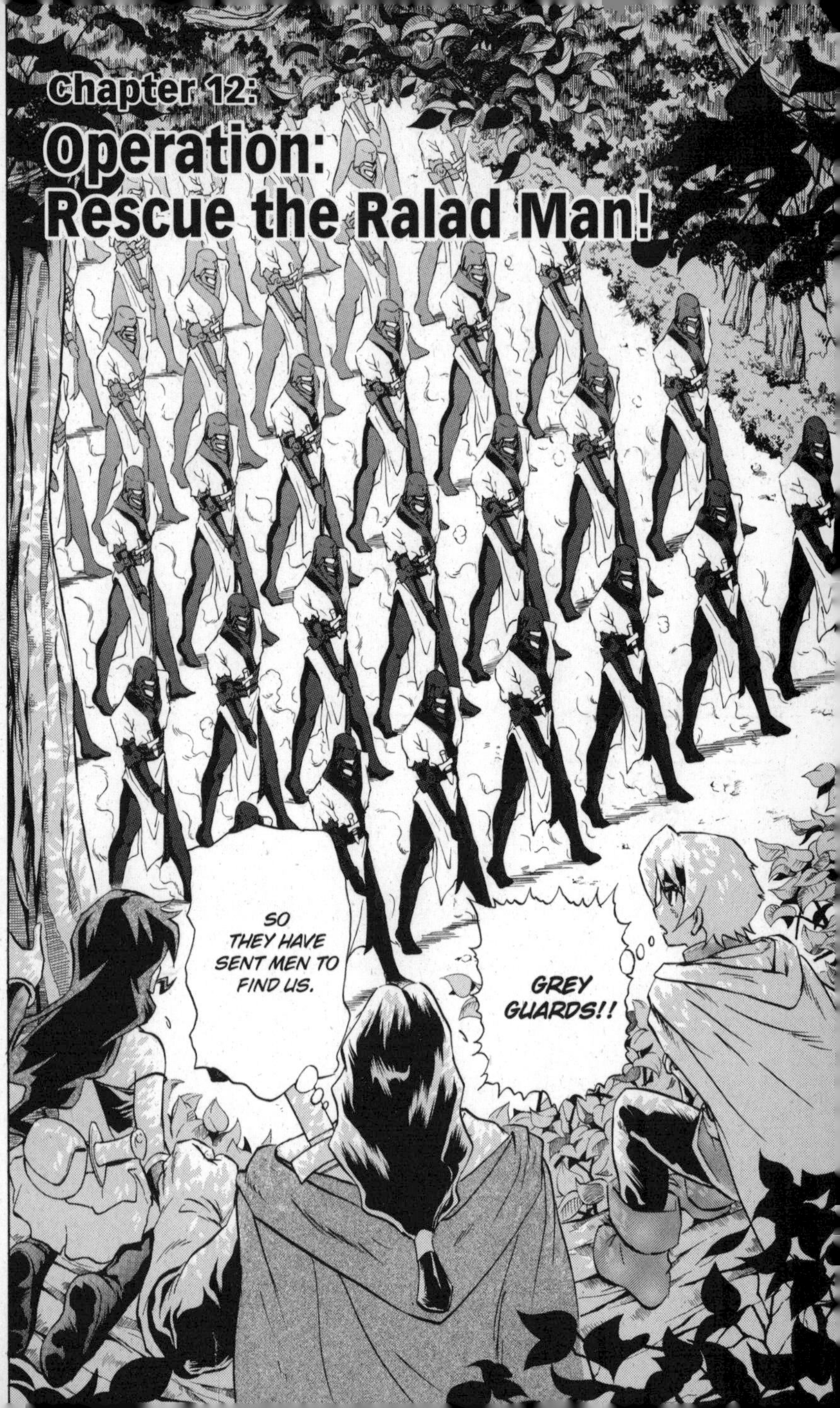
GREY GUARDS!!
SO THEY HAVE SENT MEN TO FIND US.

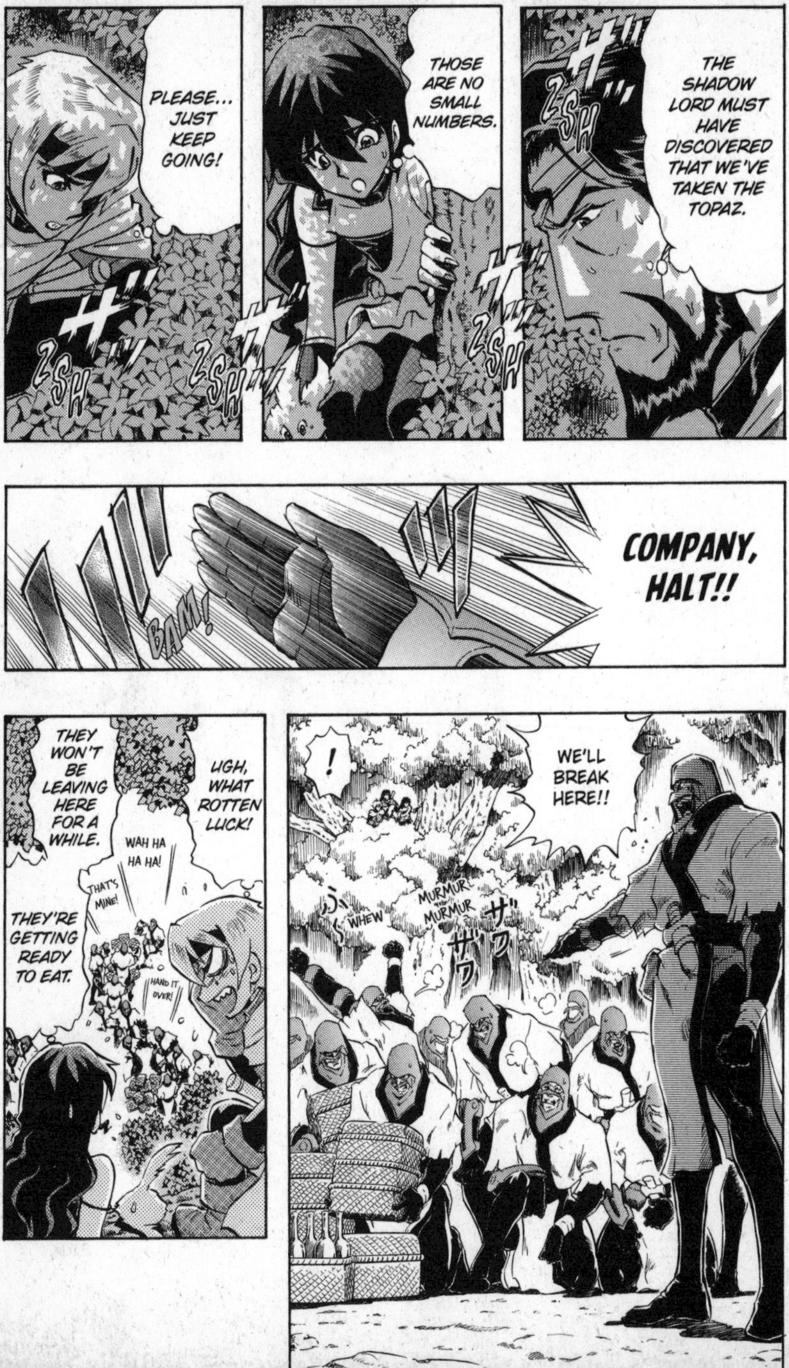
THE SHADOW LORD MUST HAVE DISCOVERED THAT WE'VE TAKEN THE TOPAZ.
ZSH
ZSH
THOSE ARE NO SMALL NUMBERS.
ZSH
PLEASE... JUST KEEP GOING!
ZSH
COMPANY, HALT!!
BAM!
WE'LL BREAK HERE!!
!
MURMUR
MURMUR
WHEW
UGH, WHAT ROTTEN LUCK!
THEY WON'T BE LEAVING HERE FOR A WHILE.
WAH HA HA HA!
THAT'S MINE!
THEY'RE GETTING READY TO EAT.
HAND IT OVER!

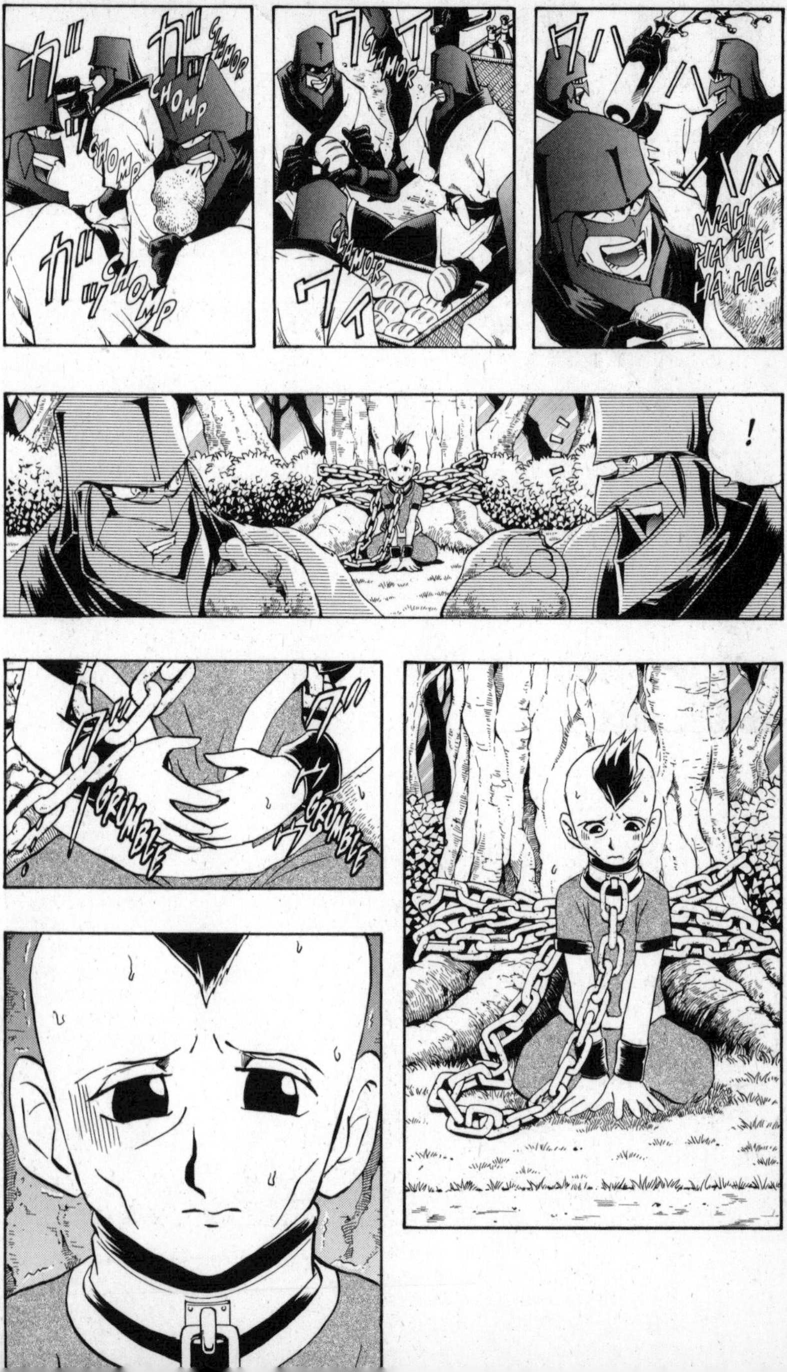
WAH HA HA HA HA!
CLAMOR
CLAMOR
CLAMOR
CHOMP
CHOMP
CHOMP
!
GRUMBLE
GRUMBLE

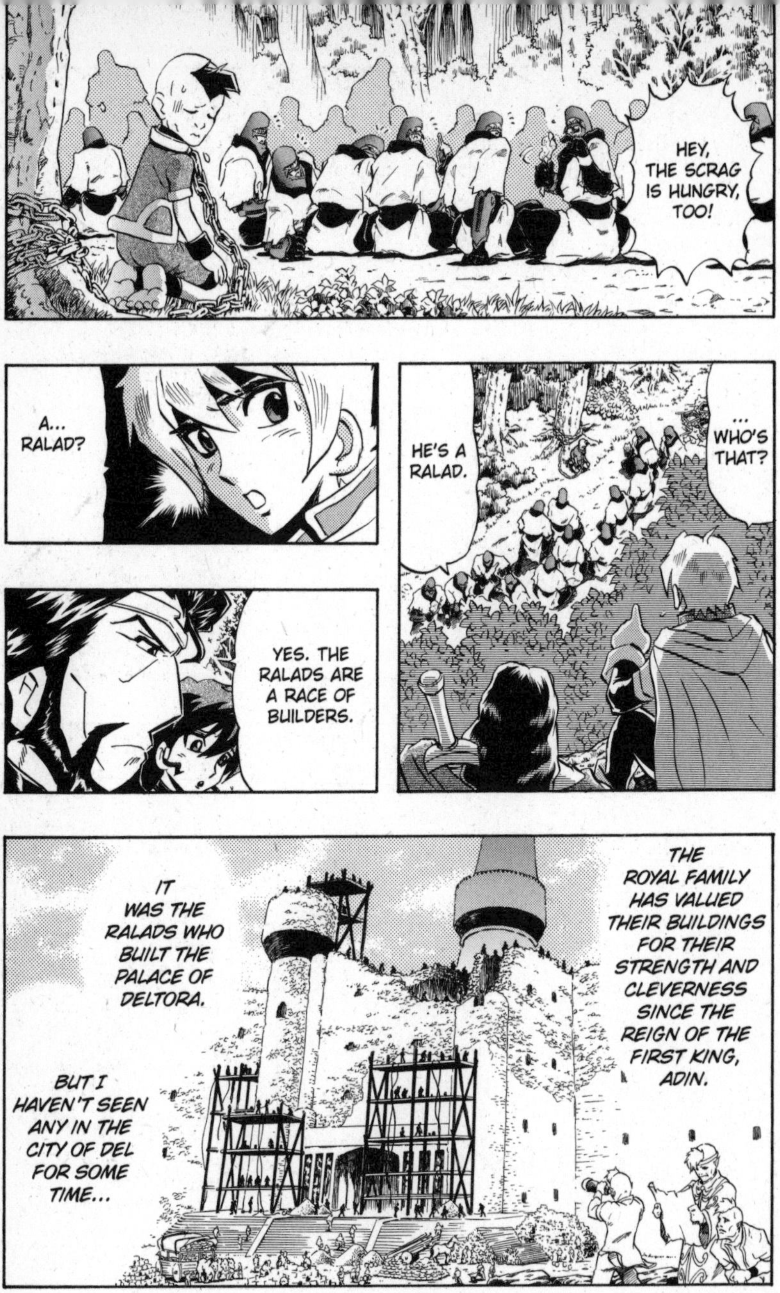
HEY, THE SCRAG IS HUNGRY, TOO!
... WHO'S THAT?
HE'S A RALAD.
A... RALAD?
YES. THE RALADS ARE A RACE OF BUILDERS.
THE ROYAL FAMILY HAS VALUED THEIR BUILDINGS FOR THEIR STRENGTH AND CLEVERNESS SINCE THE REIGN OF THE FIRST KING, ADIN.
IT WAS THE RALADS WHO BUILT THE PALACE OF DELTORA.
BUT I HAVEN'T SEEN ANY IN THE CITY OF DEL FOR SOME TIME...

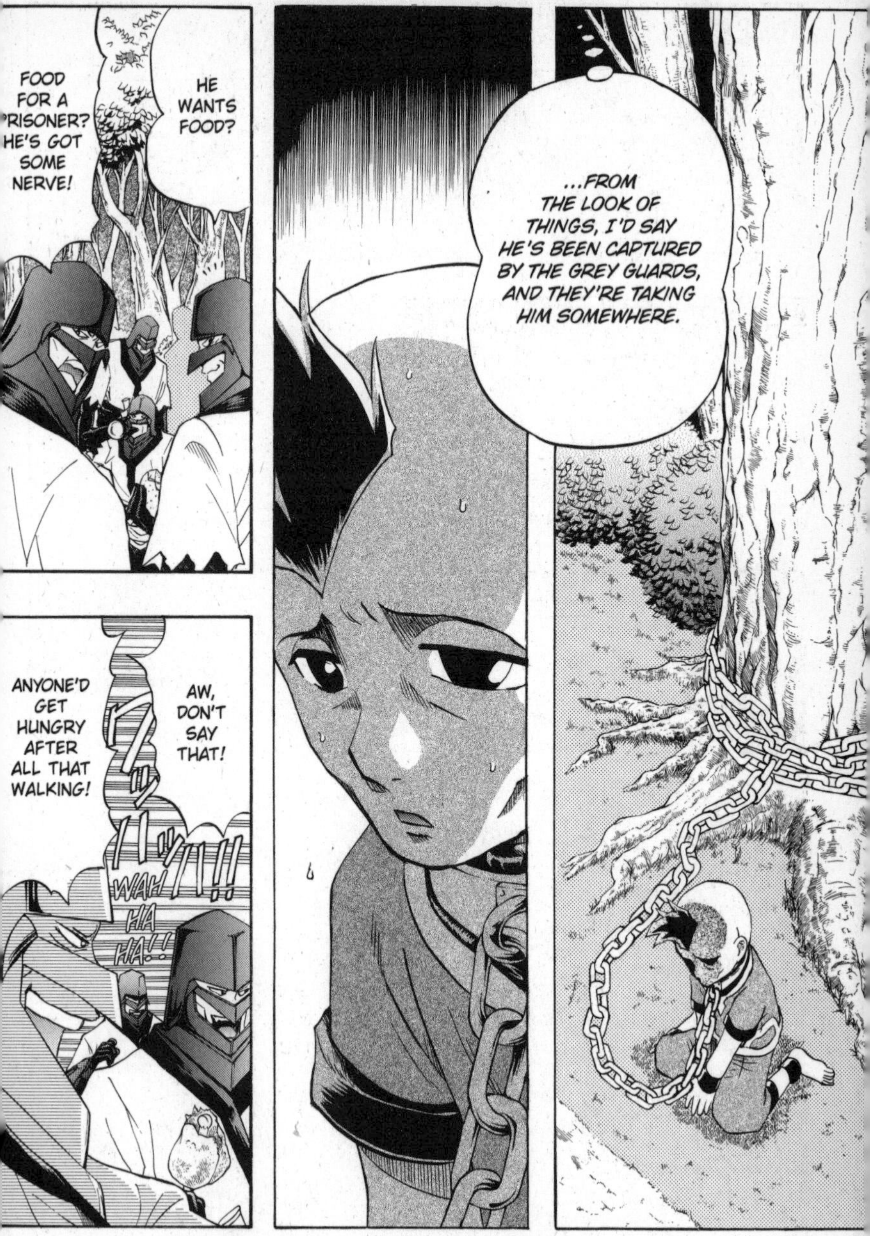
...FROM THE LOOK OF THINGS, I'D SAY HE'S BEEN CAPTURED BY THE GREY GUARDS, AND THEY'RE TAKING HIM SOMEWHERE.
HE WANTS FOOD?
FOOD FOR A PRISONER? HE'S GOT SOME NERVE!
AW, DON'T SAY THAT!
ANYONE'D GET HUNGRY AFTER ALL THAT WALKING!
WAH HA HA!!

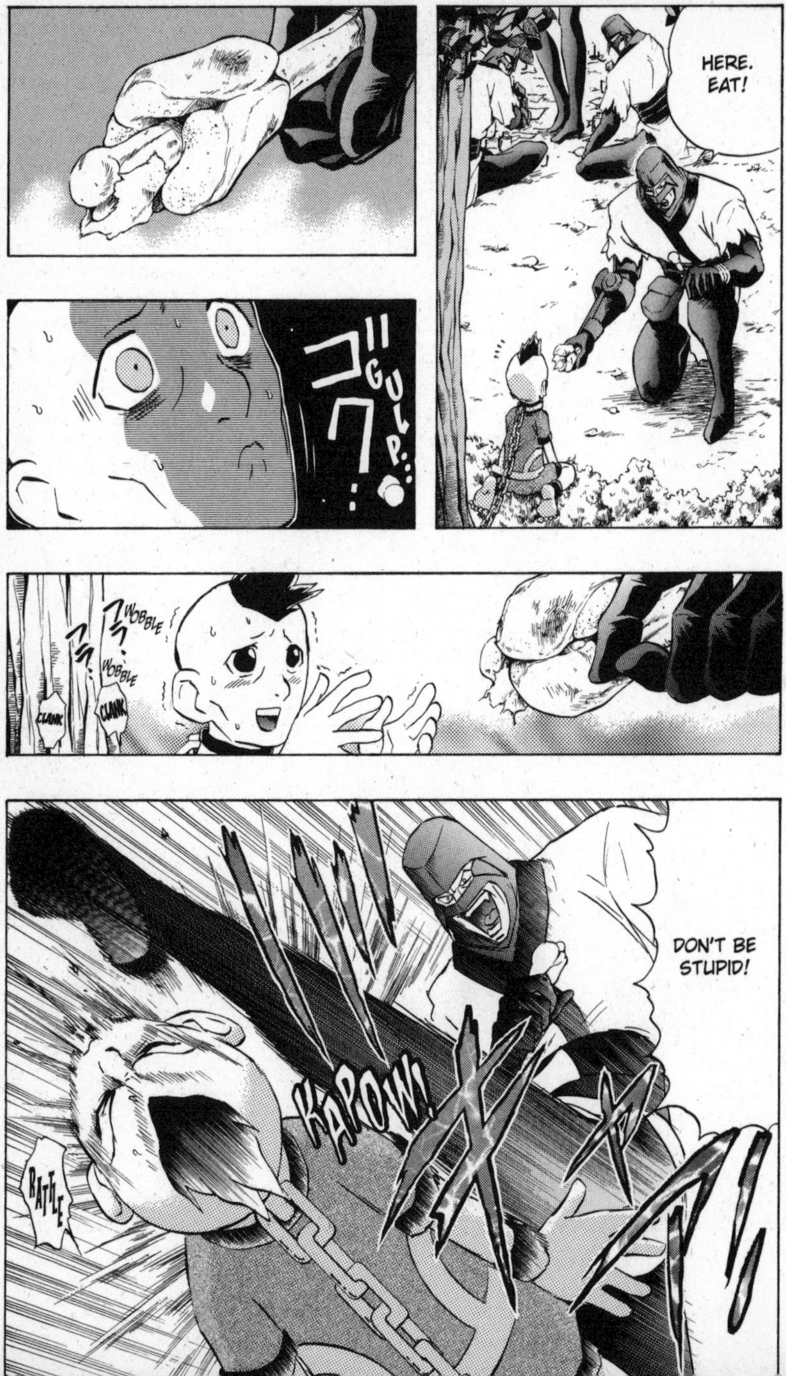
HERE. EAT!
GULP...
WOBBLE
WOBBLE
CLANK
CLANK
DON'T BE STUPID!
KAPOW!
RATTLE

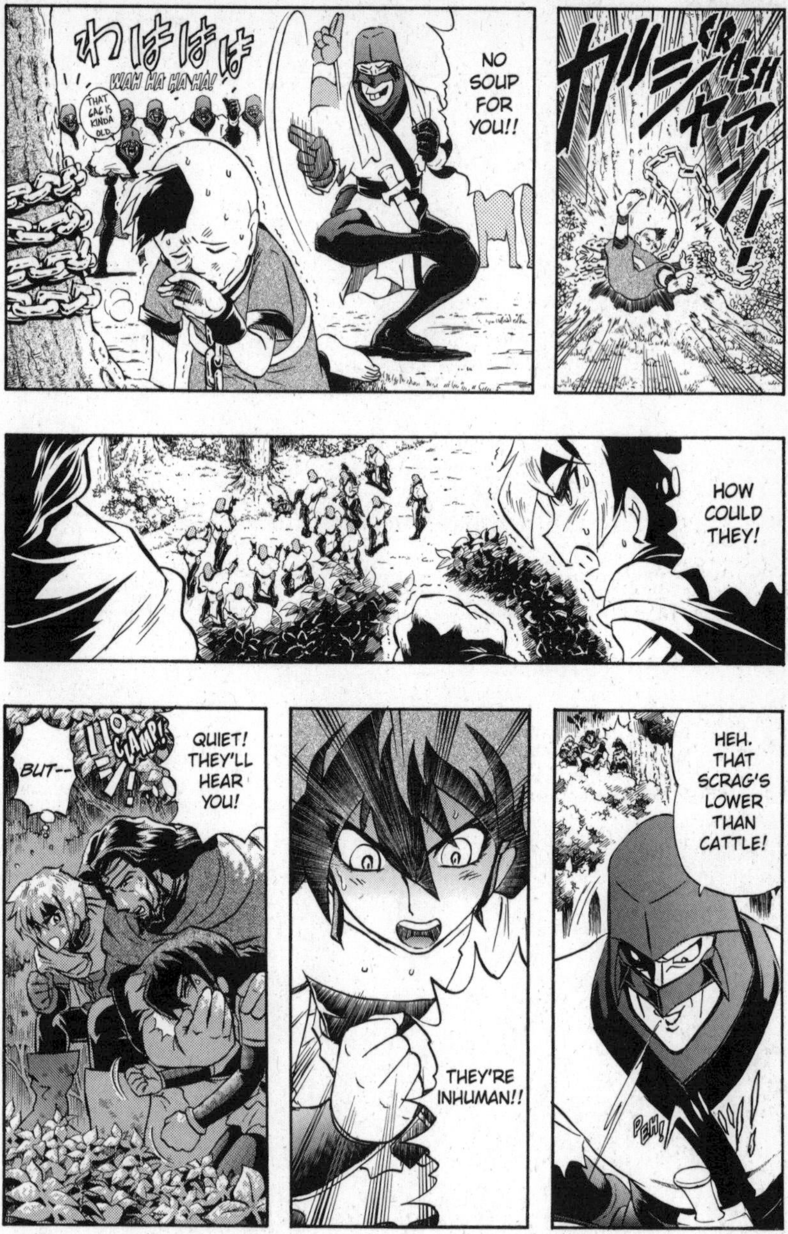

CRASH
NO SOUP FOR YOU!!
わははは
WAH HA HA HA!
THAT GAG IS KINDA OLD.
HOW COULD THEY!
HEH. THAT SCRAG'S LOWER THAN CATTLE!
PEH!
THEY'RE INHUMAN!!
QUIET! THEY'LL HEAR YOU!
CLAMP!
BUT--

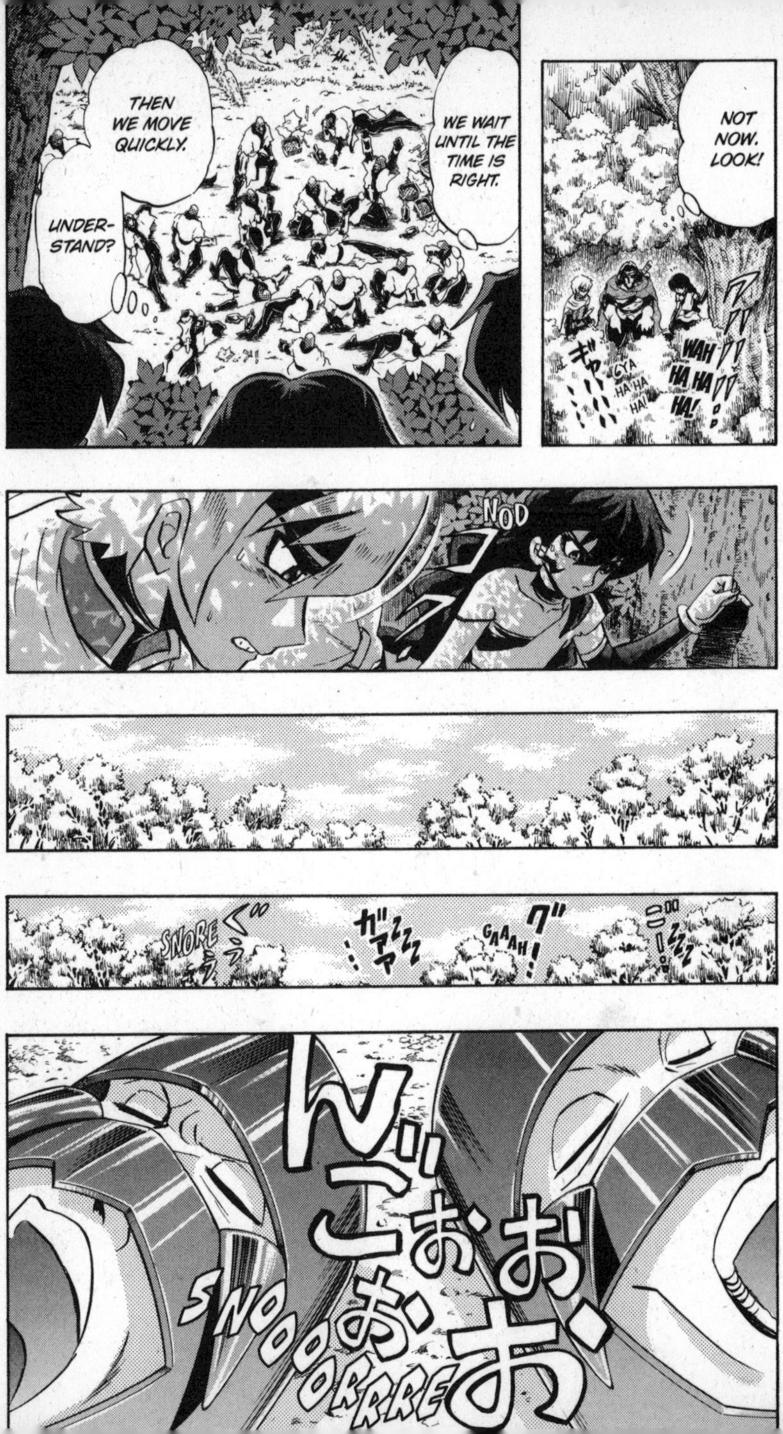
NOT NOW. LOOK!
WAH HA HA HA!
GYA HA HA HA!
WE WAIT UNTIL THE TIME IS RIGHT.
THEN WE MOVE QUICKLY.
UNDER-STAND?
NOD
GAAAH!
SNORE
SNOOOORRRE

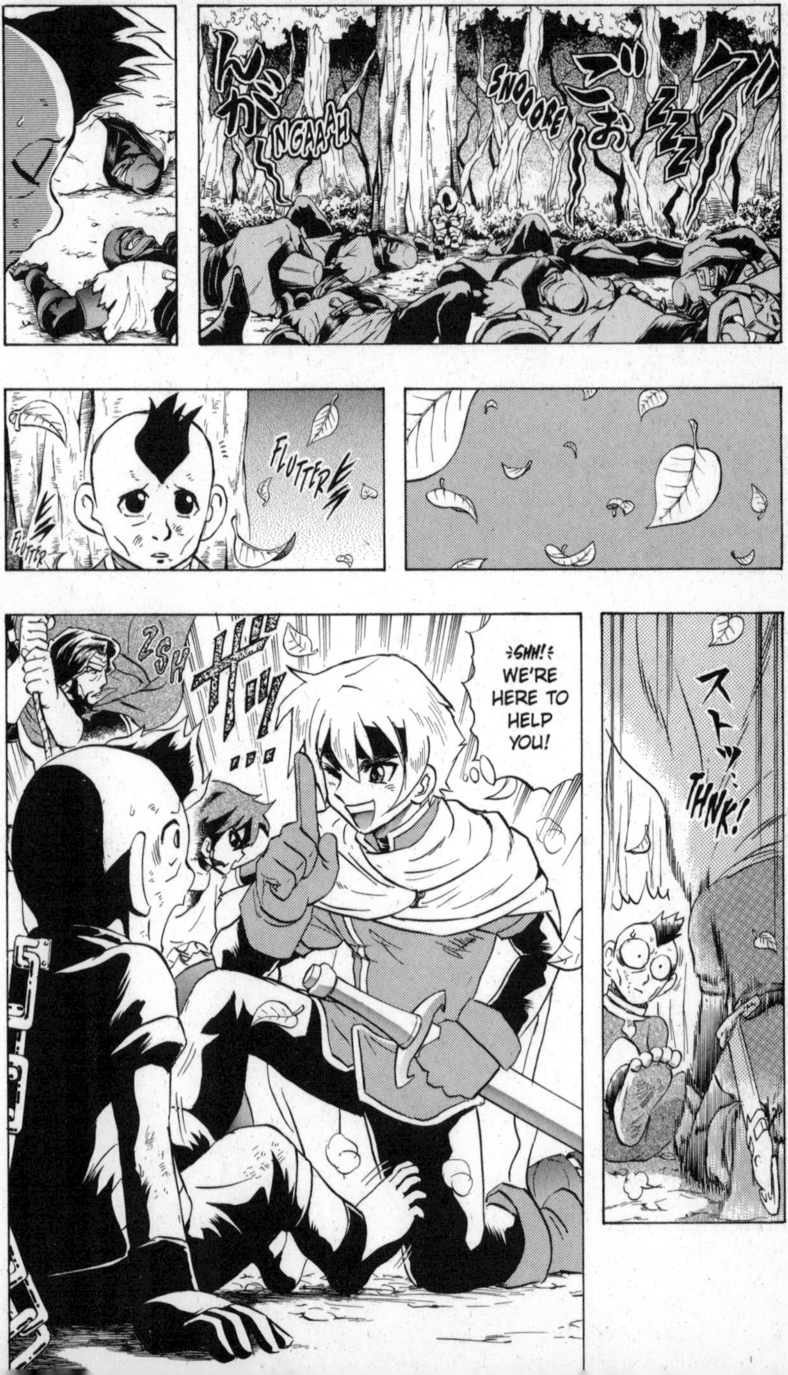
ごぉ
SNOOORE
んが
NGAAAH
FLUTTER
FLUTTER
ストッ
THNK!
SHH! WE'RE HERE TO HELP YOU!
ザッ
ZSH
...

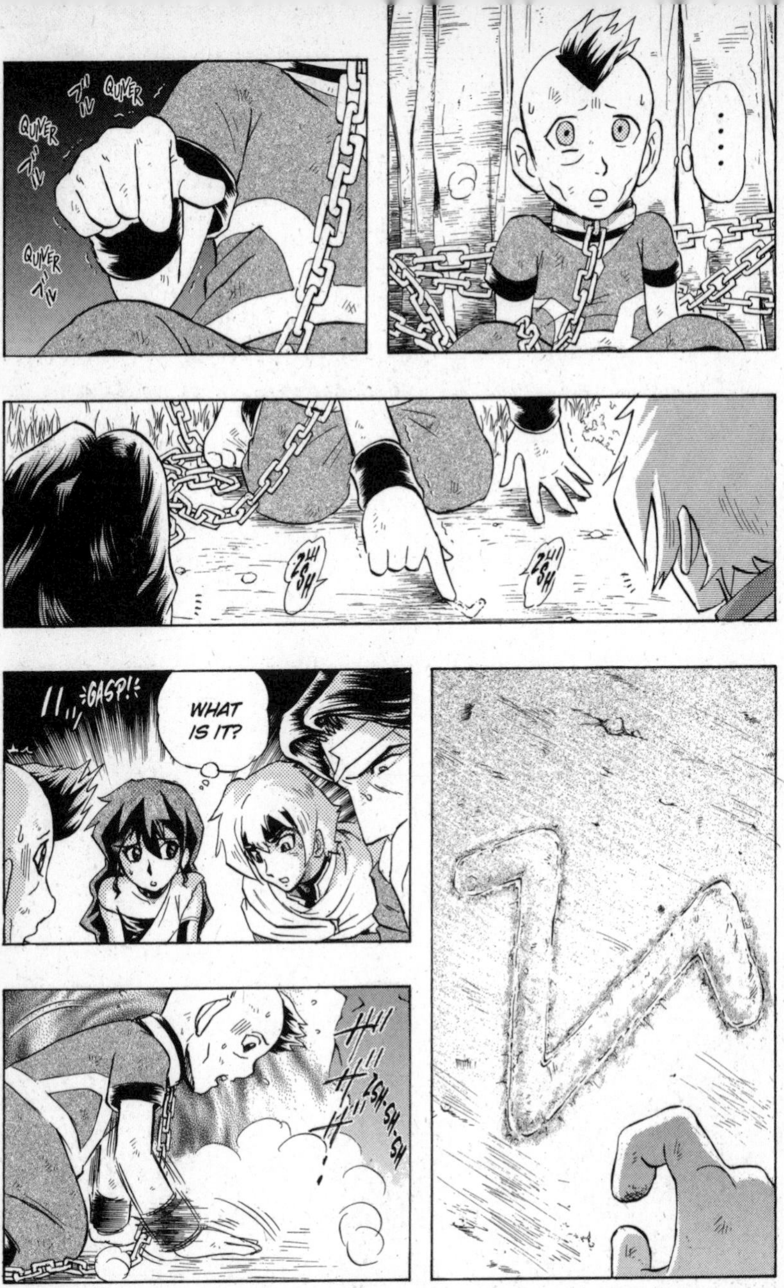
....
QUIVER
QUIVER
QUIVER
ZSH
ZSH
GASP!
WHAT IS IT?
ZSH SH SH

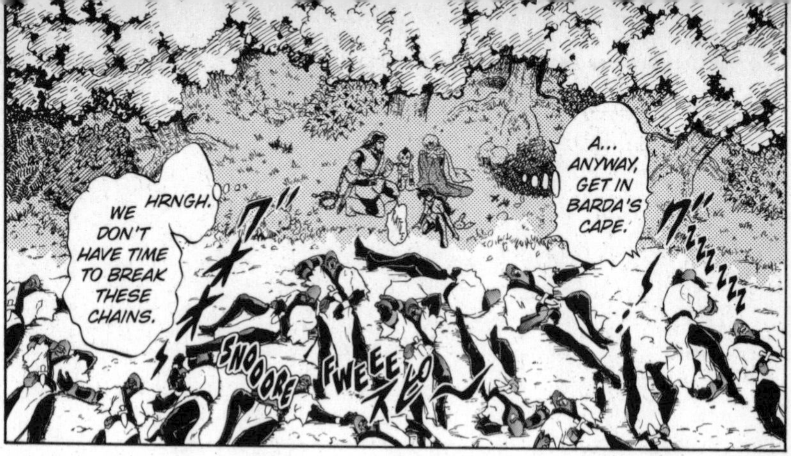
A... ANYWAY, GET IN BARDA'S CAPE.
ZZZZZ
HRNGH.
WE DON'T HAVE TIME TO BREAK THESE CHAINS.
FWEEE
SNOOORE

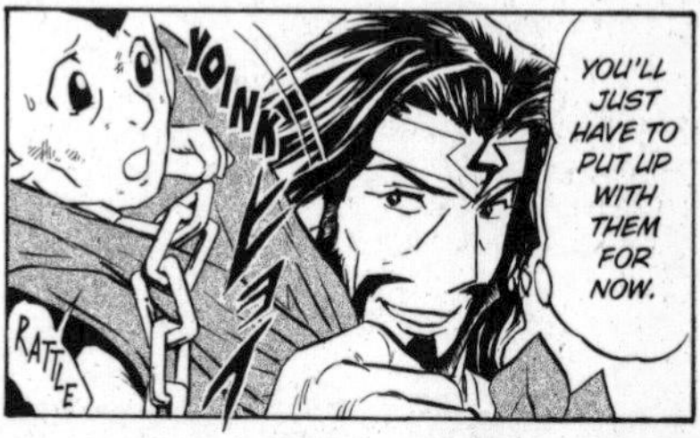
YOU'LL JUST HAVE TO PUT UP WITH THEM FOR NOW.
YOINK
RATTLE

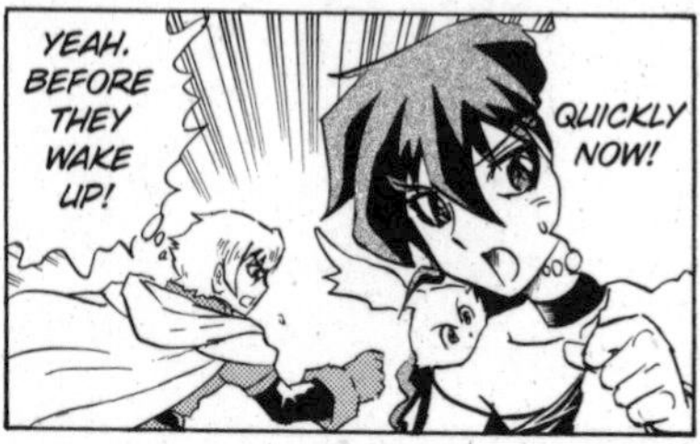
QUICKLY NOW!
YEAH. BEFORE THEY WAKE UP!

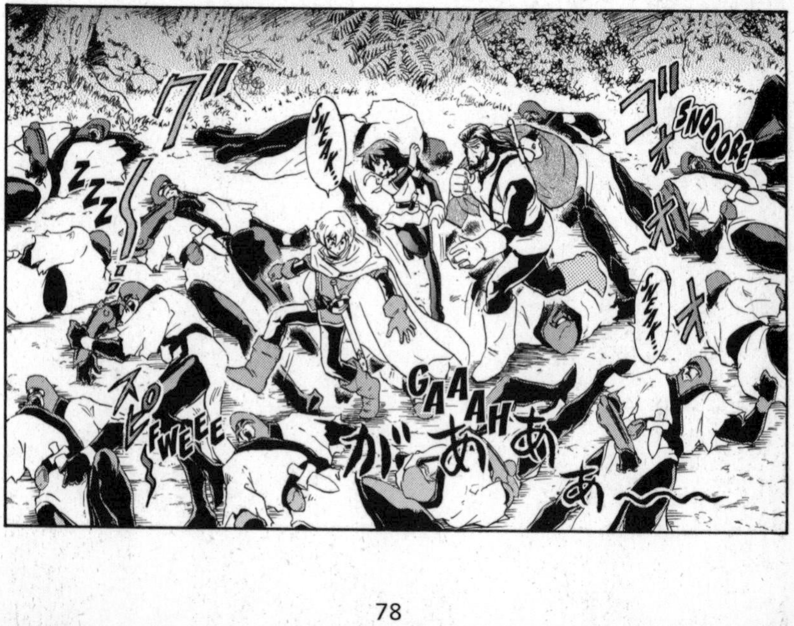
SNOOORE
SNEAK...
SNEAK...
GAAAH
FWEEE
ZZZ

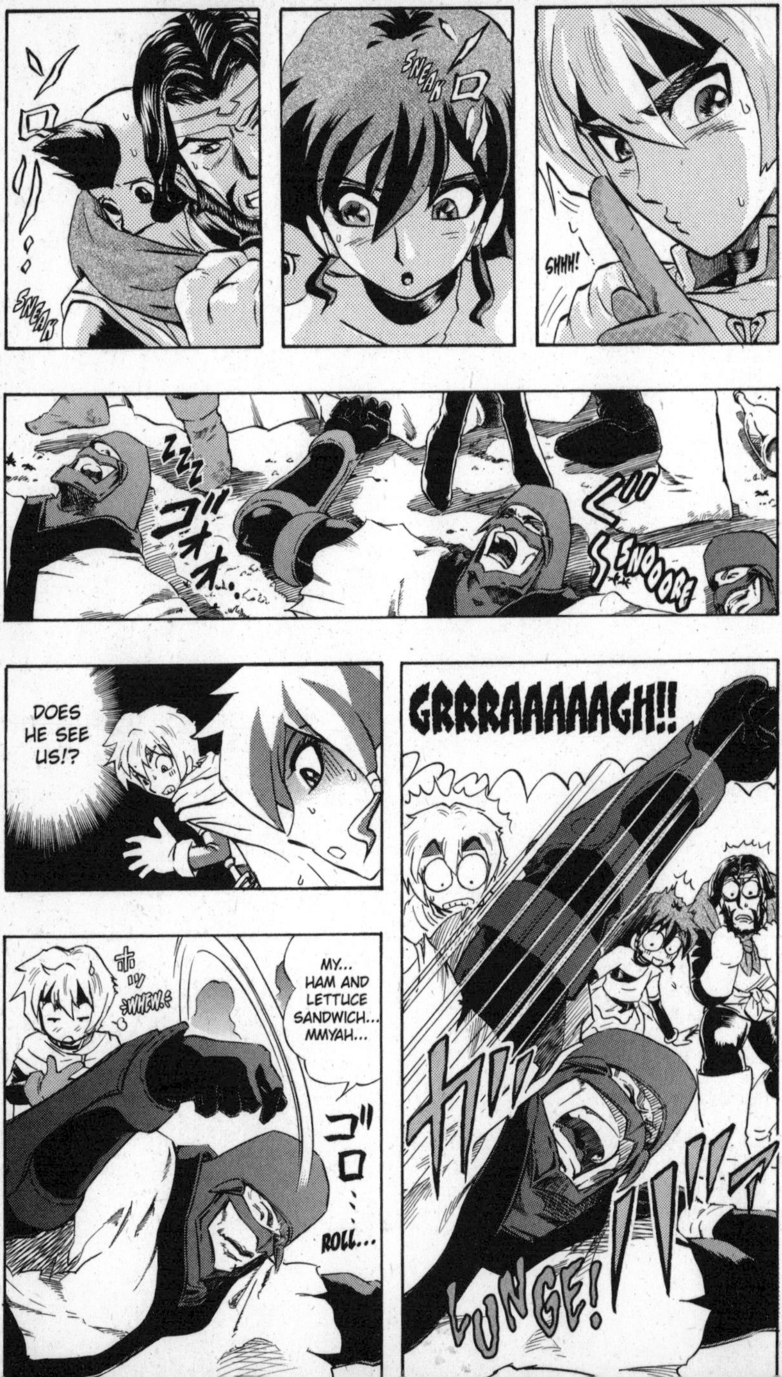
SHHH!
SNEAK
SNEAK
ZZZ
SNOOORE
GRRRAAAAAGH!!
LUNGE!
DOES HE SEE US!?
MY... HAM AND LETTUCE SANDWICH... MMYAH...
ROLL...
WHEW

OW!
WHAT
WAS THAT
FOR!?

バキッ
WHACK!

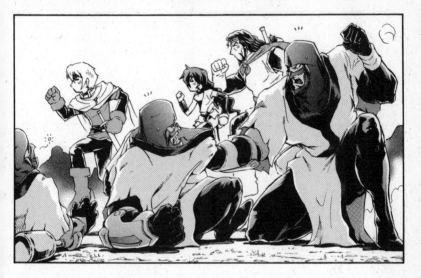

・・・

ササ…HIDE…

MY MY...
YOU'RE UP
EARLY.

HI!

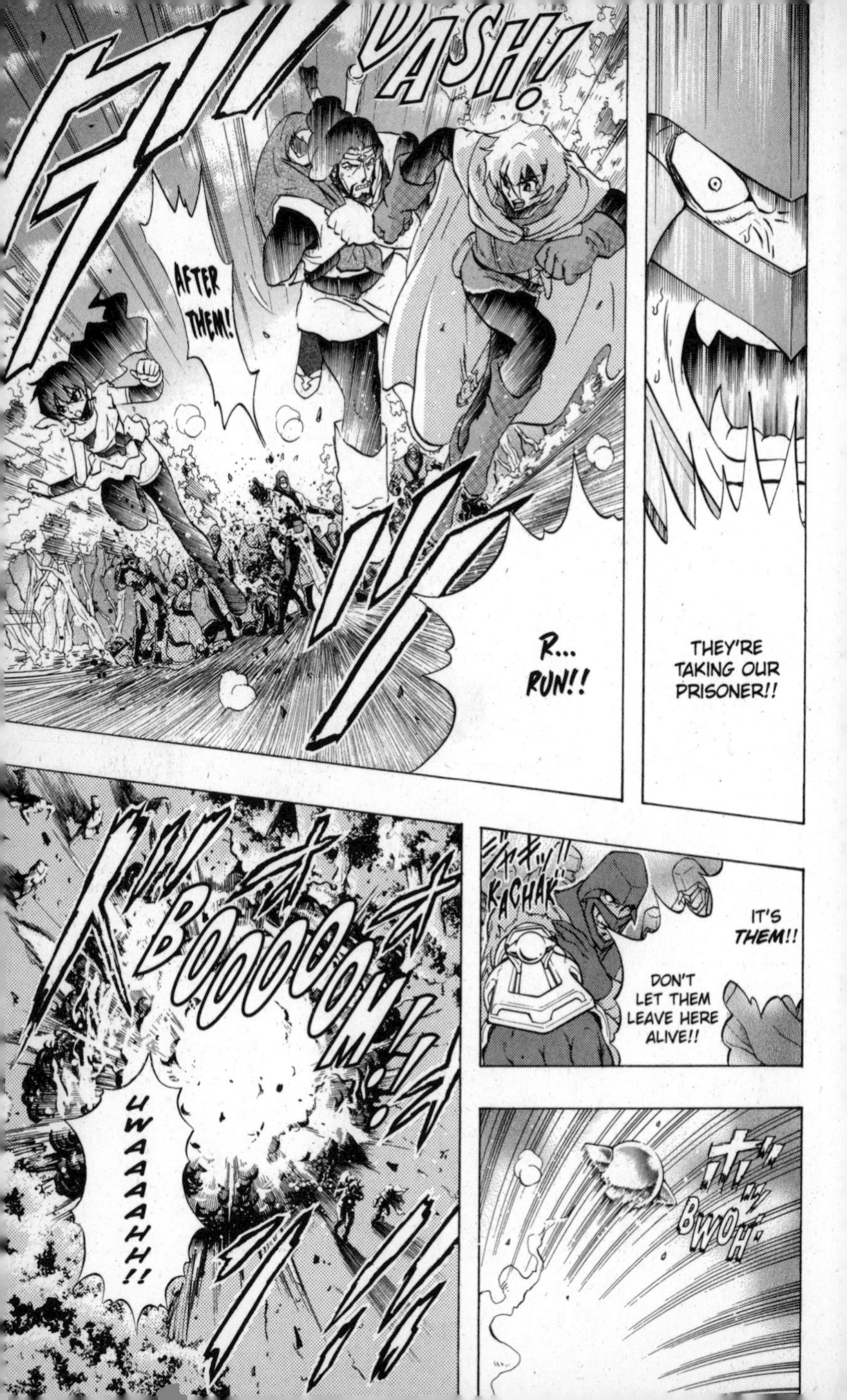
THEY'RE TAKING OUR PRISONER!!
DASH!
R... RUN!!
AFTER THEM!!
ジャキッ!!
KACHAK
IT'S THEM!!
DON'T LET THEM LEAVE HERE ALIVE!!
BWOH
BOOOOOM!!
UWAAAAAHH!!

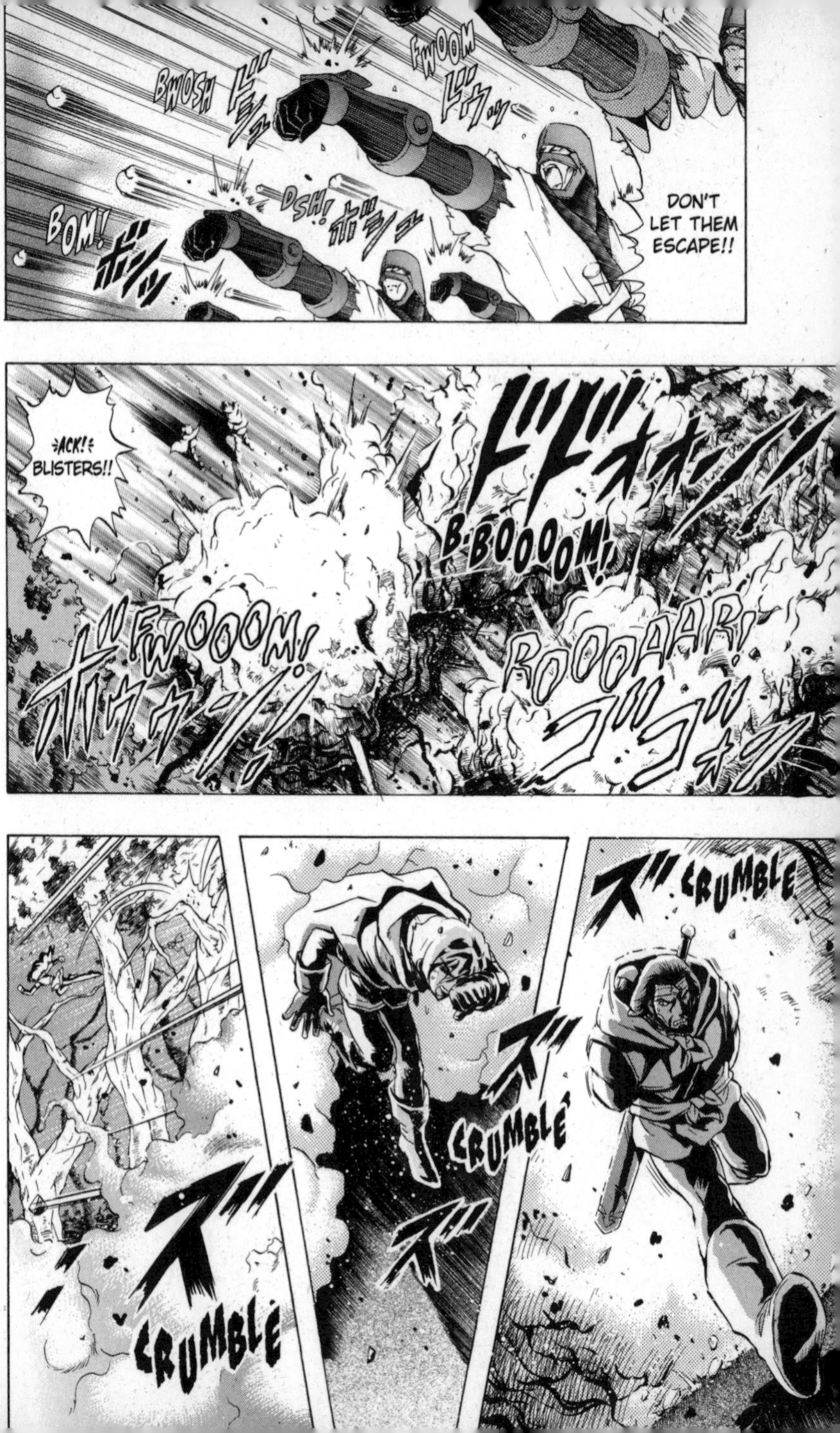
DON'T LET THEM ESCAPE!!
FWOOM
BWOSH
DSH!
BOM!
B-BOOOOM!
ROOOAAR!
FWOOOM!
ACK! BLISTERS!!
CRUMBLE
CRUMBLE
CRUMBLE

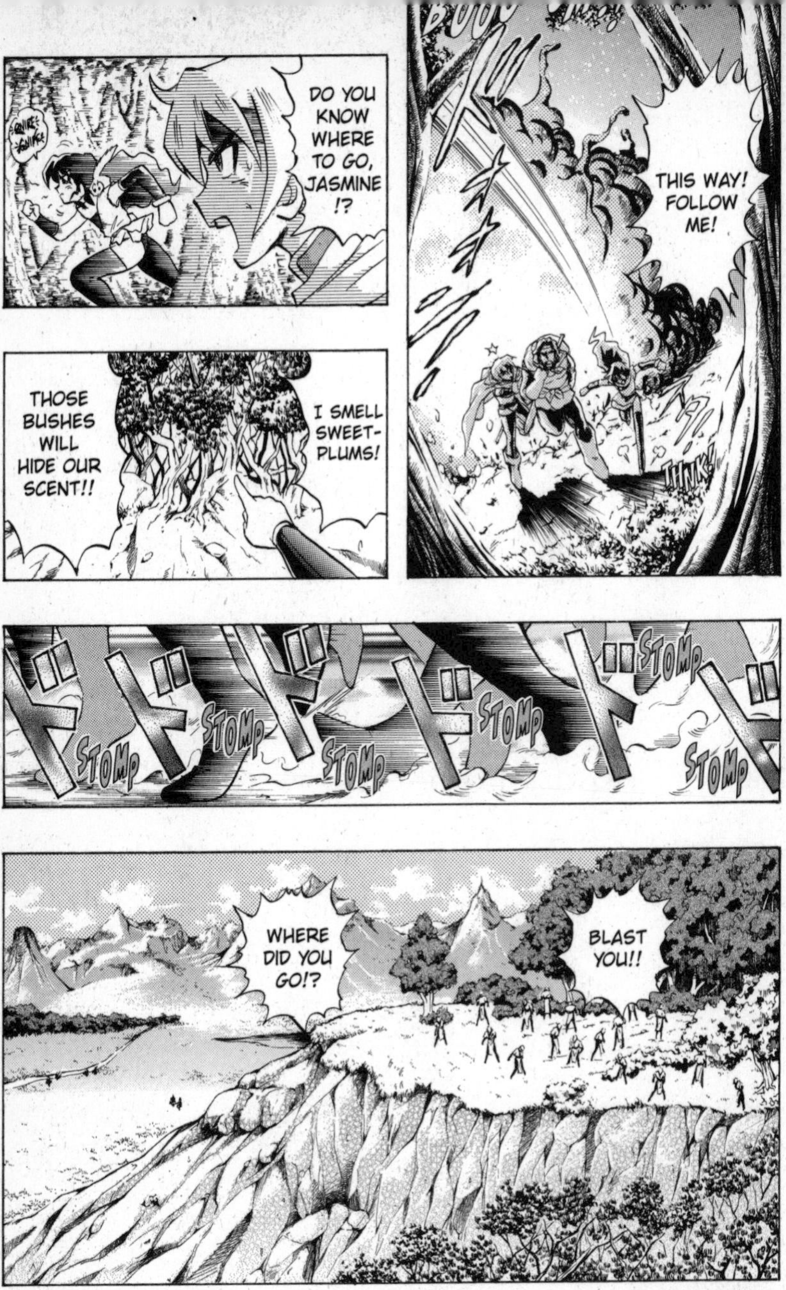
THIS WAY! FOLLOW ME!
DO YOU KNOW WHERE TO GO, JASMINE!?
I SMELL SWEET-PLUMS!
THOSE BUSHES WILL HIDE OUR SCENT!!
STOMP
STOMP
STOMP
STOMP
STOMP
STOMP
BLAST YOU!!
WHERE DID YOU GO!?

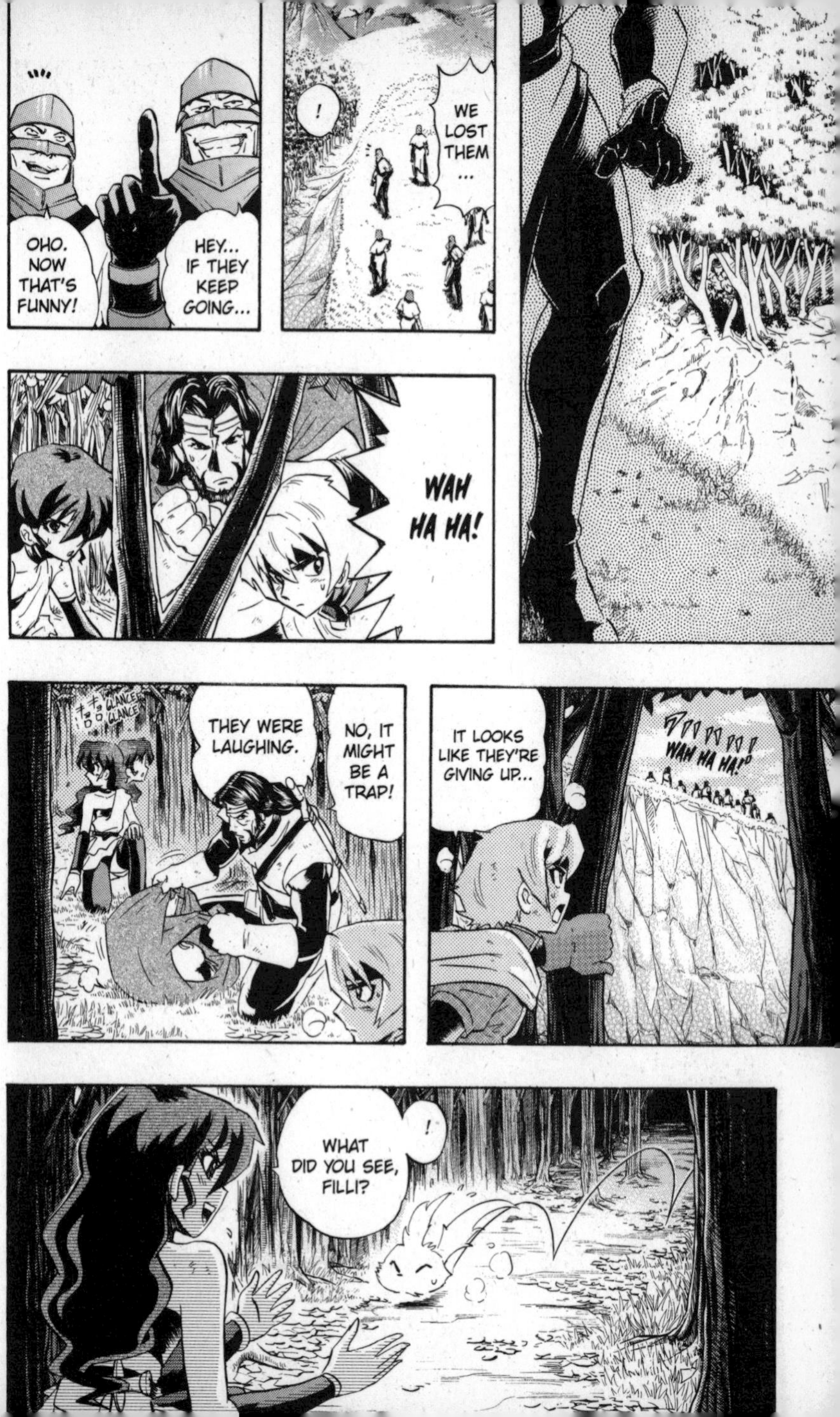
!
WE LOST THEM ...
HEY... IF THEY KEEP GOING...
OHO. NOW THAT'S FUNNY!
WAH HA HA!
WAH HA HA!
IT LOOKS LIKE THEY'RE GIVING UP...
NO, IT MIGHT BE A TRAP!
THEY WERE LAUGHING.
GLANCE GLANCE
!
WHAT DID YOU SEE, FILLI?

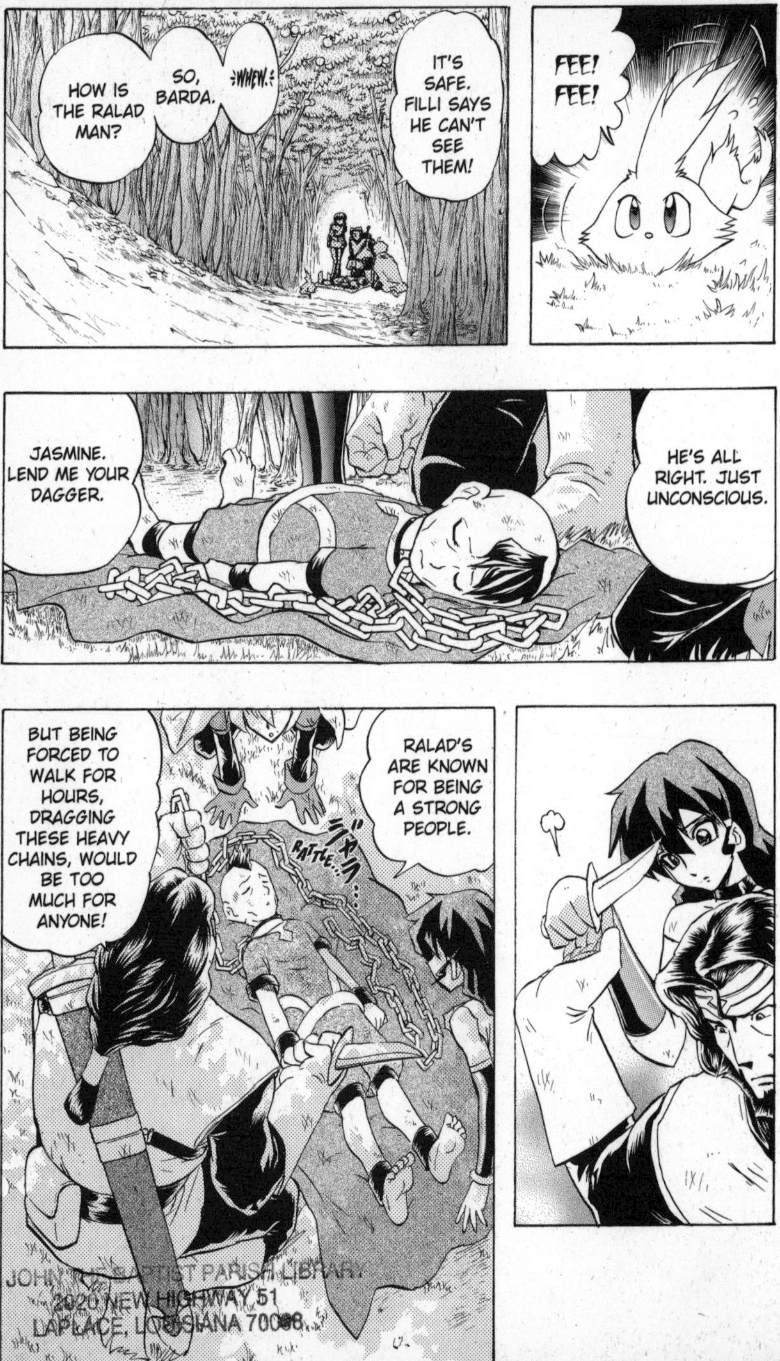
FEE! FEE!
IT'S SAFE. FILLI SAYS HE CAN'T SEE THEM!
WHEW.
SO, BARDA.
HOW IS THE RALAD MAN?
HE'S ALL RIGHT. JUST UNCONSCIOUS.
JASMINE. LEND ME YOUR DAGGER.
RALAD'S ARE KNOWN FOR BEING A STRONG PEOPLE.
RATTLE...
BUT BEING FORCED TO WALK FOR HOURS, DRAGGING THESE HEAVY CHAINS, WOULD BE TOO MUCH FOR ANYONE!

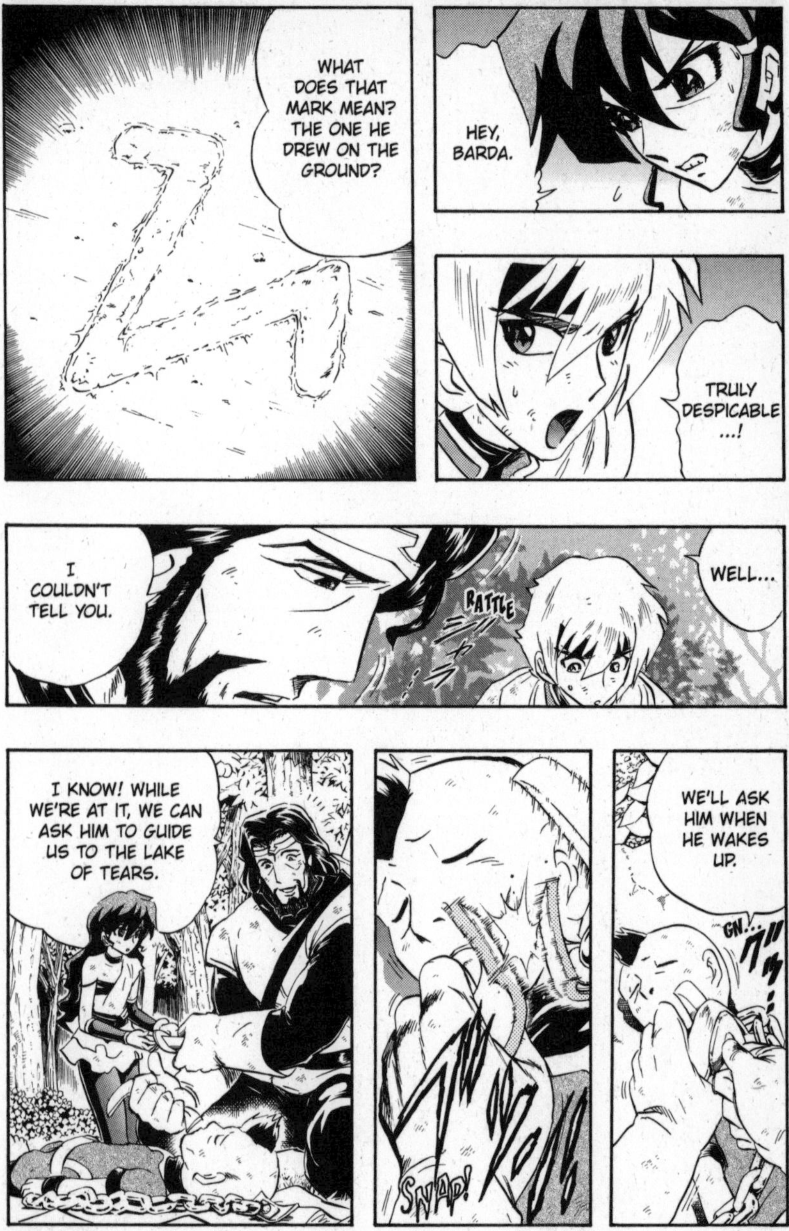
HEY, BARDA.
TRULY DESPICABLE ...!
WHAT DOES THAT MARK MEAN? THE ONE HE DREW ON THE GROUND?
WELL...
RATTLE
I COULDN'T TELL YOU.
WE'LL ASK HIM WHEN HE WAKES UP.
GN...
SNAP!
I KNOW! WHILE WE'RE AT IT, WE CAN ASK HIM TO GUIDE US TO THE LAKE OF TEARS.

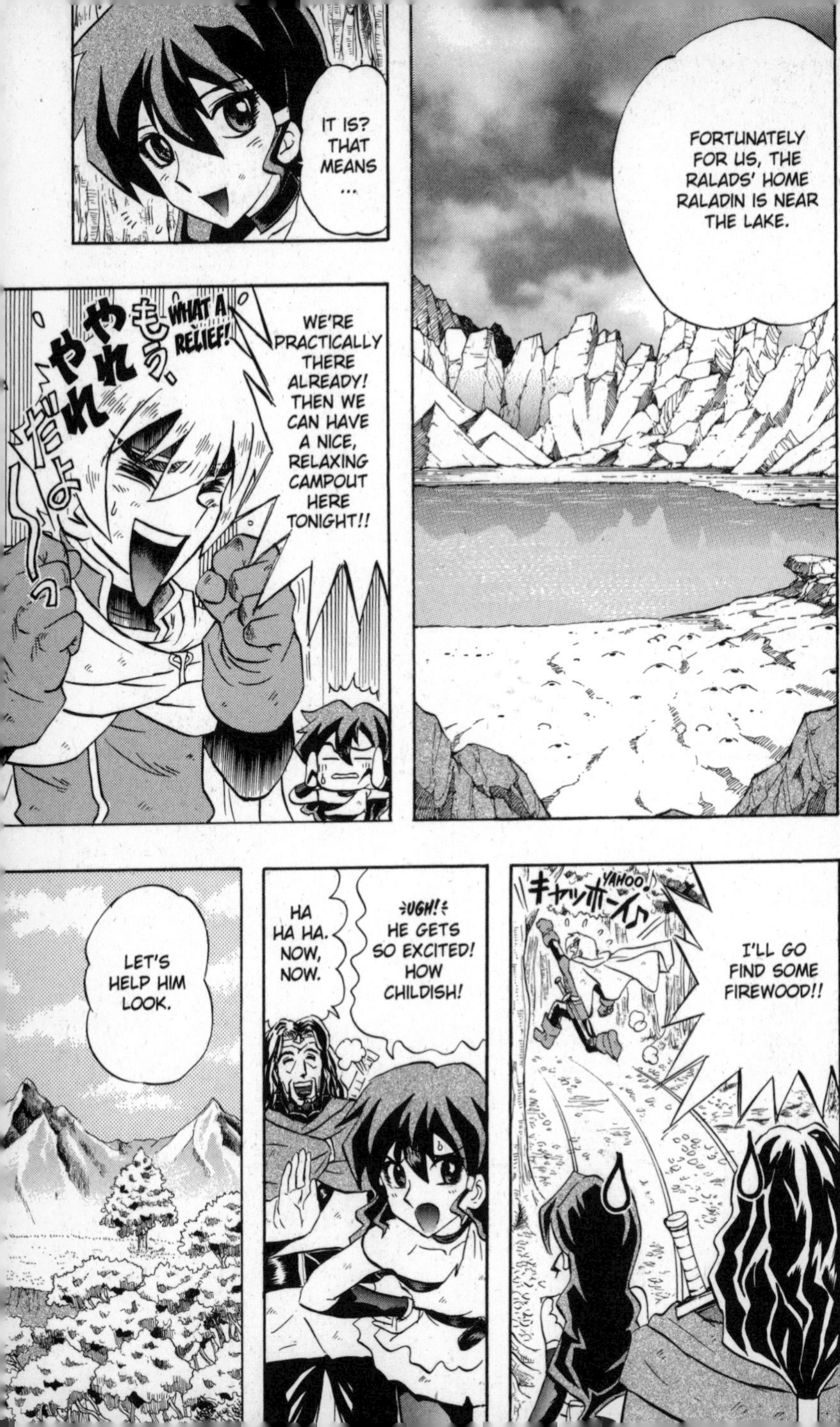
FORTUNATELY FOR US, THE RALADS' HOME RALADIN IS NEAR THE LAKE.
IT IS? THAT MEANS ...
やれやれ
WHAT A RELIEF!
WE'RE PRACTICALLY THERE ALREADY! THEN WE CAN HAVE A NICE, RELAXING CAMPOUT HERE TONIGHT!!
キャッホーイ♪
YAHOO!
I'LL GO FIND SOME FIREWOOD!!
UGH! HE GETS SO EXCITED! HOW CHILDISH!
HA HA HA. NOW, NOW.
LET'S HELP HIM LOOK.

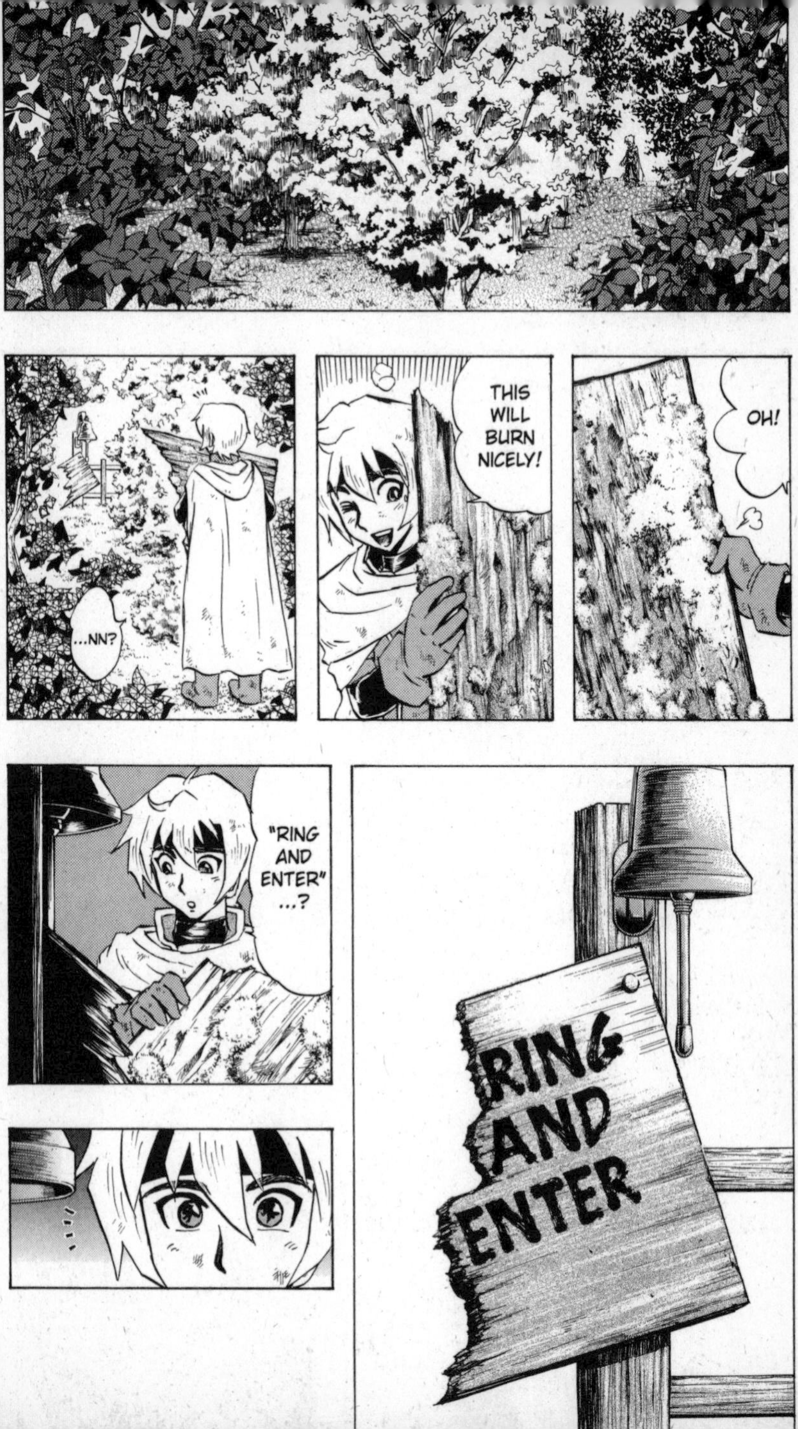
OH!
THIS WILL BURN NICELY!
...NN?
RING AND ENTER
"RING AND ENTER" ...?

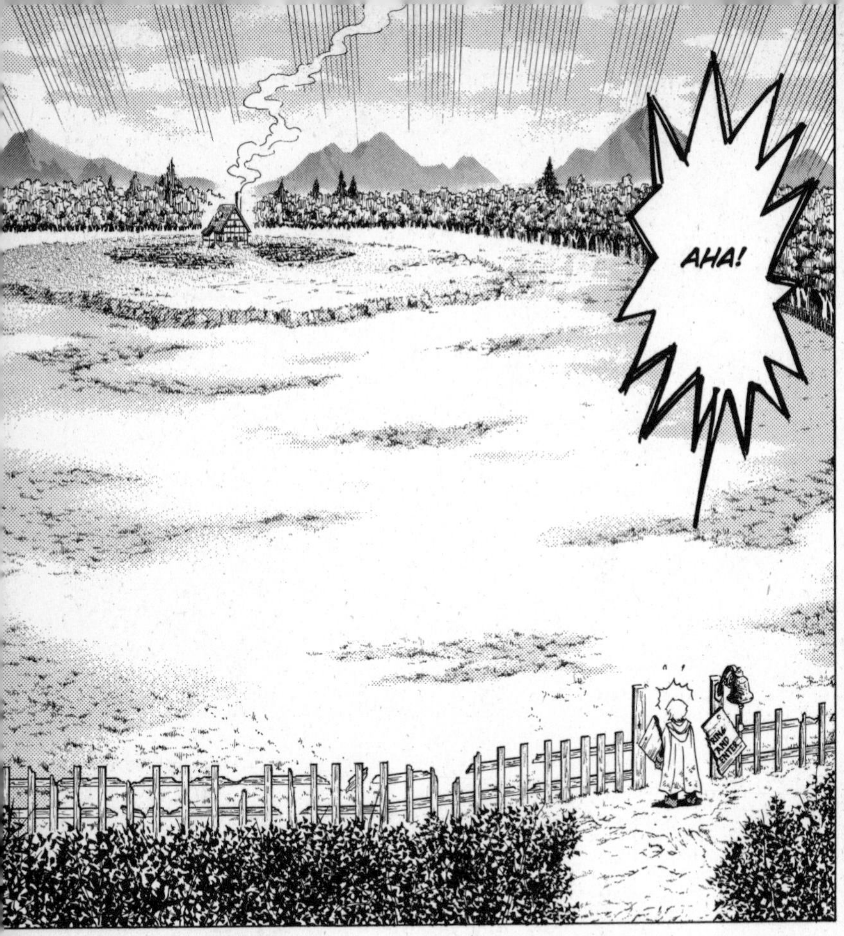
AHA!

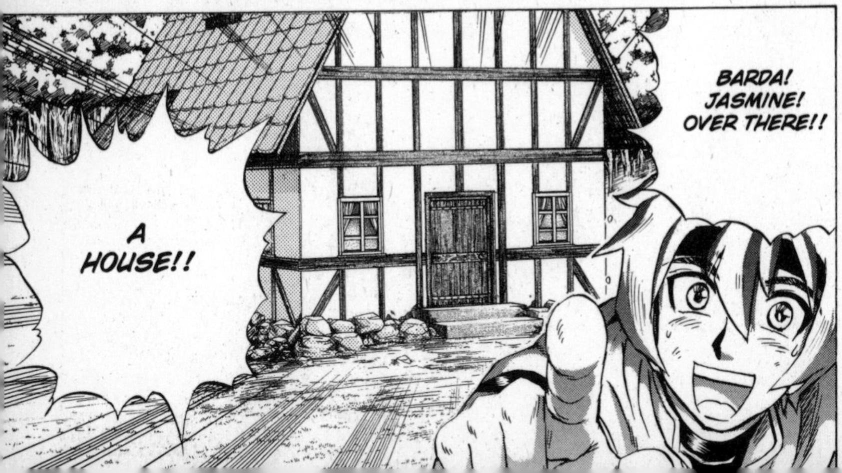
BARDA! JASMINE! OVER THERE!!
A HOUSE!!

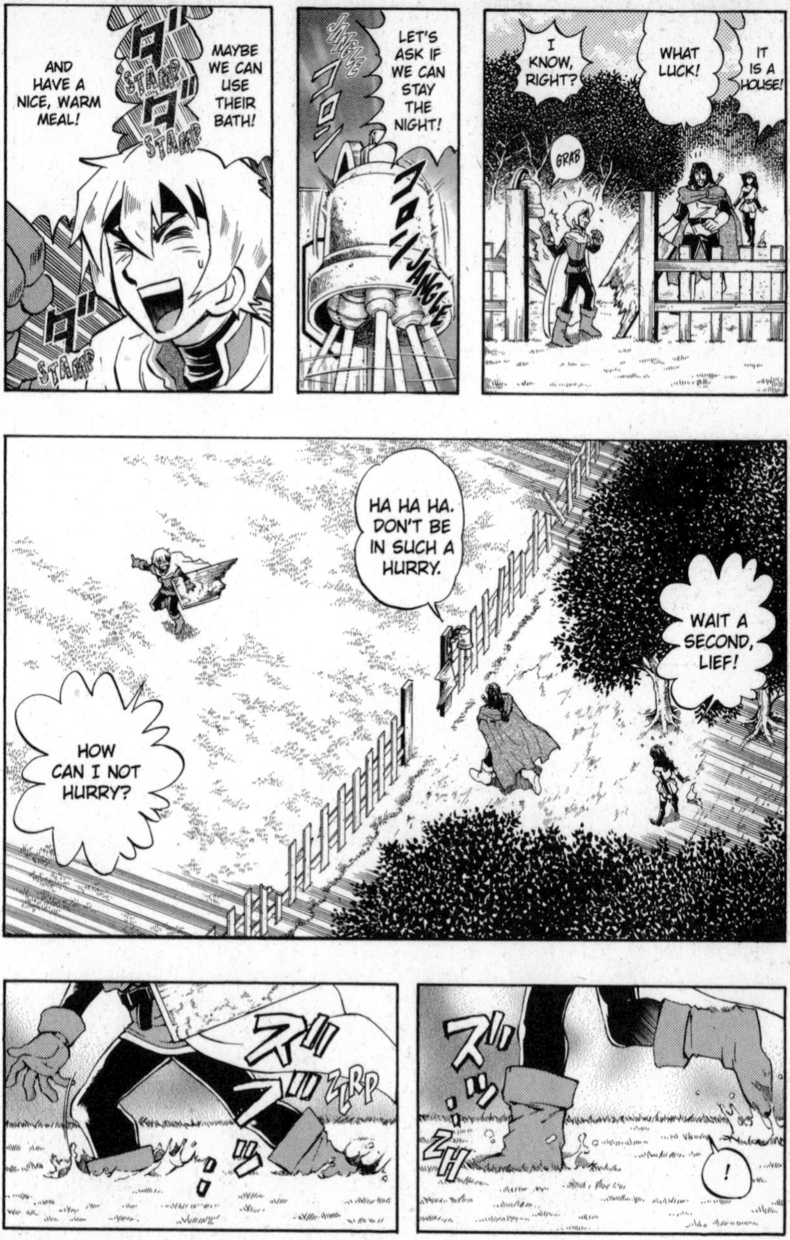
IT IS A HOUSE!
WHAT LUCK!
I KNOW, RIGHT?
GRAB
LET'S ASK IF WE CAN STAY THE NIGHT!
JANGLE
JANGLE
MAYBE WE CAN USE THEIR BATH!
STAMP
STAMP
AND HAVE A NICE, WARM MEAL!
STAMP
WAIT A SECOND, LIEF!
HA HA HA. DON'T BE IN SUCH A HURRY.
HOW CAN I NOT HURRY?
ZH
!
ZLRP

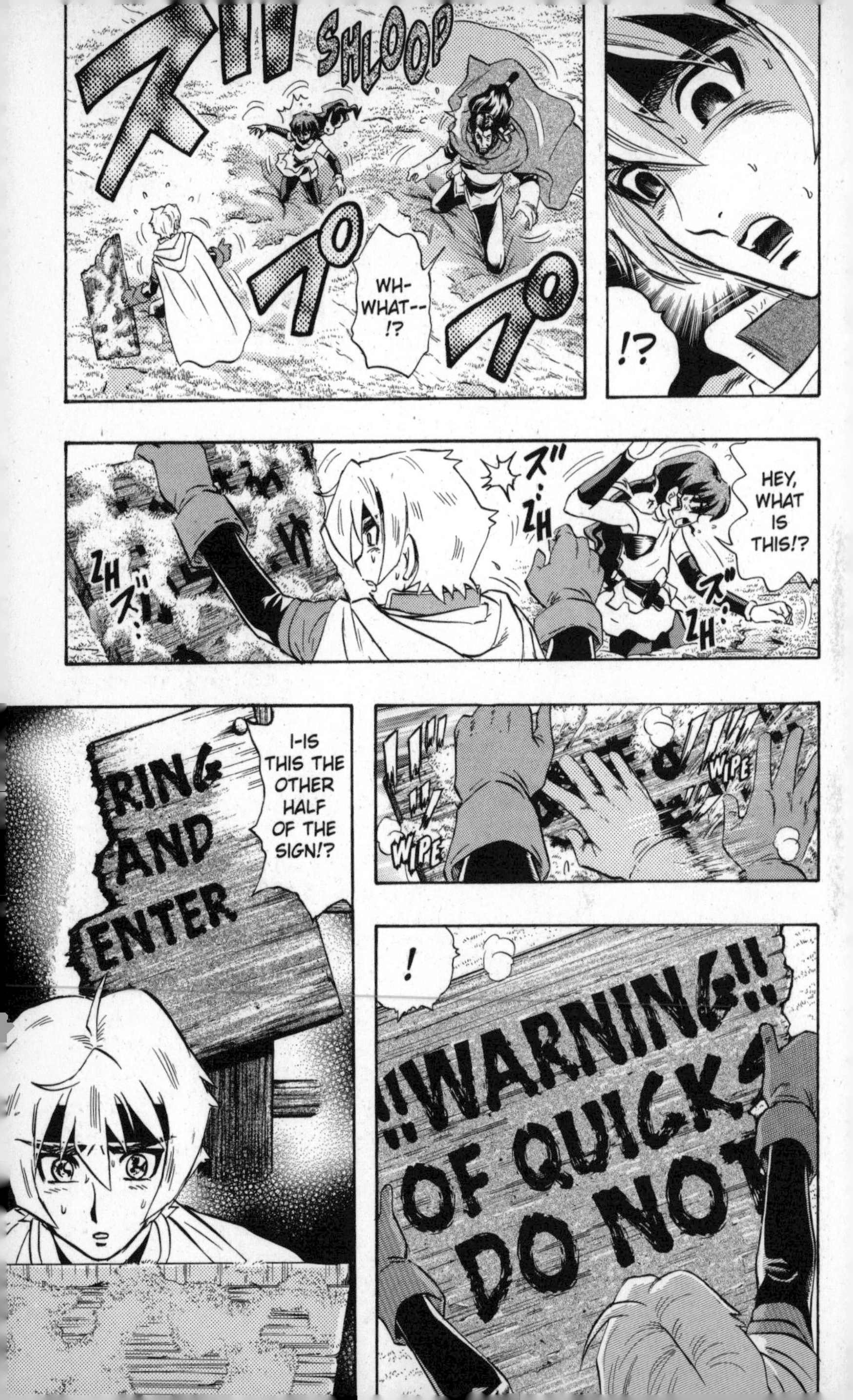

!?
ズ
SHLOOP
プ
WH- WHAT-- !?
プ
HEY, WHAT IS THIS!?
ズ
ZH
ズ
ZH
ZH
ズ
WIPE
WIPE
I-IS THIS THE OTHER HALF OF THE SIGN!?
RING AND ENTER
!
!!WARNING!!
OF QUICK
DO NOT

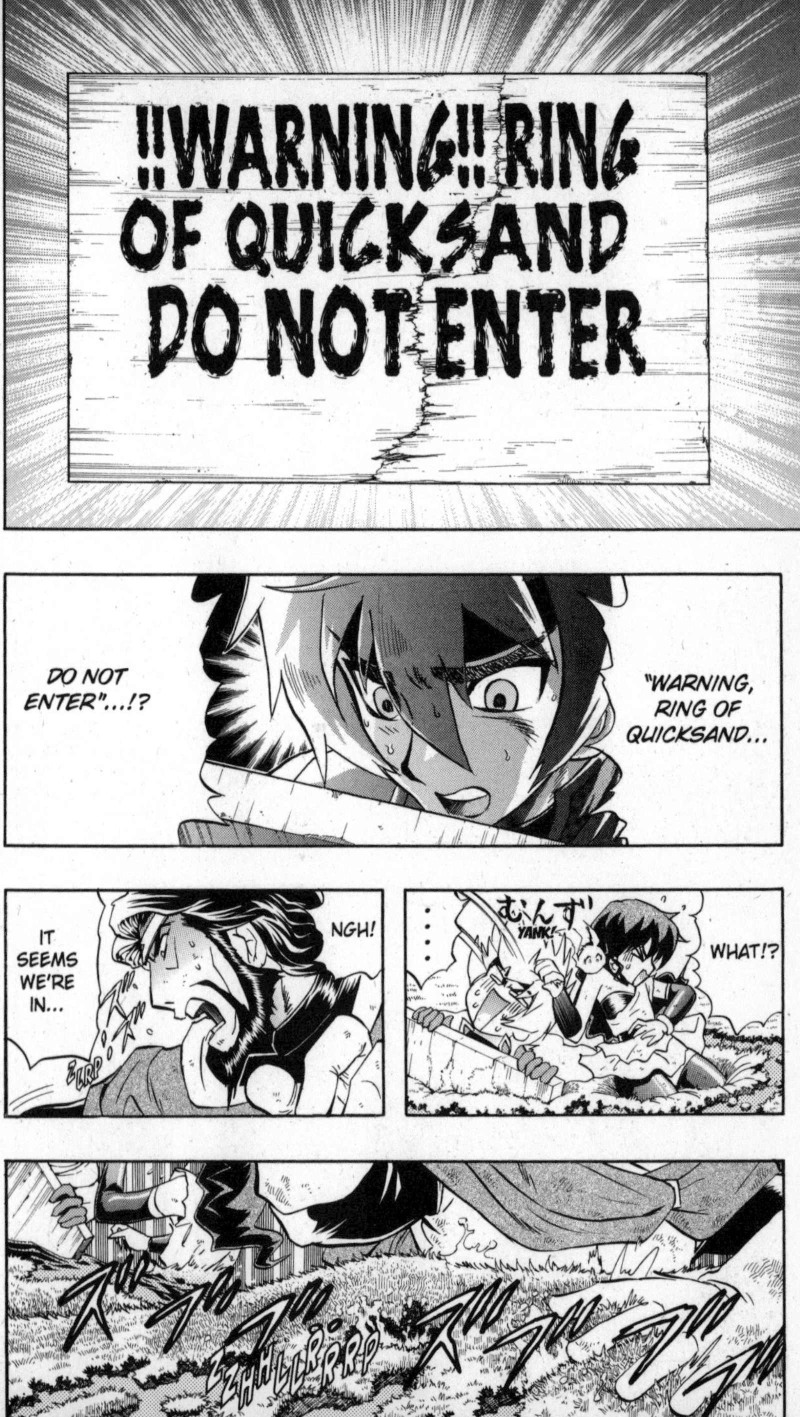
!!WARNING!! RING OF QUICKSAND DO NOT ENTER
"WARNING, RING OF QUICKSAND...
DO NOT ENTER"...!?
WHAT!?
むんず
YANK!
NGH!
IT SEEMS WE'RE IN...
ZLRP
ZHHLLRRRP

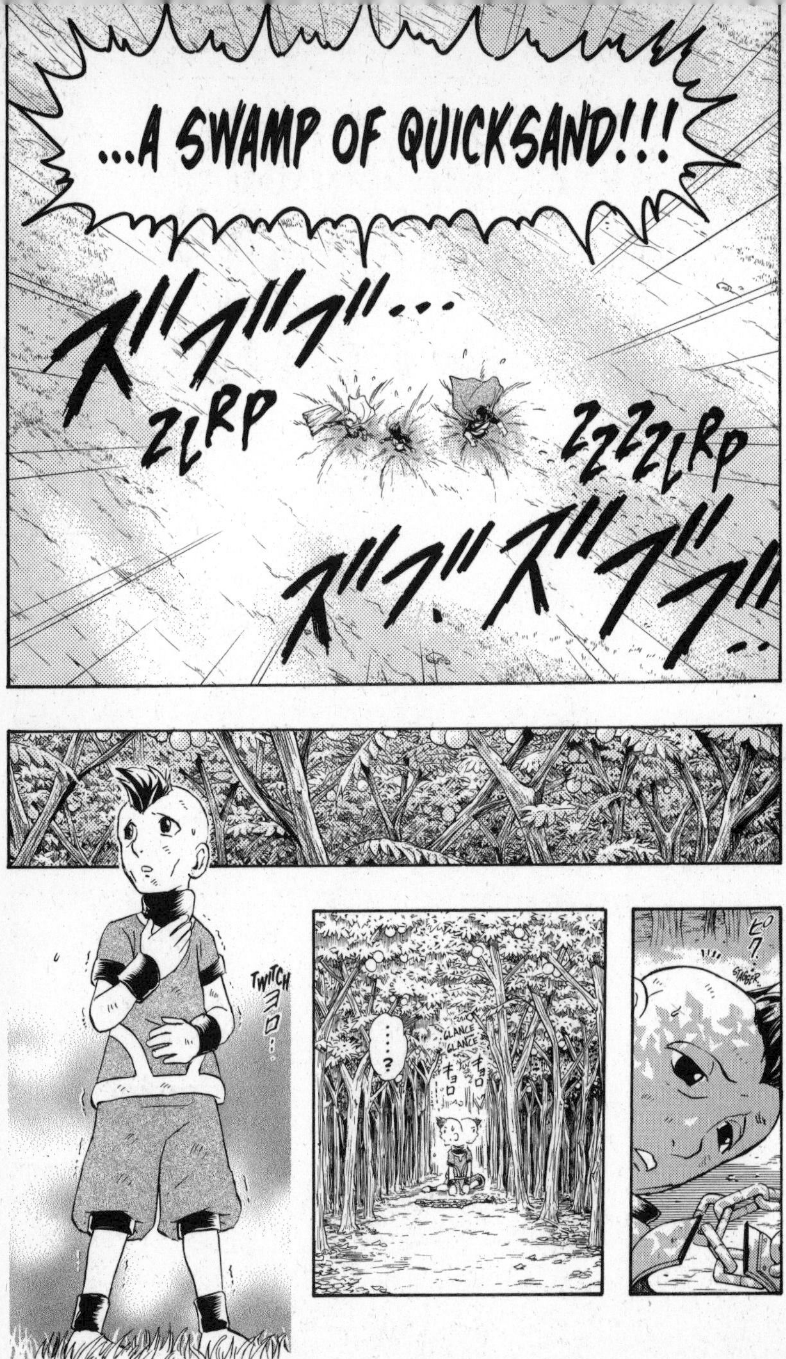
...A SWAMP OF QUICKSAND!!!
ZLRP
ZZZZLRP
STAGGER
....?
GLANCE GLANCE
TWITCH

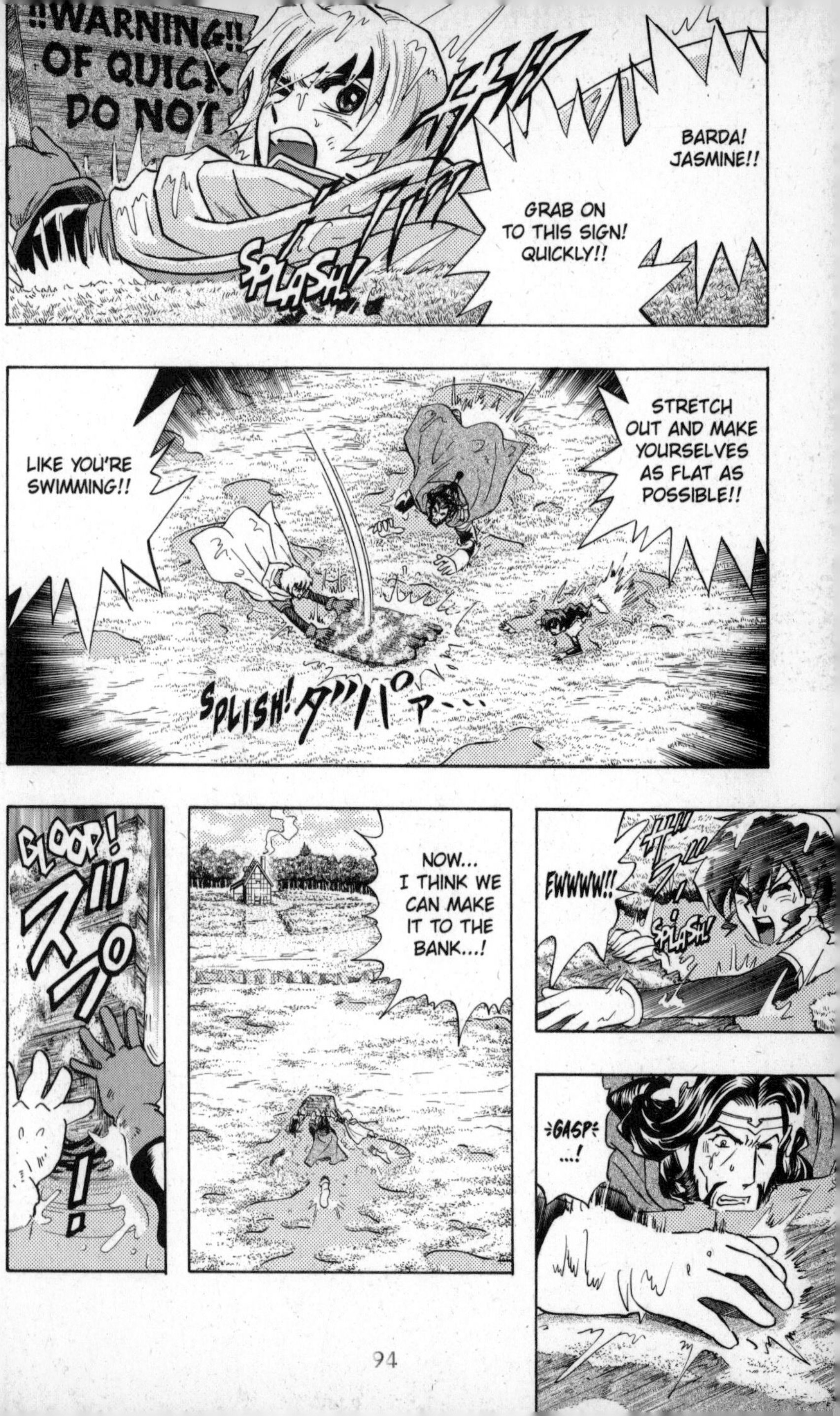
!!WARNING!!
OF QUICK
DO NOT
BARDA! JASMINE!!
GRAB ON TO THIS SIGN! QUICKLY!!
SPLASH!
STRETCH OUT AND MAKE YOURSELVES AS FLAT AS POSSIBLE!!
LIKE YOU'RE SWIMMING!!
SPLISH!
EWWWW!!
SPLASH!
GASP
...!
NOW... I THINK WE CAN MAKE IT TO THE BANK...!
GLOOP!

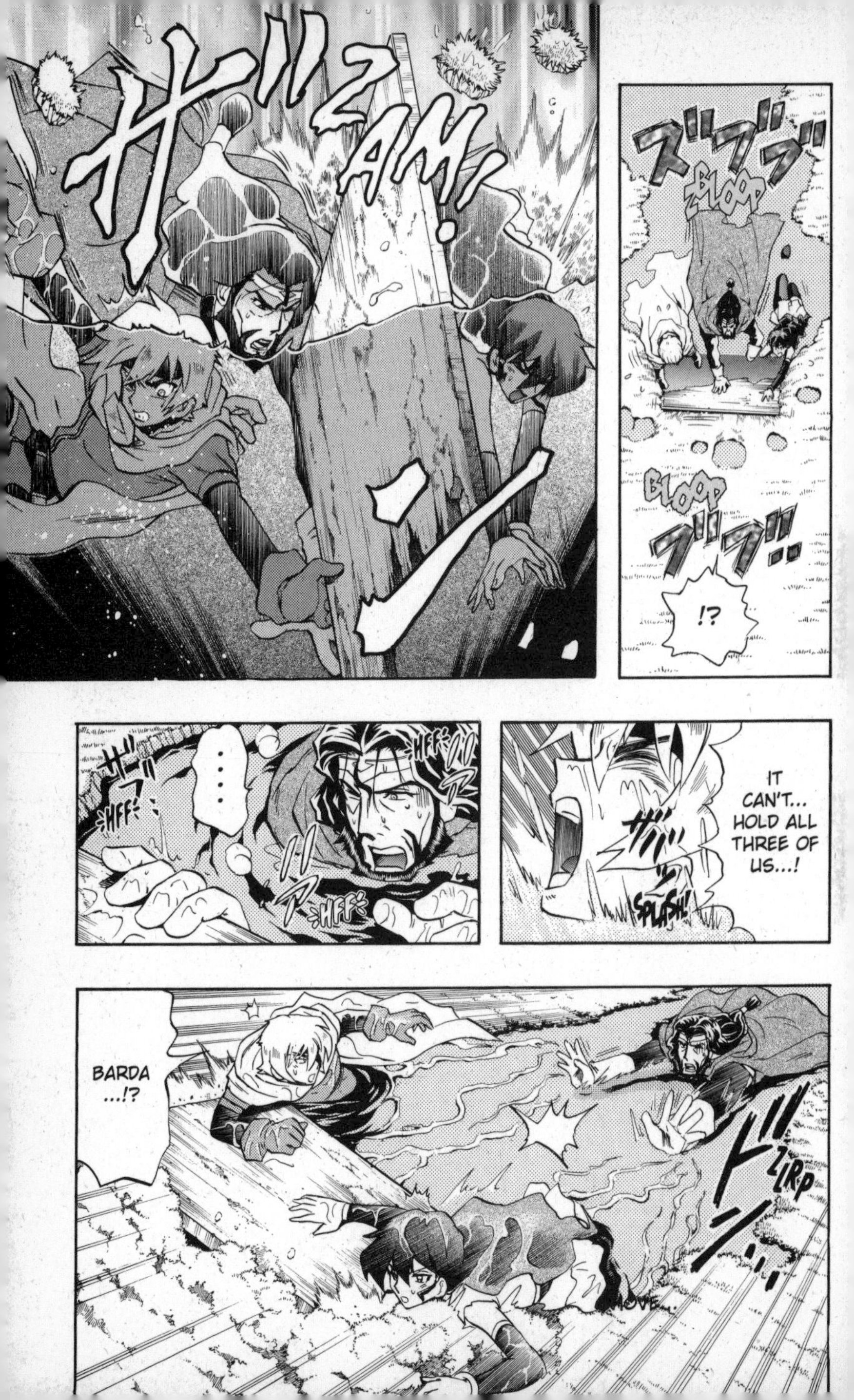
BLOOP
BLOOP
!?
WHAM!
IT CAN'T... HOLD ALL THREE OF US...!
SPLASH!
......
HFF
HFF
HFF
BARDA ...!?
ZIRP

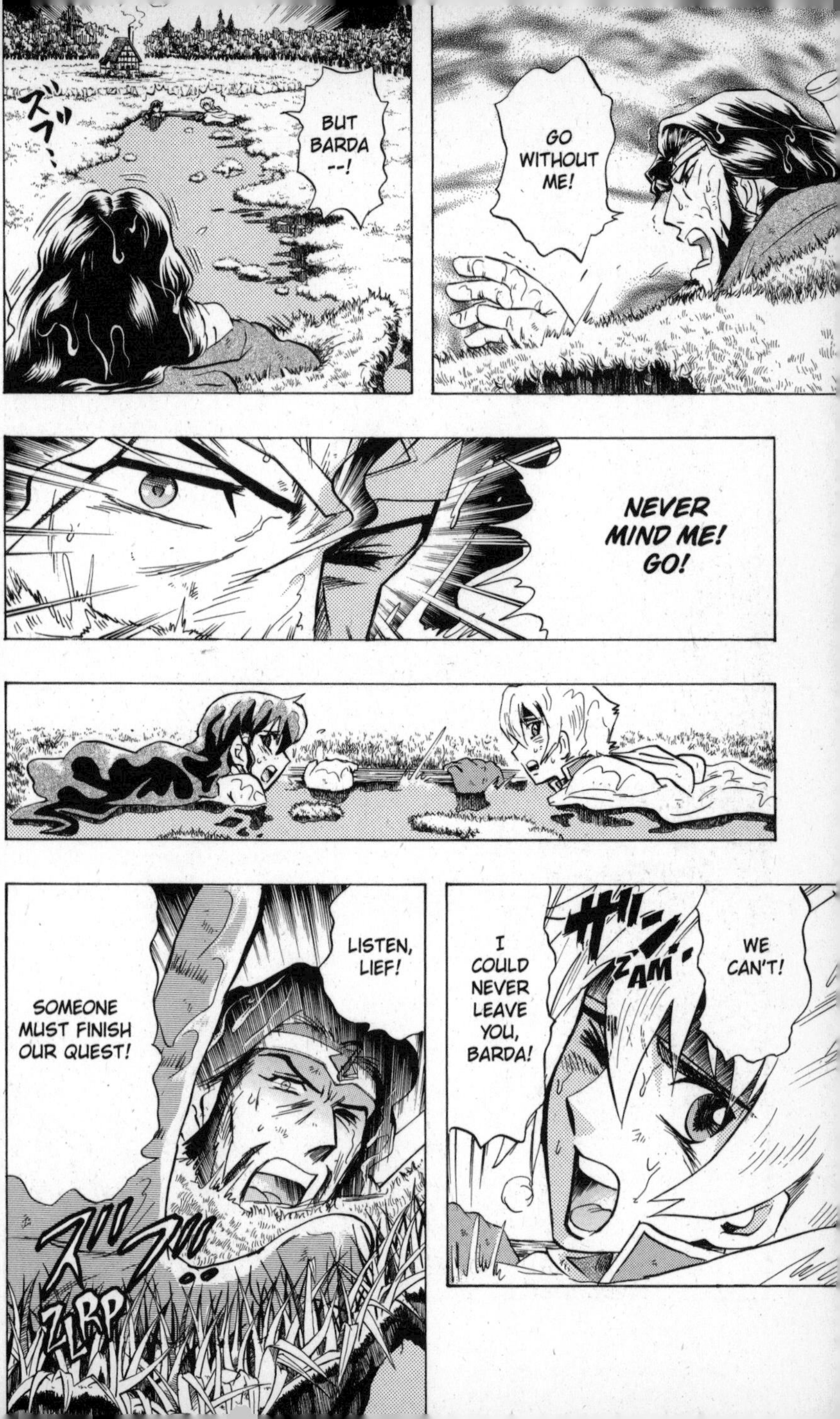
GO WITHOUT ME!
BUT BARDA --!
NEVER MIND ME! GO!
WE CAN'T!
ZAM
I COULD NEVER LEAVE YOU, BARDA!
LISTEN, LIEF!
SOMEONE MUST FINISH OUR QUEST!
ZLRP

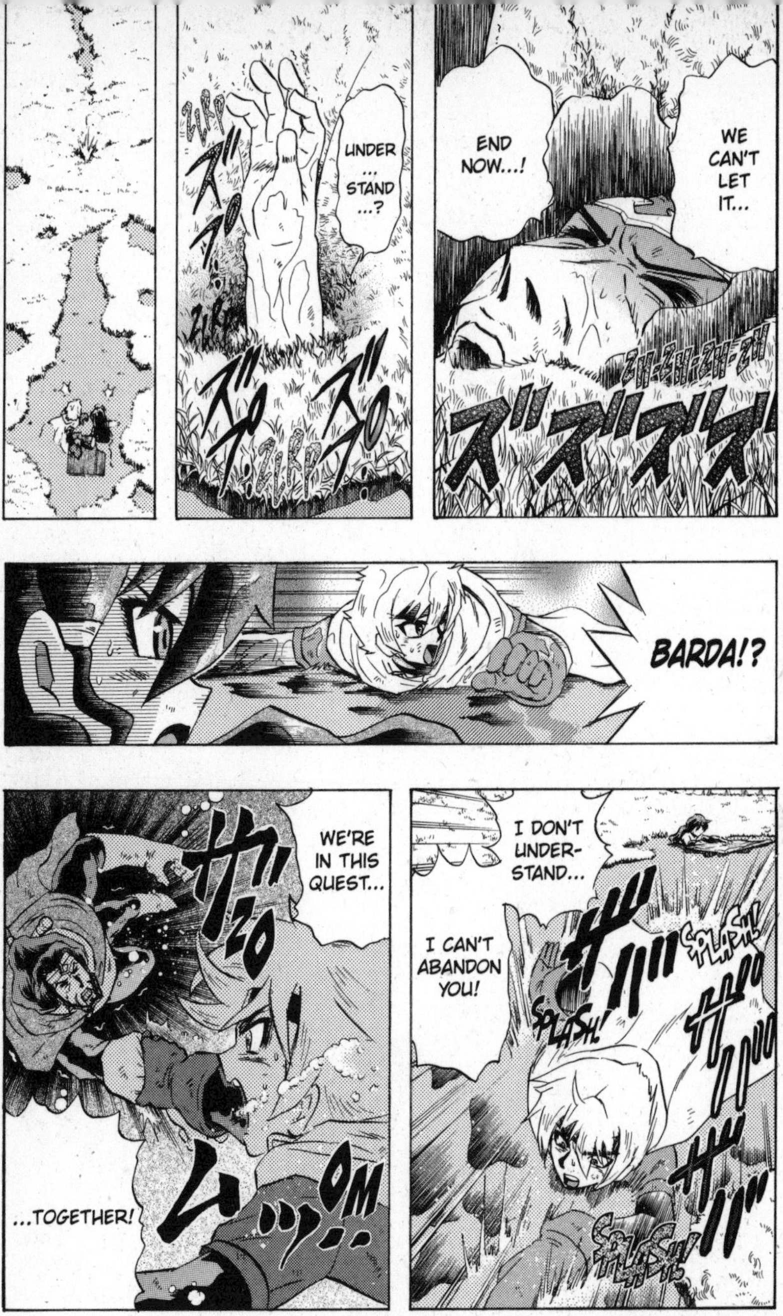

WE CAN'T LET IT...
END NOW...!
ZH-ZH-ZH-ZH
UNDER ... STAND ...?
ZLRP
ZLRP
ZLRP
BARDA!?
I DON'T UNDER-STAND...
I CAN'T ABANDON YOU!
SPLASH!
SPLASH!
WE'RE IN THIS QUEST...
...TOGETHER!
OM

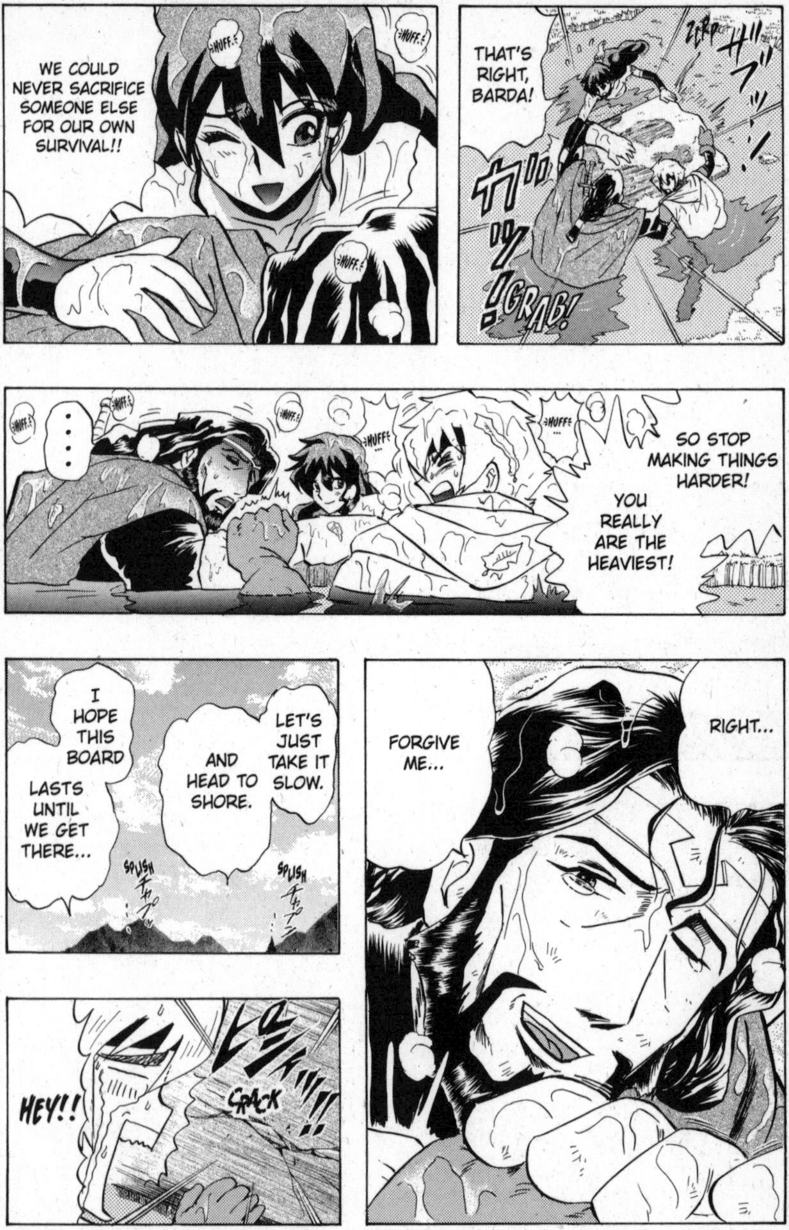
THAT'S RIGHT, BARDA!
GRAB!
WE COULD NEVER SACRIFICE SOMEONE ELSE FOR OUR OWN SURVIVAL!!
HUFF
HUFF
HUFF
SO STOP MAKING THINGS HARDER!
YOU REALLY ARE THE HEAVIEST!
HUFF
HUFF
HUFF
HUFF
HUFF
. . . .
RIGHT...
FORGIVE ME...
LET'S JUST TAKE IT SLOW.
AND HEAD TO SHORE.
I HOPE THIS BOARD LASTS UNTIL WE GET THERE...
SPLISH
SPLISH
CRACK
HEY!!

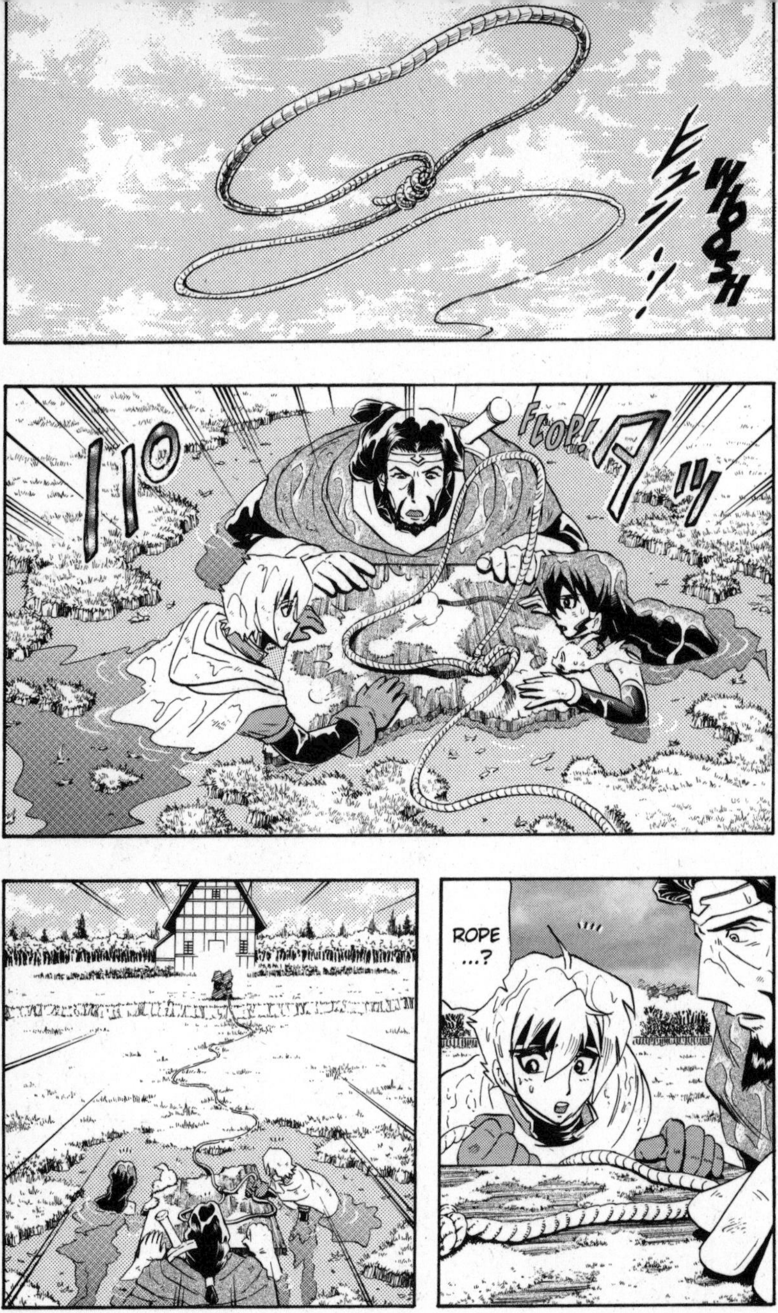
WOOSH
FLOP!
ROPE ...?

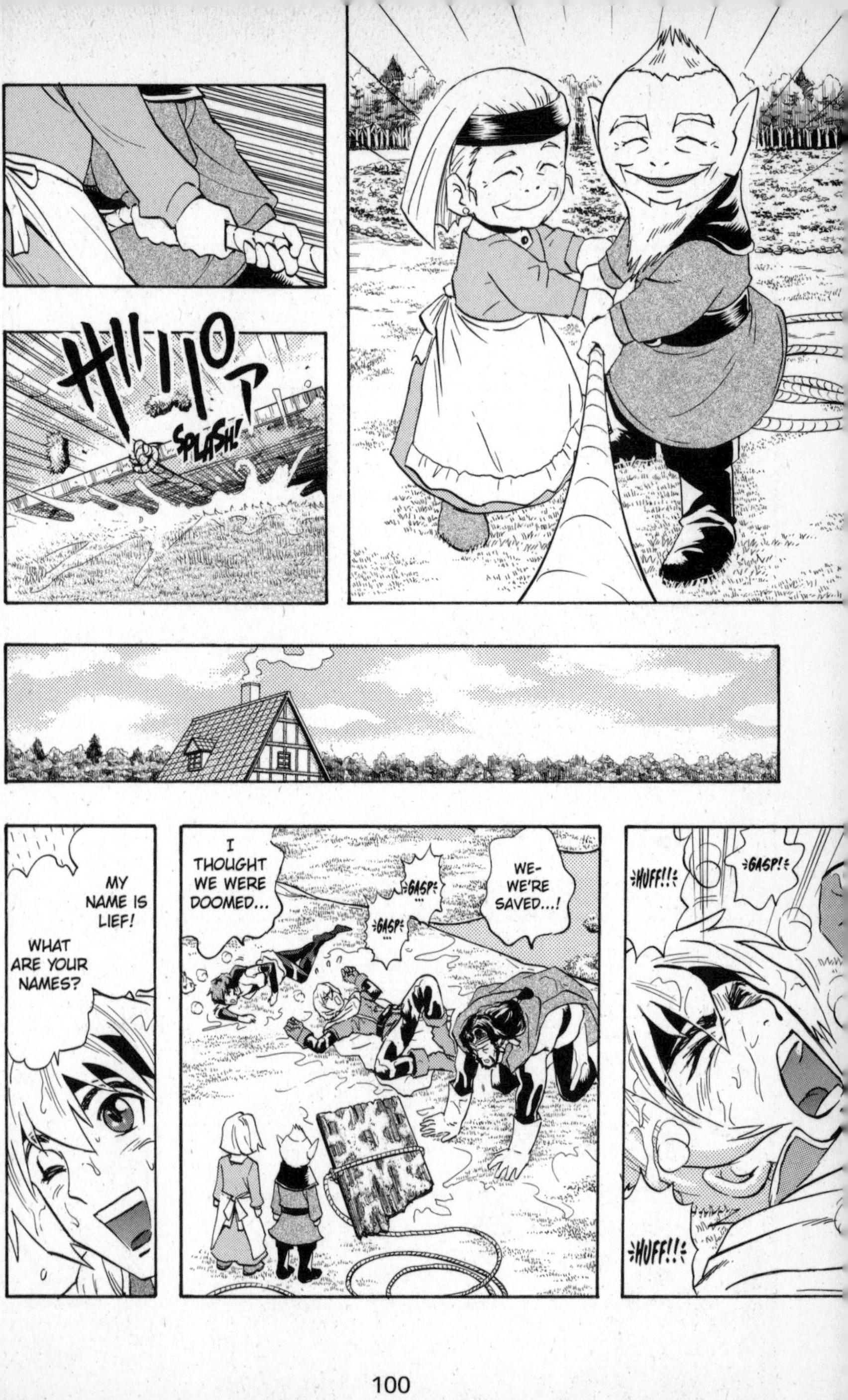
SPLASH!
HUFF!!
GASP!
HUFF!!
WE- WE'RE SAVED...!
GASP...
GASP...
I THOUGHT WE WERE DOOMED...
MY NAME IS LIEF!
WHAT ARE YOUR NAMES?

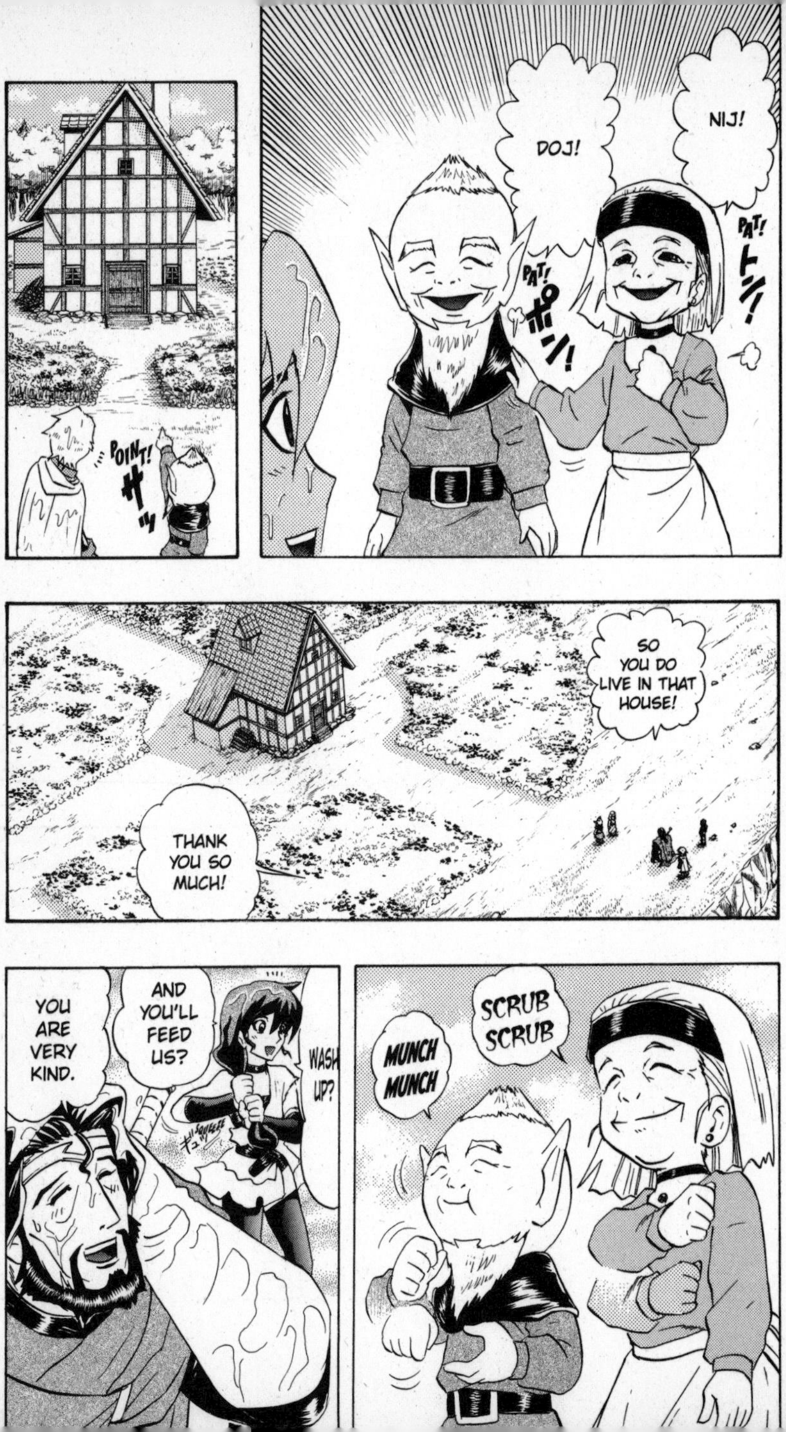
NIJ!
DOJ!
PAT!
トン!
PAT!
ポン!
POINT!
サッ
SO YOU DO LIVE IN THAT HOUSE!
THANK YOU SO MUCH!
SCRUB SCRUB
MUNCH MUNCH
WASH UP?
AND YOU'LL FEED US?
YOU ARE VERY KIND.

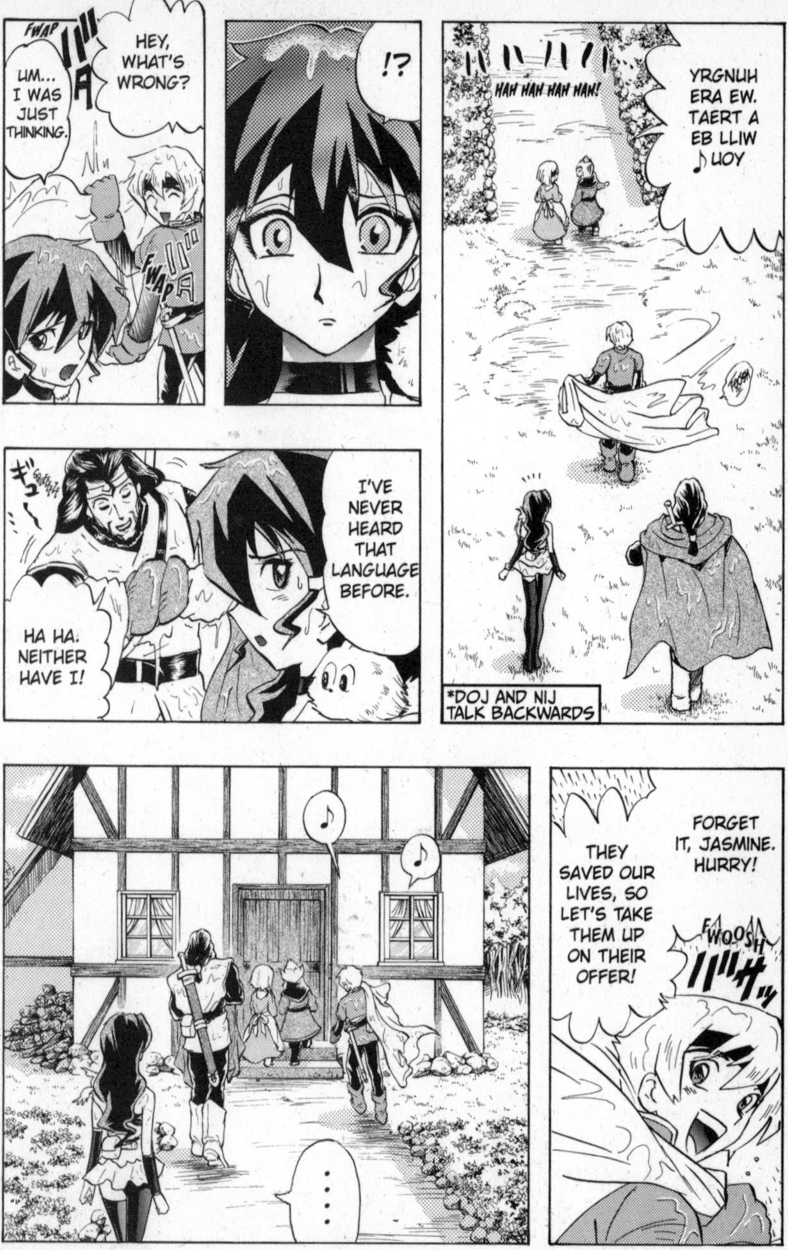
HAH HAH HAH HAN!
YRGNUH ERA EW. TAERT A EB LLIW ♪UOY
*DOJ AND NIJ TALK BACKWARDS
!?
HEY, WHAT'S WRONG?
FWAP
UM... I WAS JUST THINKING.
FWAP
I'VE NEVER HEARD THAT LANGUAGE BEFORE.
HA HA. NEITHER HAVE I!
FORGET IT, JASMINE. HURRY!
THEY SAVED OUR LIVES, SO LET'S TAKE THEM UP ON THEIR OFFER!
FWOOSH
♪
♪
....

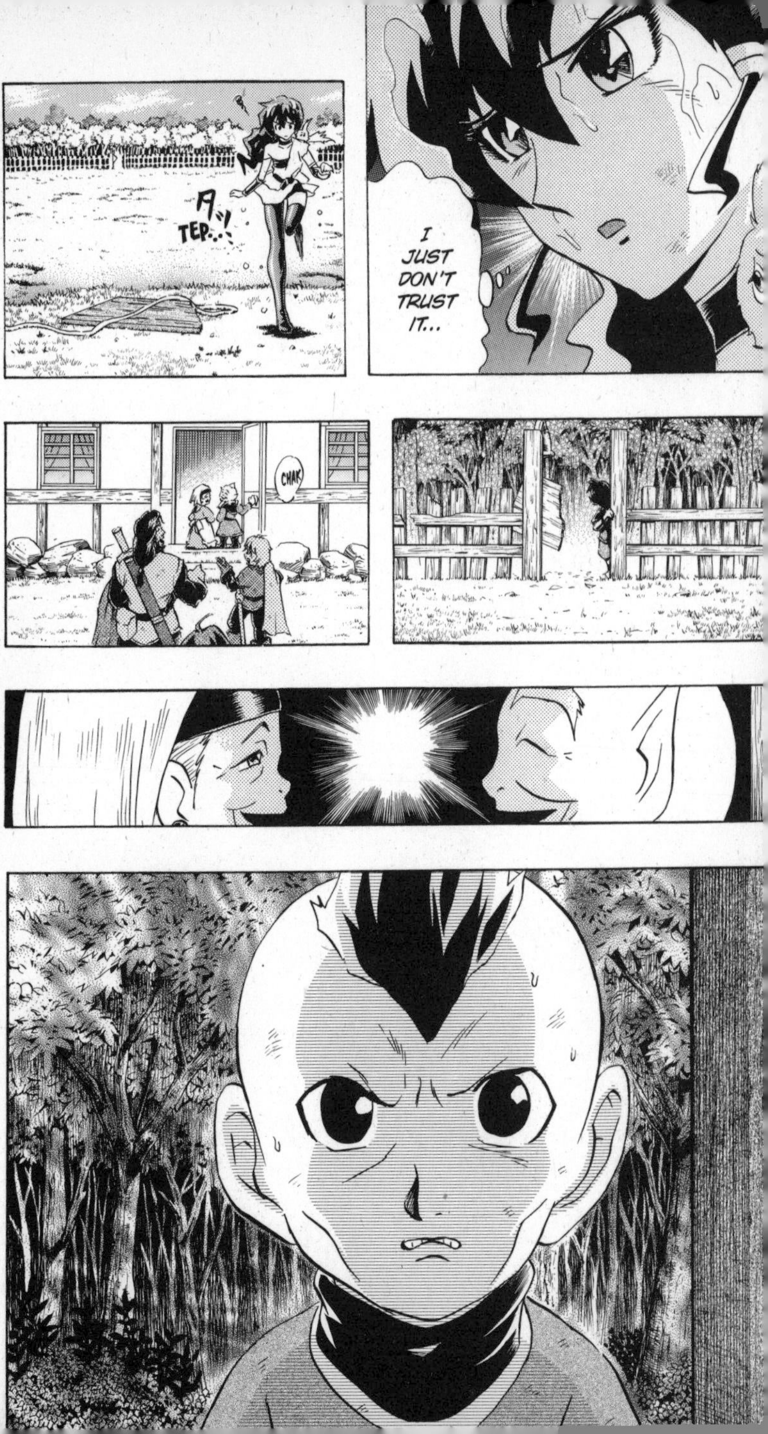
I JUST DON'T TRUST IT...
TEP...
CHAK

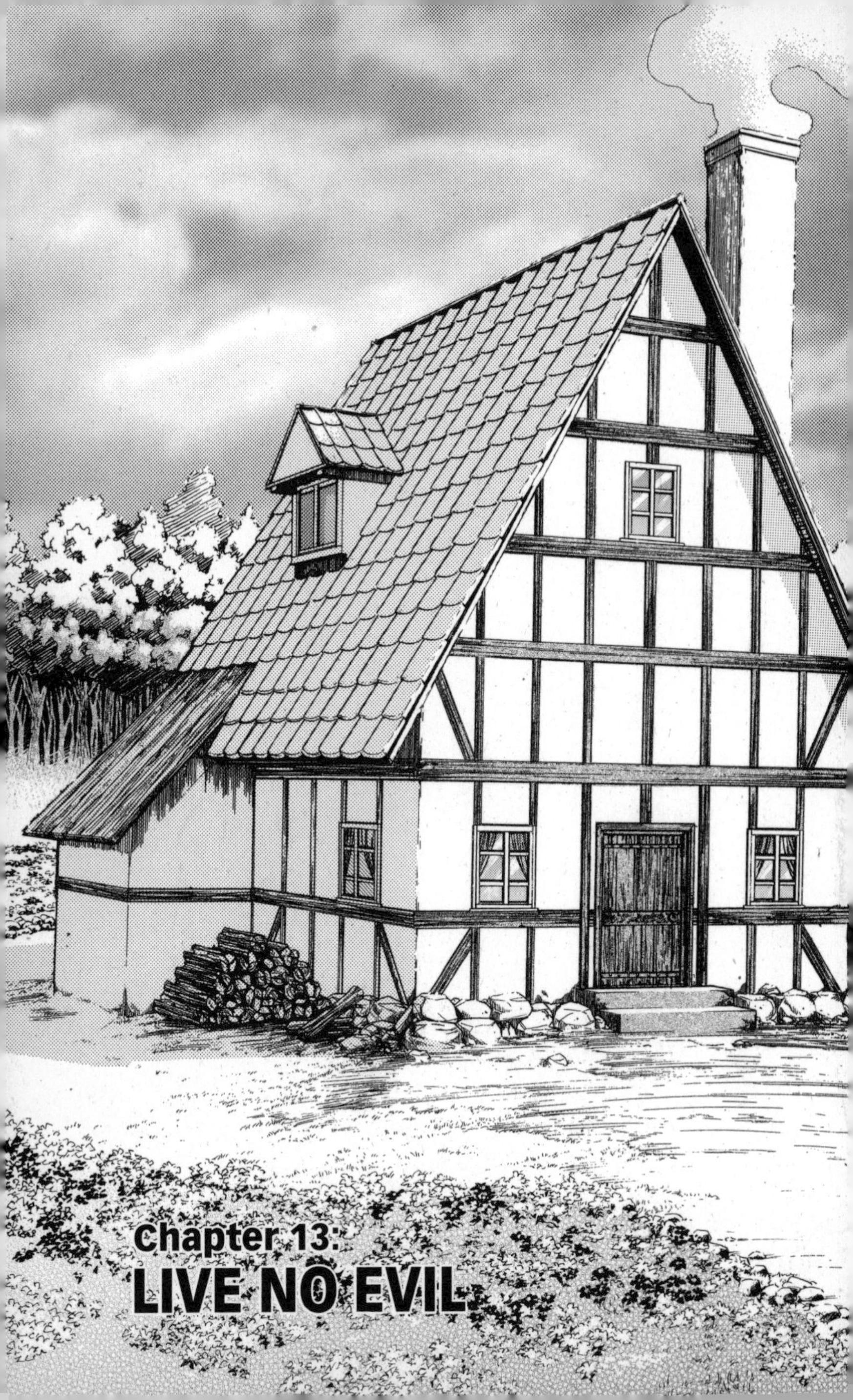
Chapter 13:
LIVE NO EVIL

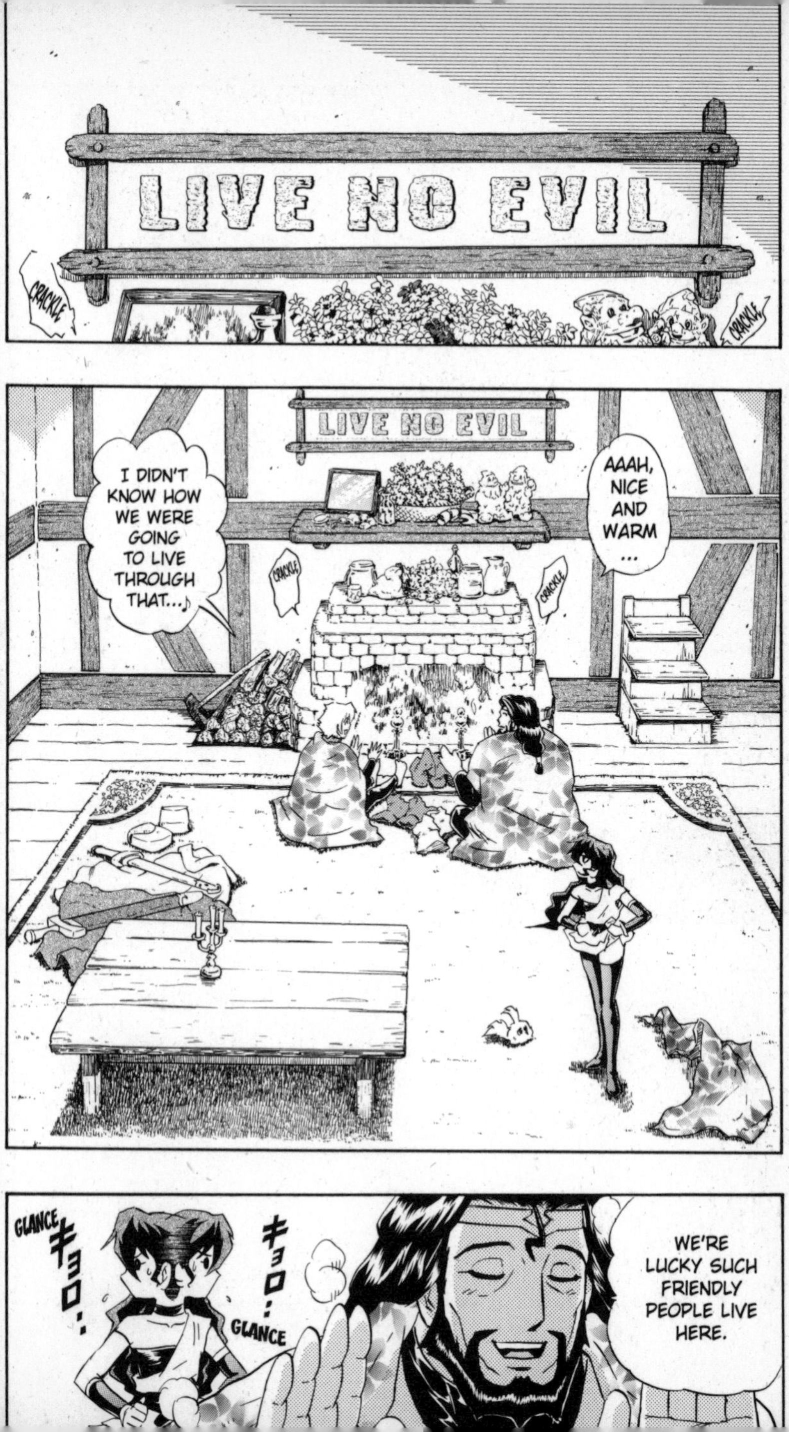
LIVE NO EVIL
CRACKLE
CRACKLE
LIVE NO EVIL
AAAH, NICE AND WARM...
CRACKLE
CRACKLE
I DIDN'T KNOW HOW WE WERE GOING TO LIVE THROUGH THAT...♪
WE'RE LUCKY SUCH FRIENDLY PEOPLE LIVE HERE.
キョロ・・
GLANCE
GLANCE
キョロ・・

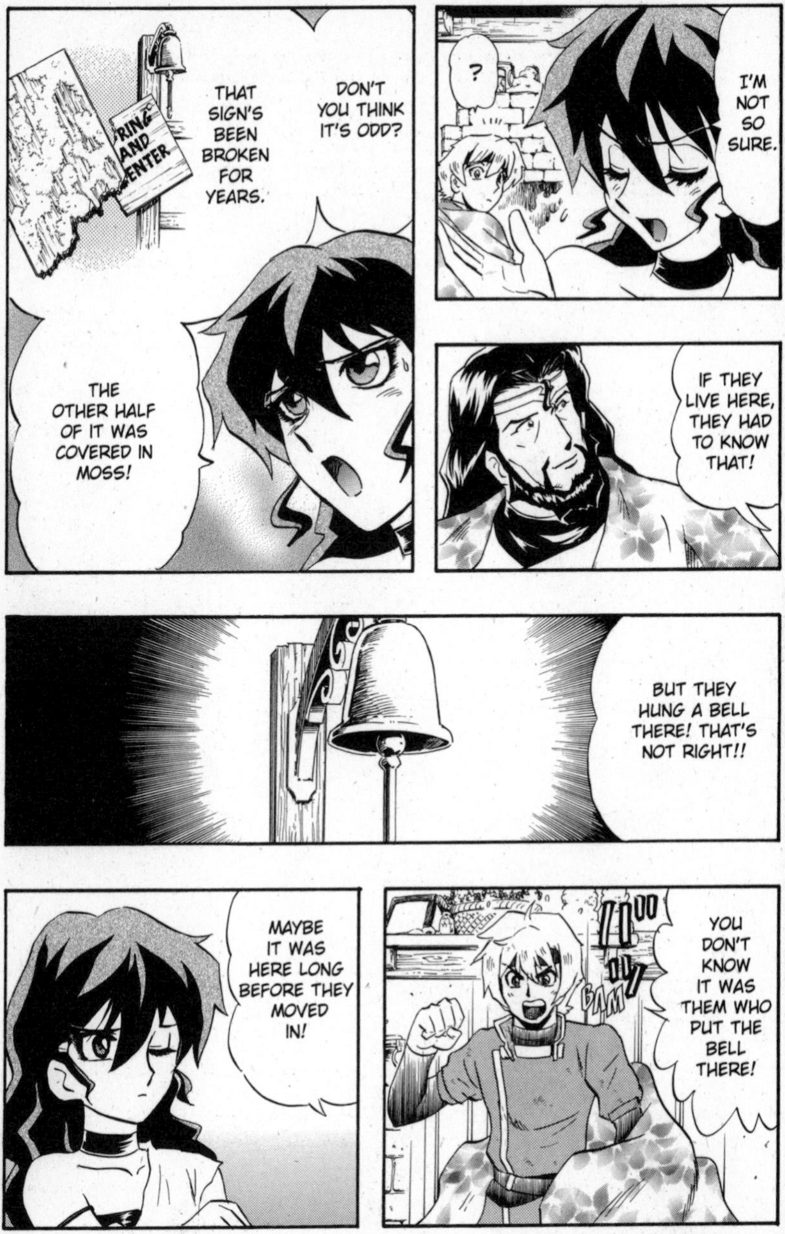
?
I'M NOT SO SURE.
IF THEY LIVE HERE, THEY HAD TO KNOW THAT!
DON'T YOU THINK IT'S ODD?
THAT SIGN'S BEEN BROKEN FOR YEARS.
RING AND ENTER
THE OTHER HALF OF IT WAS COVERED IN MOSS!
BUT THEY HUNG A BELL THERE! THAT'S NOT RIGHT!!
YOU DON'T KNOW IT WAS THEM WHO PUT THE BELL THERE!
BAM
MAYBE IT WAS HERE LONG BEFORE THEY MOVED IN!

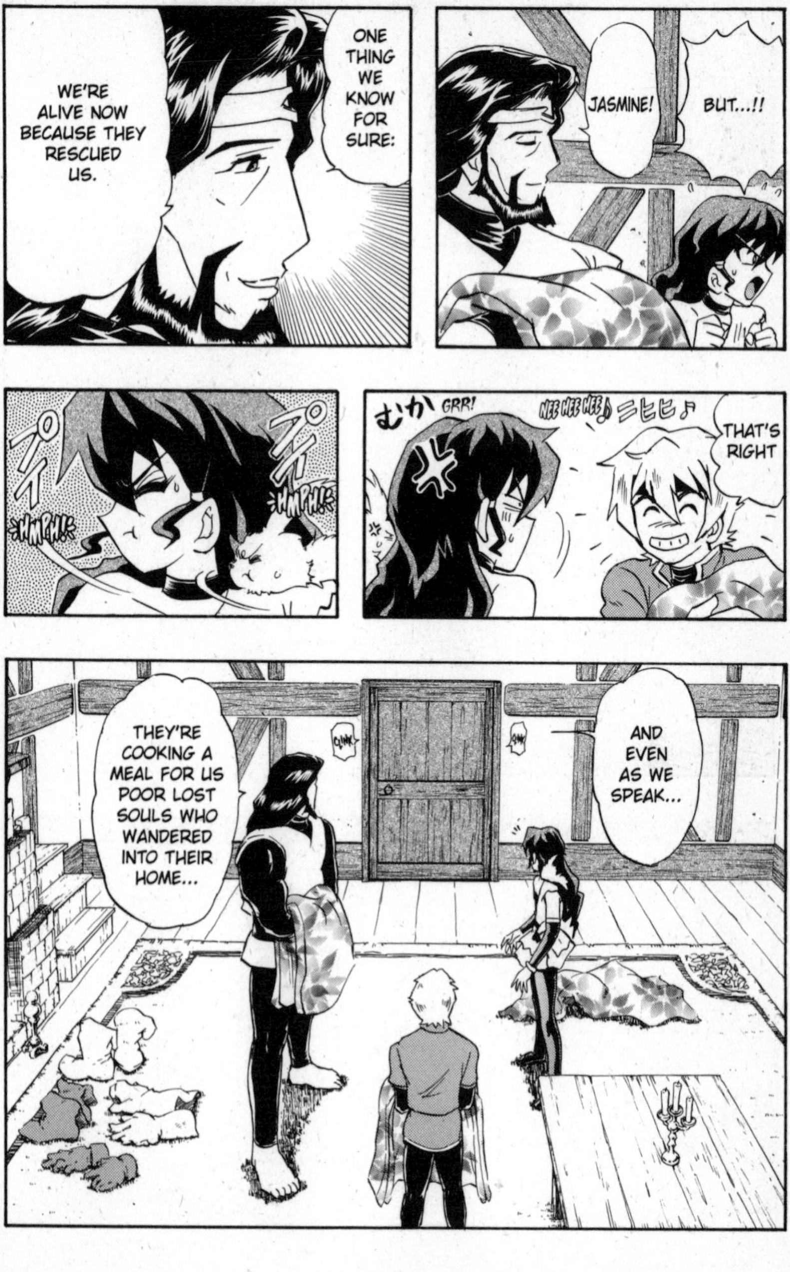
BUT...!!
JASMINE!
ONE THING WE KNOW FOR SURE:
WE'RE ALIVE NOW BECAUSE THEY RESCUED US.
THAT'S RIGHT
NEE HEE HEE♪ ニヒヒ♪
むか GRR!
HMPH!
HMPH!
AND EVEN AS WE SPEAK...
CLINK
CLINK
THEY'RE COOKING A MEAL FOR US POOR LOST SOULS WHO WANDERED INTO THEIR HOME...

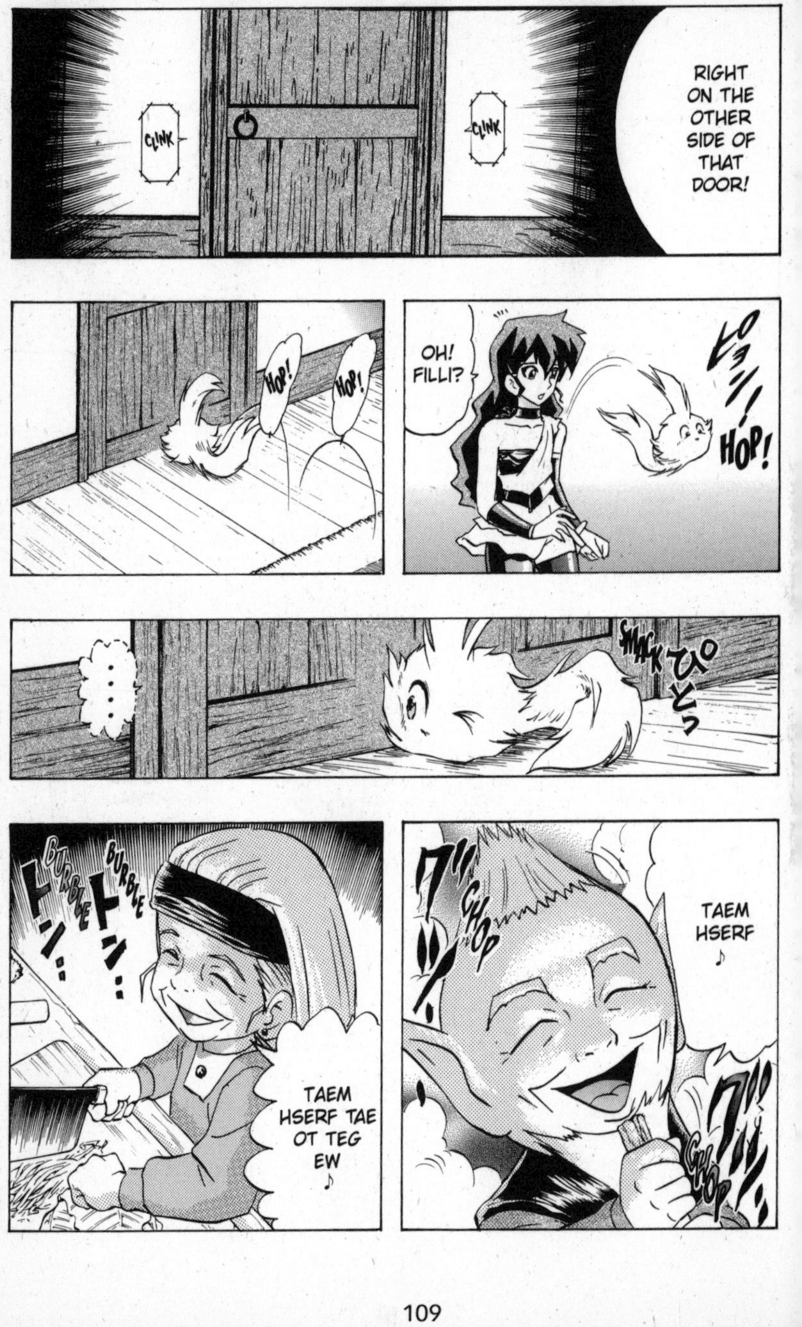
RIGHT ON THE OTHER SIDE OF THAT DOOR!
CLINK
CLINK
ピョン！
HOP!
OH! FILLI?
HOP!
HOP!
SMACK
ぴとっ
...
TAEM HSERF ♪
CHOP
CHOP
BURBLE
BURBLE
TAEM HSERF TAE OT TEG EW ♪

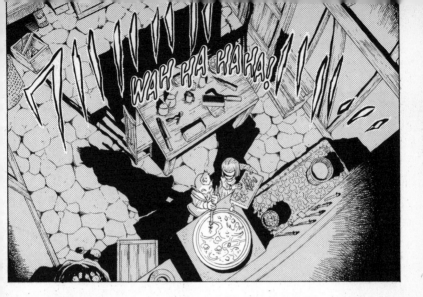

WAH HA HA HA!

FILLI...?

SLURP...

WAH
HA HA
HA HA
HA HA

...ARE YOU SCARED?

110

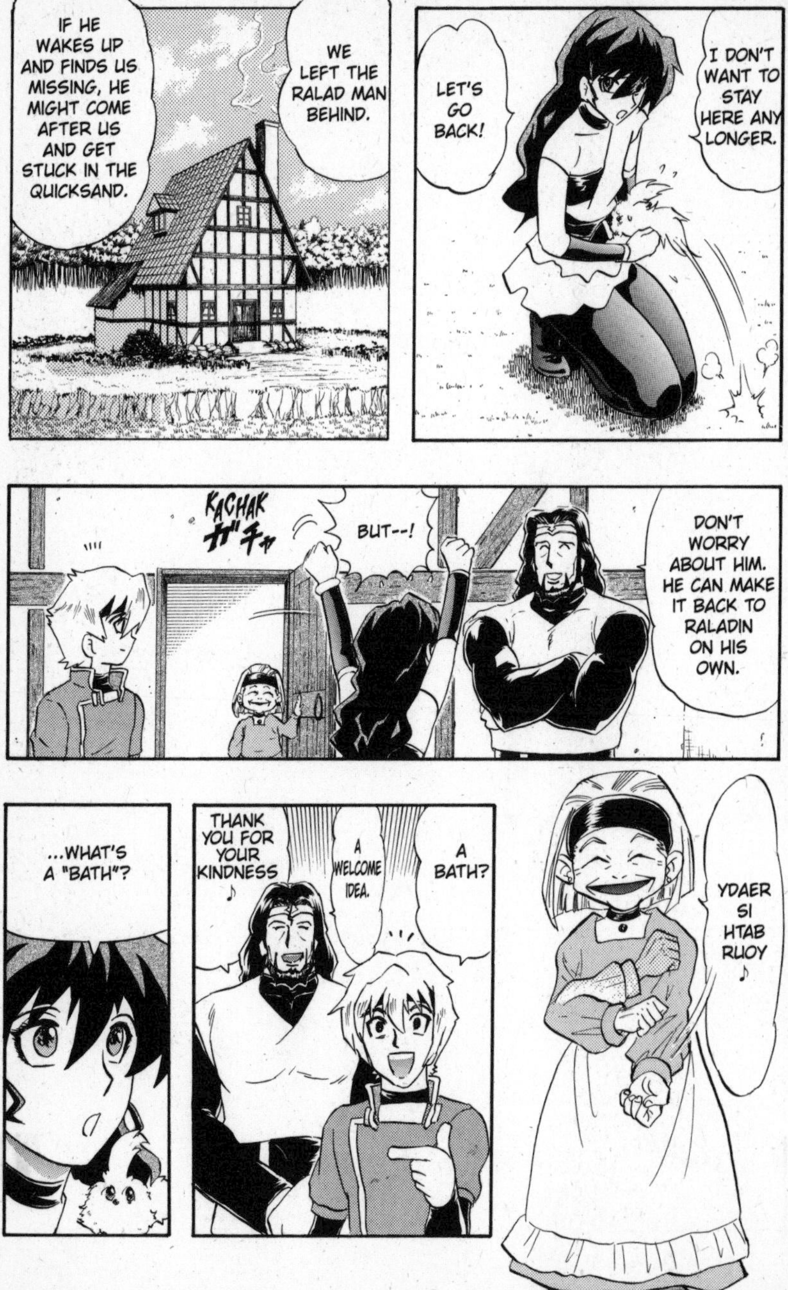
I DON'T WANT TO STAY HERE ANY LONGER.
LET'S GO BACK!
WE LEFT THE RALAD MAN BEHIND.
IF HE WAKES UP AND FINDS US MISSING, HE MIGHT COME AFTER US AND GET STUCK IN THE QUICKSAND.
DON'T WORRY ABOUT HIM. HE CAN MAKE IT BACK TO RALADIN ON HIS OWN.
BUT--!
KACHAK
ガチャ
YDAER SI HTAB RUOY ♪
A BATH?
A WELCOME IDEA.
THANK YOU FOR YOUR KINDNESS ♪
...WHAT'S A "BATH"?

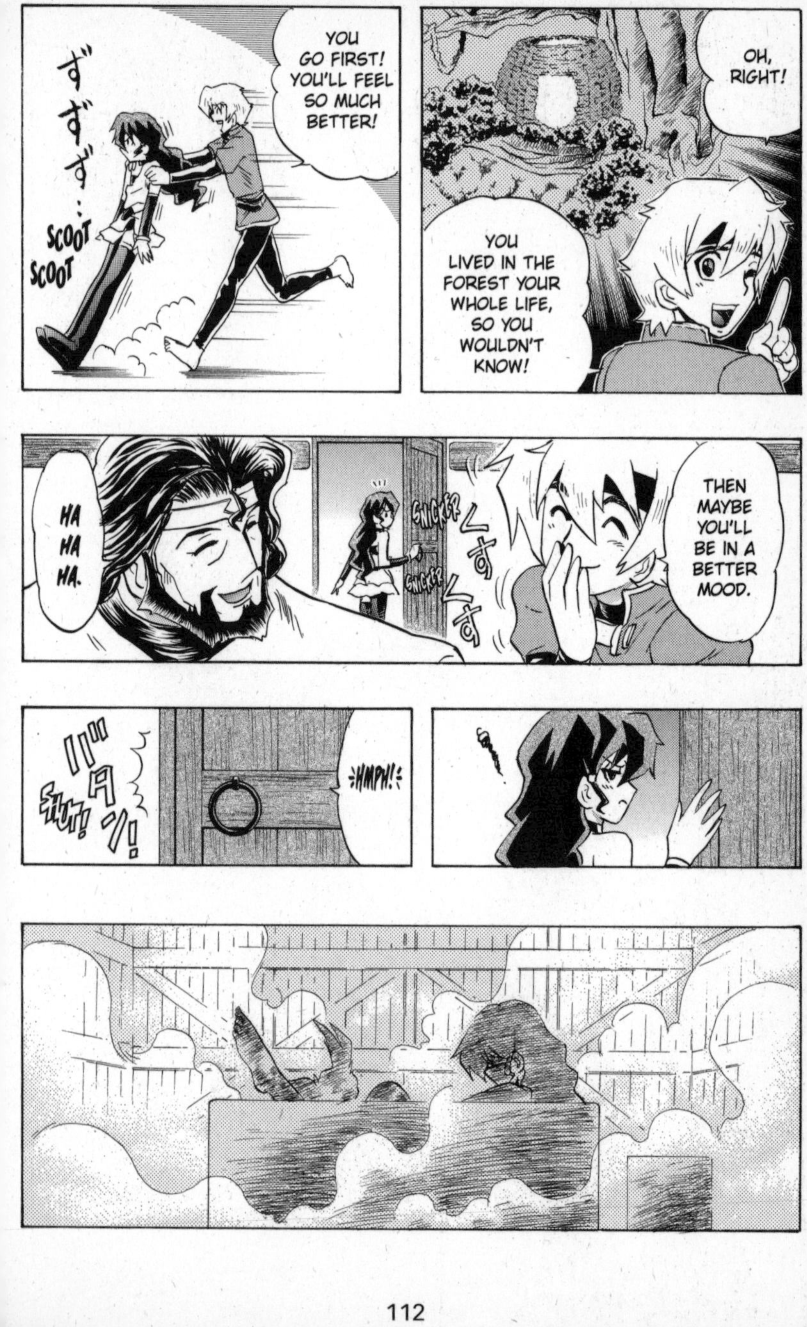
OH, RIGHT!
YOU LIVED IN THE FOREST YOUR WHOLE LIFE, SO YOU WOULDN'T KNOW!
YOU GO FIRST! YOU'LL FEEL SO MUCH BETTER!
ずずず…
SCOOT SCOOT
THEN MAYBE YOU'LL BE IN A BETTER MOOD.
くすくす
SNICKER SNICKER
HA HA HA.
HMPH!
バタン!!
SHUT!

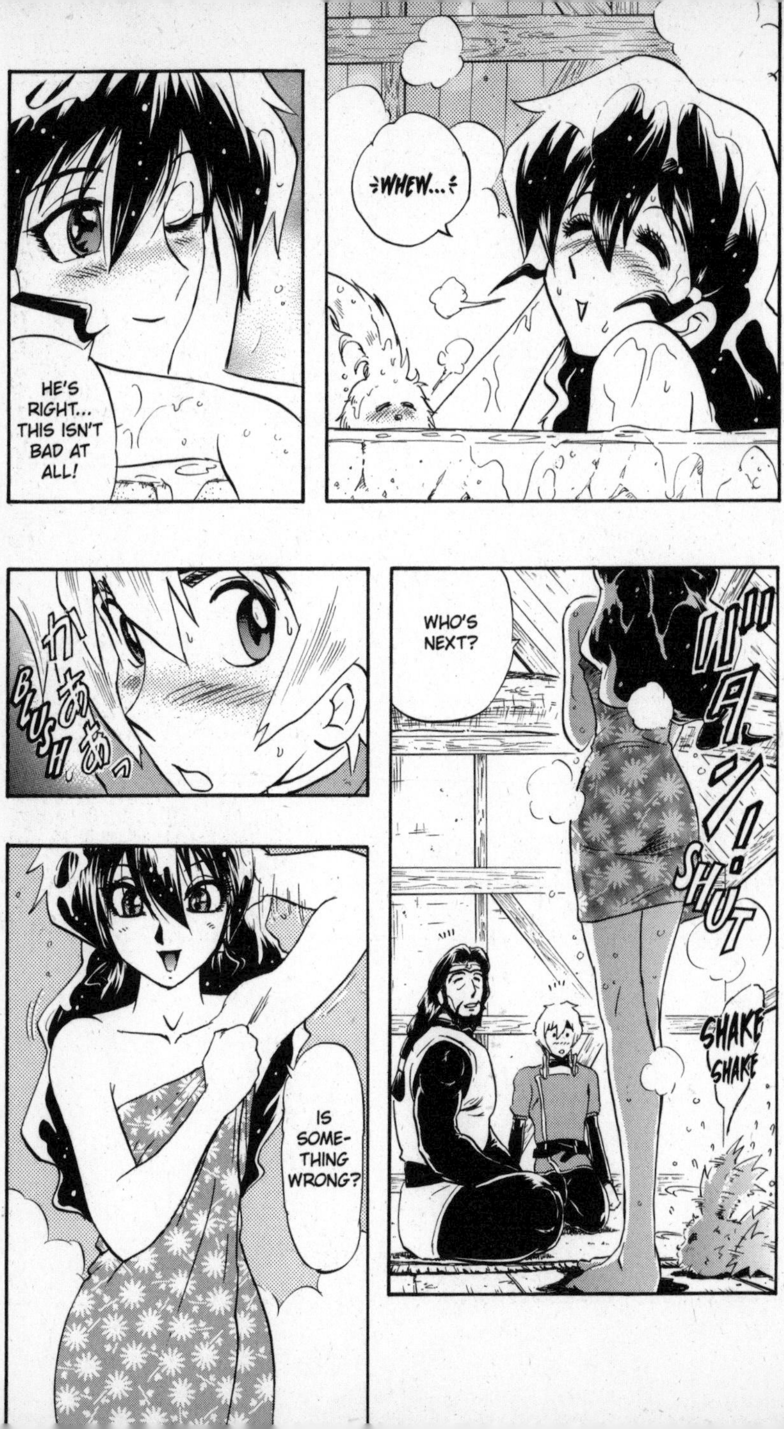

WHEW...
HE'S RIGHT... THIS ISN'T BAD AT ALL!
WHO'S NEXT?
SHUT
SHAKE SHAKE
かあああっ
BLUSH
IS SOMETHING WRONG?

PULL PULL

SHAKE

N-NOTHING!

SHAKE

OKAY!

OH...

YOU CAN GO NEXT, LIEF.

B-DMP

!!

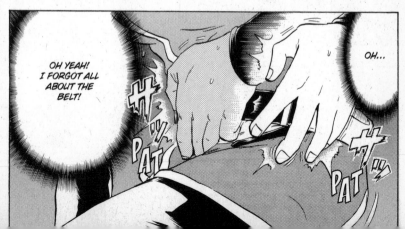

OH YEAH! I FORGOT ALL ABOUT THE BELT!

OH...

PAT

PAT

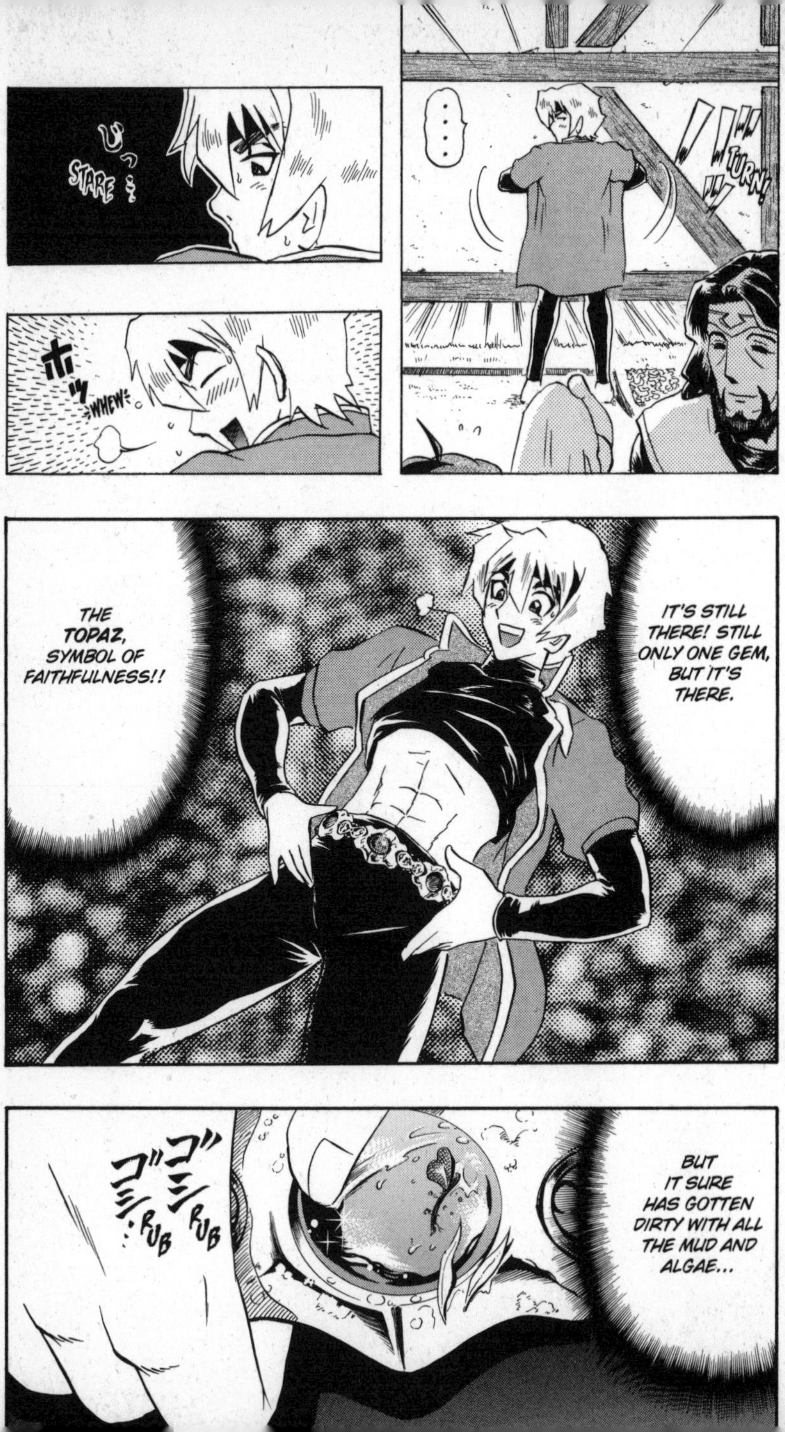
...
TURN!
STARE
ホッ
WHEW
IT'S STILL THERE! STILL ONLY ONE GEM, BUT IT'S THERE.
THE TOPAZ, SYMBOL OF FAITHFULNESS!!
BUT IT SURE HAS GOTTEN DIRTY WITH ALL THE MUD AND ALGAE...
ゴシゴシ
RUB RUB

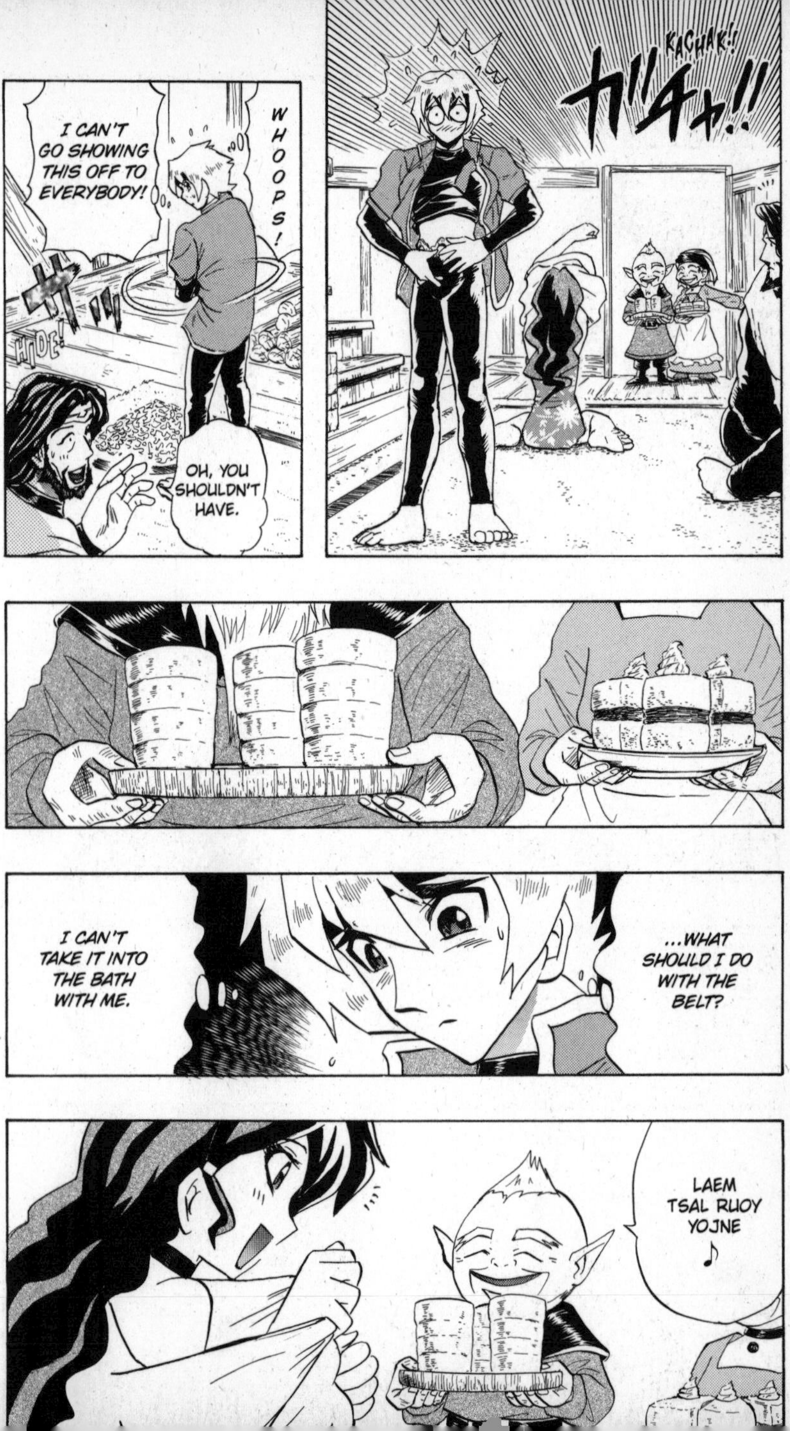
KACHAK!!
カチャ!!
WHOOPS!
I CAN'T GO SHOWING THIS OFF TO EVERYBODY!
HIDE!
OH, YOU SHOULDN'T HAVE.
...WHAT SHOULD I DO WITH THE BELT?
I CAN'T TAKE IT INTO THE BATH WITH ME.
LAEM TSAL RUOY YOJNE ♪

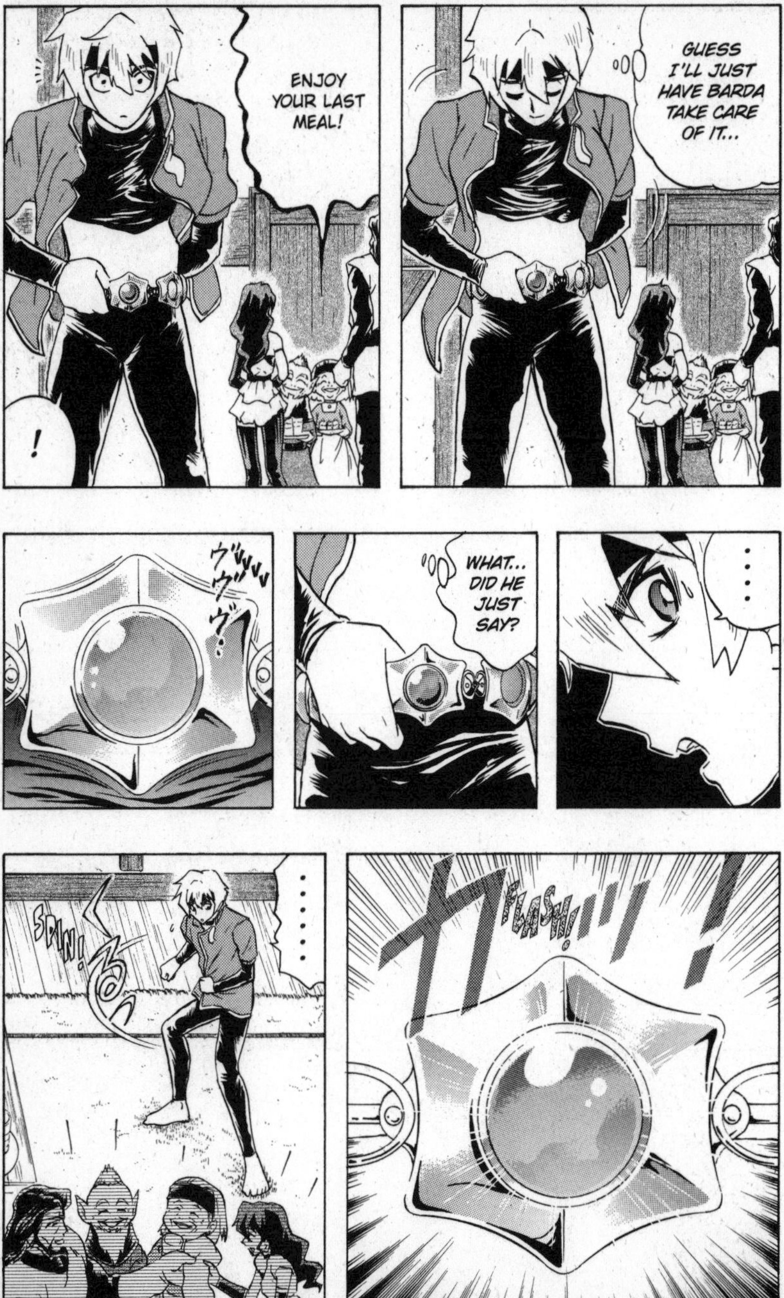
GUESS I'LL JUST HAVE BARDA TAKE CARE OF IT...
ENJOY YOUR LAST MEAL!
!
....
WHAT... DID HE JUST SAY?
FLASH!!
!
......
SPIN!

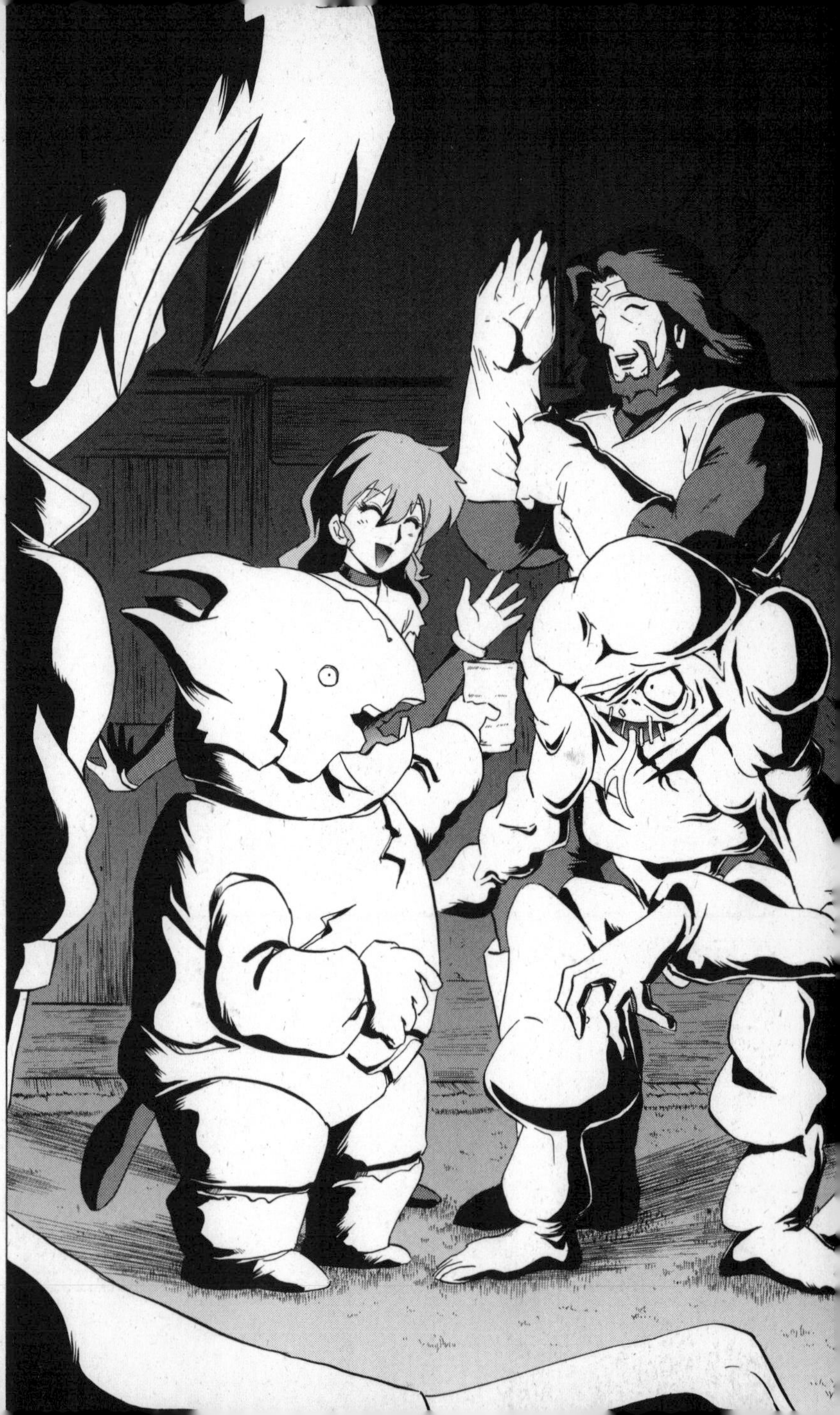

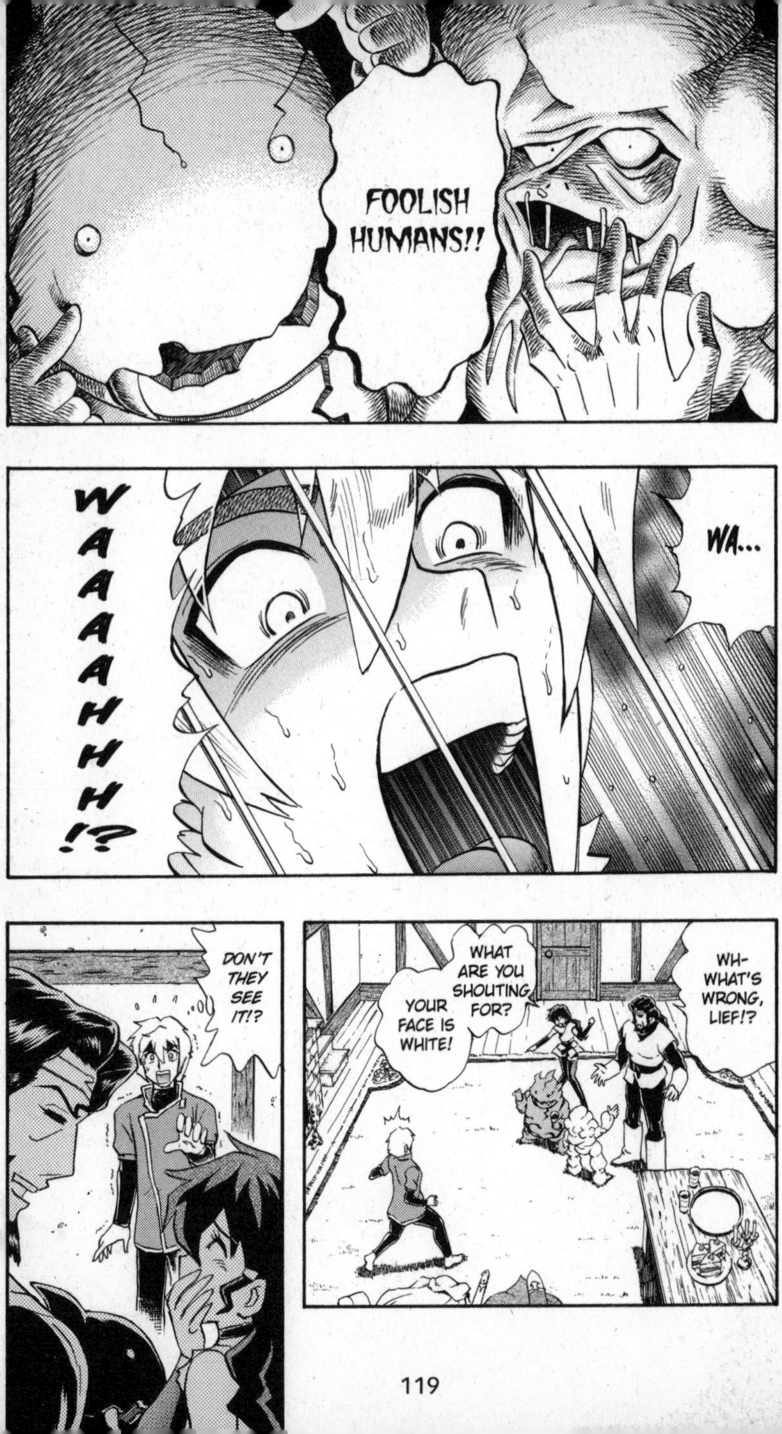
FOOLISH HUMANS!!
WA...
WAAAAHHH!?
WH- WHAT'S WRONG, LIEF!?
WHAT ARE YOU SHOUTING FOR?
YOUR FACE IS WHITE!
DON'T THEY SEE IT!?

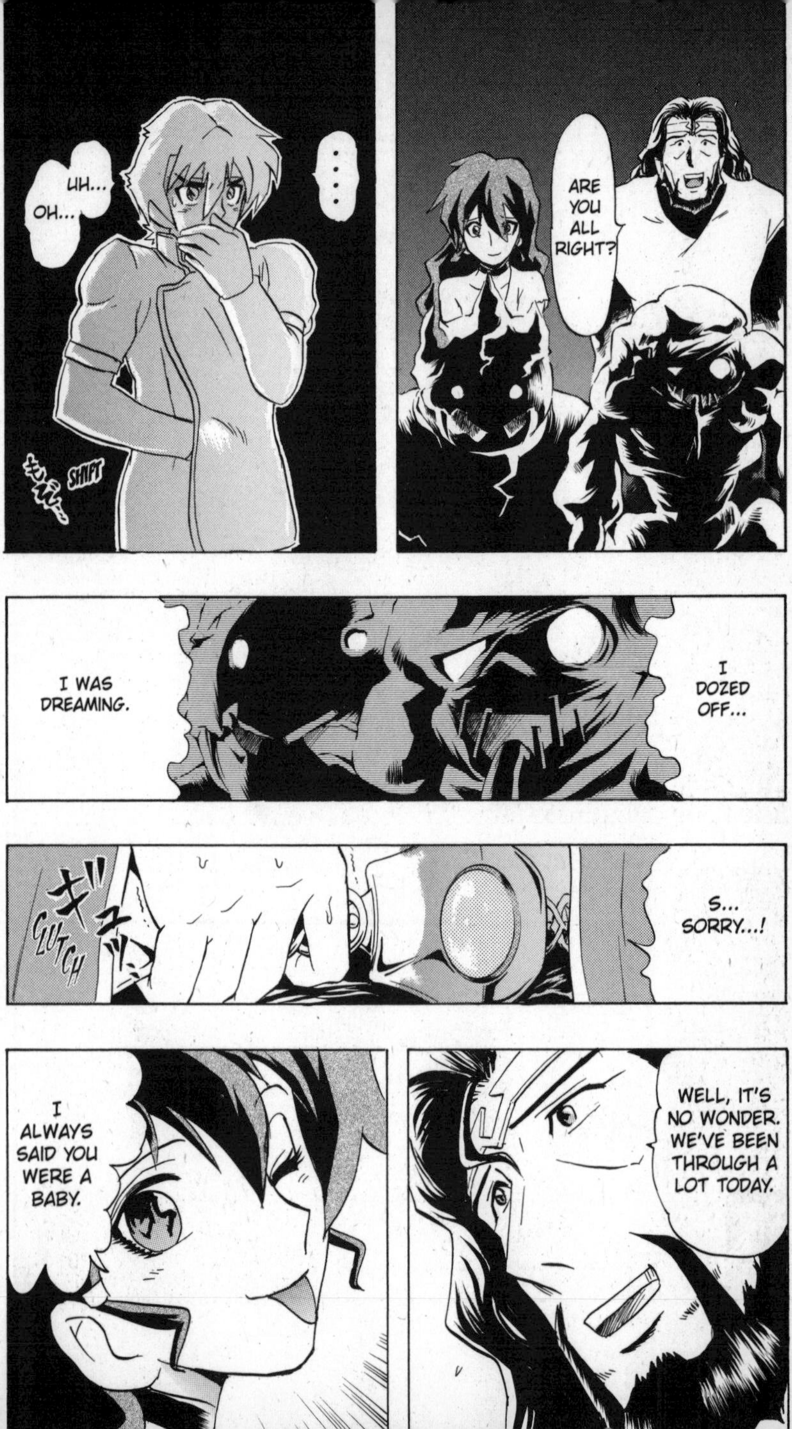
ARE YOU ALL RIGHT?
....
UH... OH...
SHIFT
I DOZED OFF...
I WAS DREAMING.
S... SORRY...!
CLUTCH
WELL, IT'S NO WONDER. WE'VE BEEN THROUGH A LOT TODAY.
I ALWAYS SAID YOU WERE A BABY.

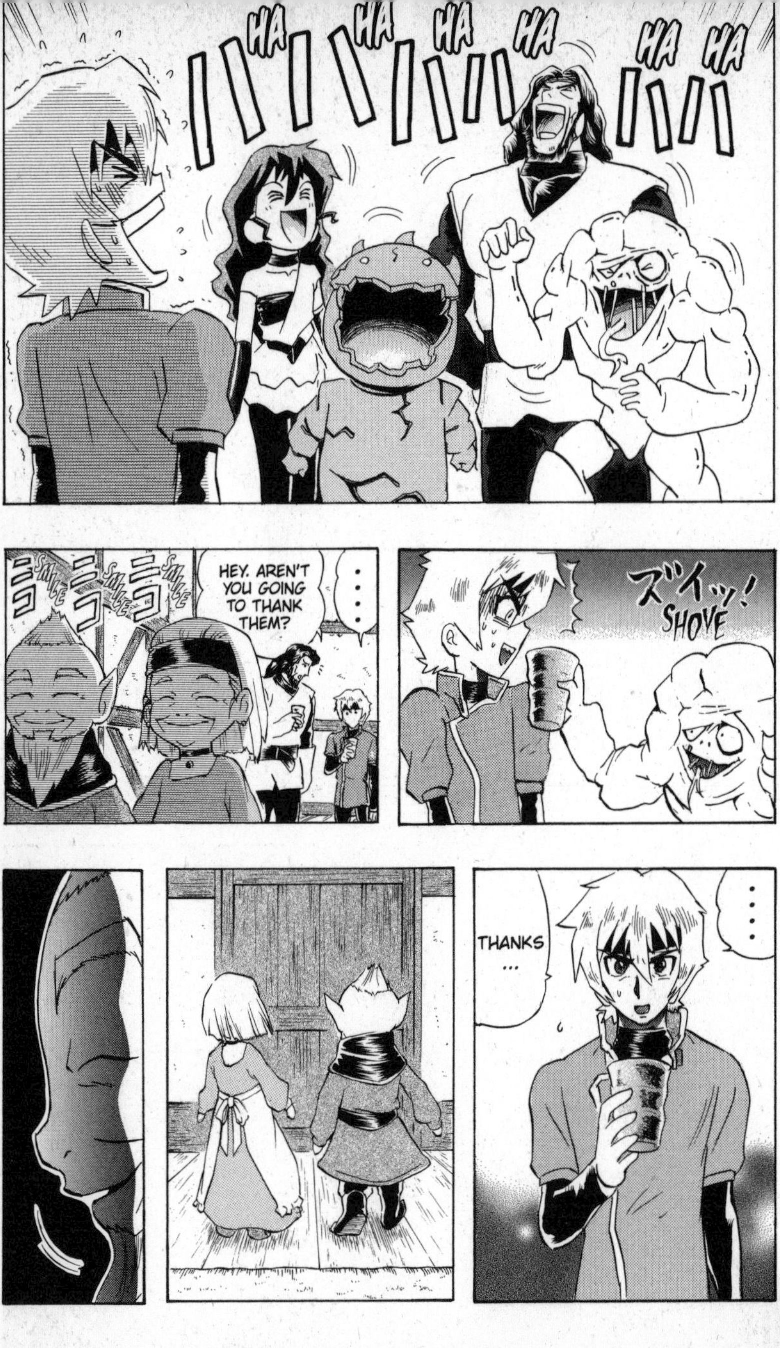
HA HA HA HA HA HA
ズイッ!
SHOVE
....
HEY. AREN'T YOU GOING TO THANK THEM?
SMILE SMILE SMILE
....
THANKS ...

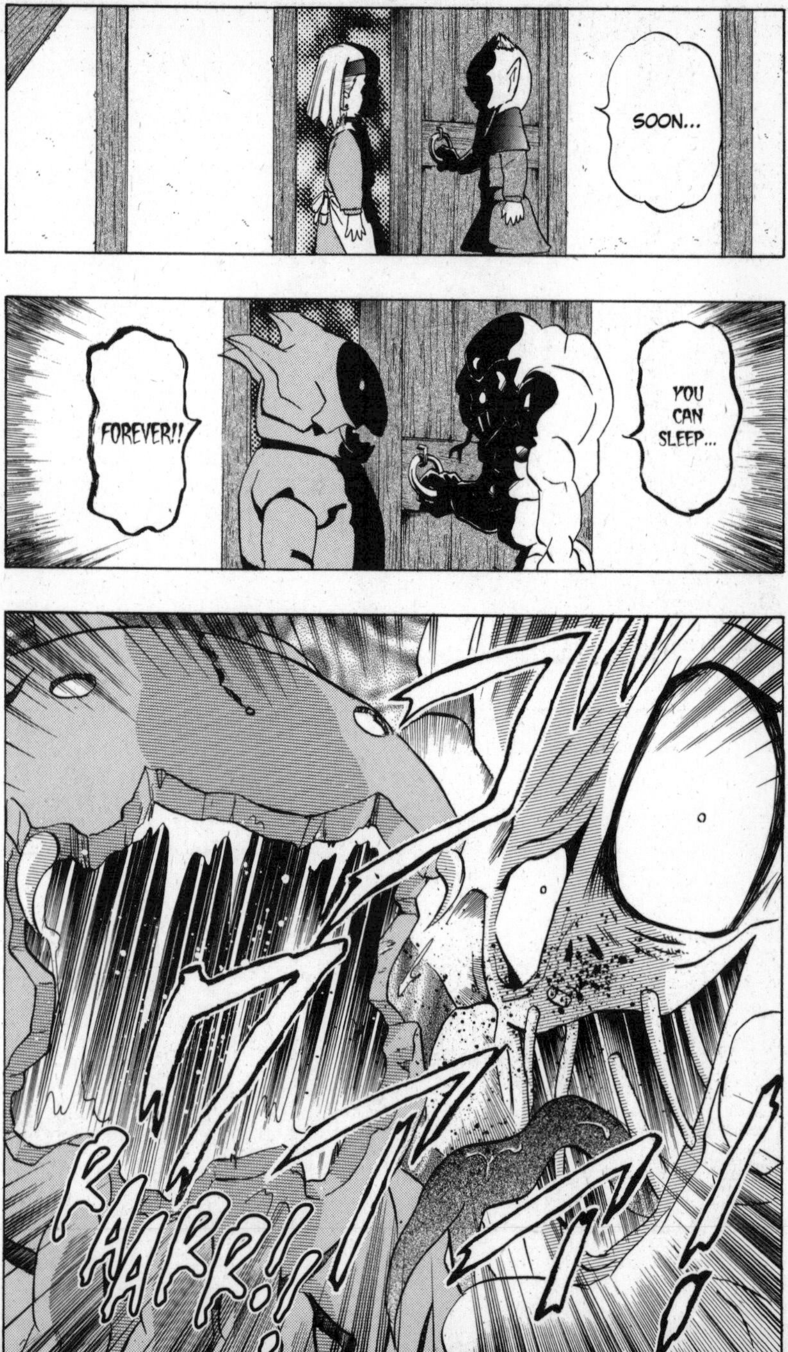
SOON...
YOU CAN SLEEP...
FOREVER!!
RAAR!!

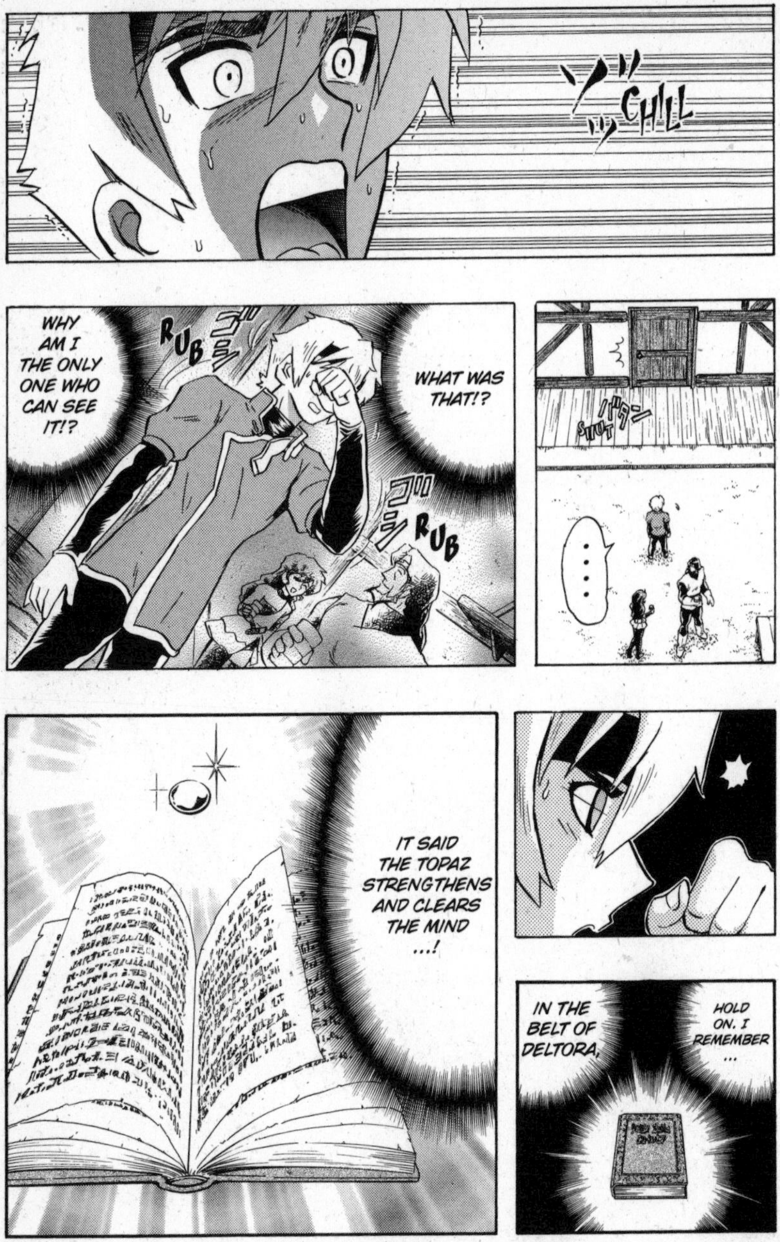
CHILL
SHUT
.....
WHAT WAS THAT!?
WHY AM I THE ONLY ONE WHO CAN SEE IT!?
RUB
RUB
HOLD ON. I REMEMBER ...
IN THE BELT OF DELTORA,
IT SAID THE TOPAZ STRENGTHENS AND CLEARS THE MIND ...!

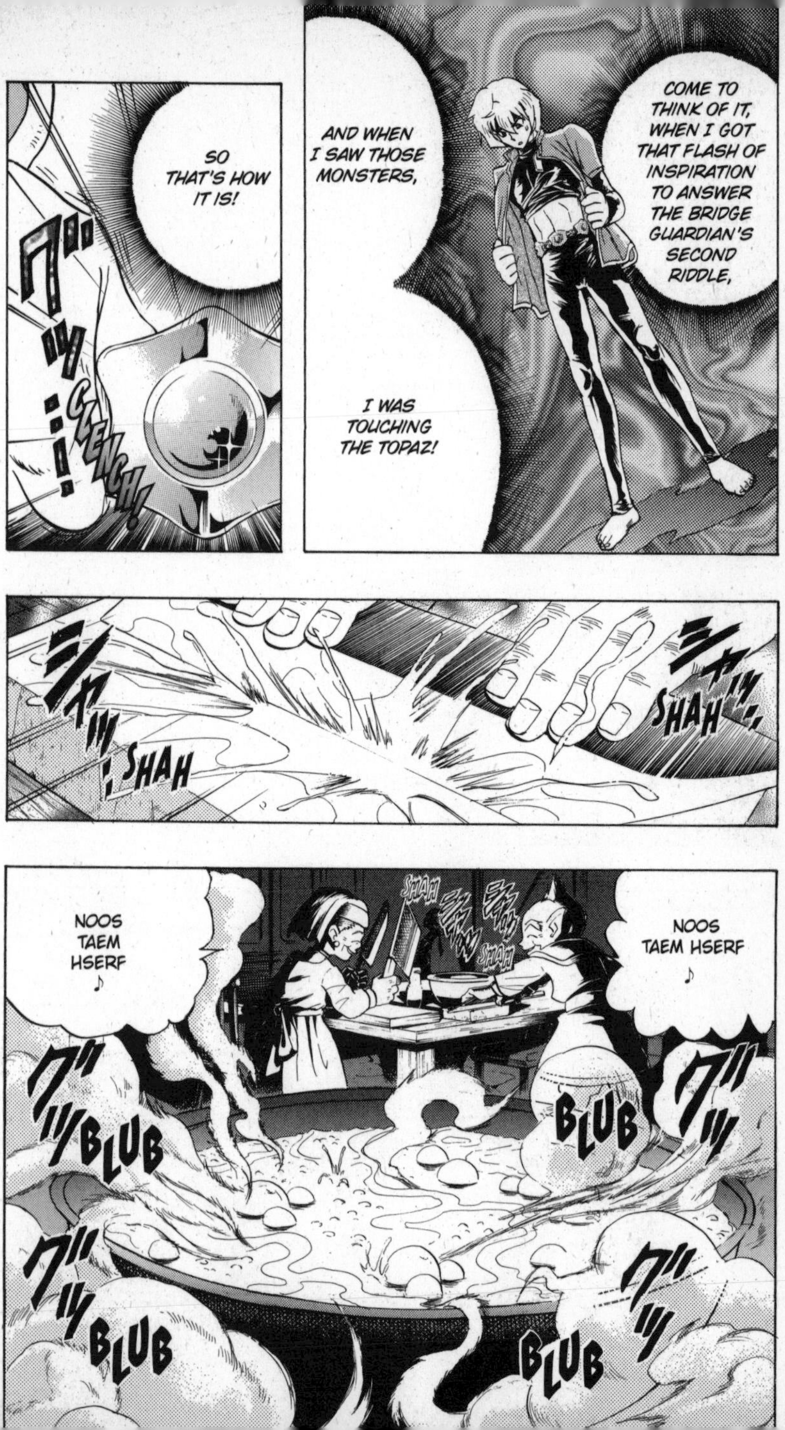
COME TO THINK OF IT, WHEN I GOT THAT FLASH OF INSPIRATION TO ANSWER THE BRIDGE GUARDIAN'S SECOND RIDDLE,
AND WHEN I SAW THOSE MONSTERS,
I WAS TOUCHING THE TOPAZ!
SO THAT'S HOW IT IS!
CLENCH!
SHAH
SHAH
NOOS TAEM HSERF ♪
NOOS TAEM HSERF ♪
SHAH
SHAH
BLUB
BLUB
BLUB
BLUB

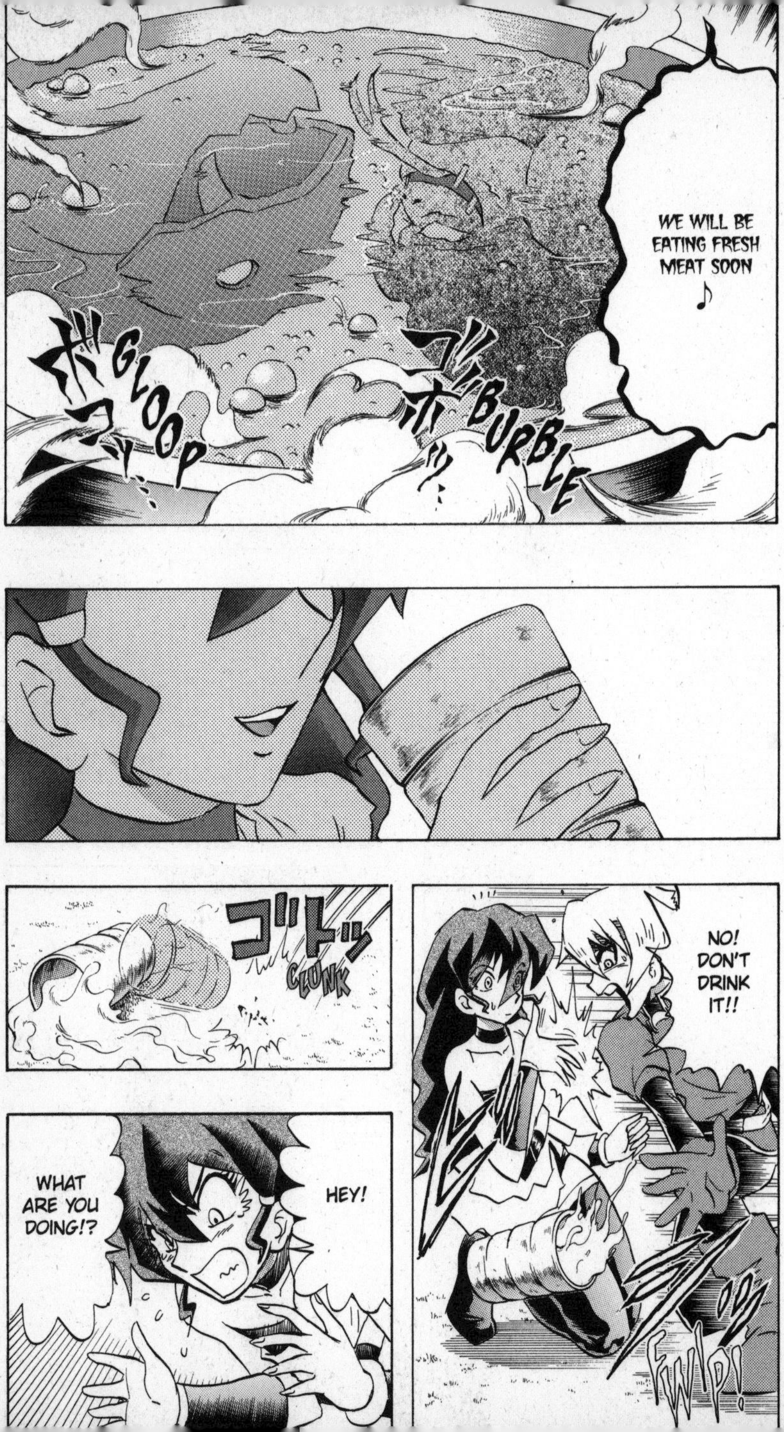
WE WILL BE EATING FRESH MEAT SOON ♪
BURBLE
GLOOP
NO! DON'T DRINK IT!!
FWIP!
ゴトッ
CLUNK
HEY!
WHAT ARE YOU DOING!?

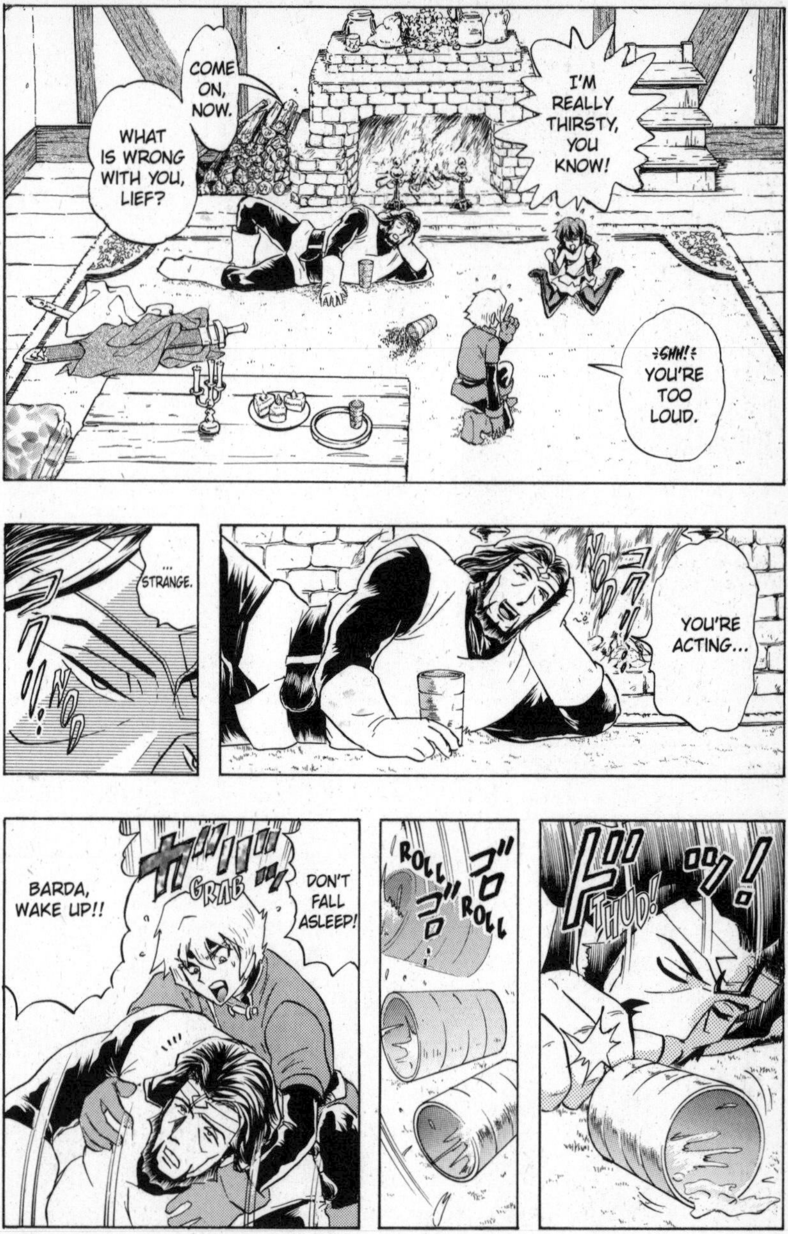
I'M REALLY THIRSTY, YOU KNOW!
COME ON, NOW.
WHAT IS WRONG WITH YOU, LIEF?
SHH! YOU'RE TOO LOUD.
NOD
YOU'RE ACTING...
NOD
... STRANGE.
THUD!
ROLL
ROLL
DON'T FALL ASLEEP!
GRAB
BARDA, WAKE UP!!

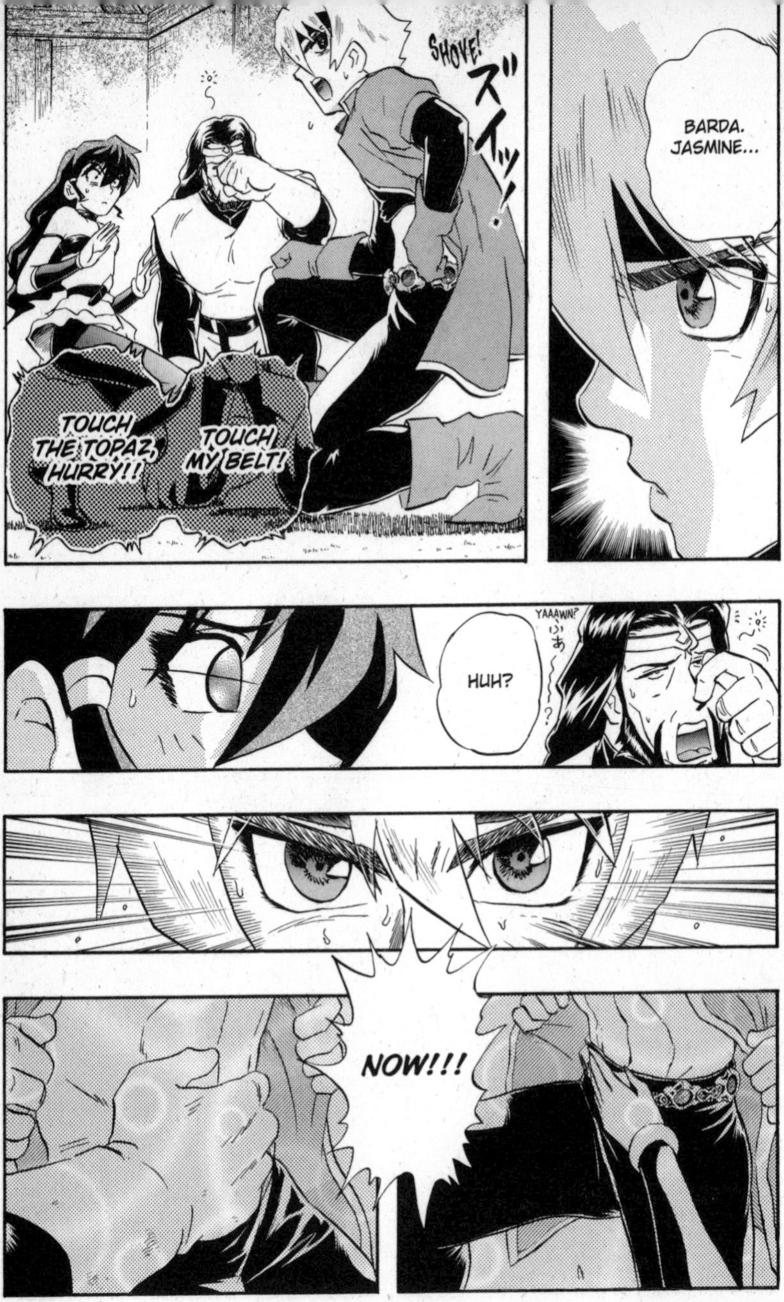
BARDA. JASMINE...
SHOVE!
ズイッ!
TOUCH MY BELT!
TOUCH THE TOPAZ, HURRY!!
YAAAWN?
ふあ~?
HUH?
NOW!!!

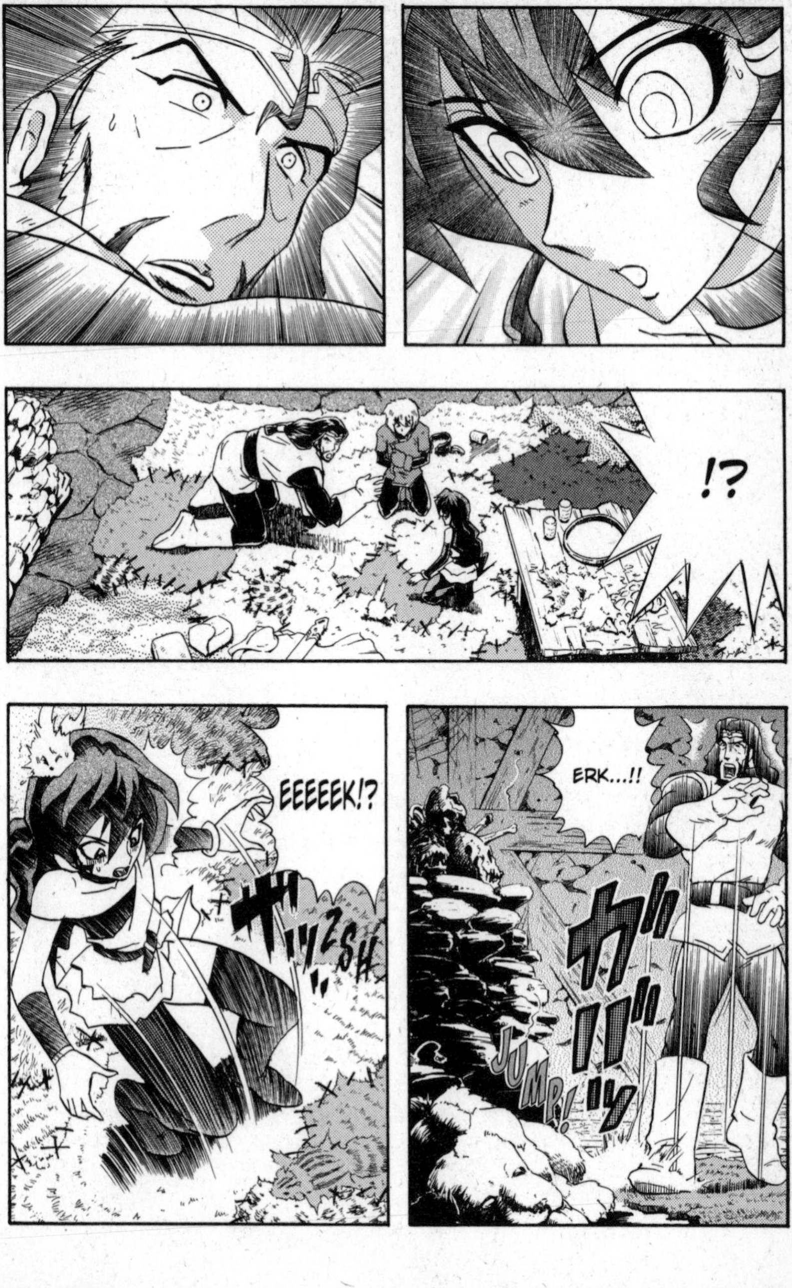
!?
ERK...!!
JUMP!
EEEEEK!?
ZSH

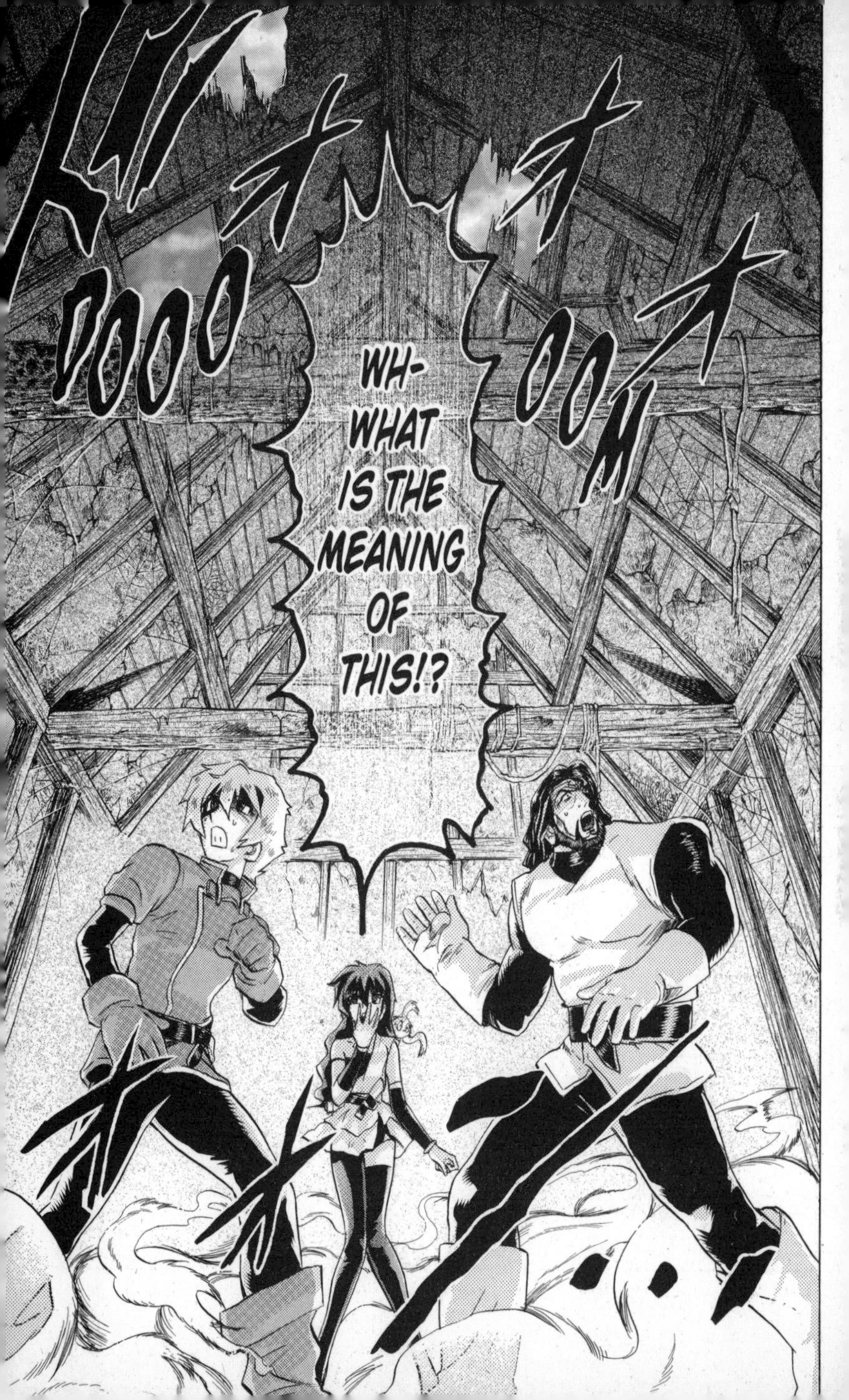
DOOOOOM
WH-WHAT IS THE MEANING OF THIS!?

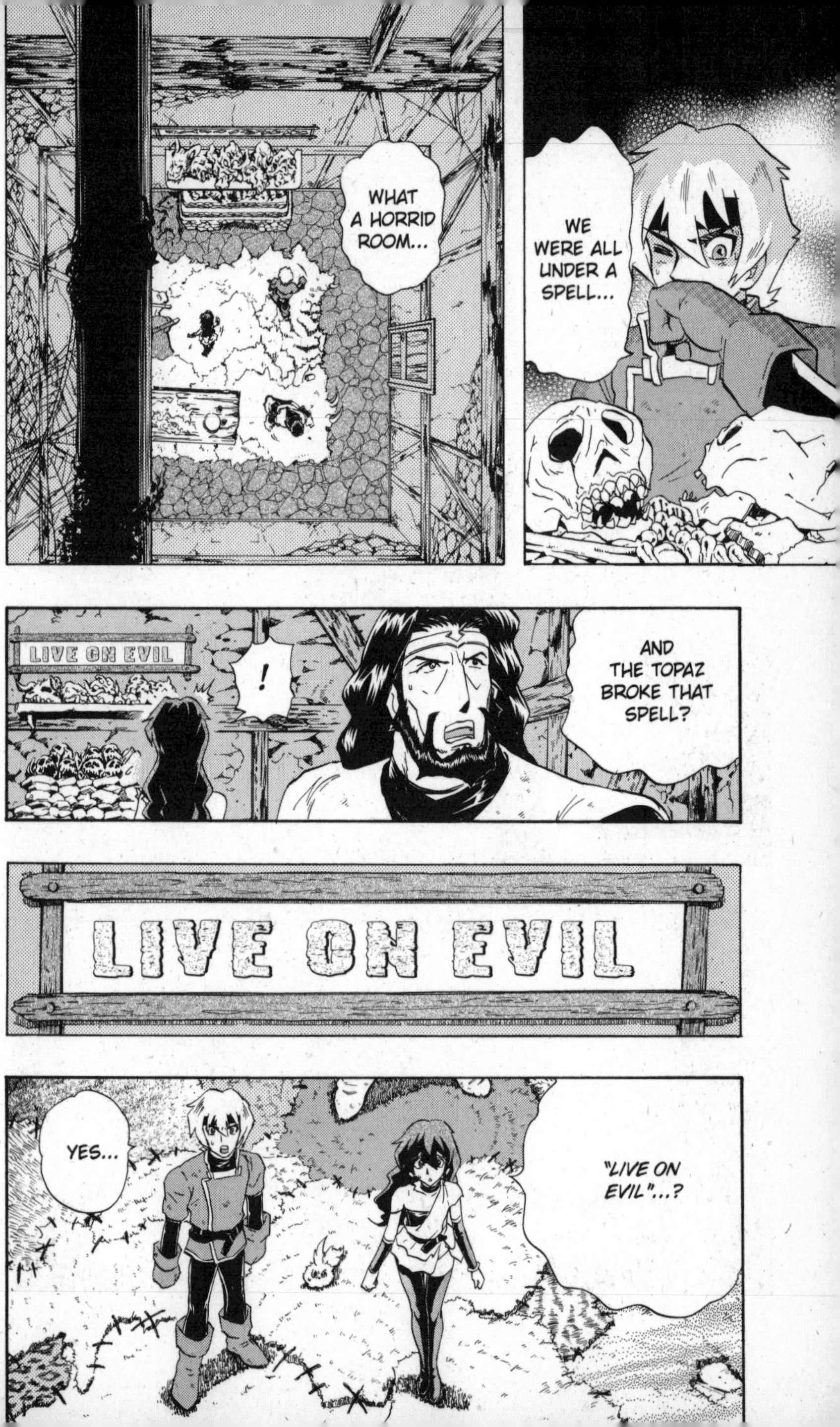
WE WERE ALL UNDER A SPELL...
WHAT A HORRID ROOM...
AND THE TOPAZ BROKE THAT SPELL?
!
LIVE ON EVIL
LIVE ON EVIL
"LIVE ON EVIL"...?
YES...

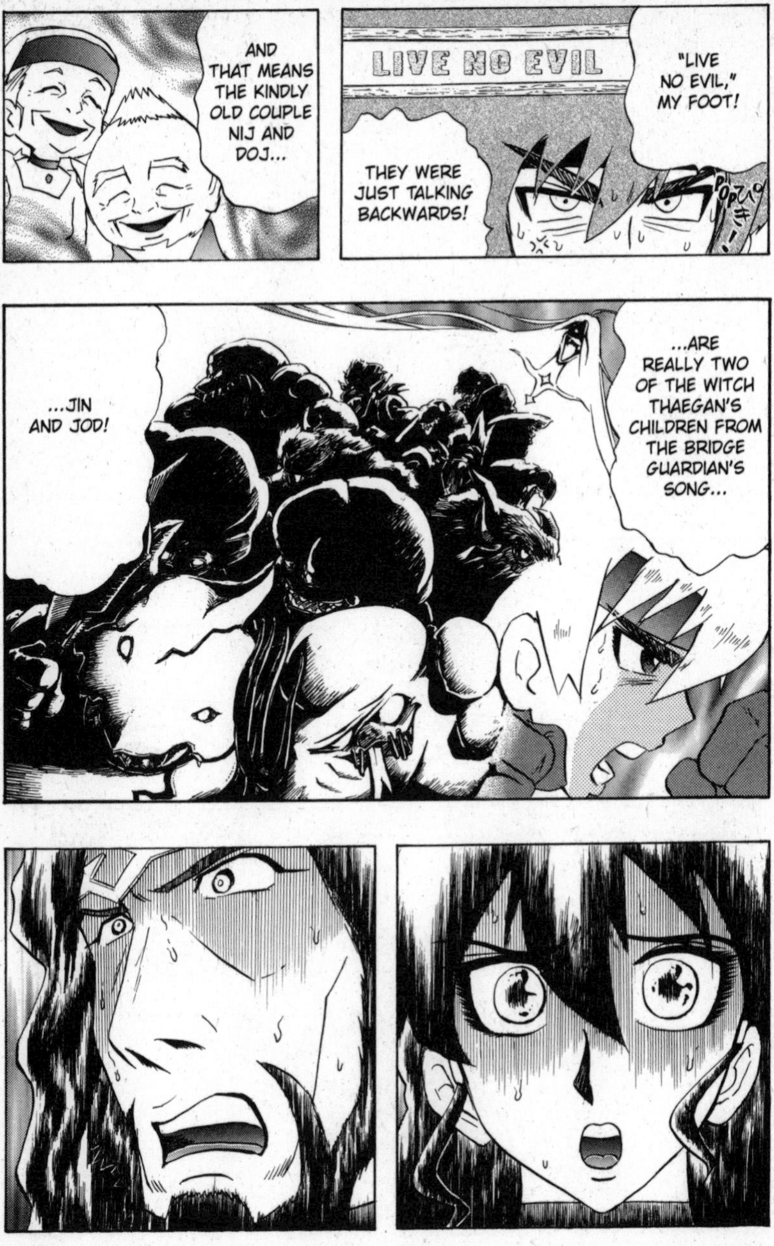
"LIVE NO EVIL," MY FOOT!
LIVE NO EVIL
THEY WERE JUST TALKING BACKWARDS!
POP
AND THAT MEANS THE KINDLY OLD COUPLE NIJ AND DOJ...
...ARE REALLY TWO OF THE WITCH THAEGAN'S CHILDREN FROM THE BRIDGE GUARDIAN'S SONG...
...JIN AND JOD!

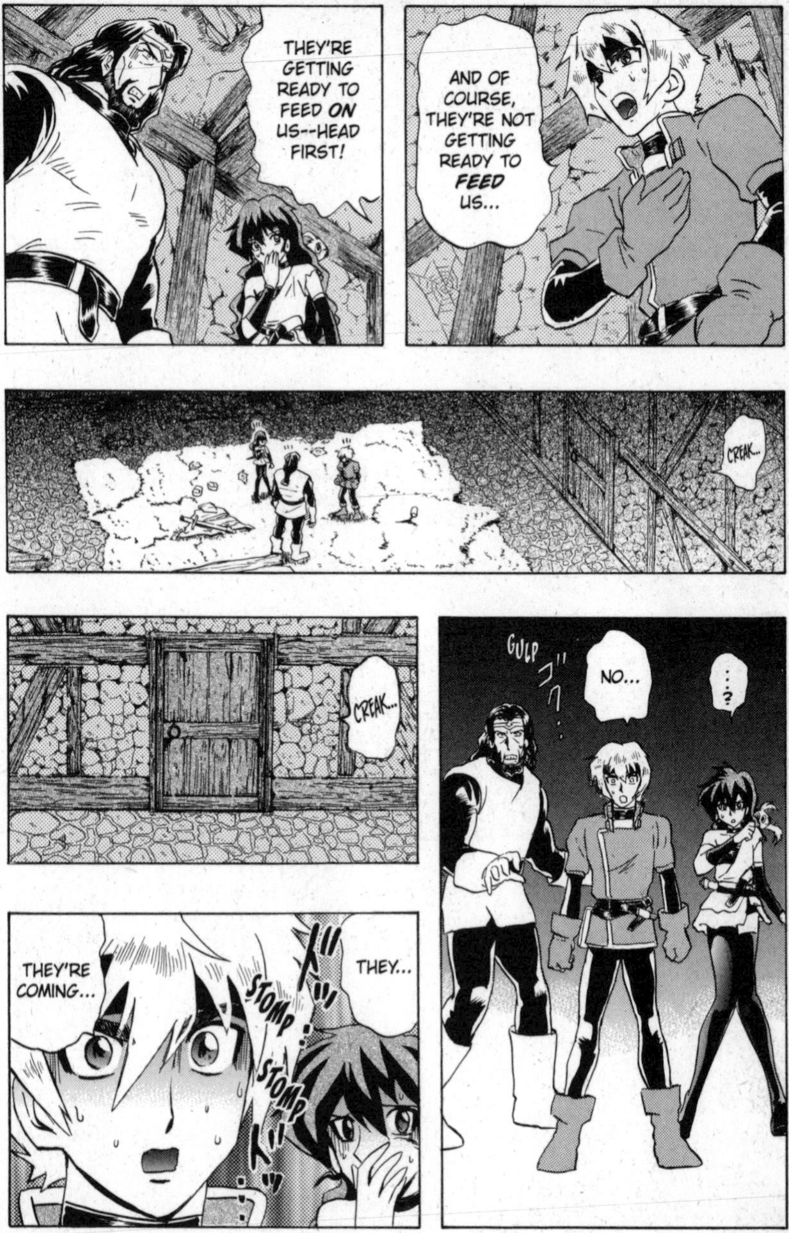
AND OF COURSE, THEY'RE NOT GETTING READY TO FEED US...
THEY'RE GETTING READY TO FEED ON US--HEAD FIRST!
CREAK...
GULP
NO...
...?
CREAK...
THEY...
THEY'RE COMING...
STOMP
STOMP

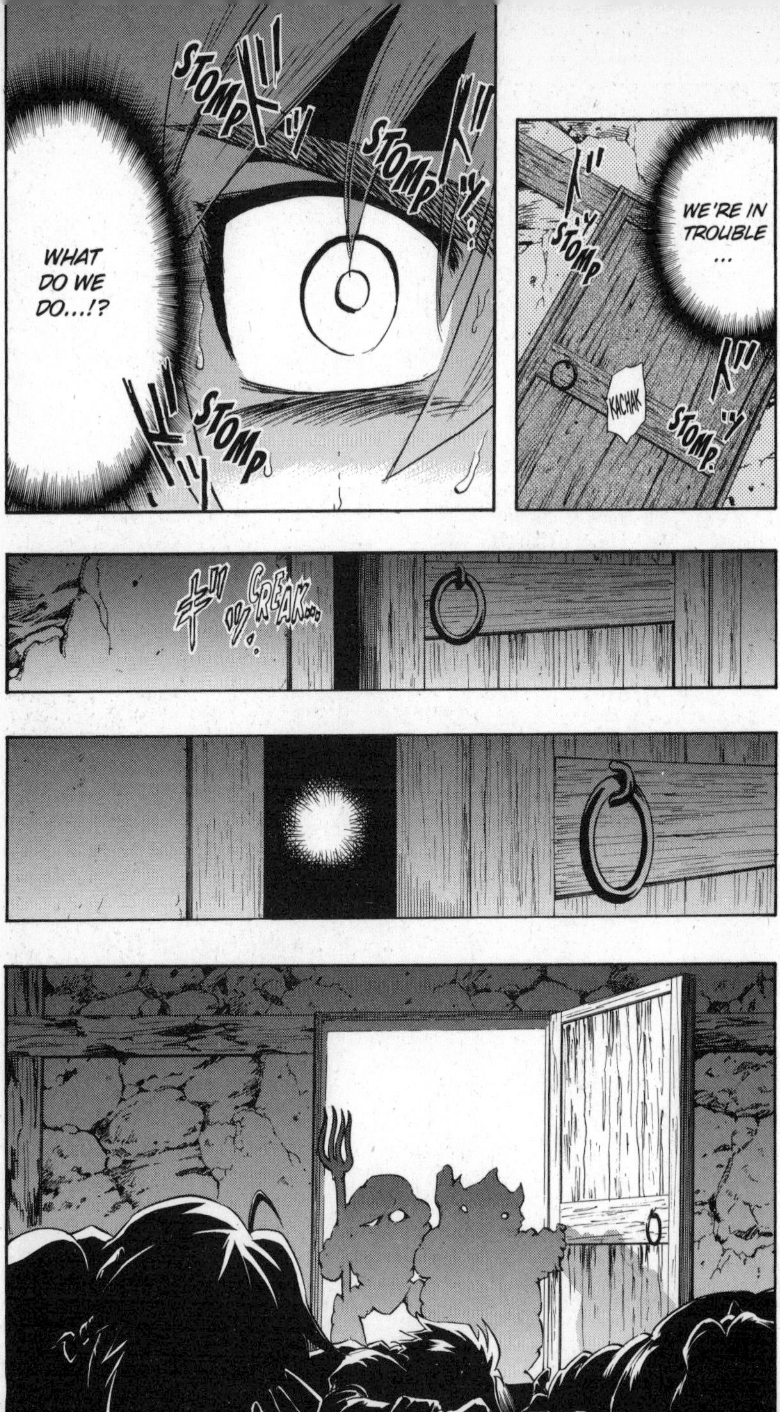
WE'RE IN TROUBLE ...
STOMP
KACHAK
STOMP
STOMP
STOMP
WHAT DO WE DO...!?
STOMP
CREAK...

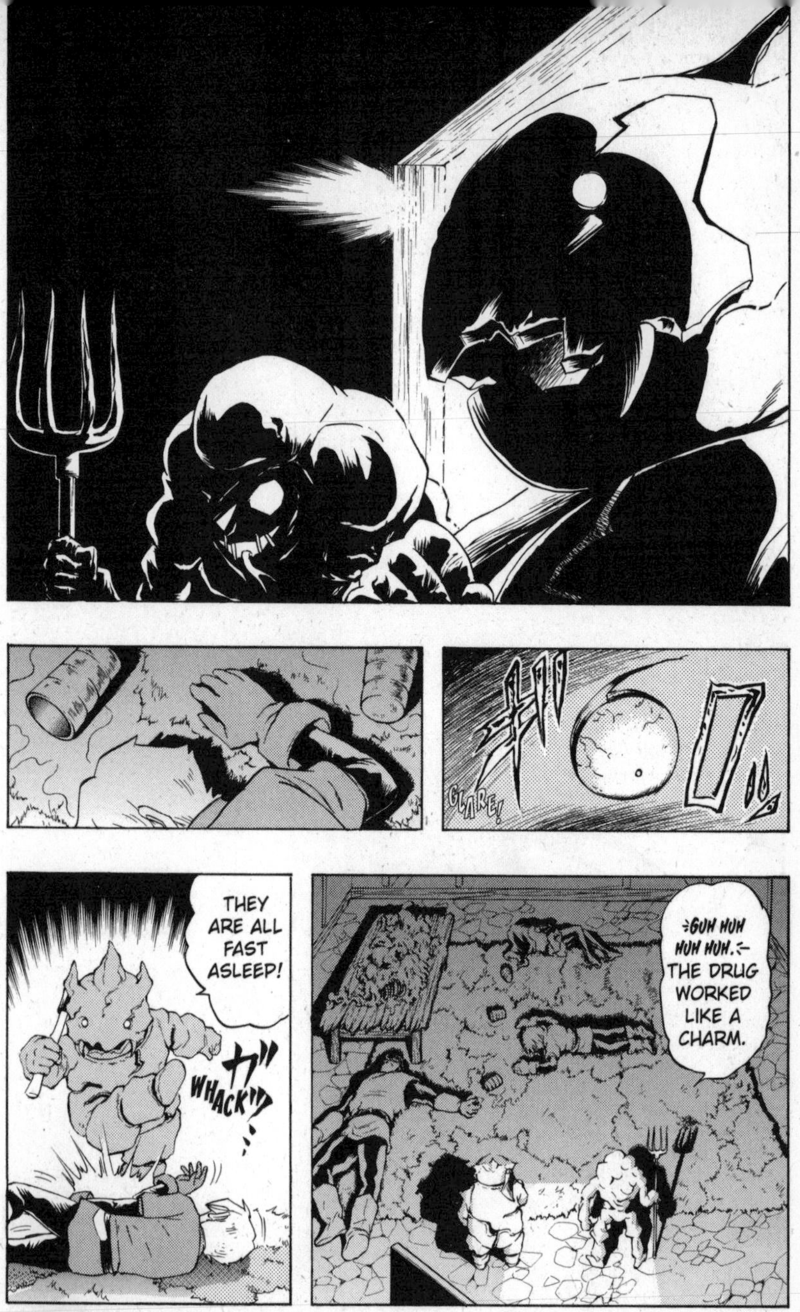
GLARE!
≈GUH HUH HUH HUH.≈ THE DRUG WORKED LIKE A CHARM.
THEY ARE ALL FAST ASLEEP!
WHACK!!

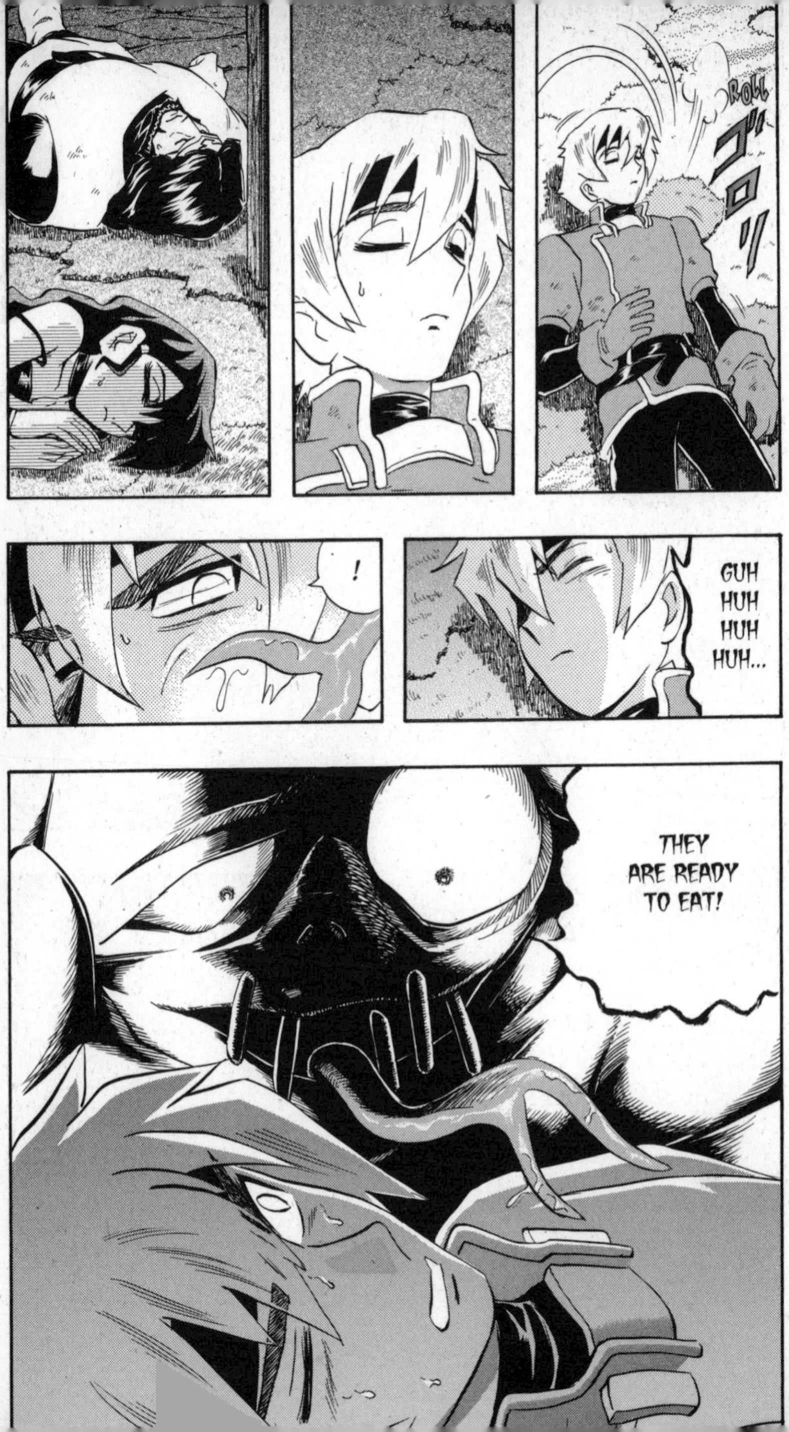
ROLL
ゴロリ
GUH HUH HUH HUH...
!
THEY ARE READY TO EAT!

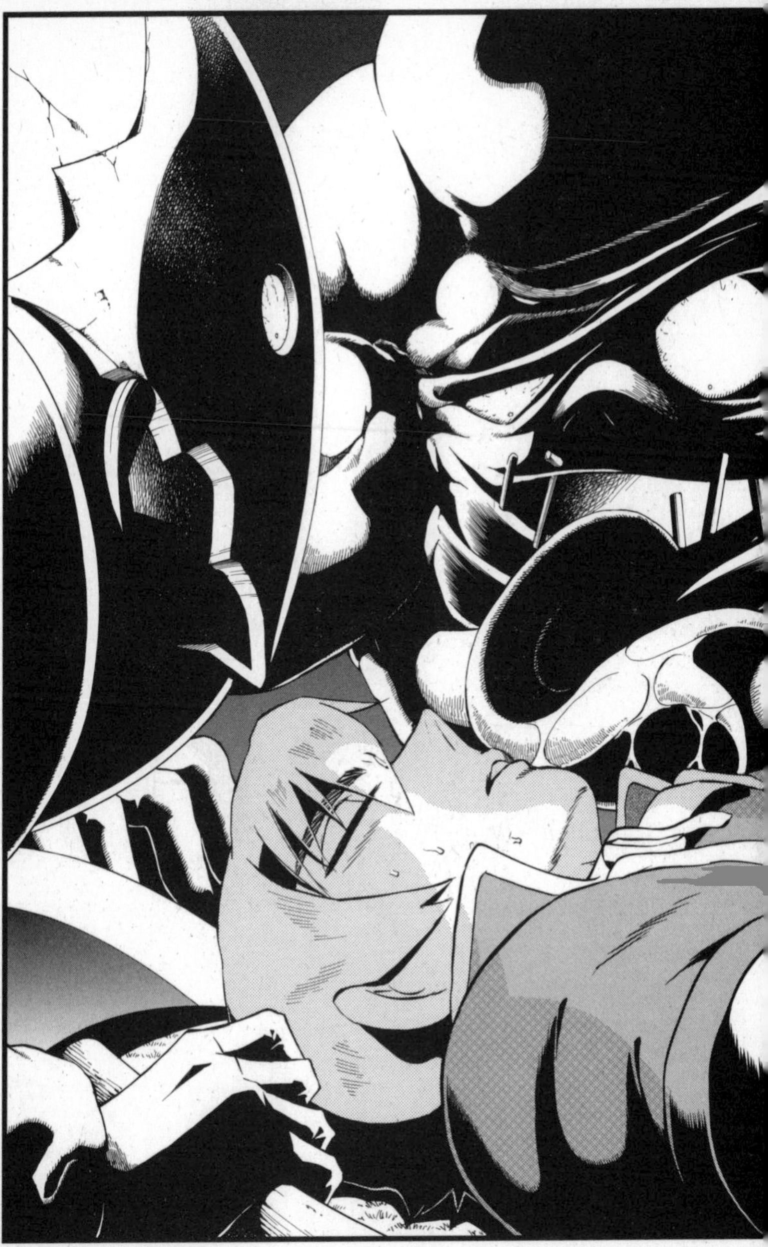

Chapter 14:
The White House of Terror

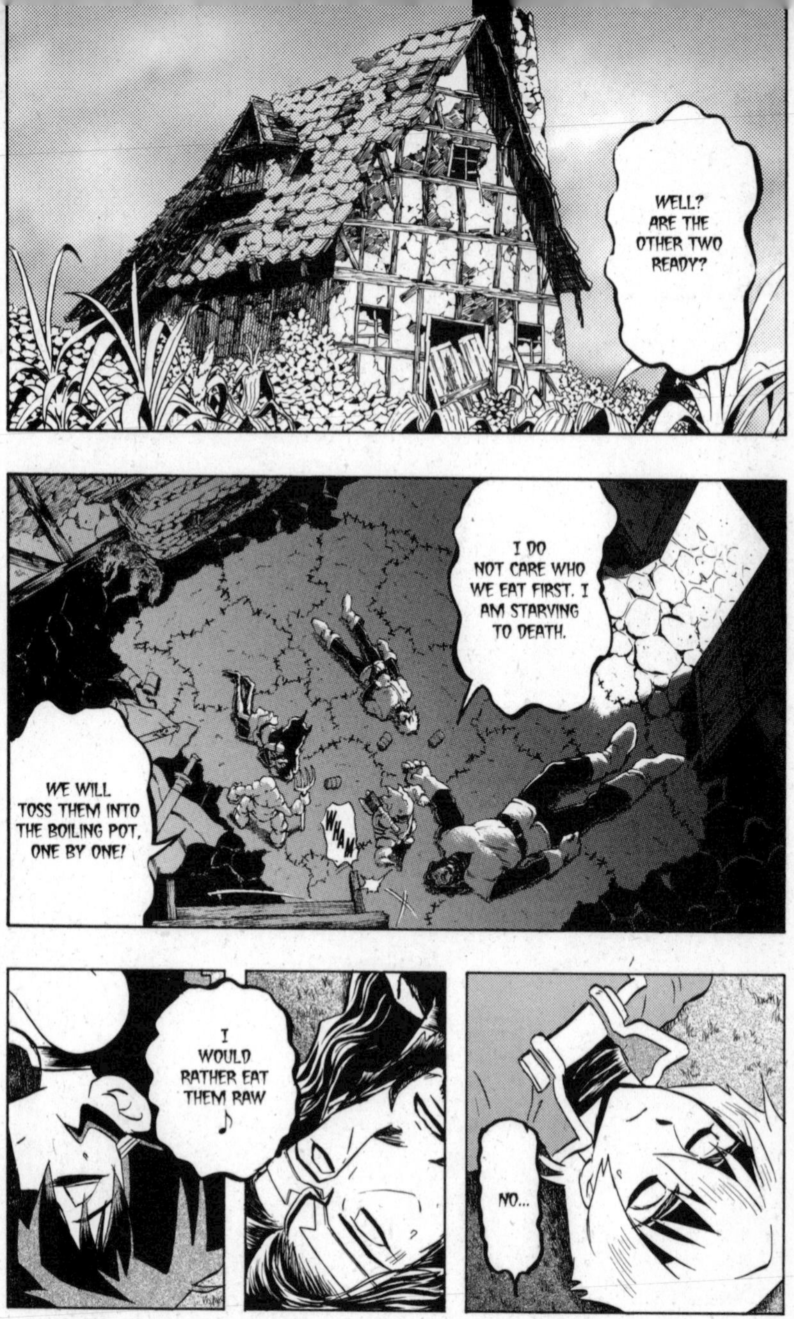
WELL? ARE THE OTHER TWO READY?
I DO NOT CARE WHO WE EAT FIRST. I AM STARVING TO DEATH.
WHAM
WE WILL TOSS THEM INTO THE BOILING POT, ONE BY ONE!
NO...
I WOULD RATHER EAT THEM RAW ♪

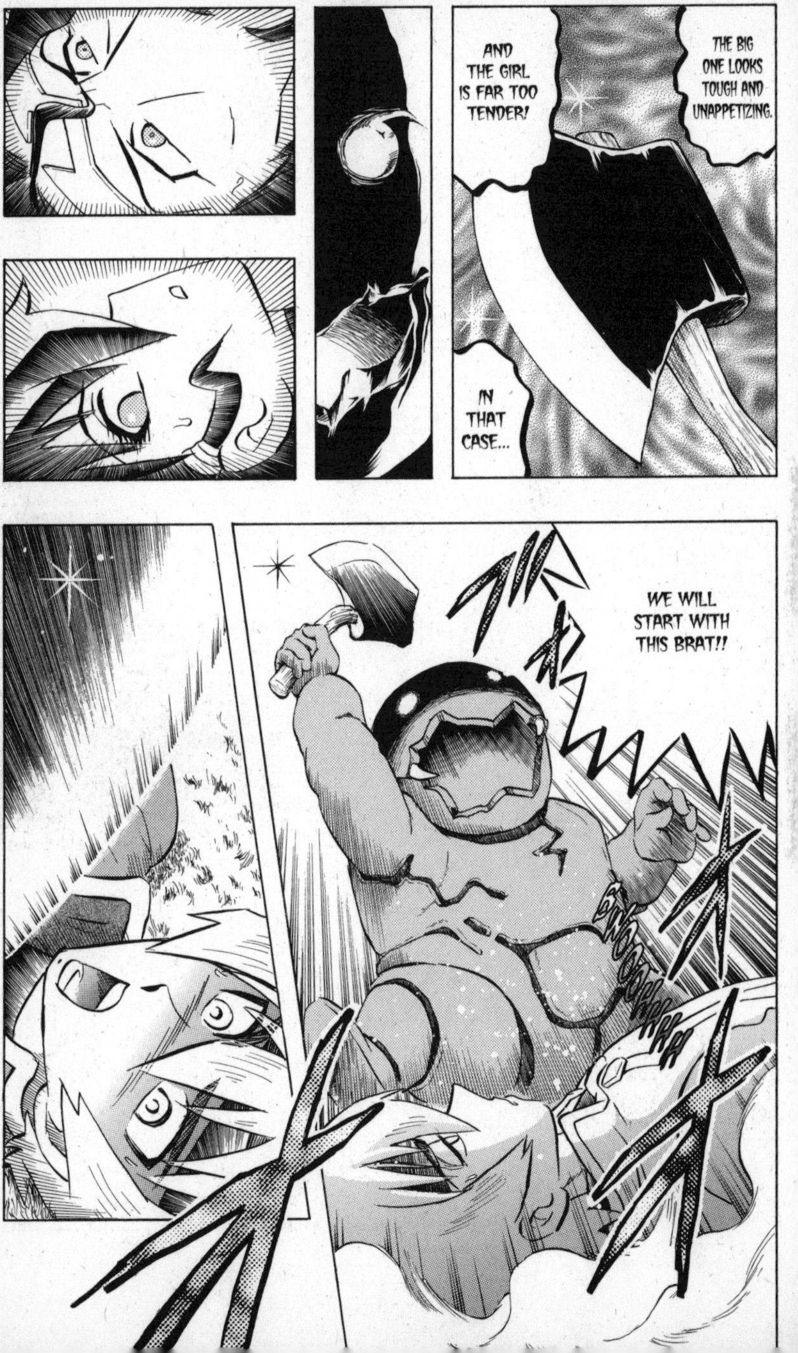
THE BIG ONE LOOKS TOUGH AND UNAPPETIZING.
AND THE GIRL IS FAR TOO TENDER!
IN THAT CASE...
WE WILL START WITH THIS BRAT!!

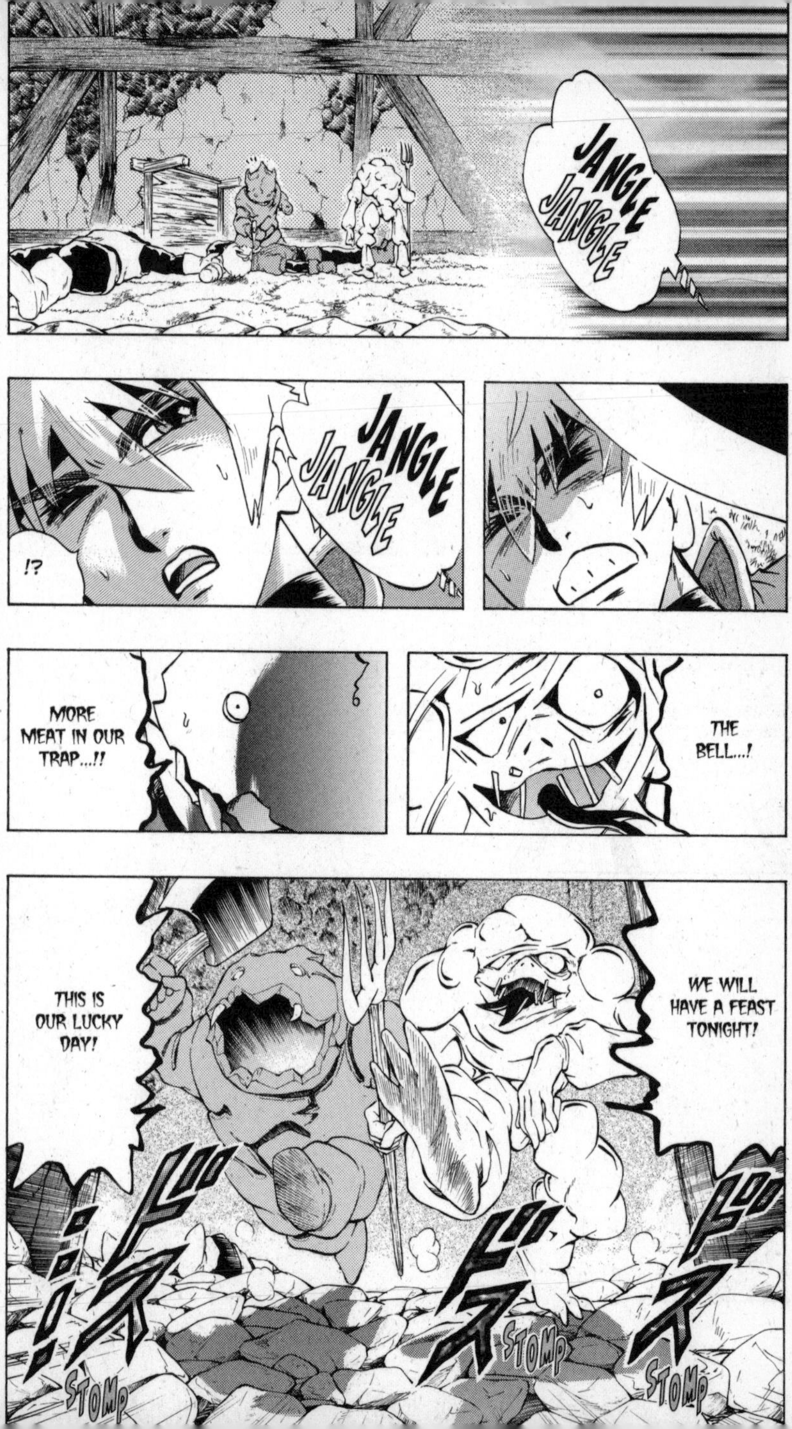
JANGLE JANGLE
JANGLE JANGLE
!?
THE BELL...!
MORE MEAT IN OUR TRAP...!!
WE WILL HAVE A FEAST TONIGHT!
THIS IS OUR LUCKY DAY!
STOMP
STOMP
STOMP

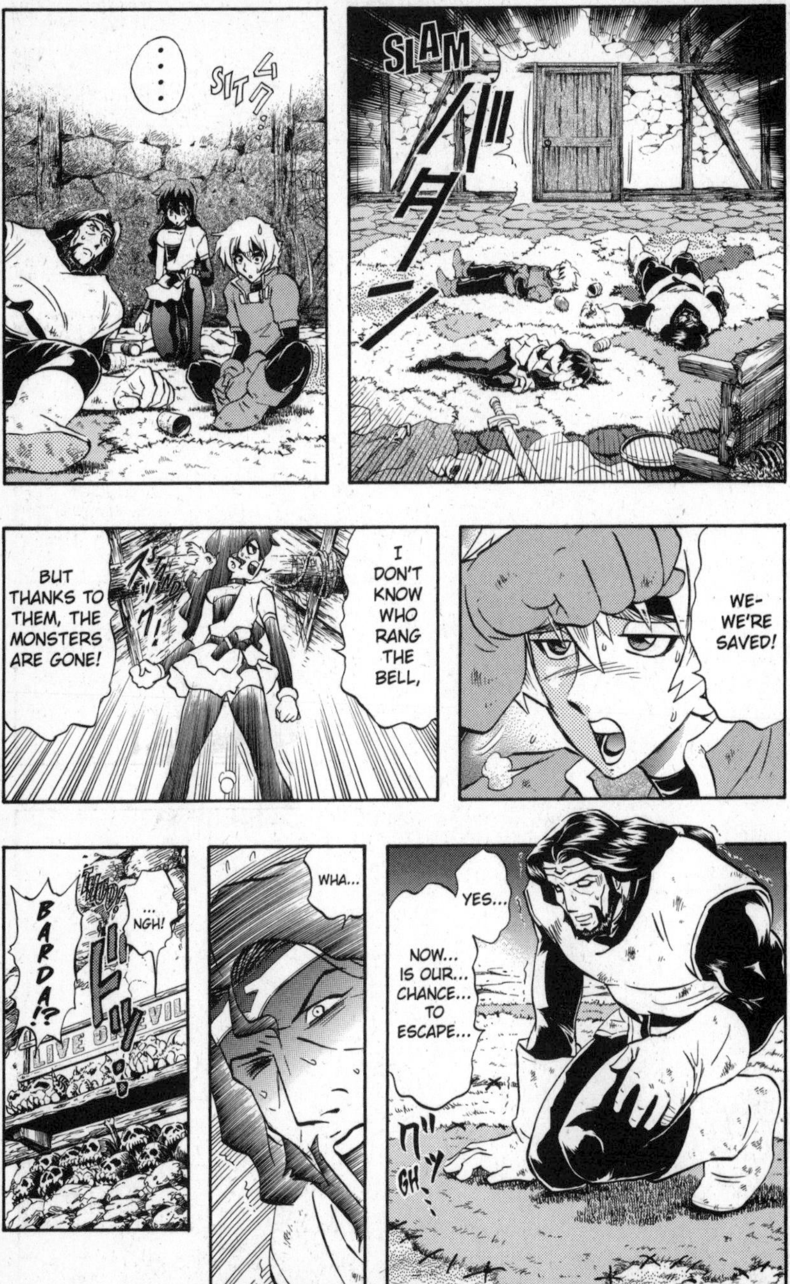
SLAM
...
SIT
WE- WE'RE SAVED!
I DON'T KNOW WHO RANG THE BELL,
BUT THANKS TO THEM, THE MONSTERS ARE GONE!
STAND
YES...
NOW... IS OUR... CHANCE... TO ESCAPE...
GH
WHA...
...NGH!
BARDA!?
THUD

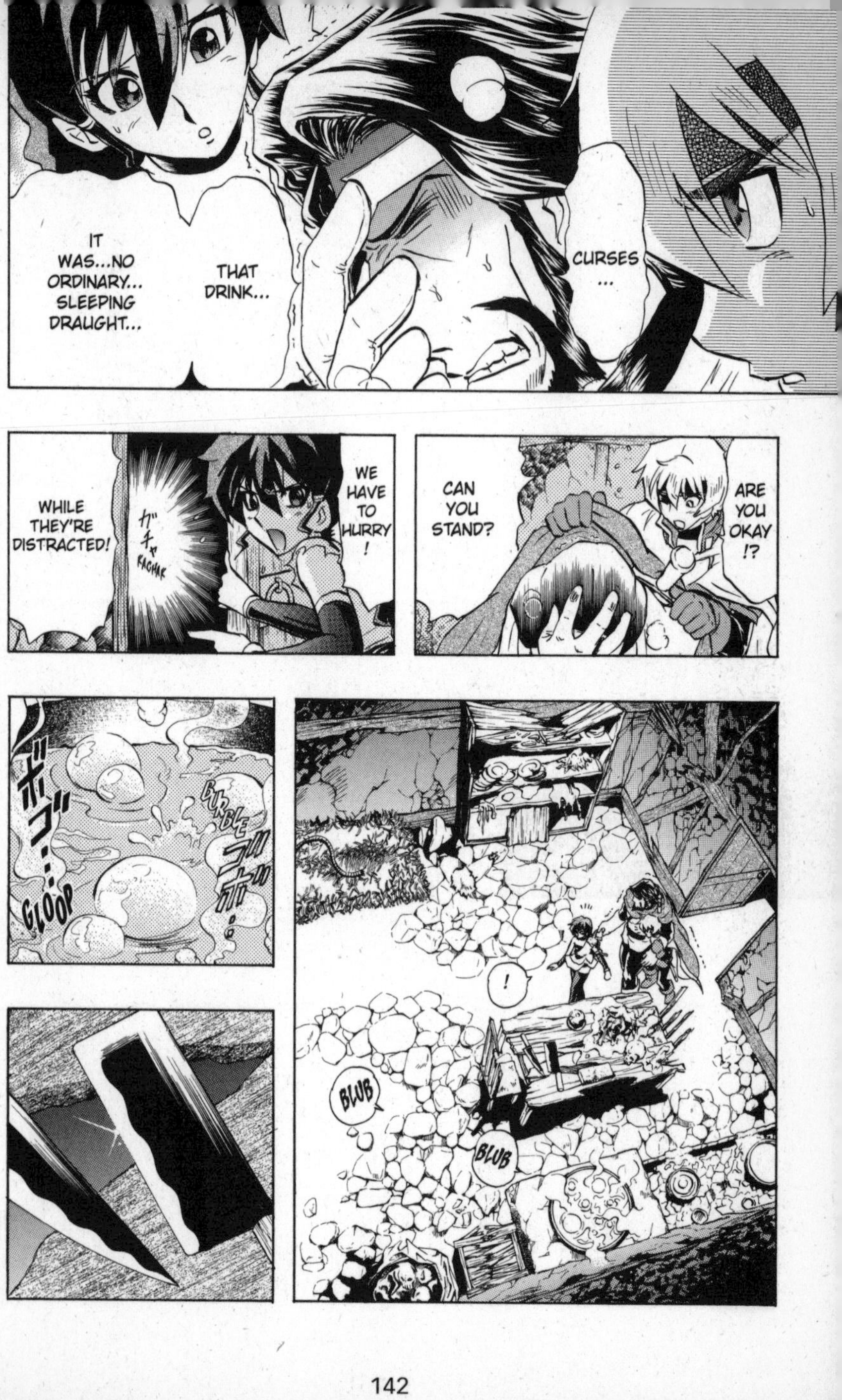
CURSES...
THAT DRINK...
IT WAS...NO ORDINARY... SLEEPING DRAUGHT...
ARE YOU OKAY!?
CAN YOU STAND?
WE HAVE TO HURRY!
ガチャ KACHAK
WHILE THEY'RE DISTRACTED!
!
BLUB
BLUB
BUBBLE
GLOOP

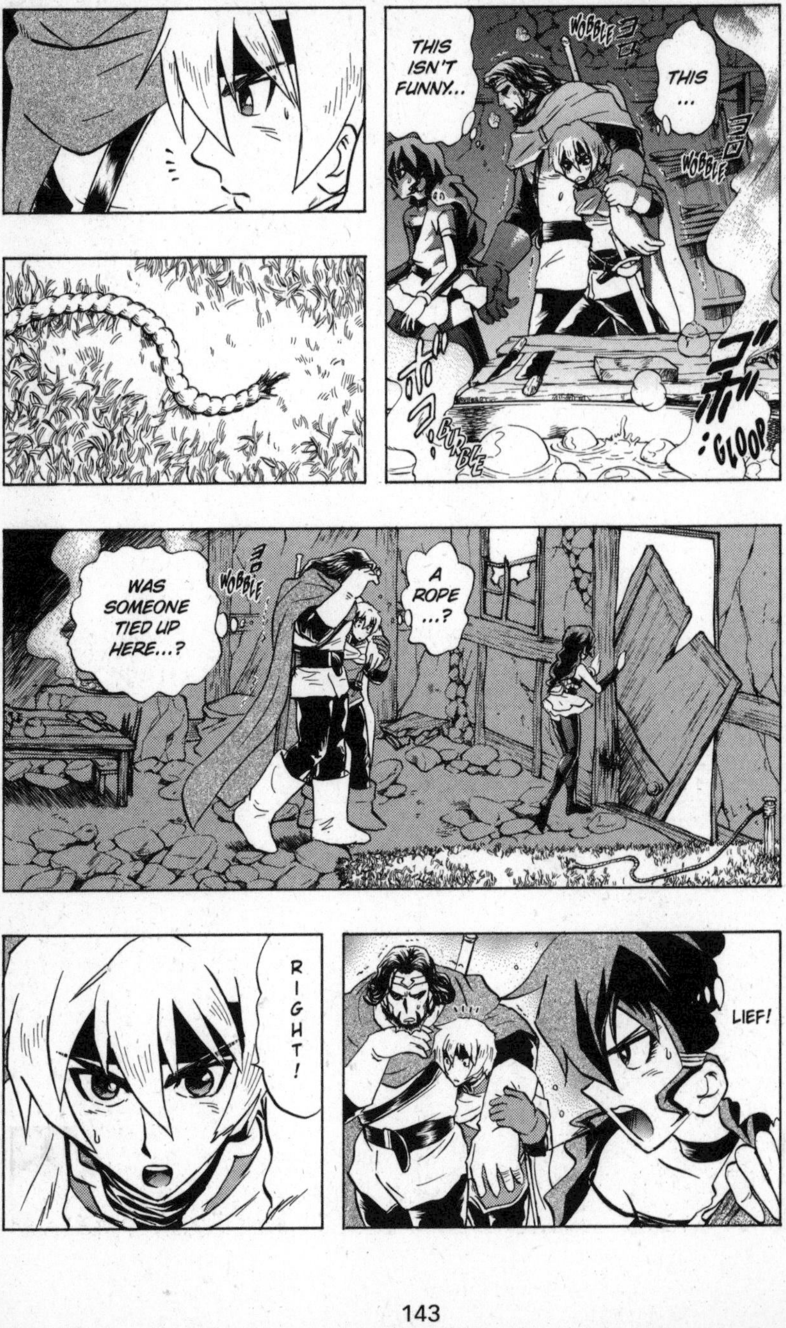
WOBBLE
THIS ...
THIS ISN'T FUNNY...
WOBBLE
GLOOP
BURBLE
A ROPE ...?
WOBBLE
WAS SOMEONE TIED UP HERE...?
LIEF!
RIGHT!

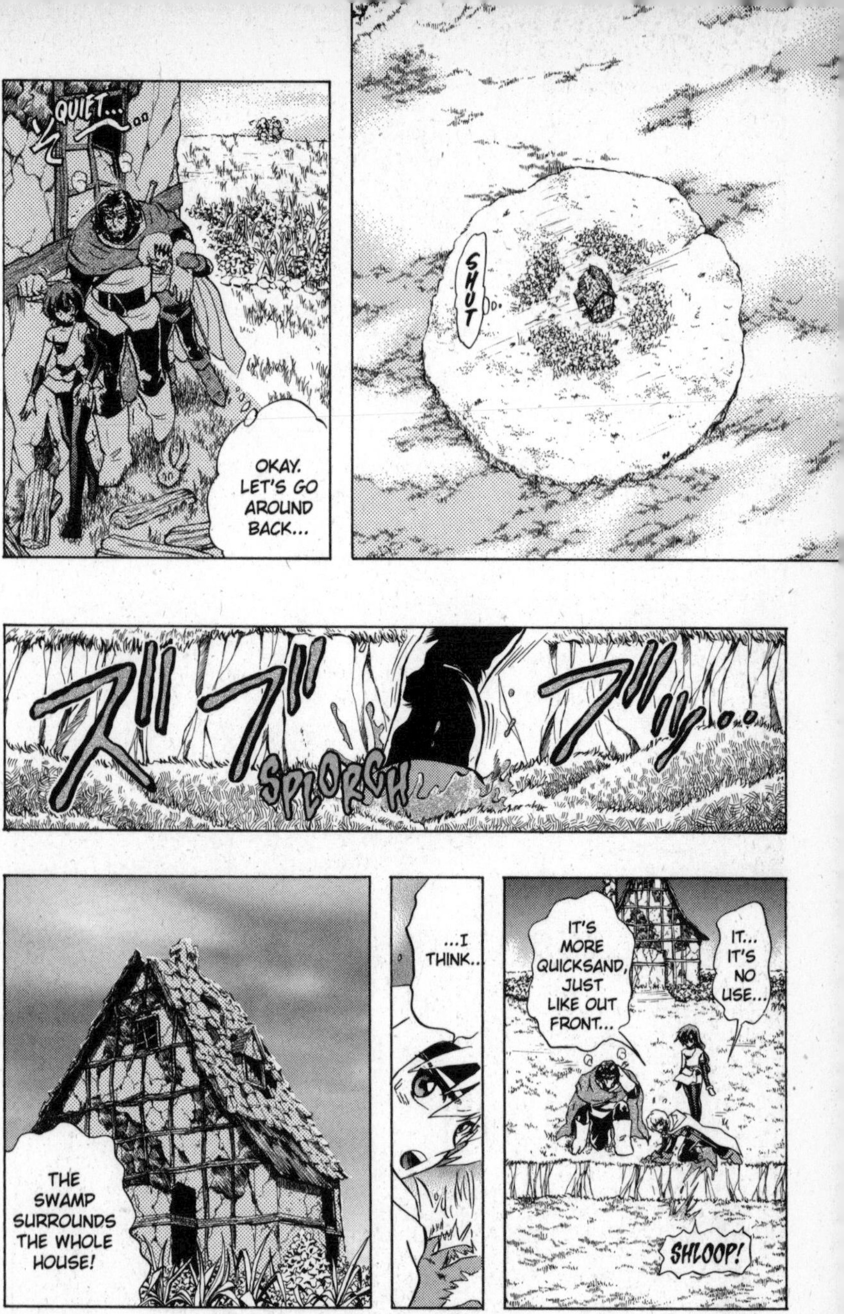
SHUT
QUIET...
OKAY. LET'S GO AROUND BACK...
SPLORCH
IT... IT'S NO USE...
IT'S MORE QUICKSAND, JUST LIKE OUT FRONT...
SHLOOP!
...I THINK...
THE SWAMP SURROUNDS THE WHOLE HOUSE!

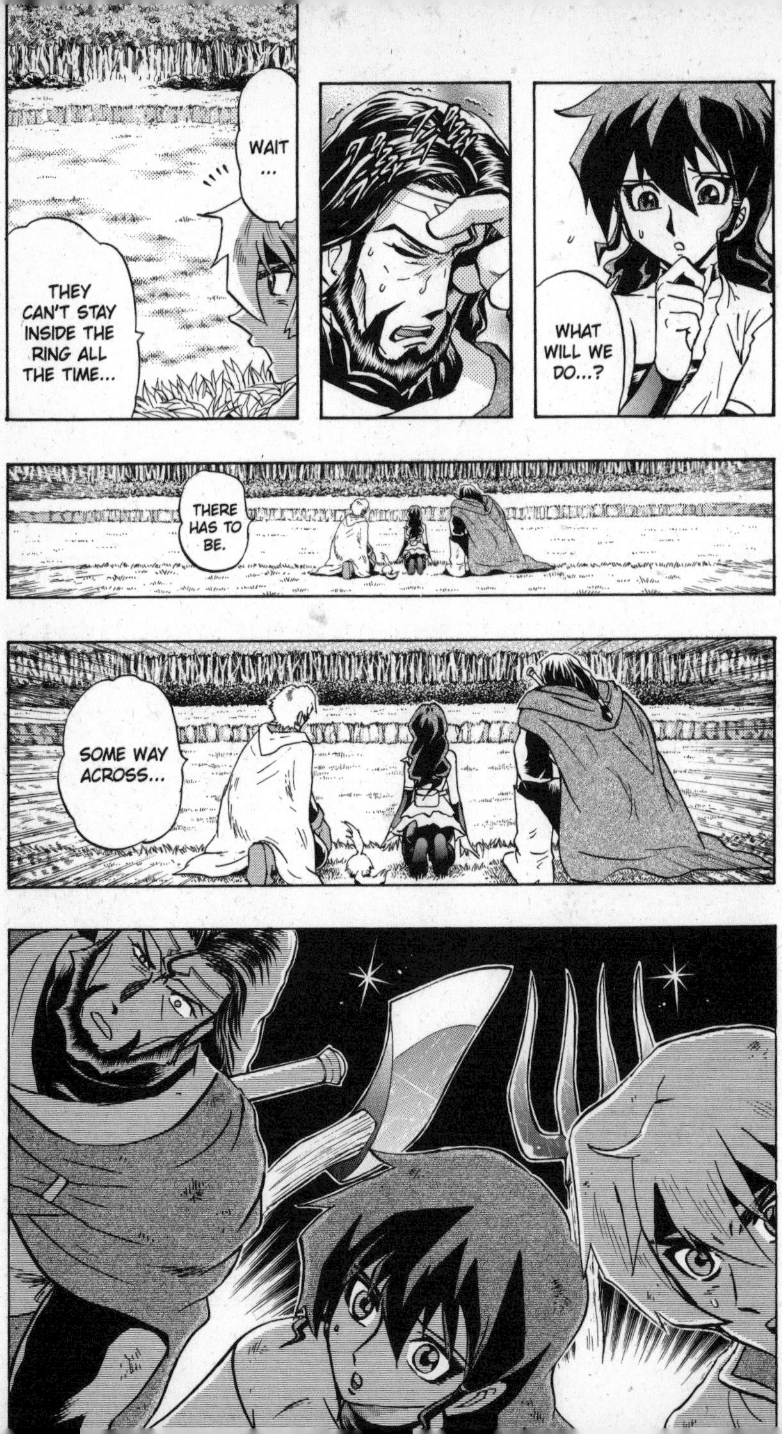
WHAT WILL WE DO...?
WAIT ...
THEY CAN'T STAY INSIDE THE RING ALL THE TIME...
THERE HAS TO BE.
SOME WAY ACROSS...

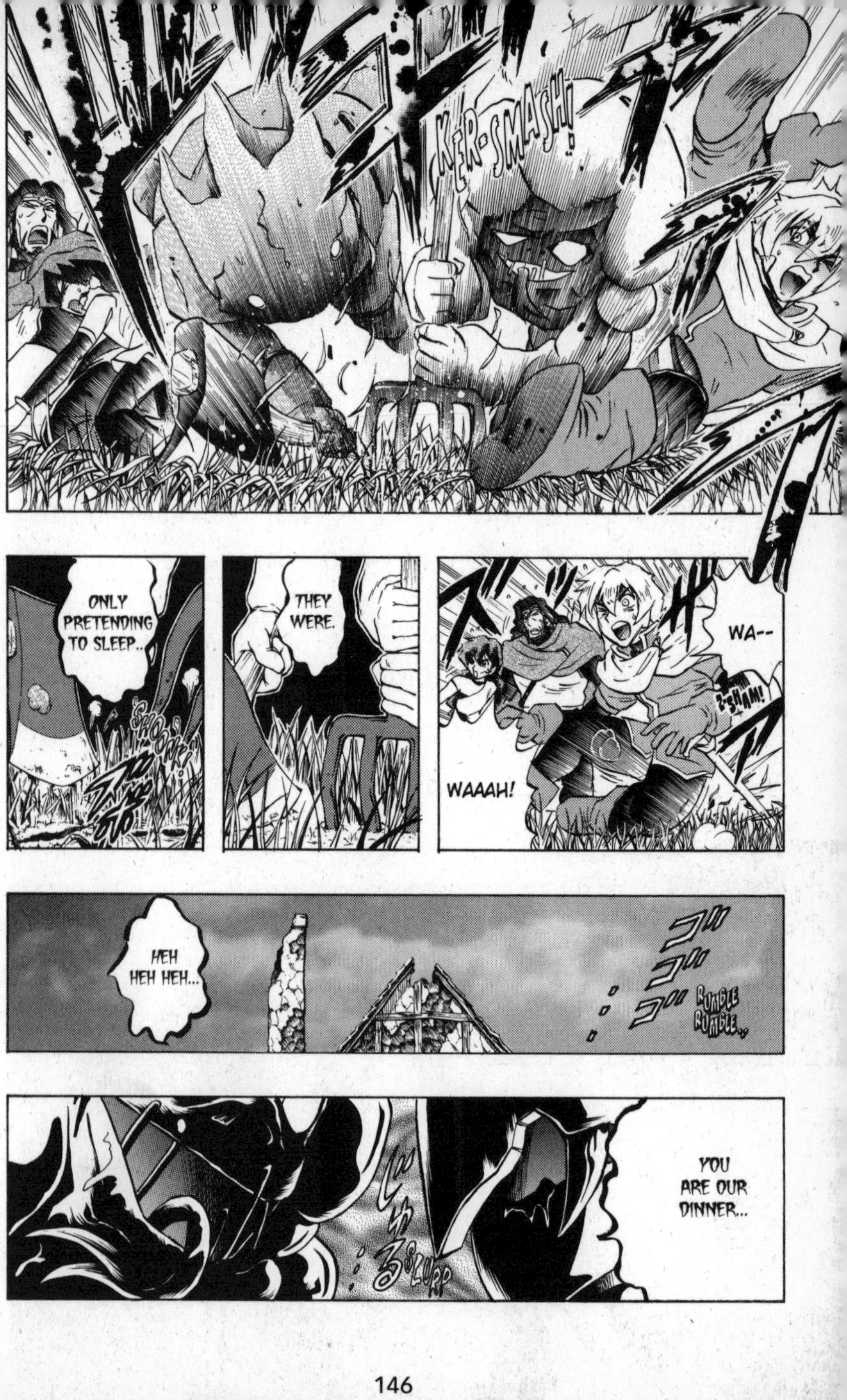
KER-SMASH!
WA--
Z-SHAM!
WAAAH!
THEY WERE.
ONLY PRETENDING TO SLEEP...
SHOOOK!
RUMBLE RUMBLE...
HEH HEH HEH...
YOU ARE OUR DINNER...
SLURP

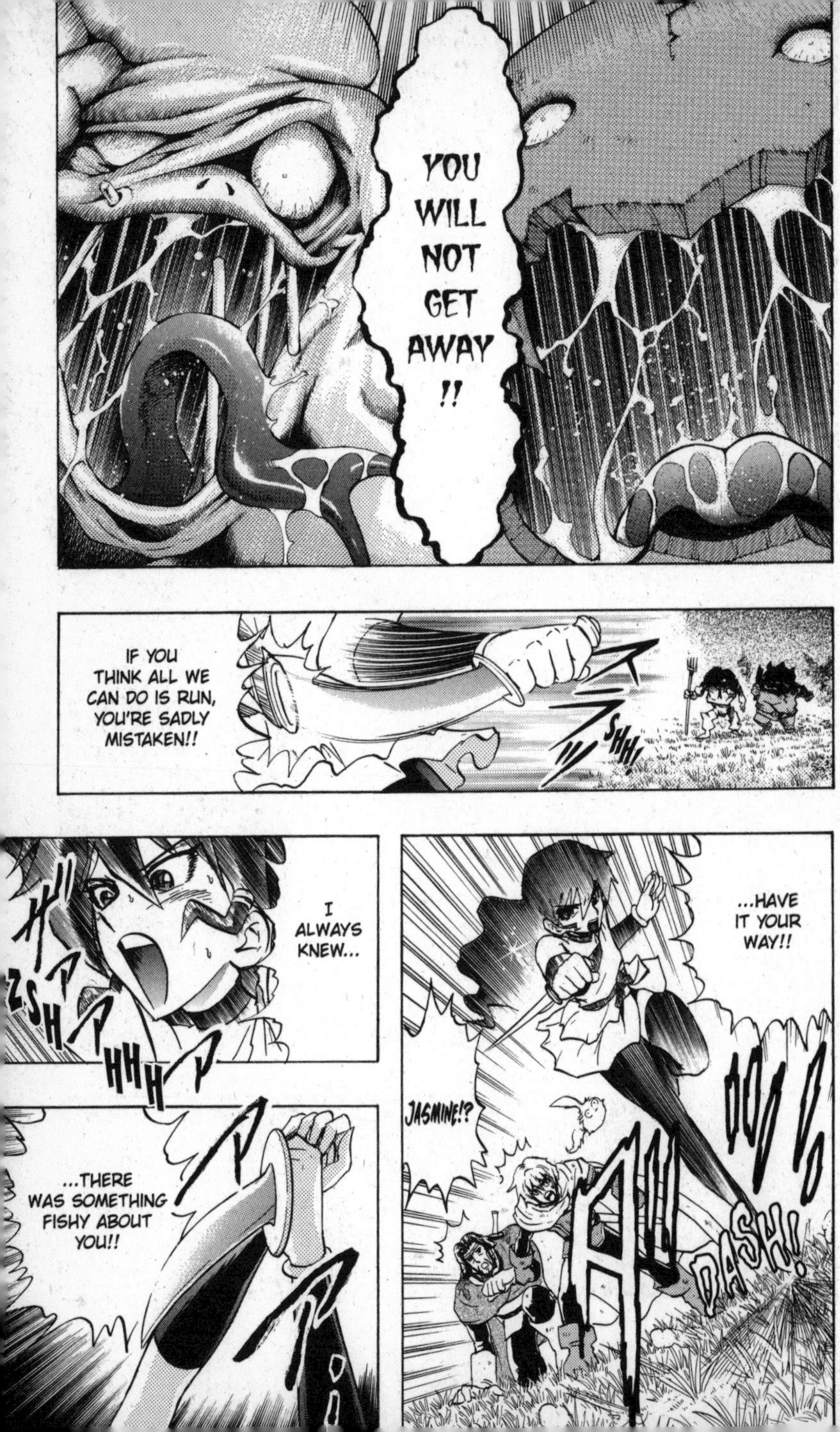
YOU WILL NOT GET AWAY !!
IF YOU THINK ALL WE CAN DO IS RUN, YOU'RE SADLY MISTAKEN!!
SHH!
...HAVE IT YOUR WAY!!
JASMINE!?
DASH!
I ALWAYS KNEW...
ZSHHHH
...THERE WAS SOMETHING FISHY ABOUT YOU!!

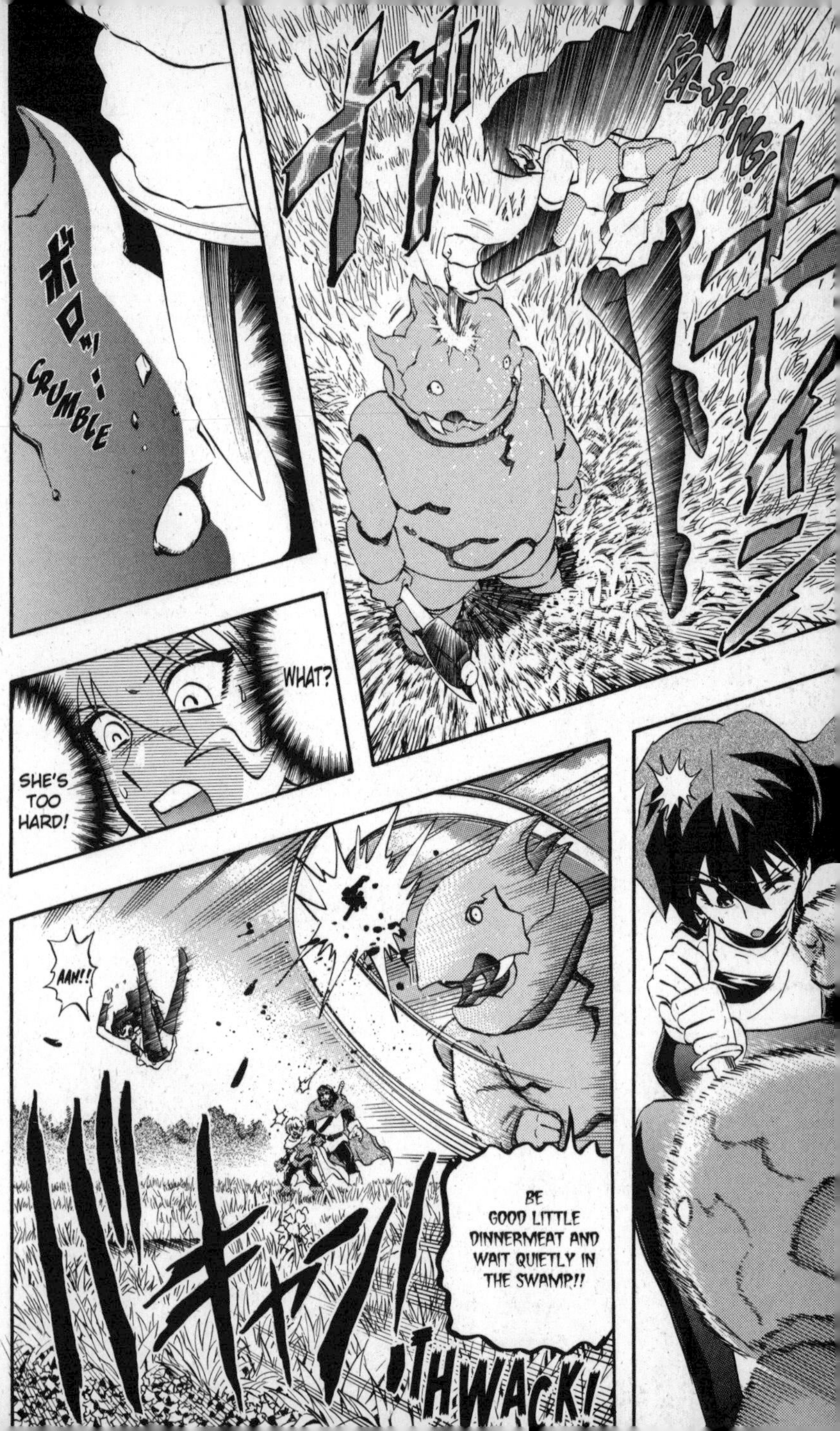

KA-SHING!
ボロッ…
CRUMBLE
WHAT?
SHE'S TOO HARD!
AAN!!
BE GOOD LITTLE DINNERMEAT AND WAIT QUIETLY IN THE SWAMP!!
THWACK!

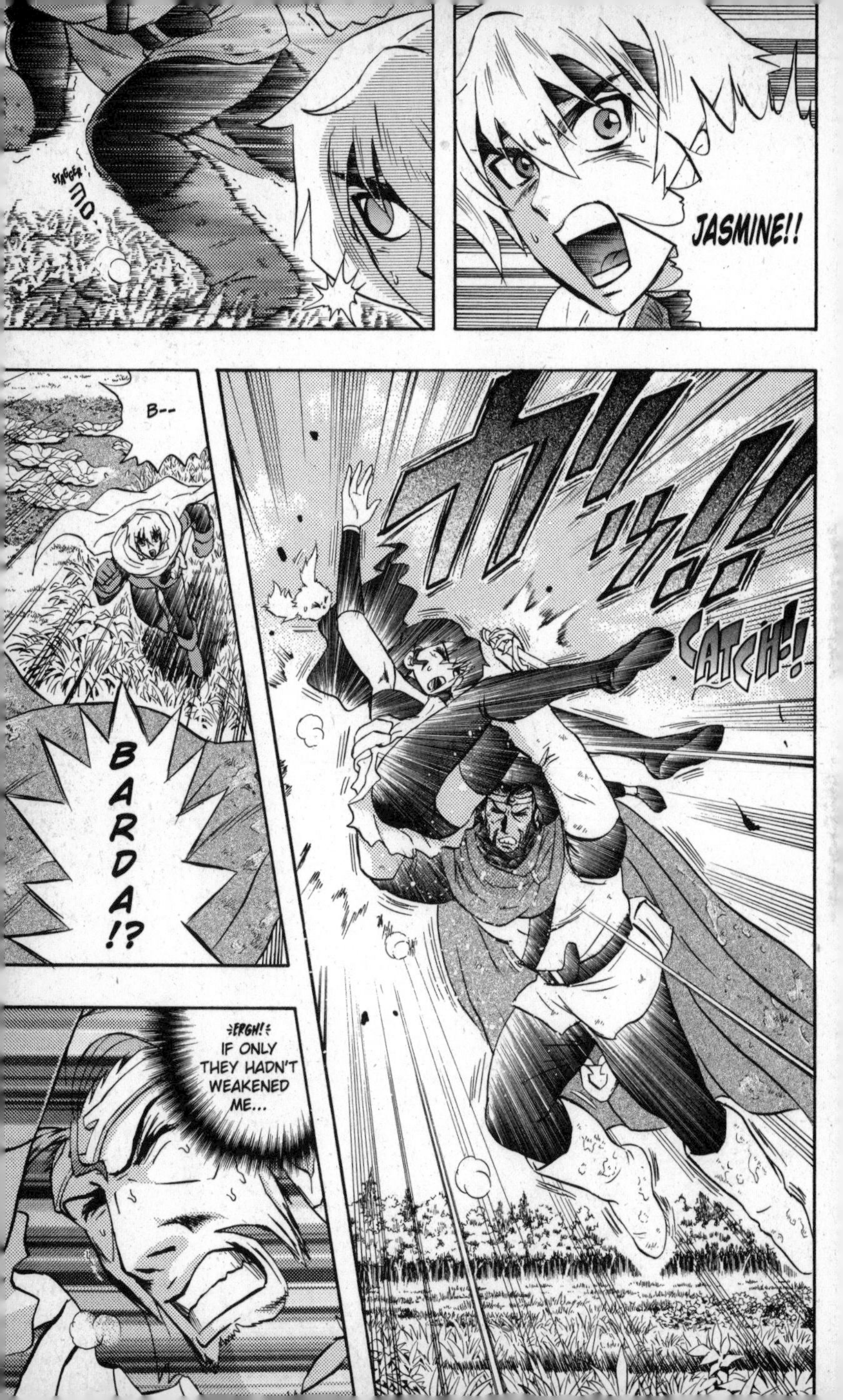
JASMINE!!
STAGGER
B--
CATCH!!
BARDA!?
ERGH!
IF ONLY THEY HADN'T WEAKENED ME...

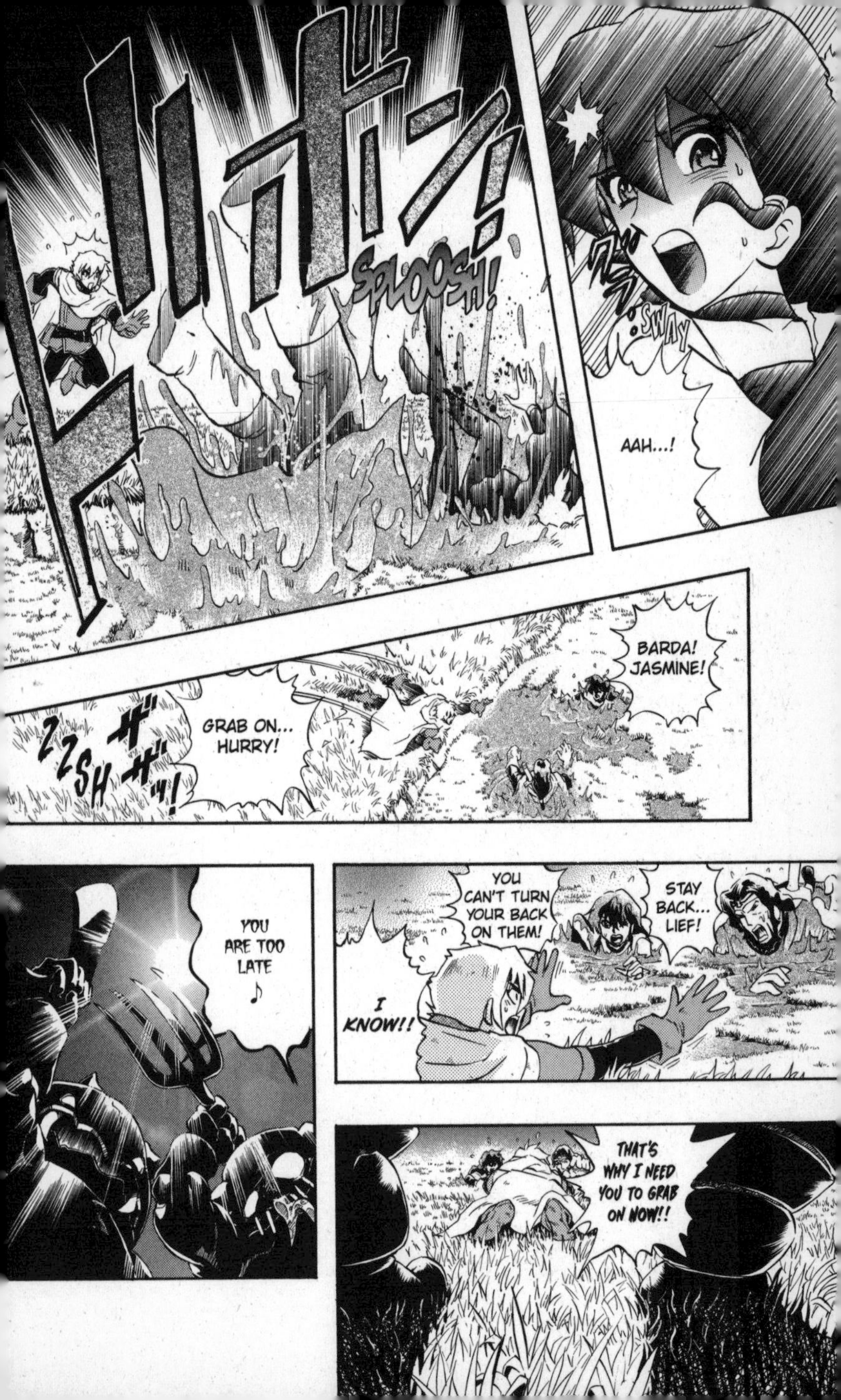
SWAY
AAH...!
SPLOOSH!
BARDA! JASMINE!
GRAB ON... HURRY!
ZZSH
STAY BACK... LIEF!
YOU CAN'T TURN YOUR BACK ON THEM!
I KNOW!!
THAT'S WHY I NEED YOU TO GRAB ON NOW!!
YOU ARE TOO LATE ♪

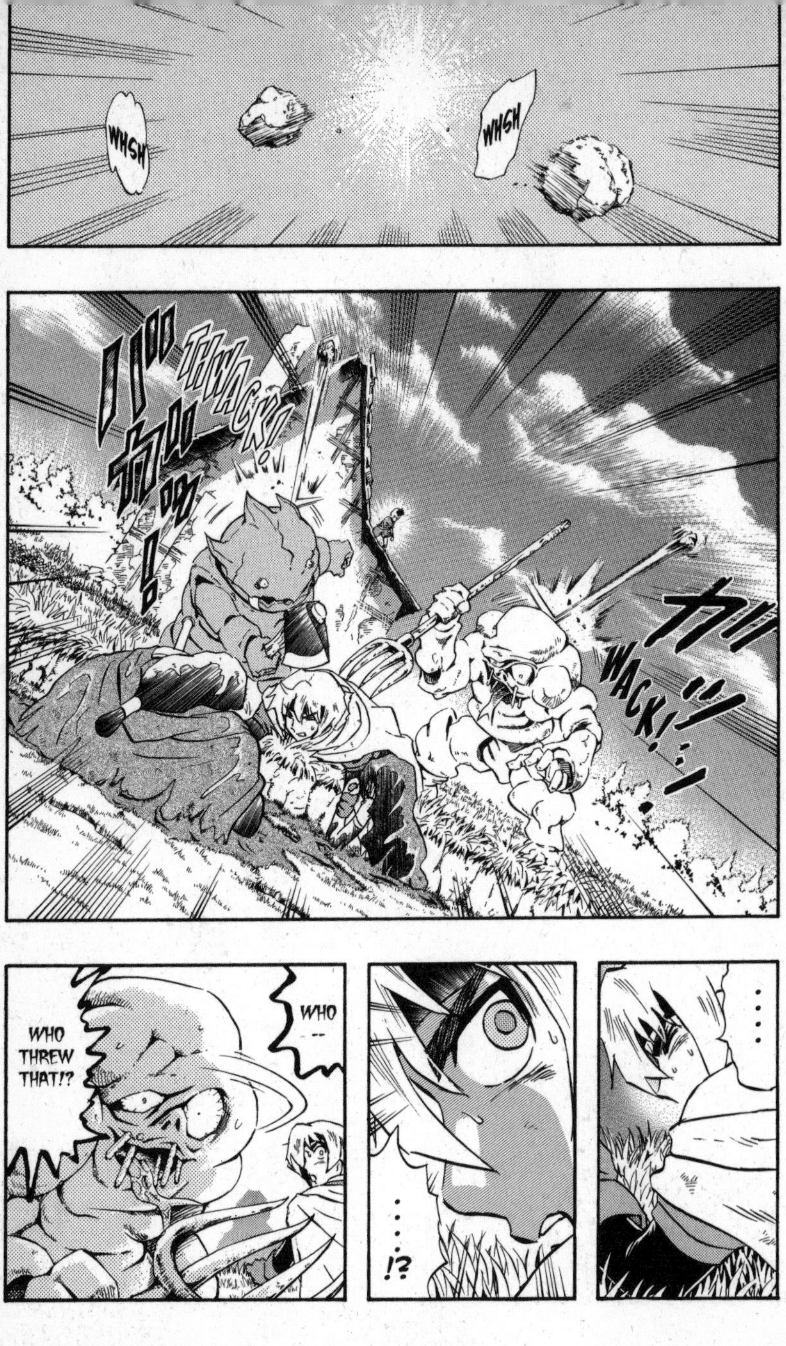

WHSH
WHSH
THWACK!
WACK!
....
....!?
WHO --
WHO THREW THAT!?

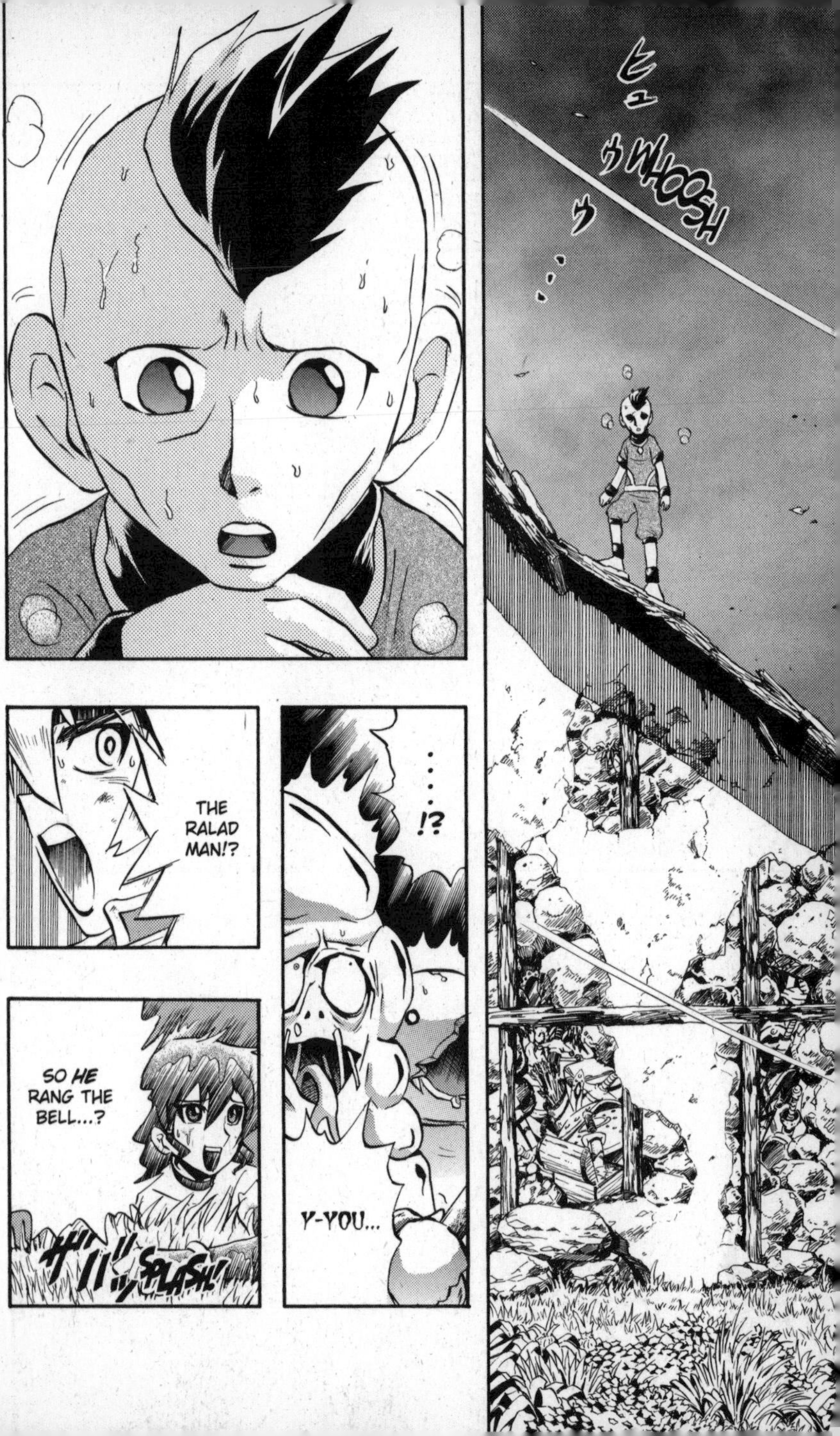

ヒュゥゥ
WHOOSH
...!?
Y-YOU...
THE RALAD MAN!?
SO HE RANG THE BELL...?
ザバッ
SPLASH!

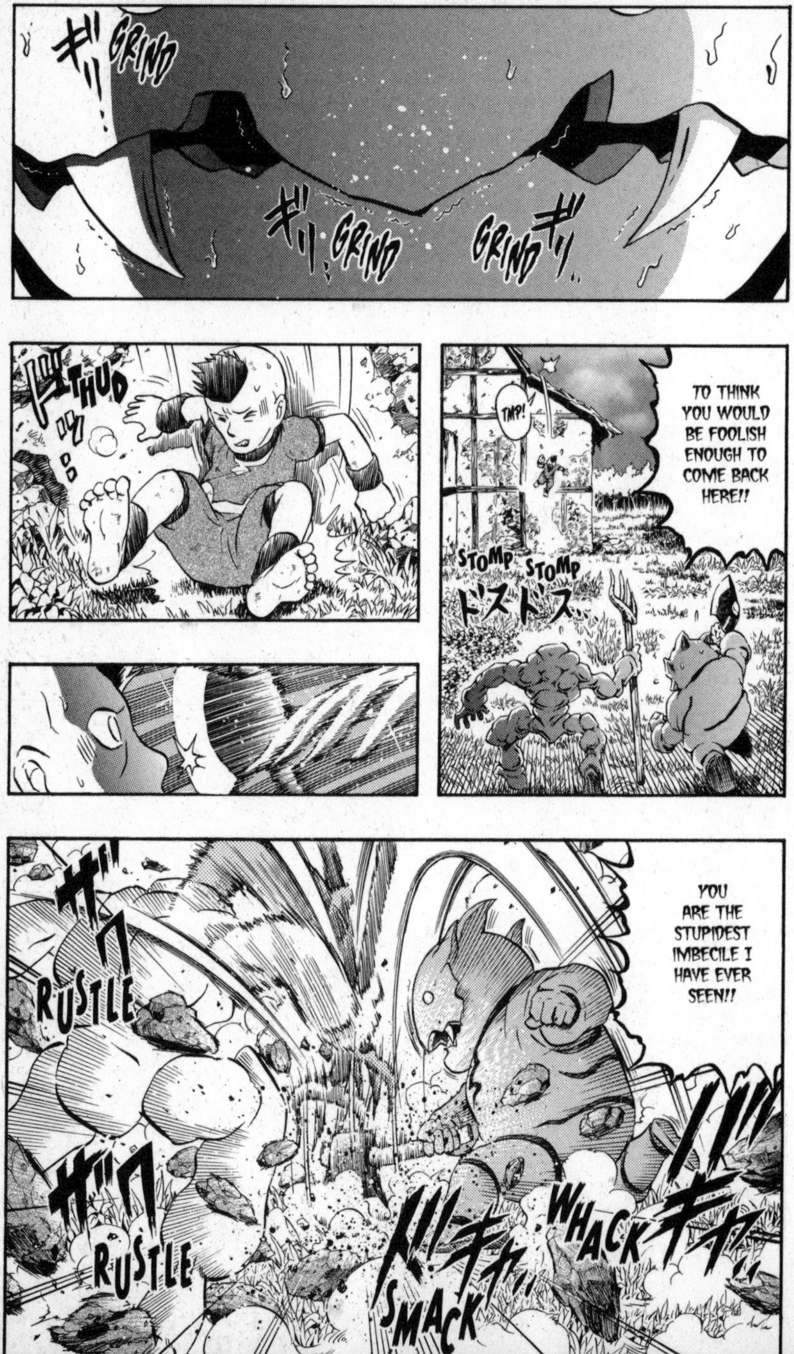
GRIND ギリ
ギリ GRIND
ギリ GRIND
TMP!
TO THINK YOU WOULD BE FOOLISH ENOUGH TO COME BACK HERE!!
STOMP STOMP
ドスドス
ドサッ THUD
YOU ARE THE STUPIDEST IMBECILE I HAVE EVER SEEN!!
ザワ RUSTLE
WHACK
SMACK
ザワ RUSTLE

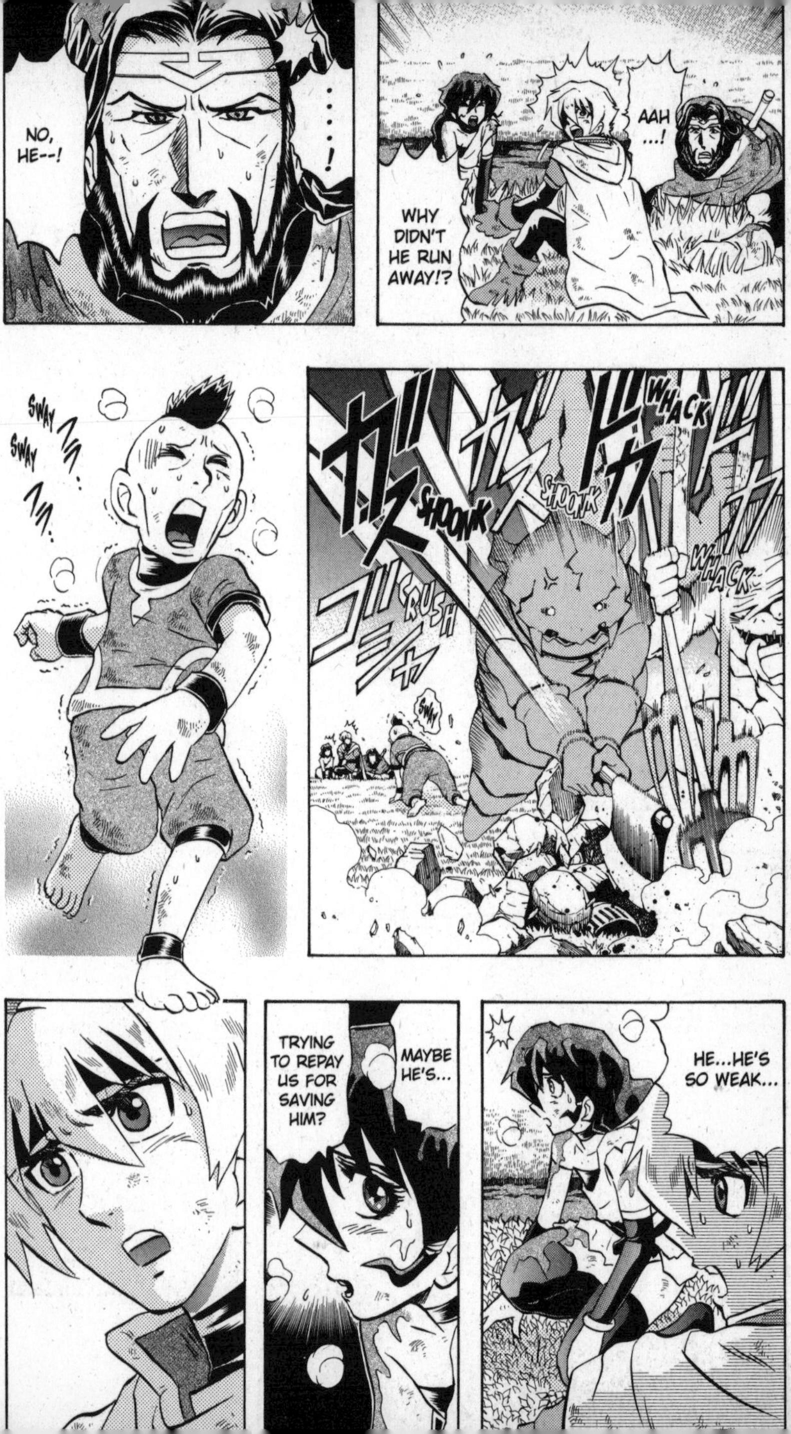
AAH ...!
WHY DIDN'T HE RUN AWAY!?
...!
NO, HE--!
WHACK
WHACK
SHOONK
SHOONK
CRUSH
SWAY
SWAY
SWAY
HE...HE'S SO WEAK...
MAYBE HE'S...
TRYING TO REPAY US FOR SAVING HIM?

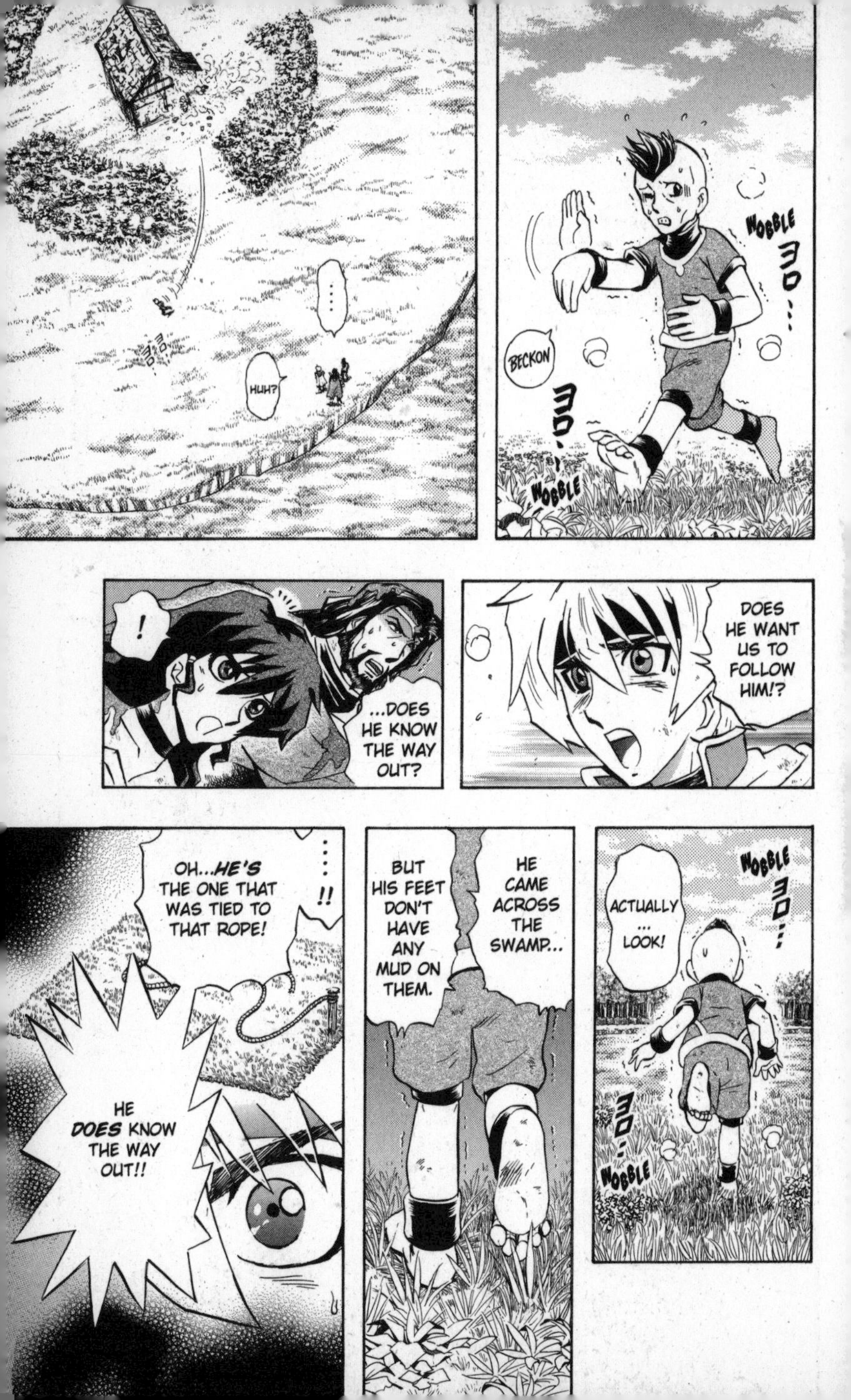
WOBBLE
ヨロ...
BECKON
ヨロ、
WOBBLE
......
HUH?
DOES HE WANT US TO FOLLOW HIM!?
!
...DOES HE KNOW THE WAY OUT?
WOBBLE
ヨロ...
ACTUALLY ... LOOK!
ヨロ...
WOBBLE
HE CAME ACROSS THE SWAMP...
BUT HIS FEET DON'T HAVE ANY MUD ON THEM.
....!!
OH...HE'S THE ONE THAT WAS TIED TO THAT ROPE!
HE DOES KNOW THE WAY OUT!!

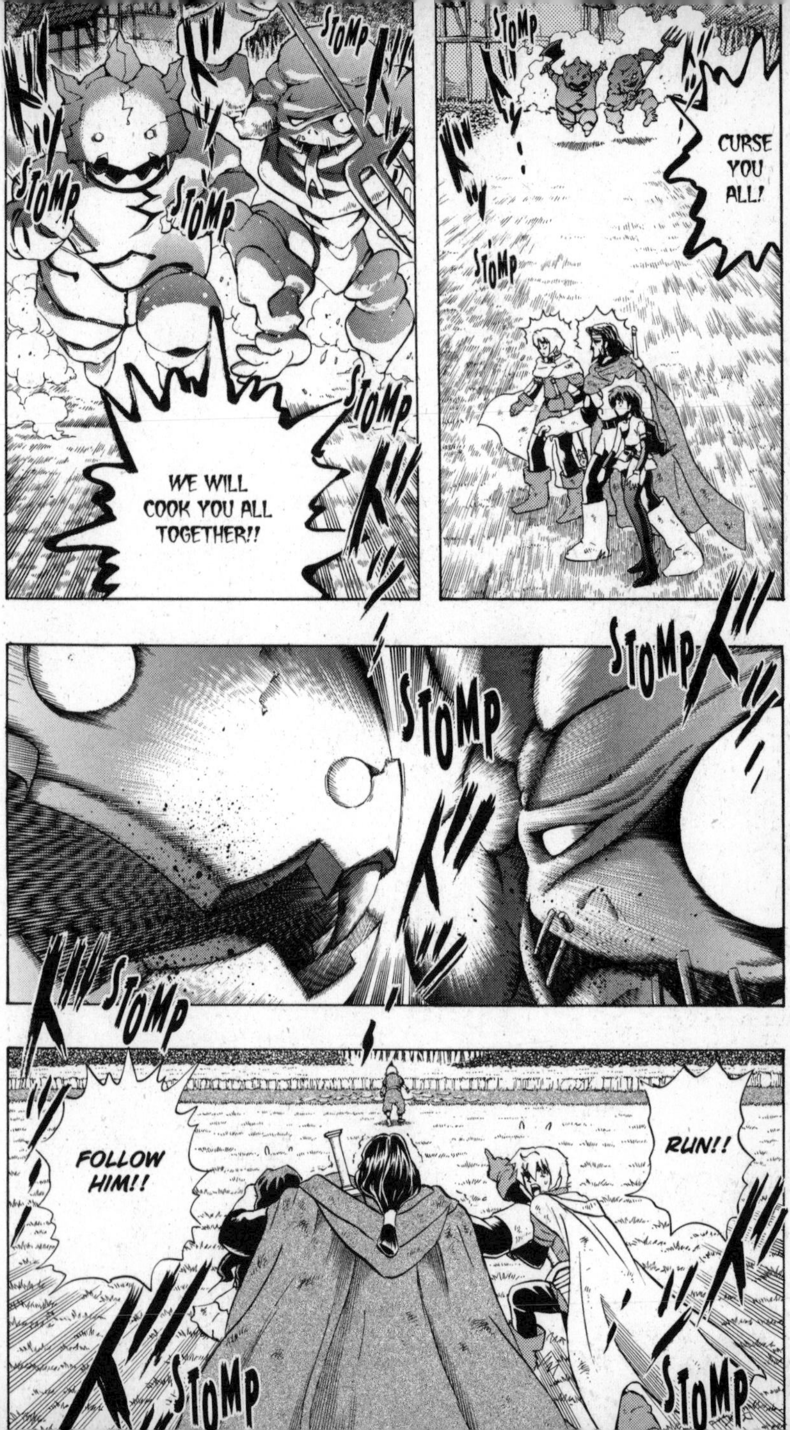
STOMP
CURSE YOU ALL!
STOMP
STOMP
STOMP
STOMP
STOMP
WE WILL COOK YOU ALL TOGETHER!!
STOMP
STOMP
STOMP
STOMP
RUN!!
FOLLOW HIM!!
STOMP
STOMP

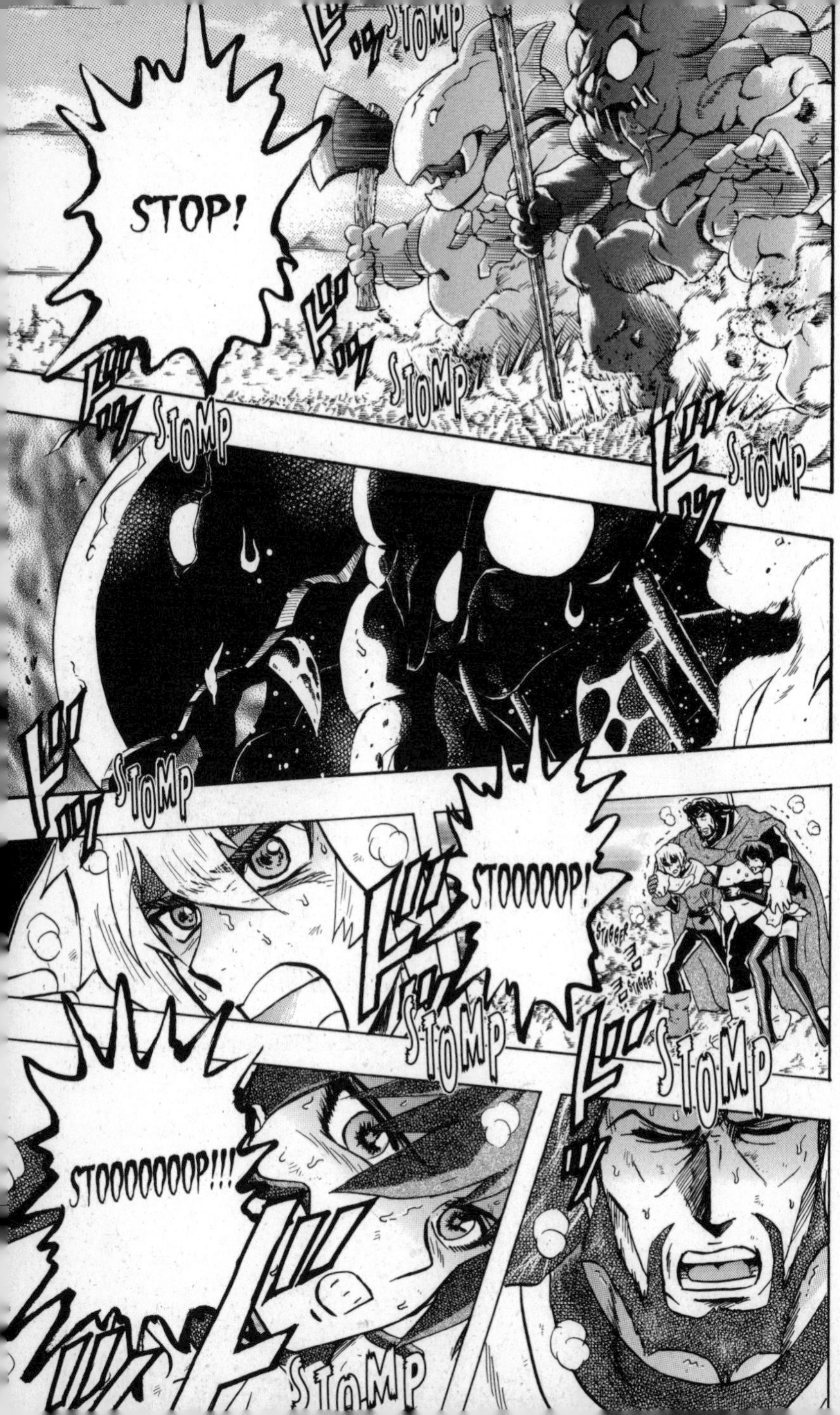
STOMP
STOP!
STOMP
STOMP
STOMP
STOMP
STAGGER
STAGGER
STOOOOOP!
STOMP
STOMP
STOOOOOOP!!!
STOMP

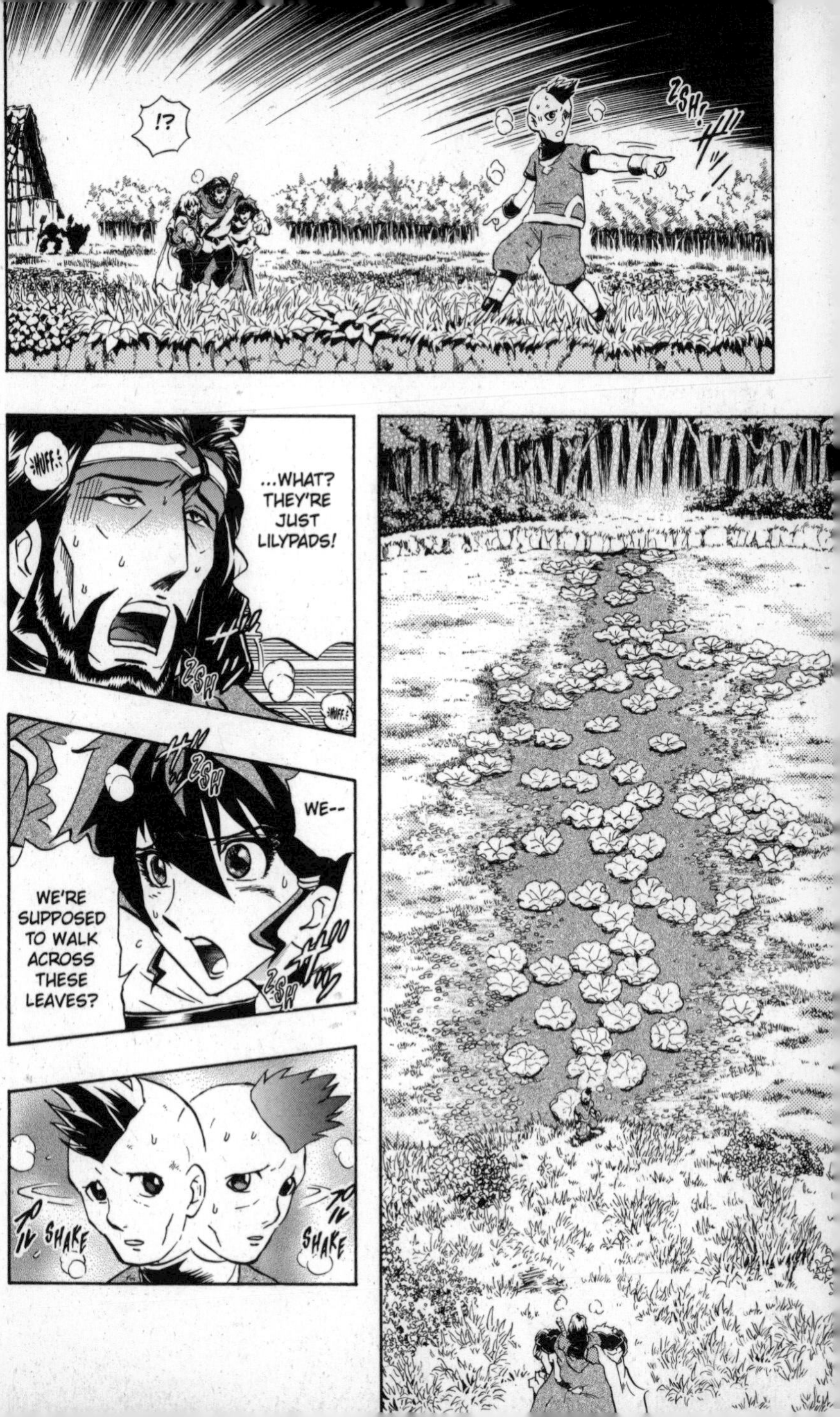
ZSH!
!?
HUFF
...WHAT? THEY'RE JUST LILYPADS!
ZSH
HUFF
ZSH
WE--
WE'RE SUPPOSED TO WALK ACROSS THESE LEAVES?
ZSH
SHAKE
SHAKE

TMP!

...

HUH? HE'S WALKING BETWEEN THE LEAVES!

I GET IT!

SPLISH SPLISH SPLISH SPLISH

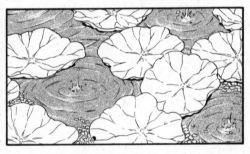

...

!!

SNIFF!

SNIFF!

WAVE!

THE LEAVES ARE CAMOUFLAGE! THERE ARE STEPPING STONES, BUT ONLY INBETWEEN THEM!!

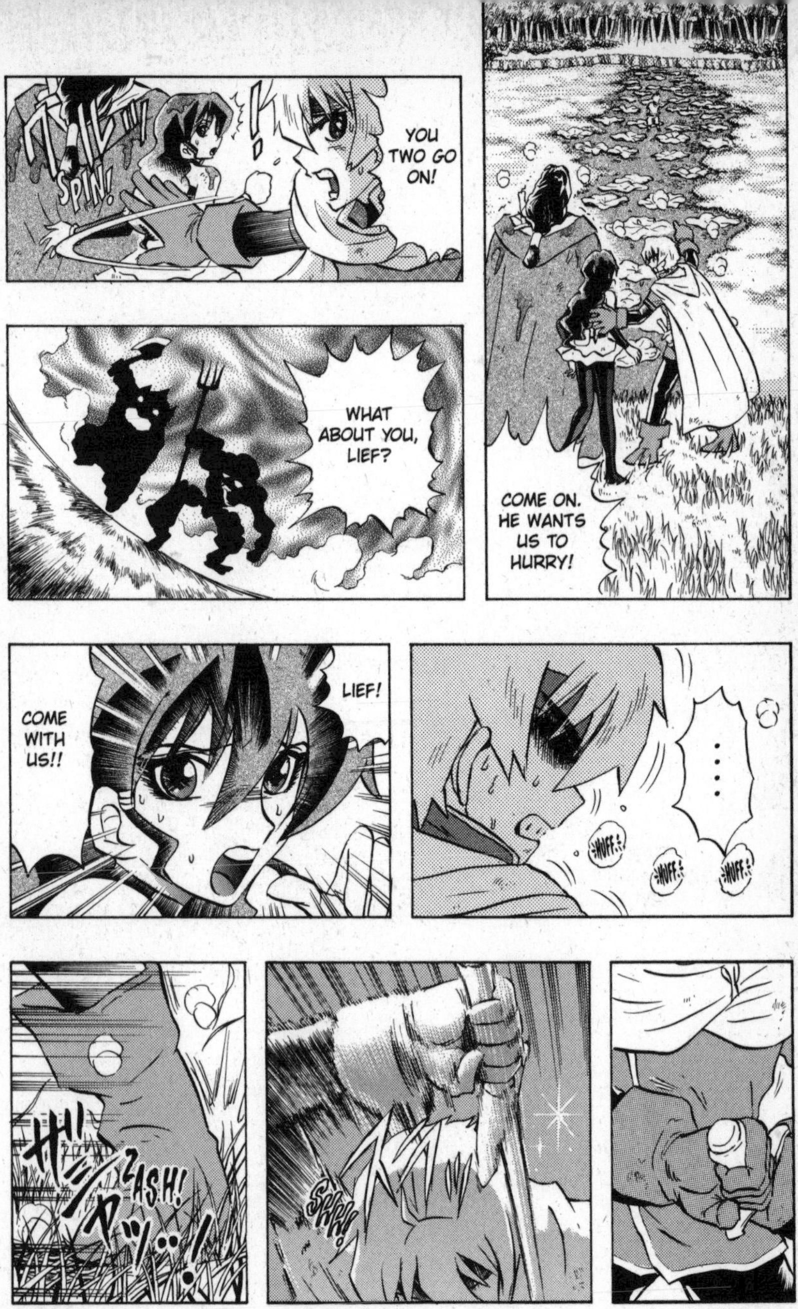
COME ON. HE WANTS US TO HURRY!
SPIN!
YOU TWO GO ON!
WHAT ABOUT YOU, LIEF?
.....
HUFF!
HUFF!
HUFF!
LIEF!
COME WITH US!!
SHING!
ZASH!

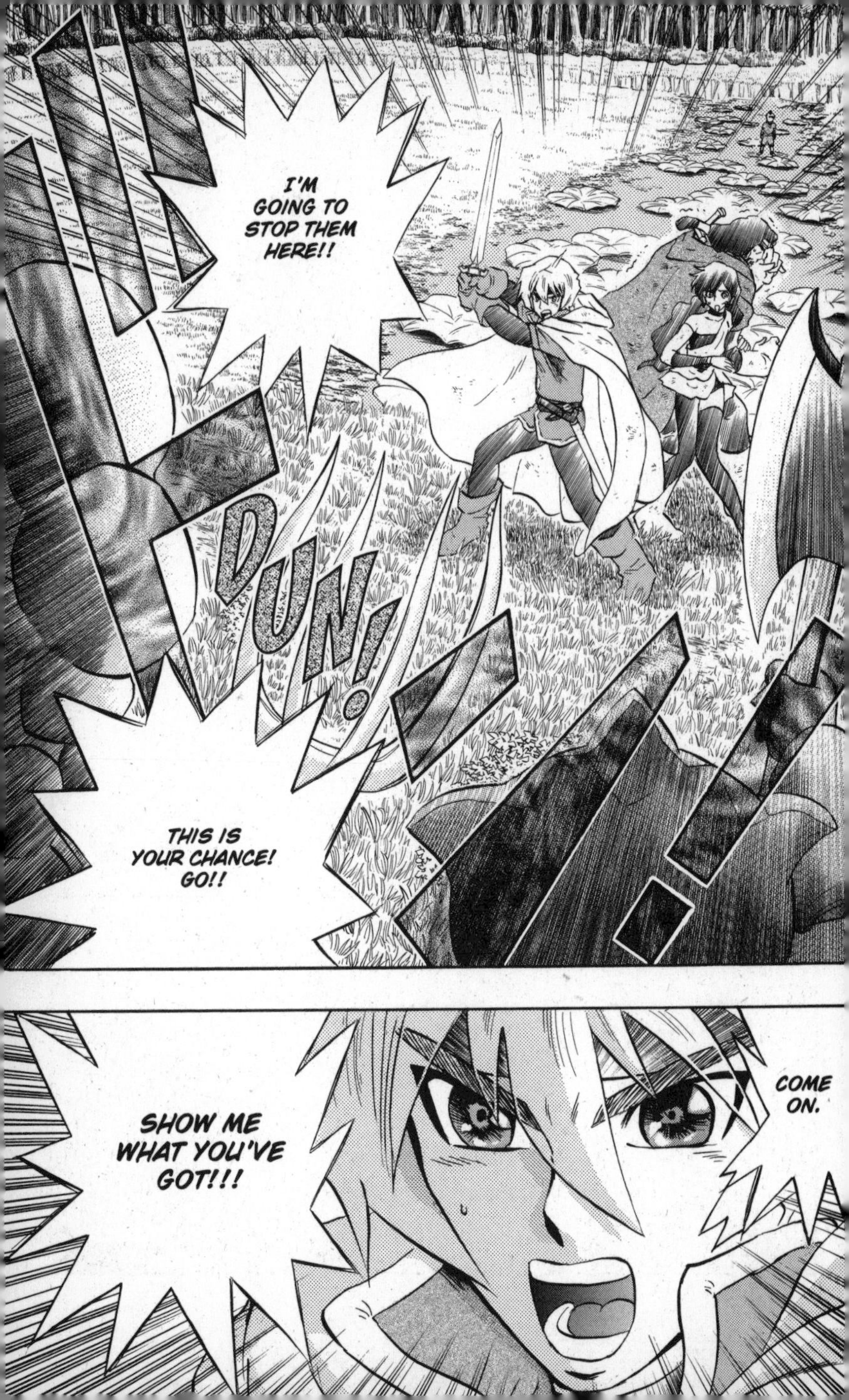
I'M GOING TO STOP THEM HERE!!
DUN!
THIS IS YOUR CHANCE! GO!!
COME ON.
SHOW ME WHAT YOU'VE GOT!!!

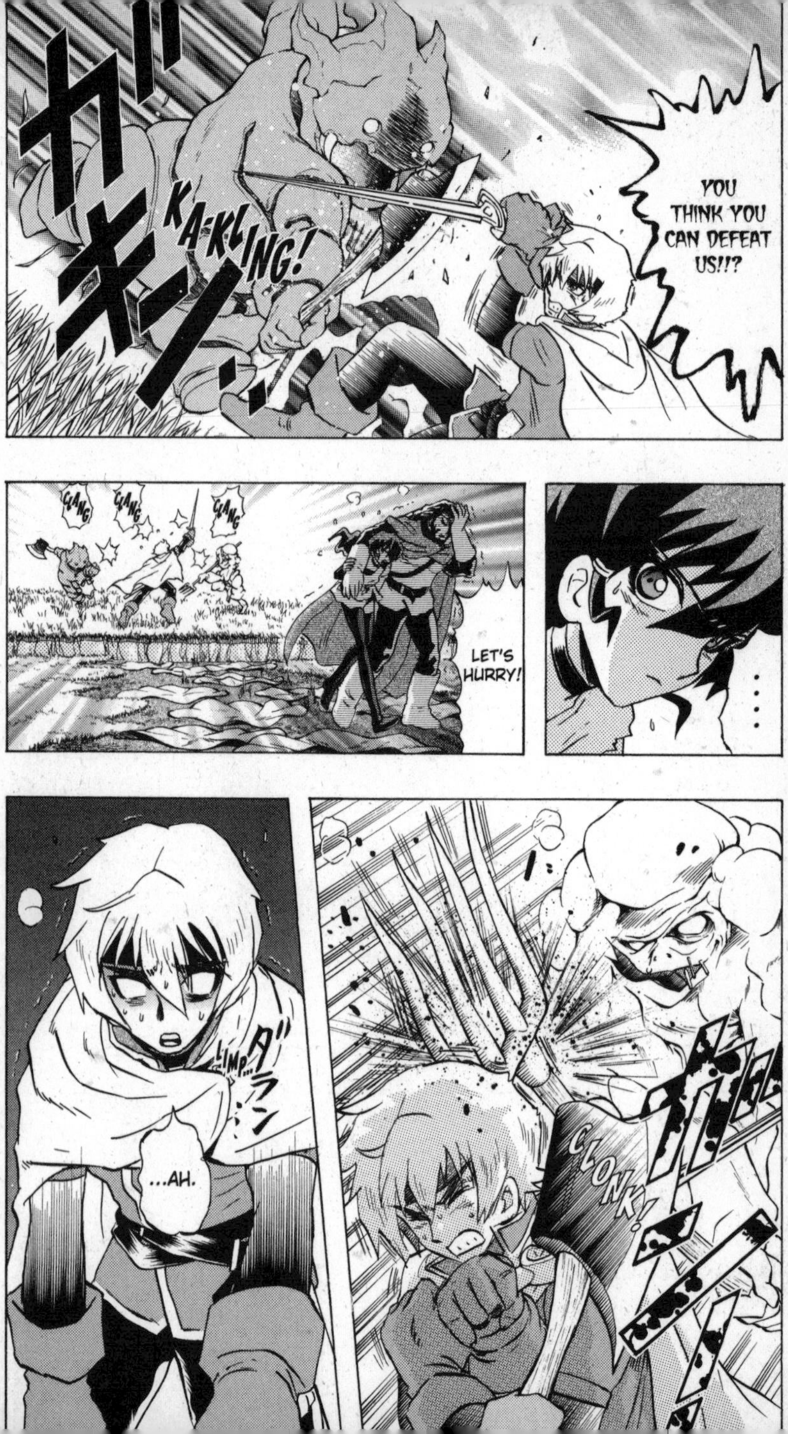

YOU THINK YOU CAN DEFEAT US!!?
KA-KLING!
....
CLANG
CLANG
CLANG
LET'S HURRY!
CLONK!
LIMP...
...AH.

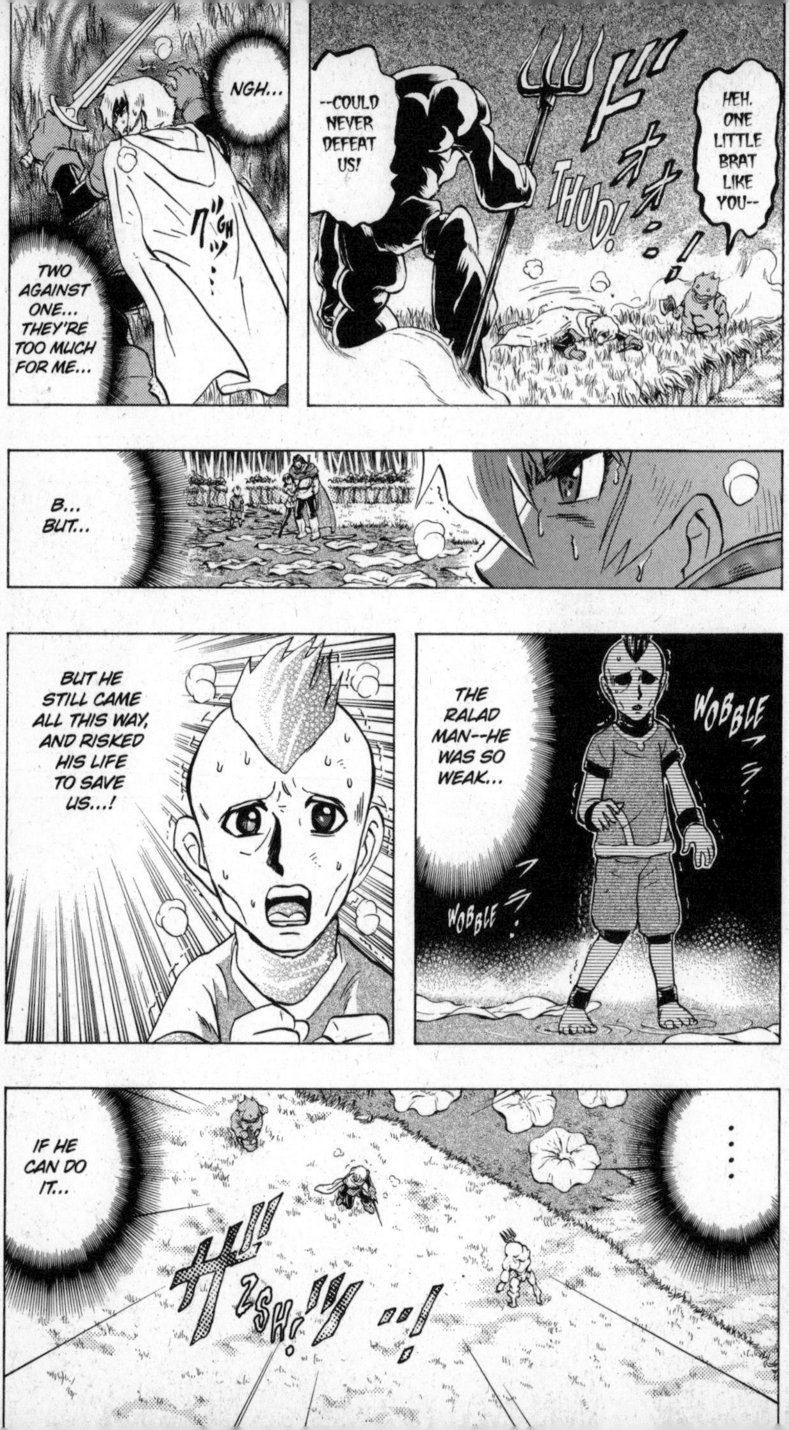
HEH. ONE LITTLE BRAT LIKE YOU--
--COULD NEVER DEFEAT US!
THUD!
NGH...
GH
TWO AGAINST ONE... THEY'RE TOO MUCH FOR ME...
B... BUT...
THE RALAD MAN--HE WAS SO WEAK...
WOBBLE
WOBBLE
BUT HE STILL CAME ALL THIS WAY, AND RISKED HIS LIFE TO SAVE US...!
....
IF HE CAN DO IT...
ZSH!

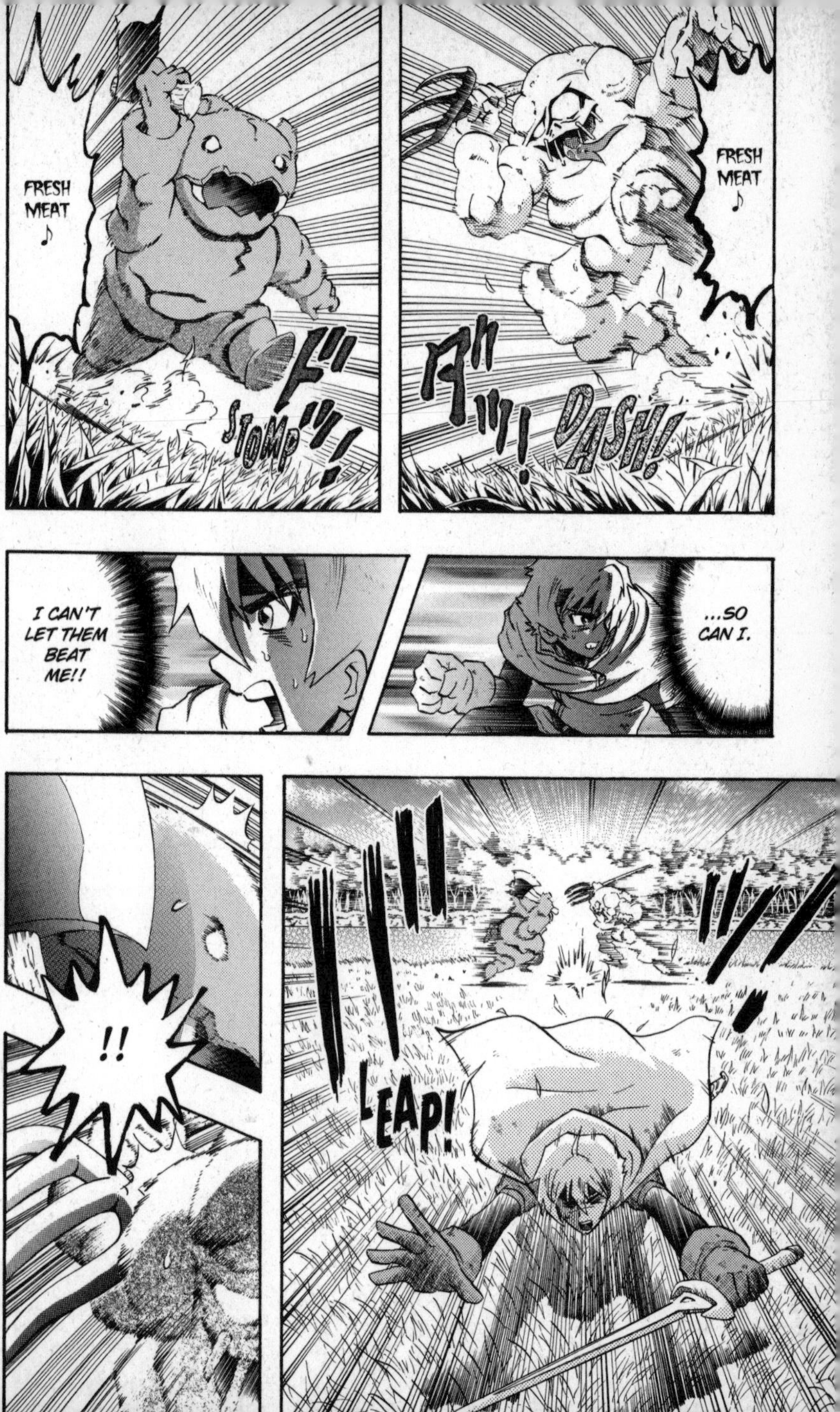
FRESH MEAT ♪
DASH!
FRESH MEAT ♪
STOMP
...SO CAN I.
I CAN'T LET THEM BEAT ME!!
LEAP!
!!

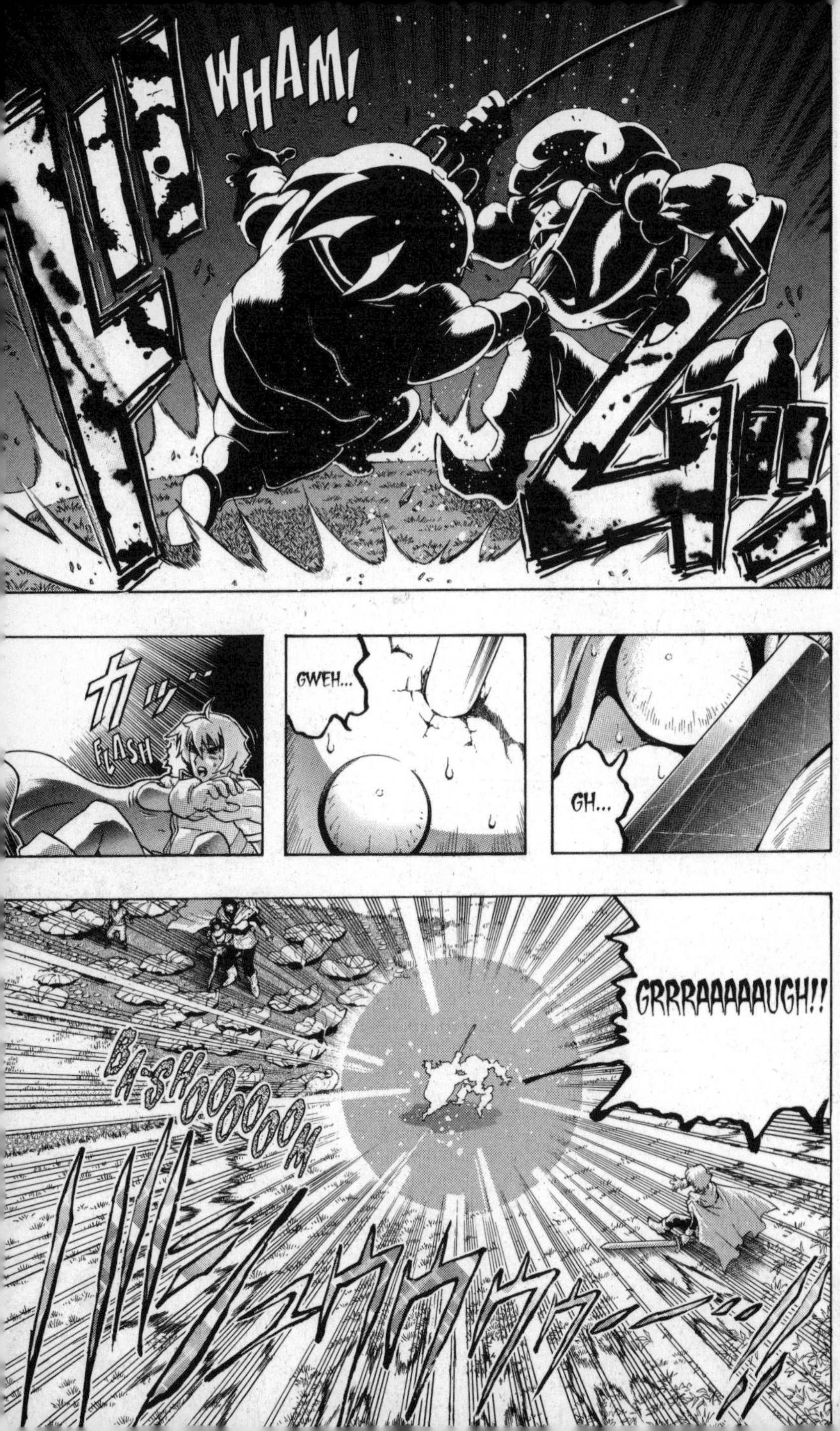
WHAM!
GH...
GWEH...
カッ
FLASH
GRRRAAAAAUGH!!
BA-SHOOOOOOM

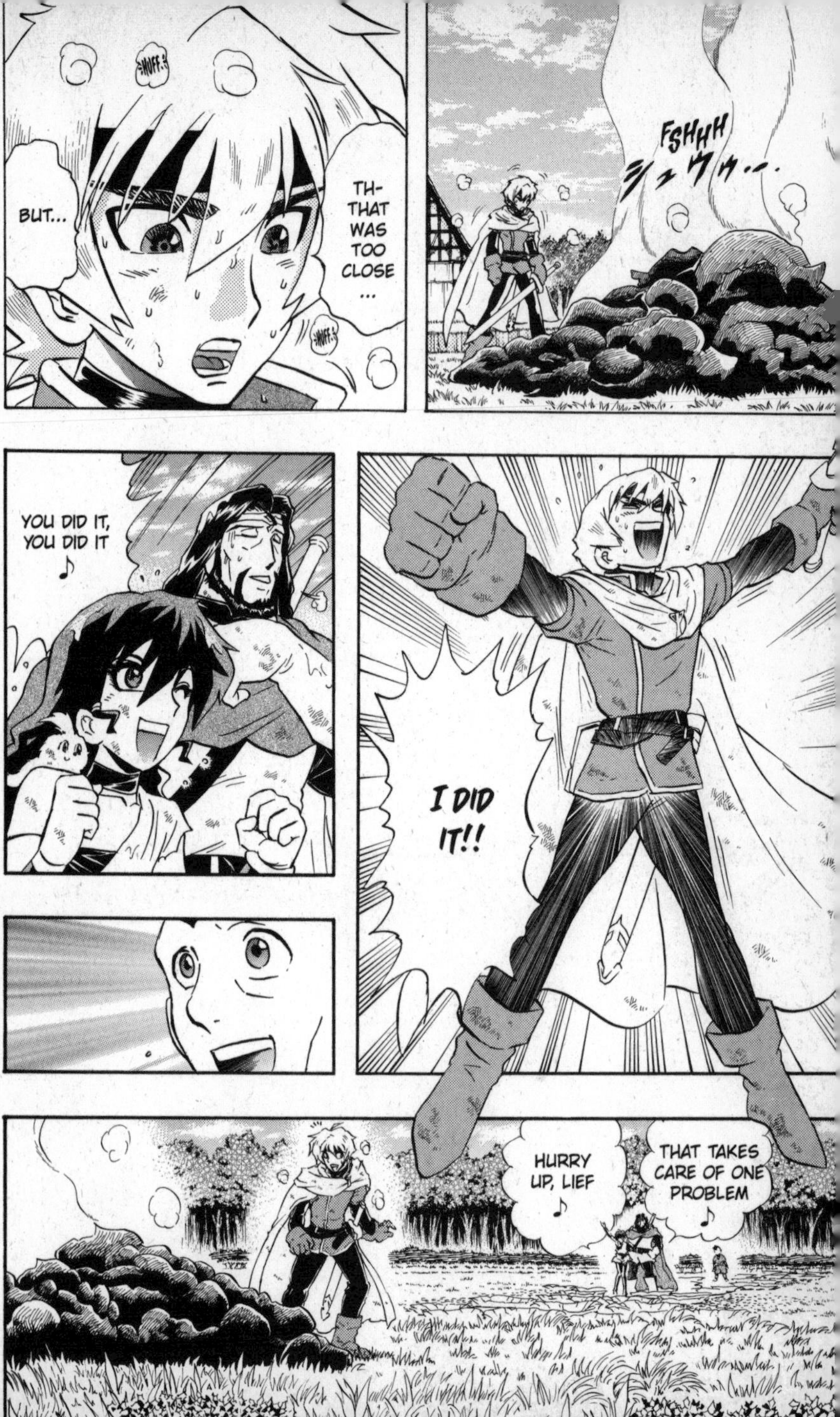
FSHHH
HUFF
TH-THAT WAS TOO CLOSE ...
BUT...
HUFF
I DID IT!!
YOU DID IT, YOU DID IT ♪
THAT TAKES CARE OF ONE PROBLEM ♪
HURRY UP, LIEF ♪

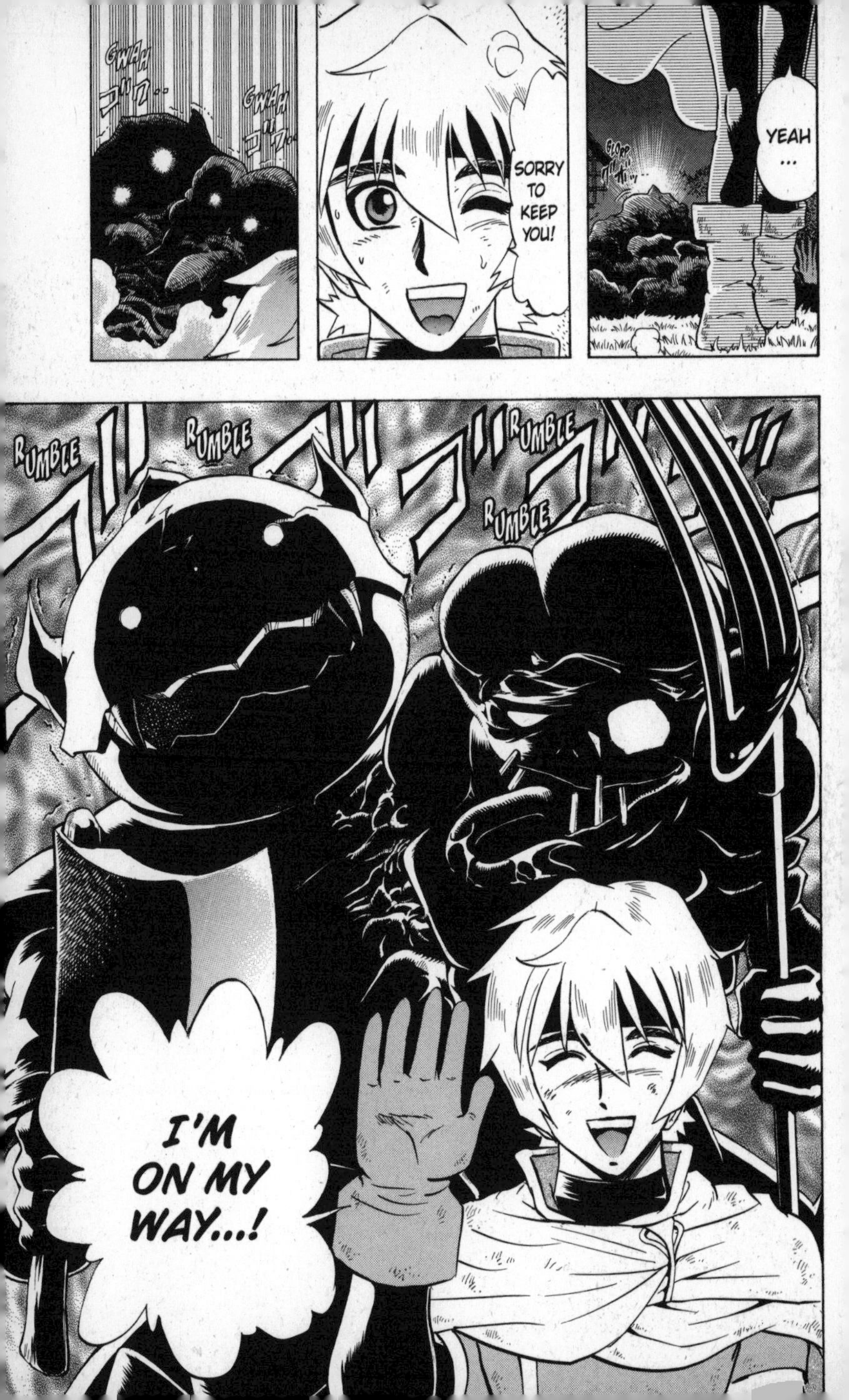
YEAH ...
GLORP
SORRY TO KEEP YOU!
GWAH
GWAH
RUMBLE
RUMBLE
RUMBLE
RUMBLE
I'M ON MY WAY...!

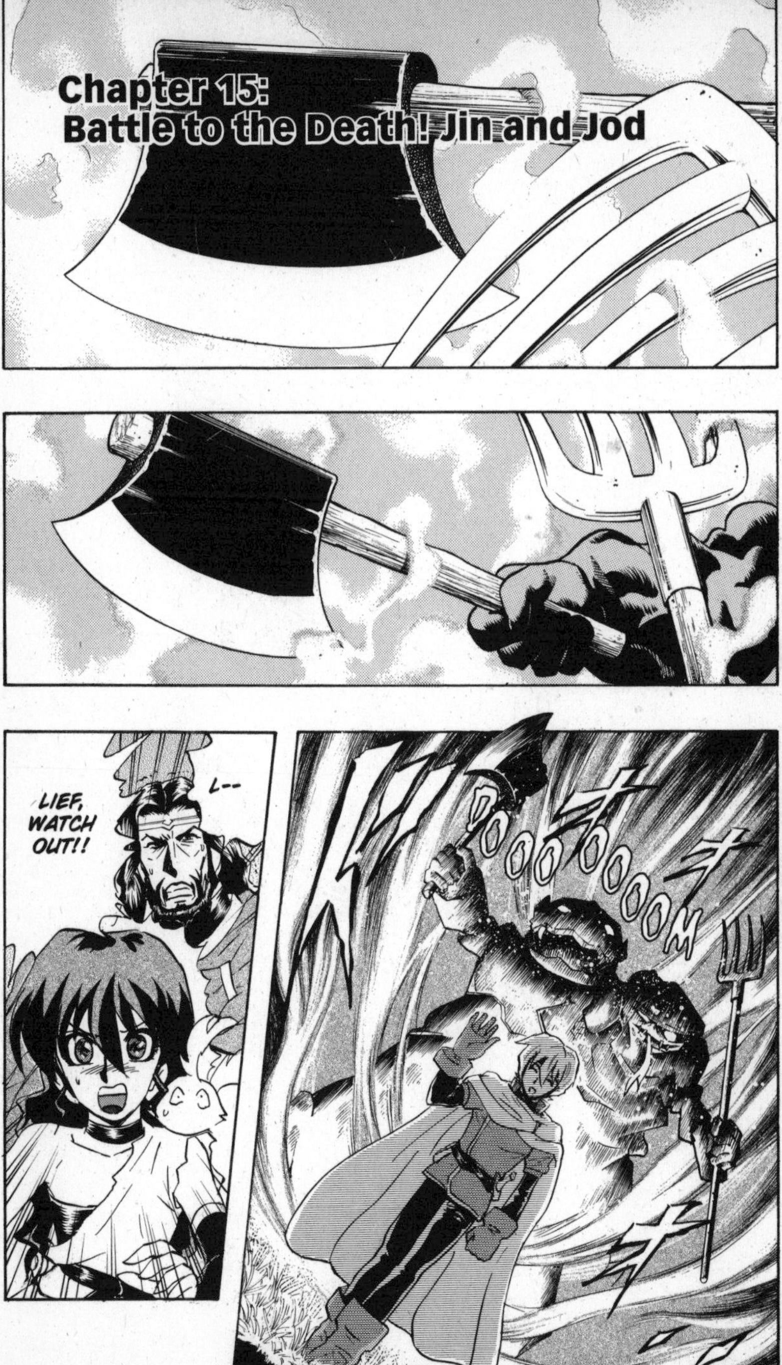
Chapter 15:
Battle to the Death! Jin and Jod
DOOOOOOOM
L--
LIEF, WATCH OUT!!

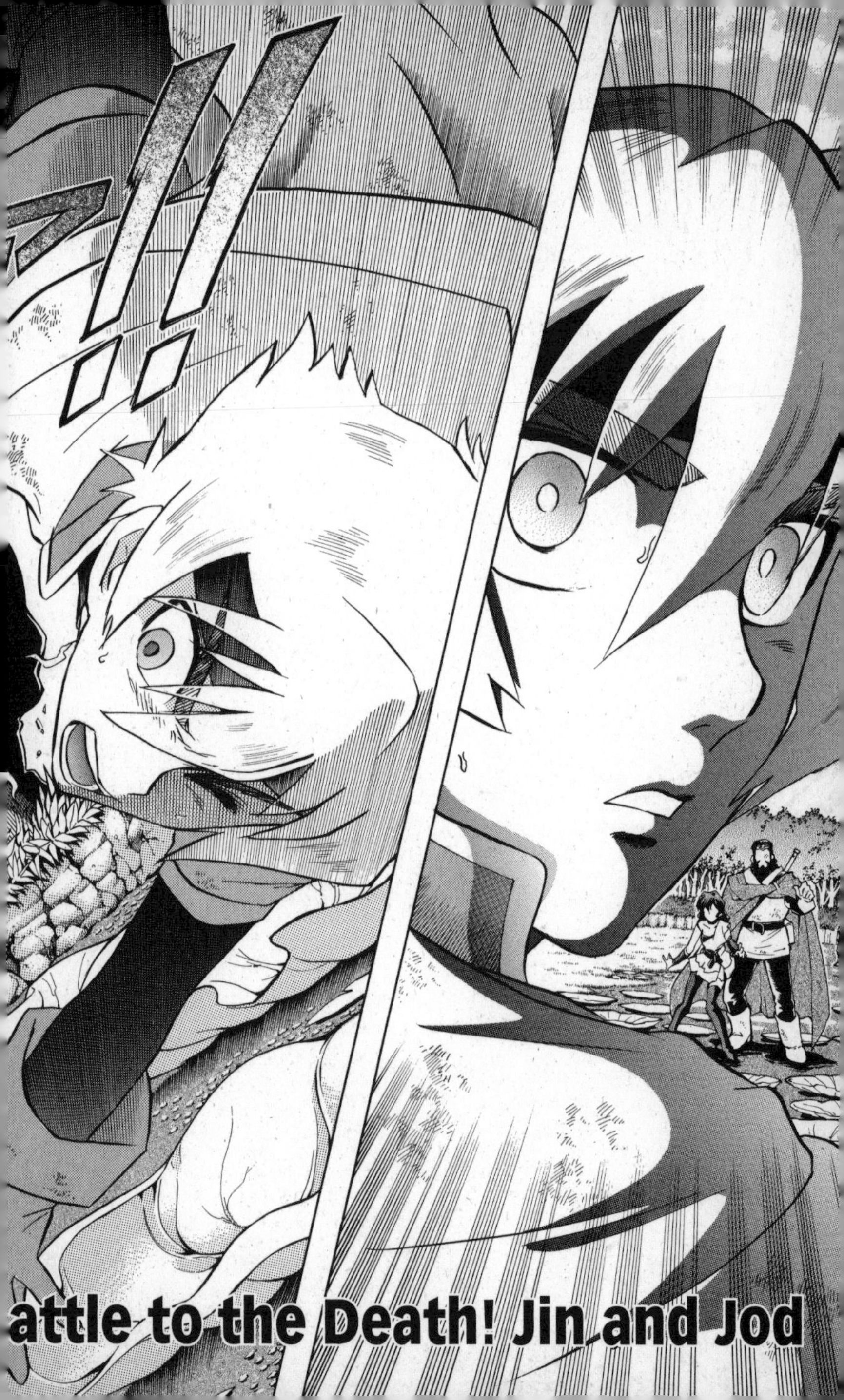
attle to the Death! Jin and Jod

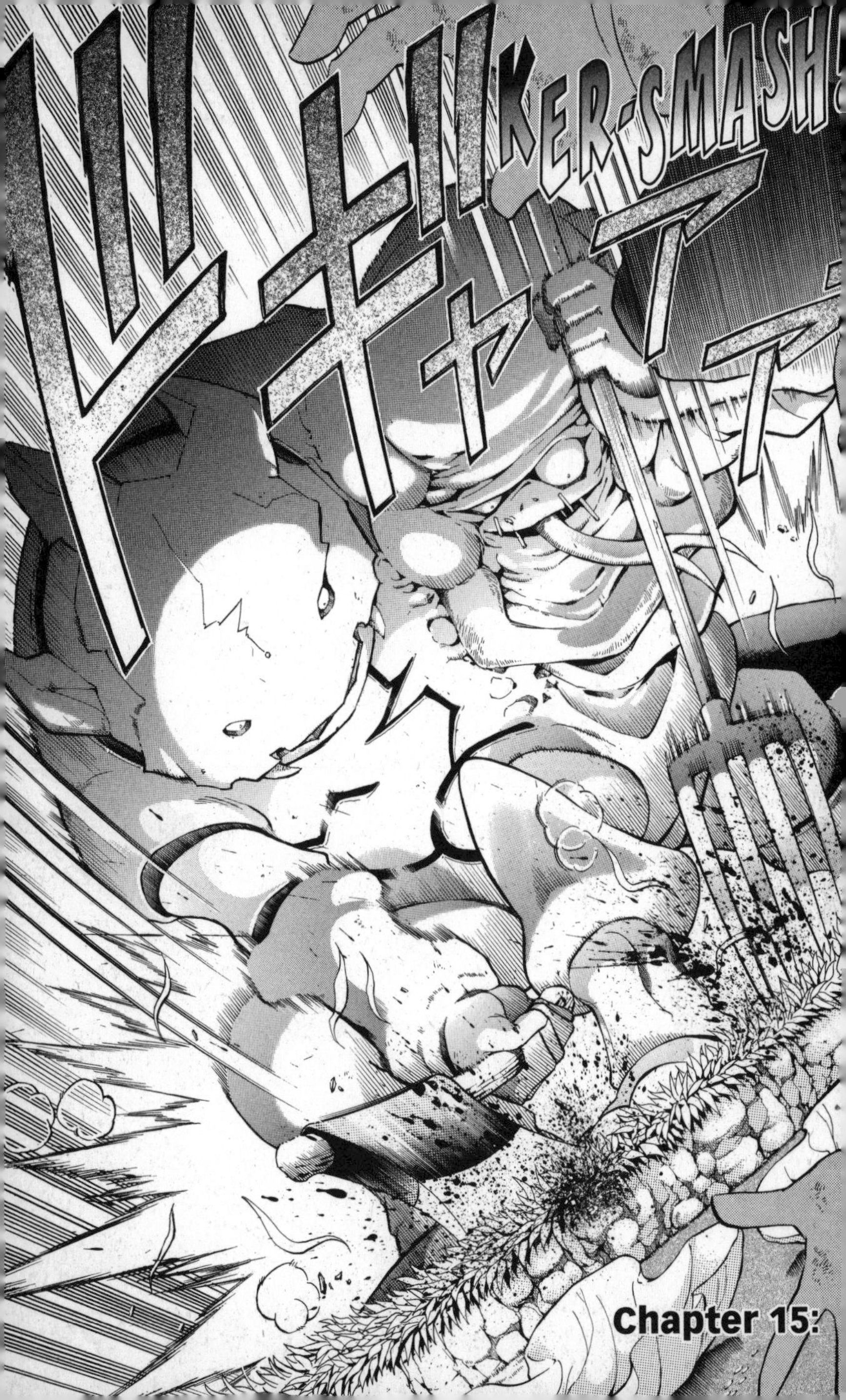
KER-SMASH!

Chapter 15:

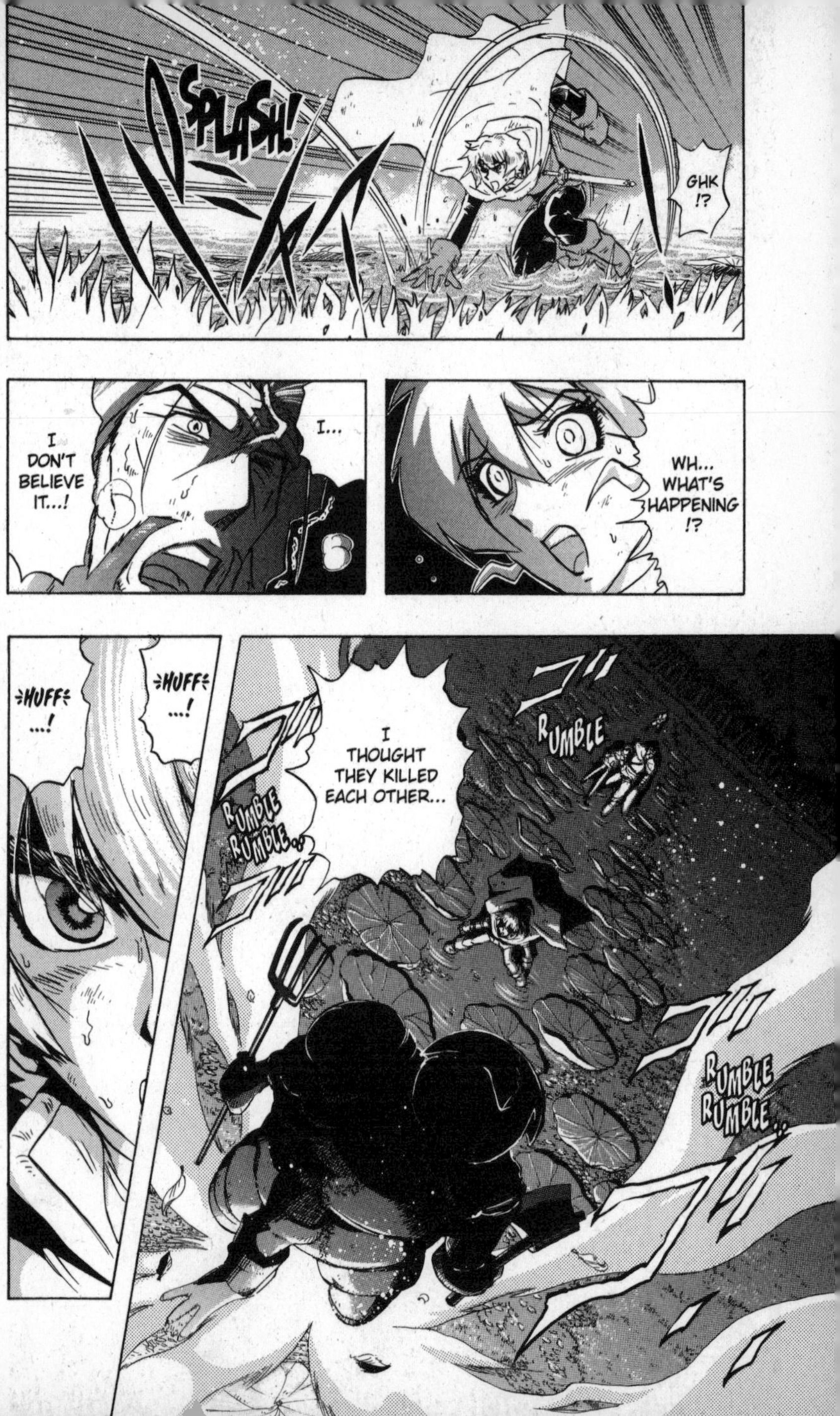
SPLASH!
GHK !?
WH... WHAT'S HAPPENING !?
I...
I DON'T BELIEVE IT...!
RUMBLE
I THOUGHT THEY KILLED EACH OTHER...
RUMBLE RUMBLE...
RUMBLE RUMBLE...
HUFF ...!
HUFF ...!

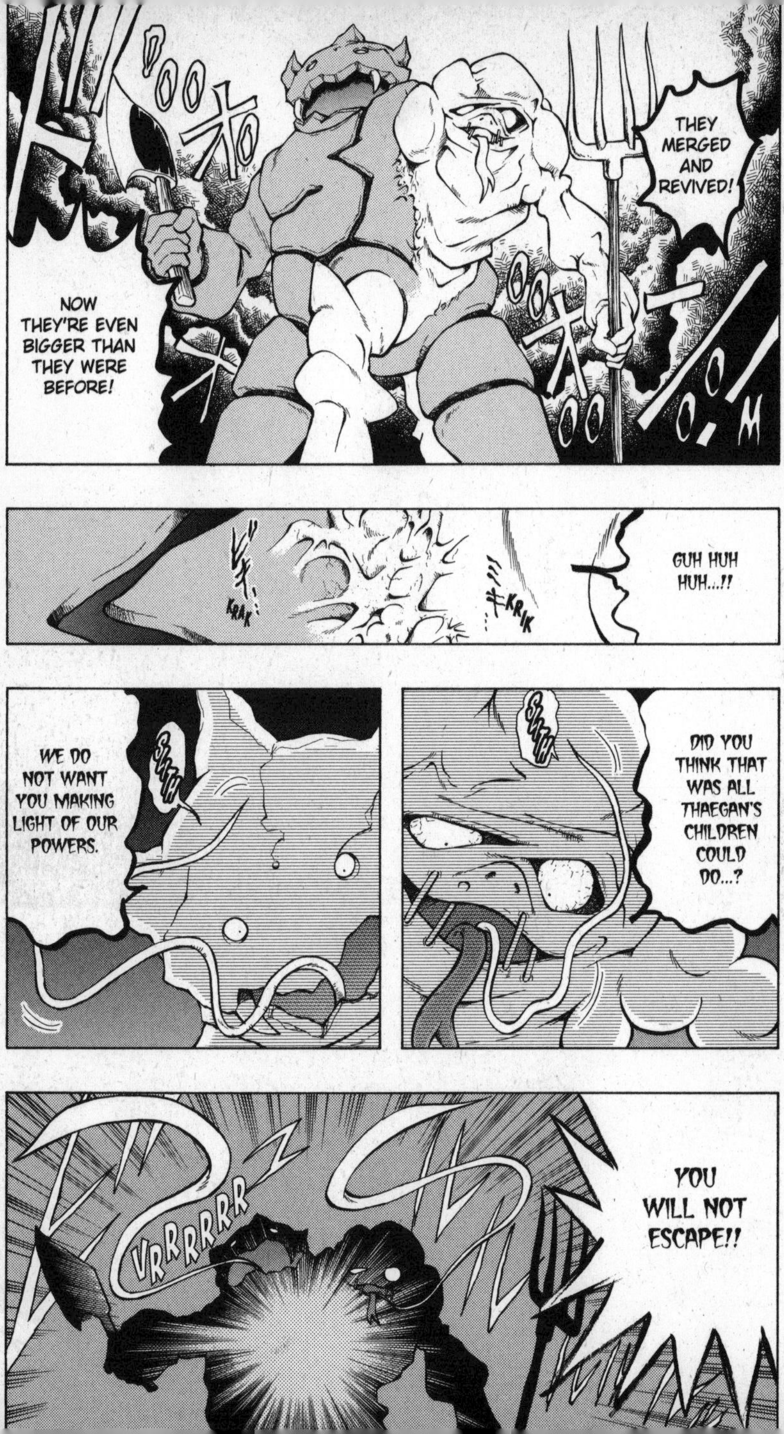
THEY MERGED AND REVIVED!
NOW THEY'RE EVEN BIGGER THAN THEY WERE BEFORE!
GUH HUH HUH...!!
KRIK
KRAK
DID YOU THINK THAT WAS ALL THAEGAN'S CHILDREN COULD DO...?
WE DO NOT WANT YOU MAKING LIGHT OF OUR POWERS.
YOU WILL NOT ESCAPE!!
VRRRRRR

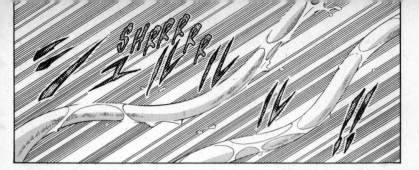

SHRRRR ILFR II

WHA --!?

FWAH...

FWIP!

DAAAZE...

ERGH ...!

THIS IS THE WORST POSSIBLE TIME FOR MY EYES TO GO DIM...!

LIEF!!

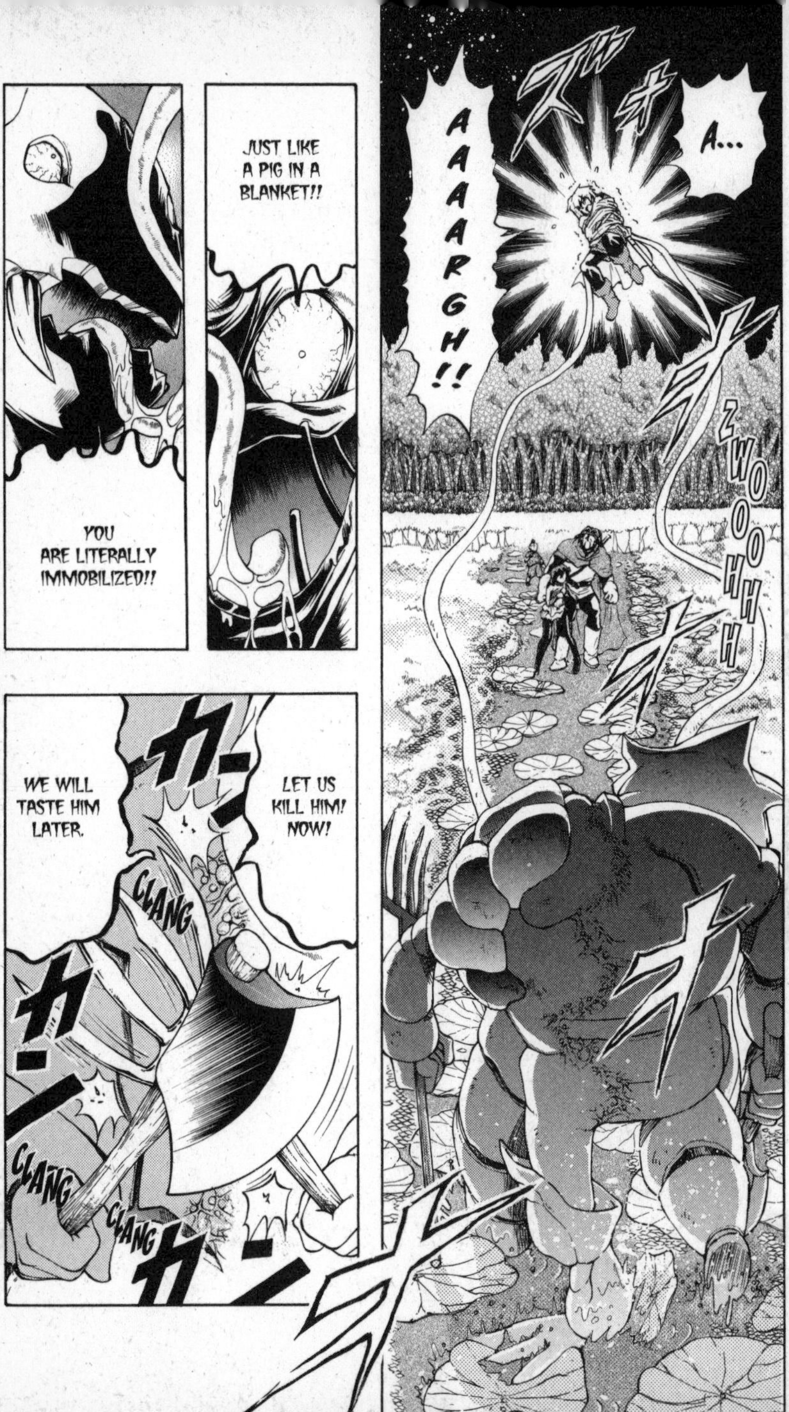
A...
AAAARGH!!
ZWOOOHHHH
JUST LIKE A PIG IN A BLANKET!!
YOU ARE LITERALLY IMMOBILIZED!!
LET US KILL HIM! NOW!
WE WILL TASTE HIM LATER.
CLANG
CLANG
CLANG

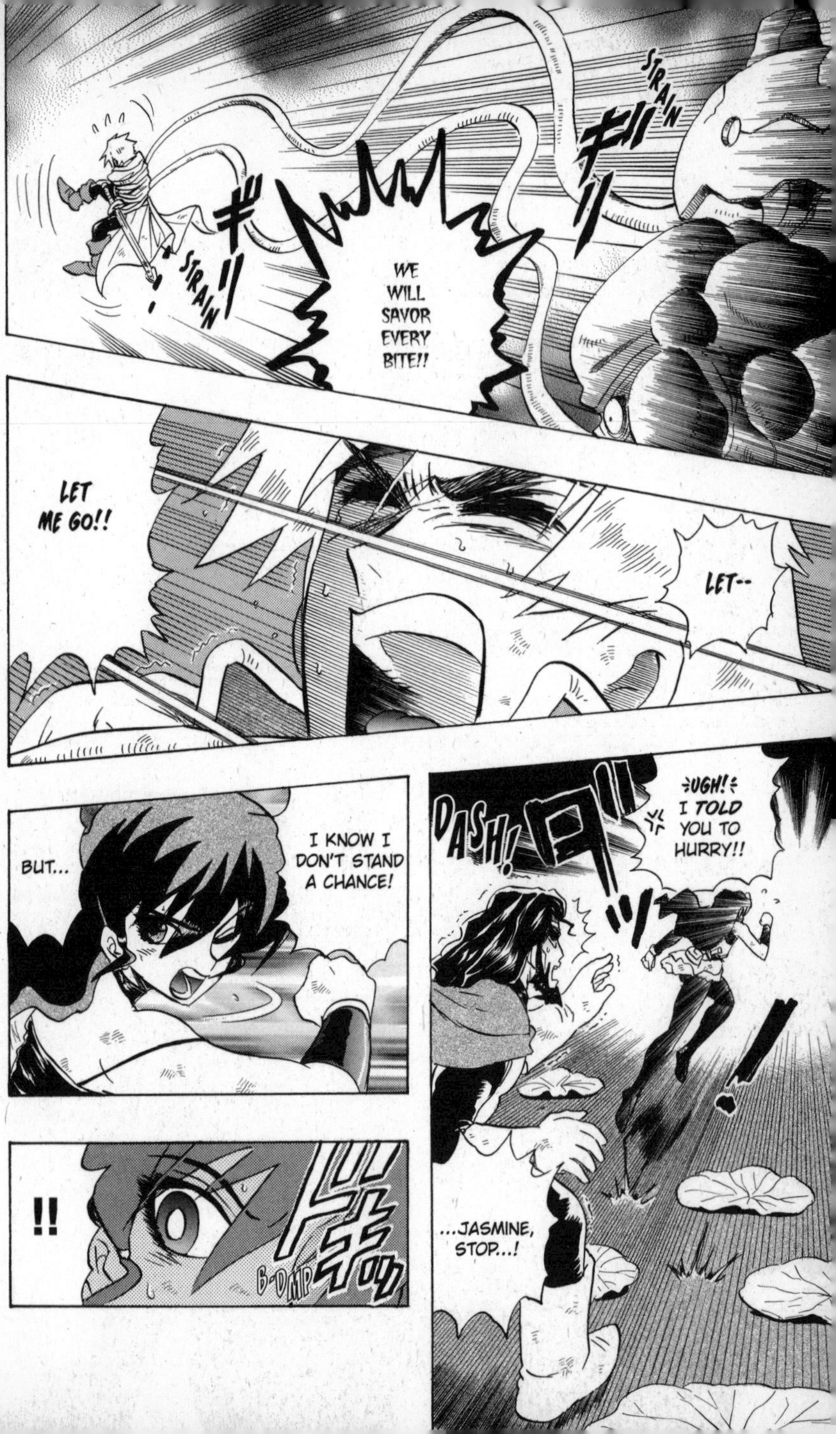
STRAIN
STRAIN
WE WILL SAVOR EVERY BITE!!
LET--
LET ME GO!!
UGH! I TOLD YOU TO HURRY!!
DASH!
...JASMINE, STOP...!
I KNOW I DON'T STAND A CHANCE!
BUT...
!!
B-DMP

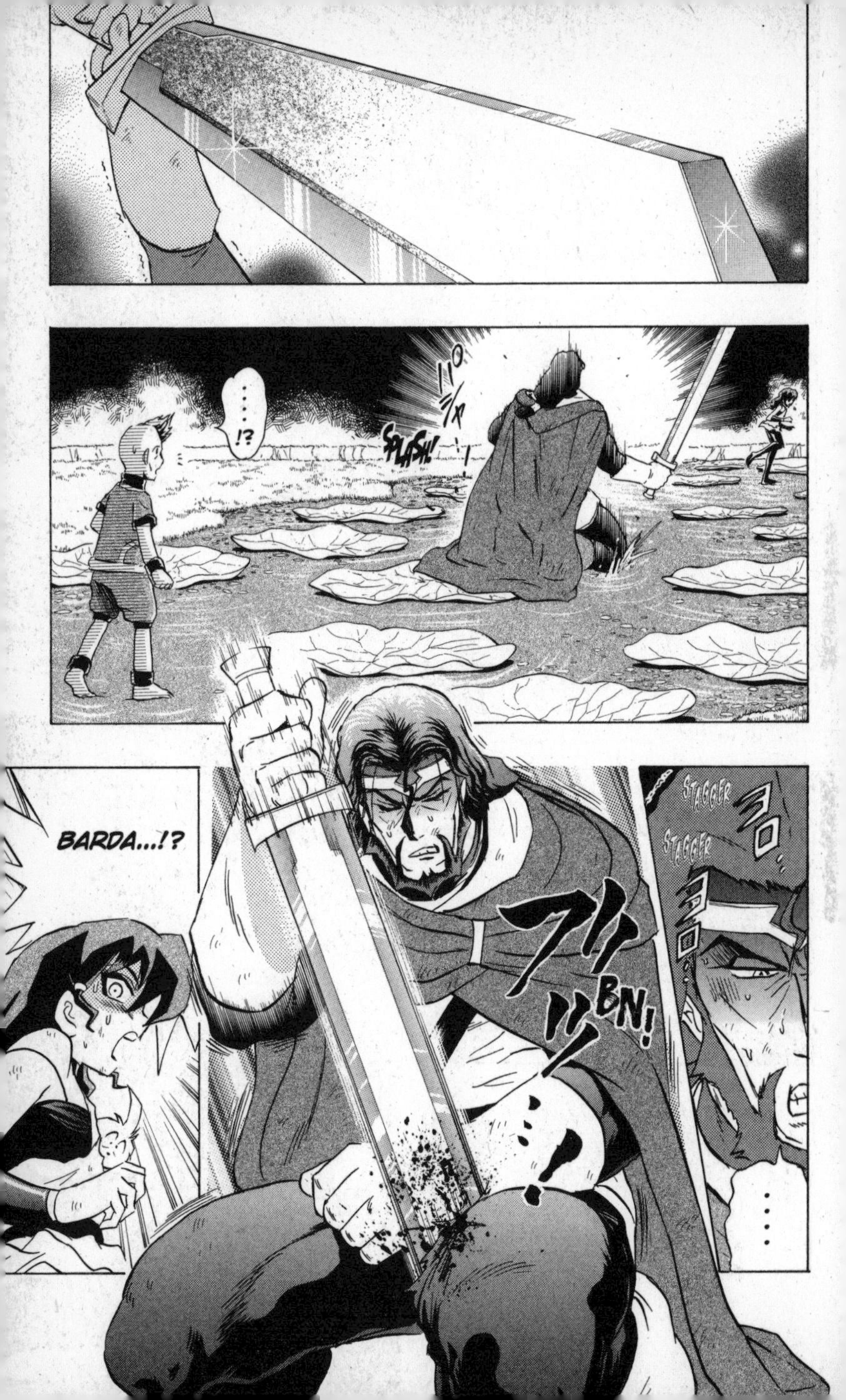

パシャ
SPLASH!
...!?
ヨロ
STAGGER
ヨロ
STAGGER
....
ブン
BN!
...!
BARDA...!?

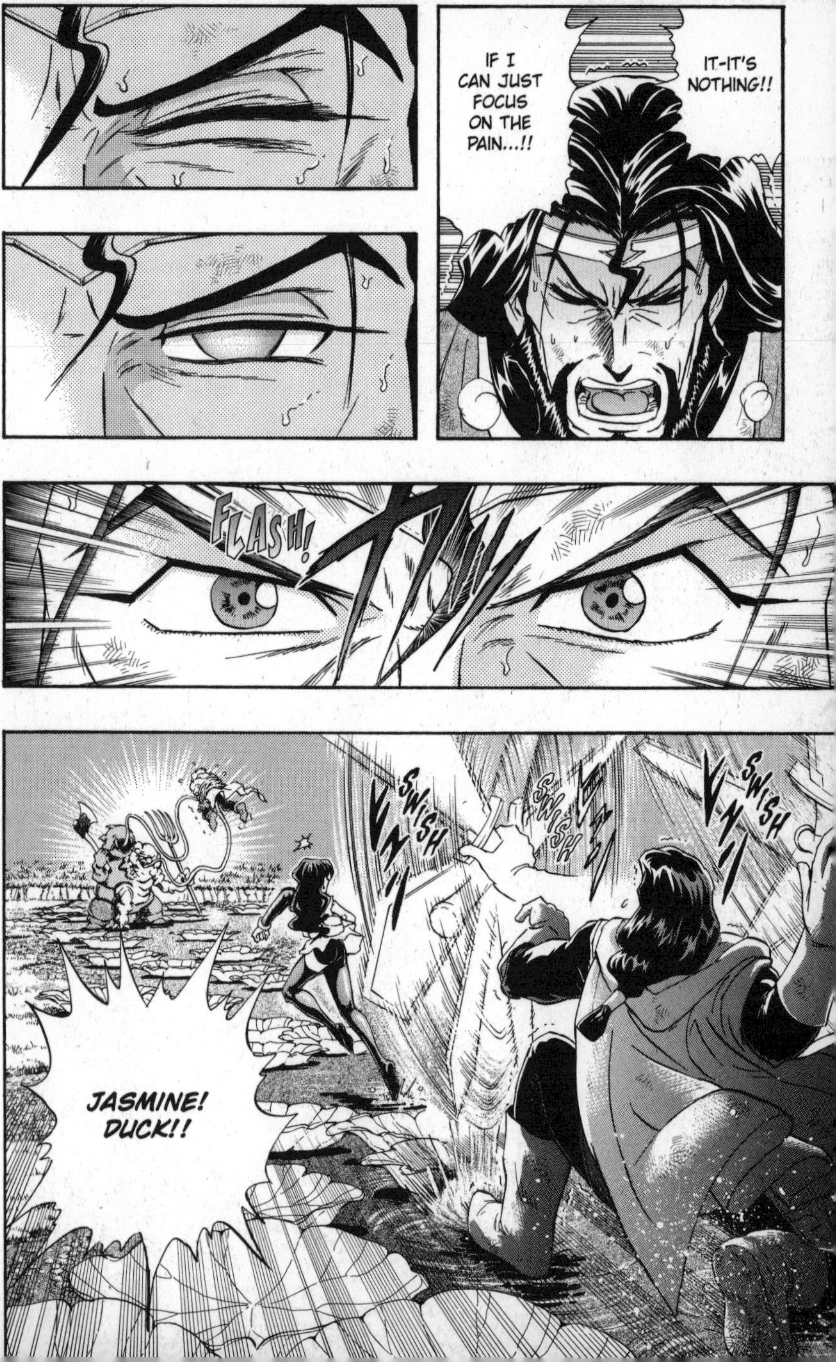
IT-IT'S NOTHING!!
IF I CAN JUST FOCUS ON THE PAIN...!!
FLASH!
SWISH
SWISH
SWISH
JASMINE! DUCK!!

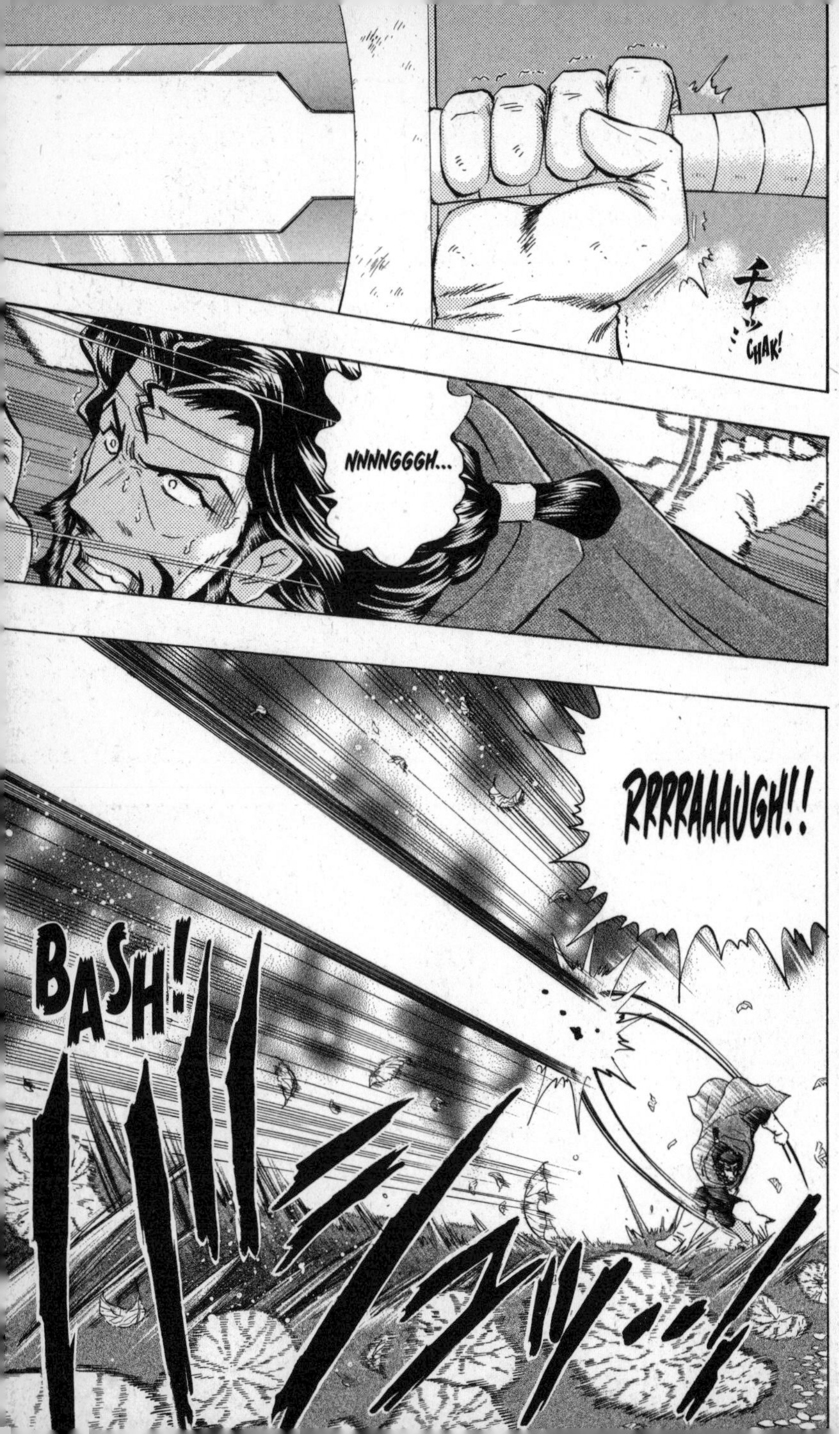
CHAK!
NNNNGGGH...
RRRRAAAUGH!!
BASH!!

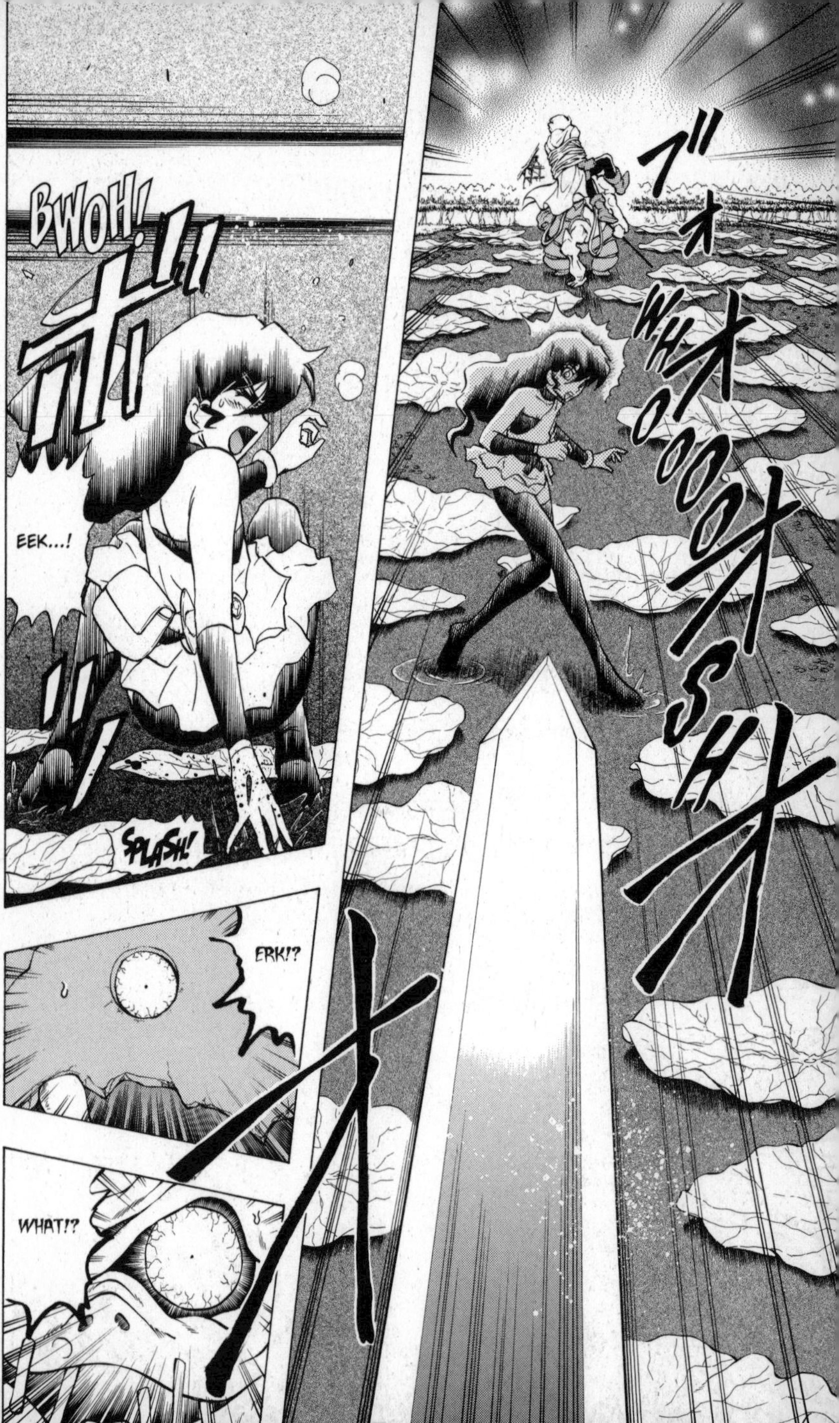
WHOOOOSH
BWOH!
EEK...!
SPLASH!
ERK!?
WHAT!?

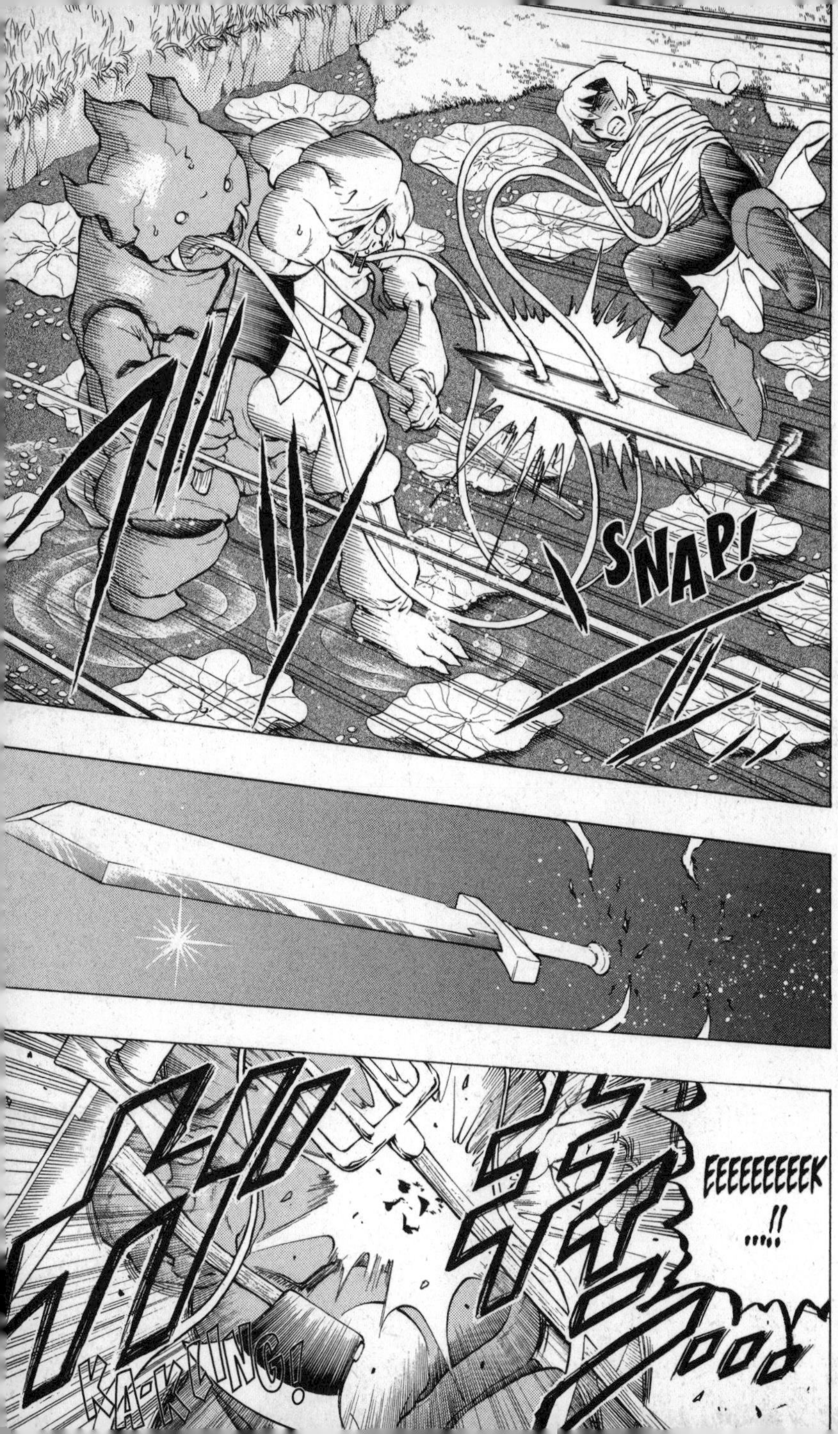
SNAP!
EEEEEEEEK
...!!
KA-KLING!

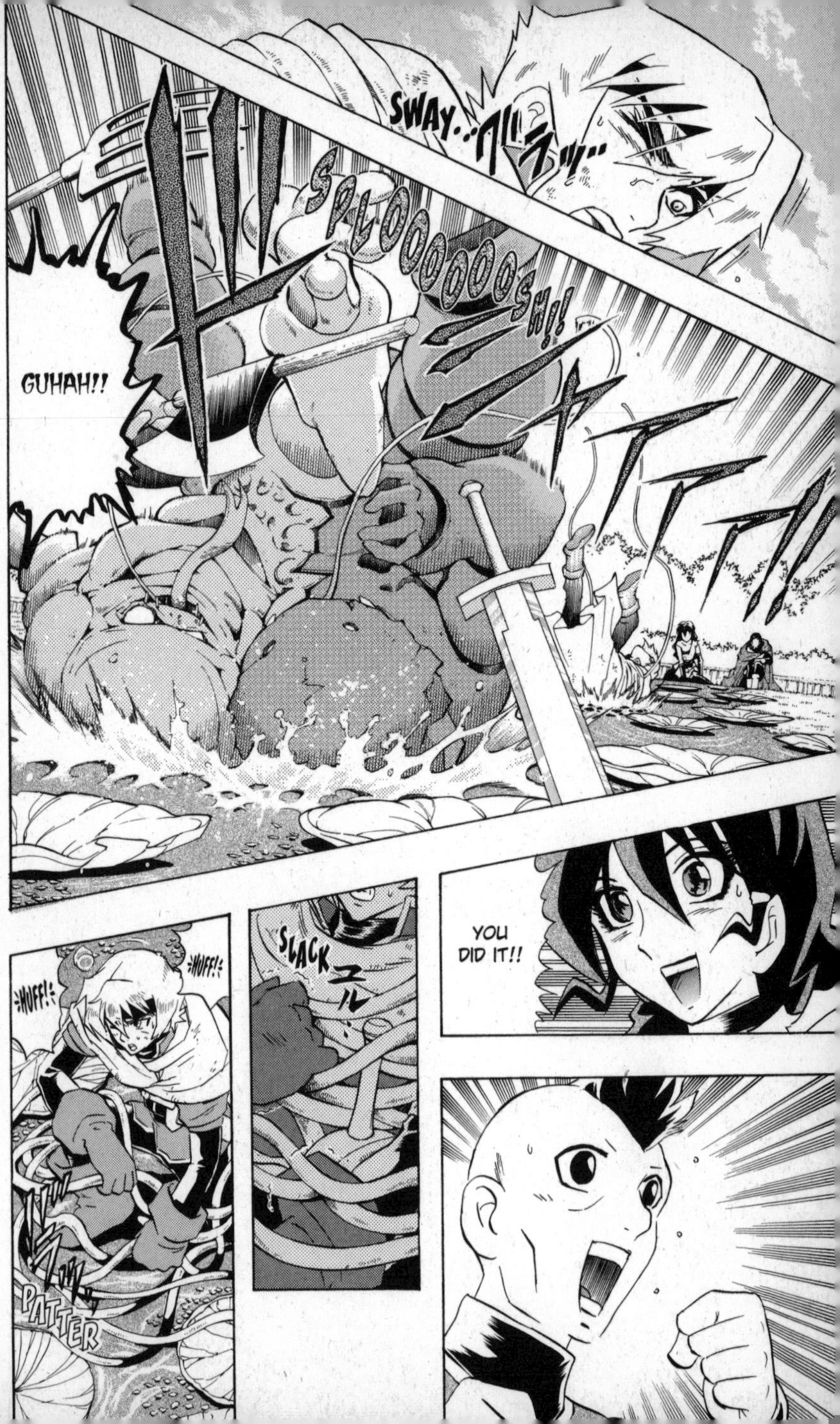
SWAY...
SPLOOOOOOOSH!!
GUHAH!!
YOU DID IT!!
SLACK
HUFF!
HUFF!
PATTER

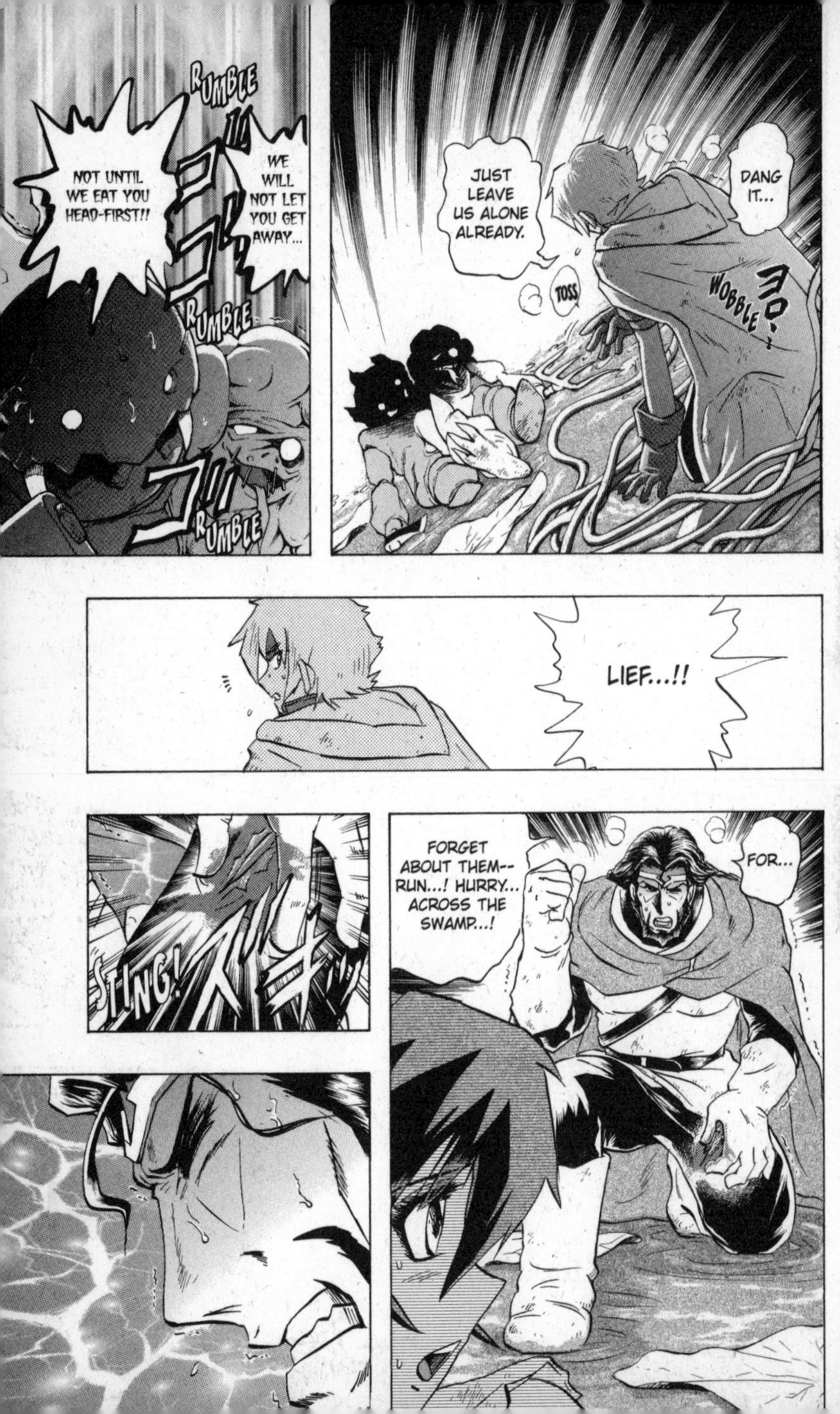
DANG IT...
JUST LEAVE US ALONE ALREADY.
TOSS
WOBBLE
RUMBLE
WE WILL NOT LET YOU GET AWAY...
NOT UNTIL WE EAT YOU HEAD-FIRST!!
RUMBLE
RUMBLE
LIEF...!!
FOR...
FORGET ABOUT THEM-- RUN...! HURRY... ACROSS THE SWAMP...!
STING!

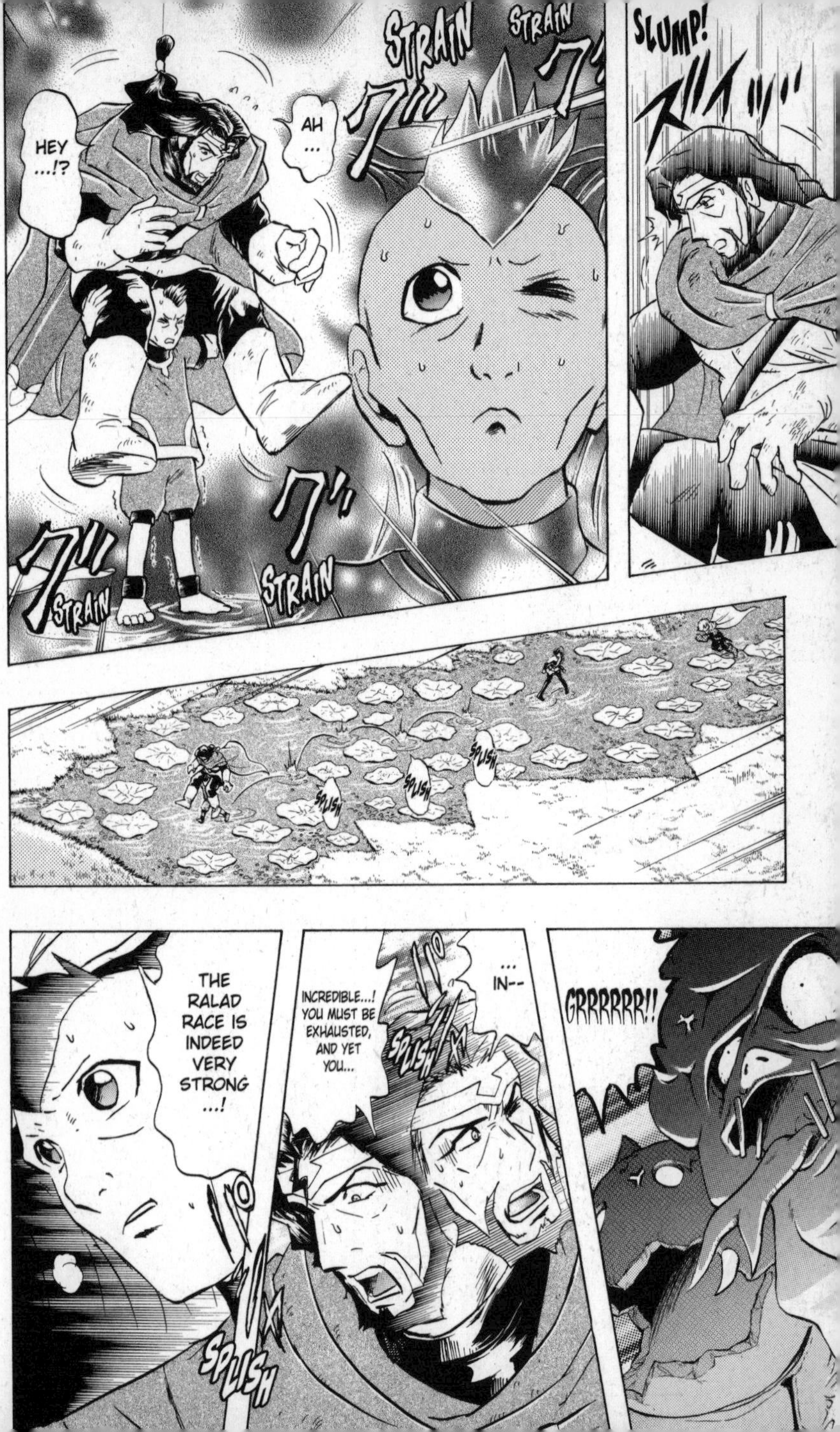
SLUMP!
STRAIN
STRAIN
AH ...
HEY ...!?
STRAIN
STRAIN
SPLISH
SPLISH
SPLISH
GRRRRRR!!
... IN--
INCREDIBLE...! YOU MUST BE EXHAUSTED, AND YET YOU...
SPLISH
THE RALAD RACE IS INDEED VERY STRONG ...!
SPLISH

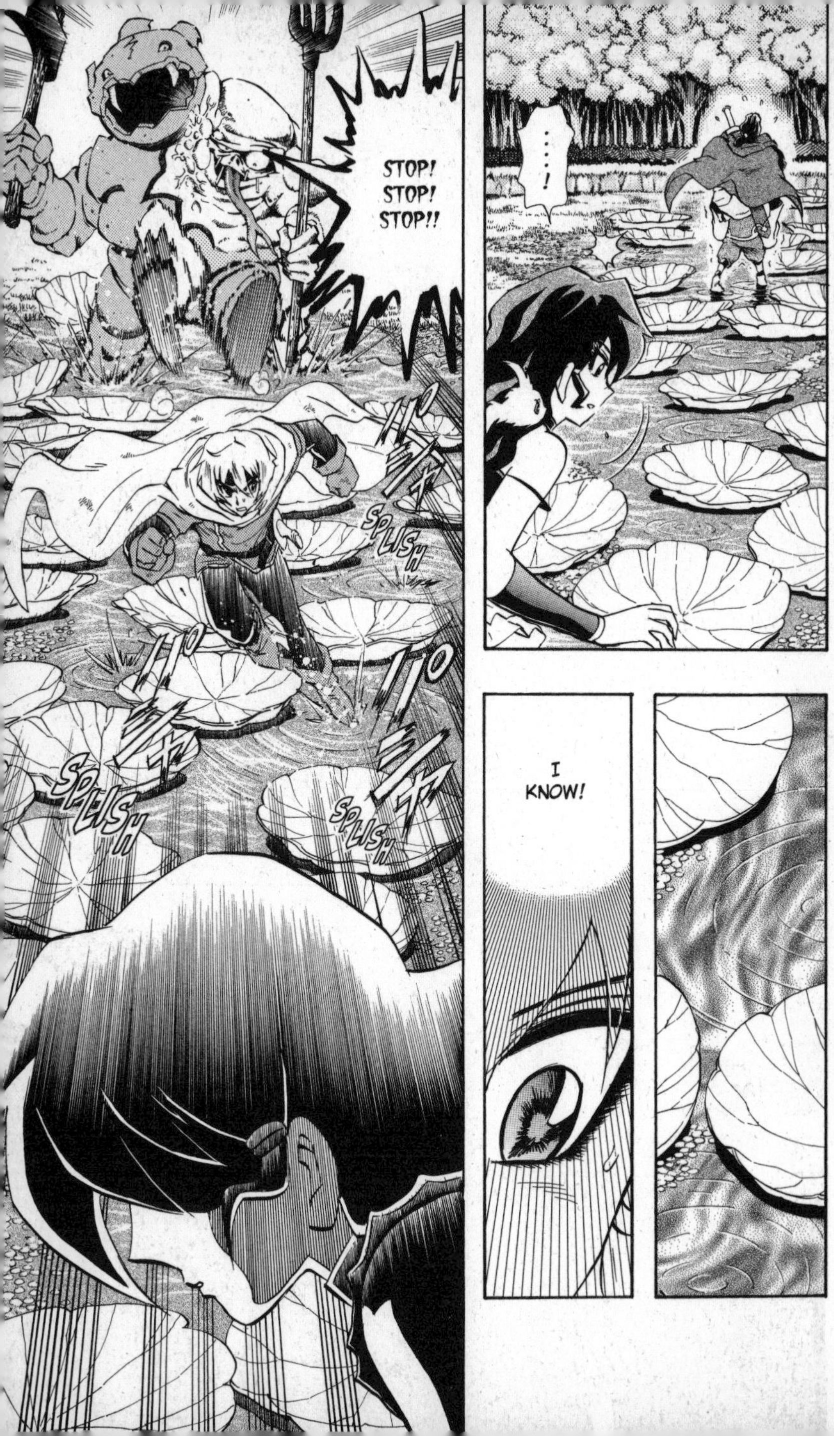

.....!
I KNOW!
STOP! STOP! STOP!!
パシャ
SPLISH
パシャ
SPLISH
パシャ
SPLISH

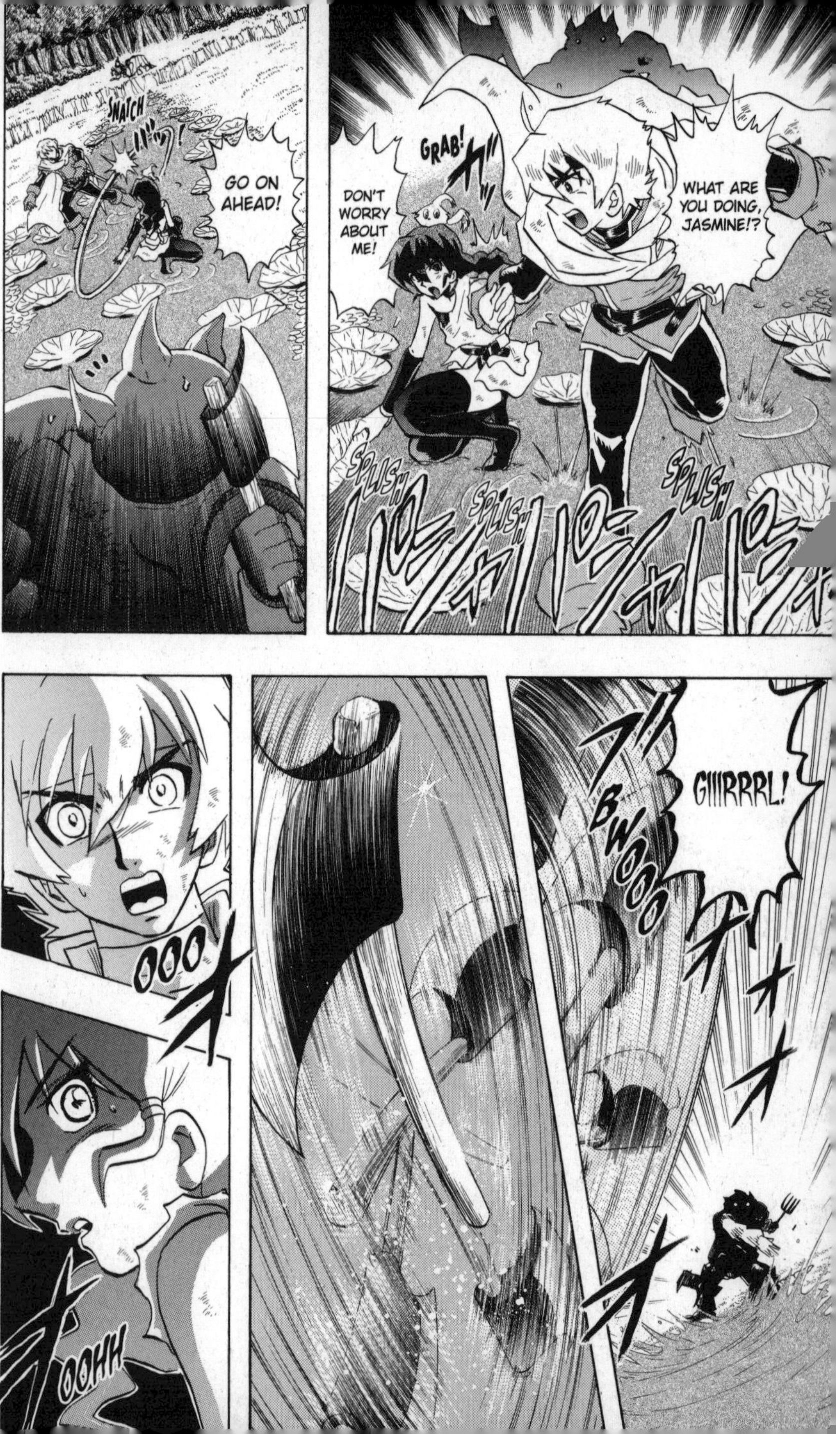
WHAT ARE YOU DOING, JASMINE!?
GRAB!
DON'T WORRY ABOUT ME!
SPLISH
SPLISH
SPLISH
SNATCH
GO ON AHEAD!
GIIIRRRL!
BWOOOO
OOO
OOHH

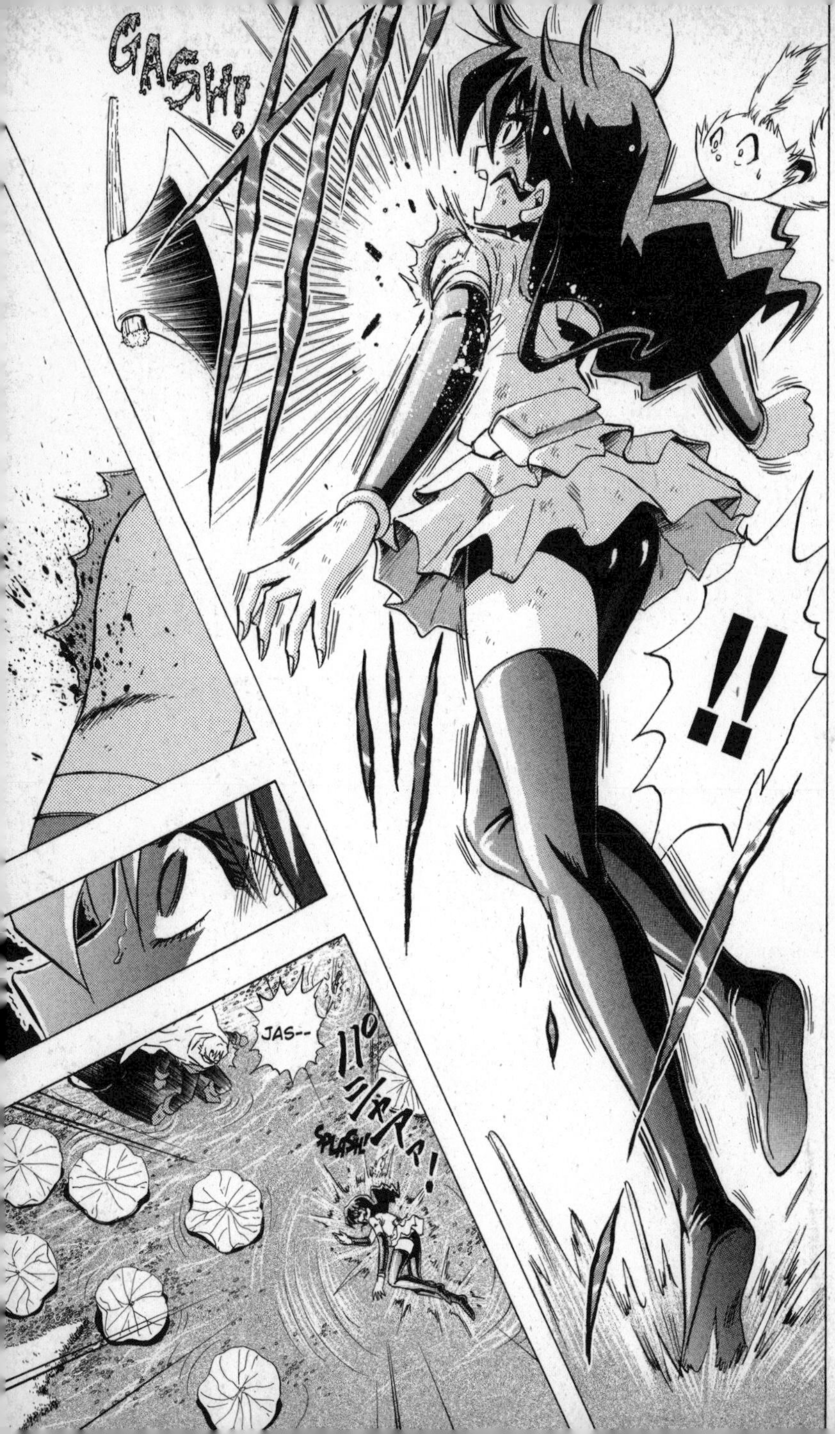
GASH!
!!
JAS--
パシャアァ!
SPLASH!

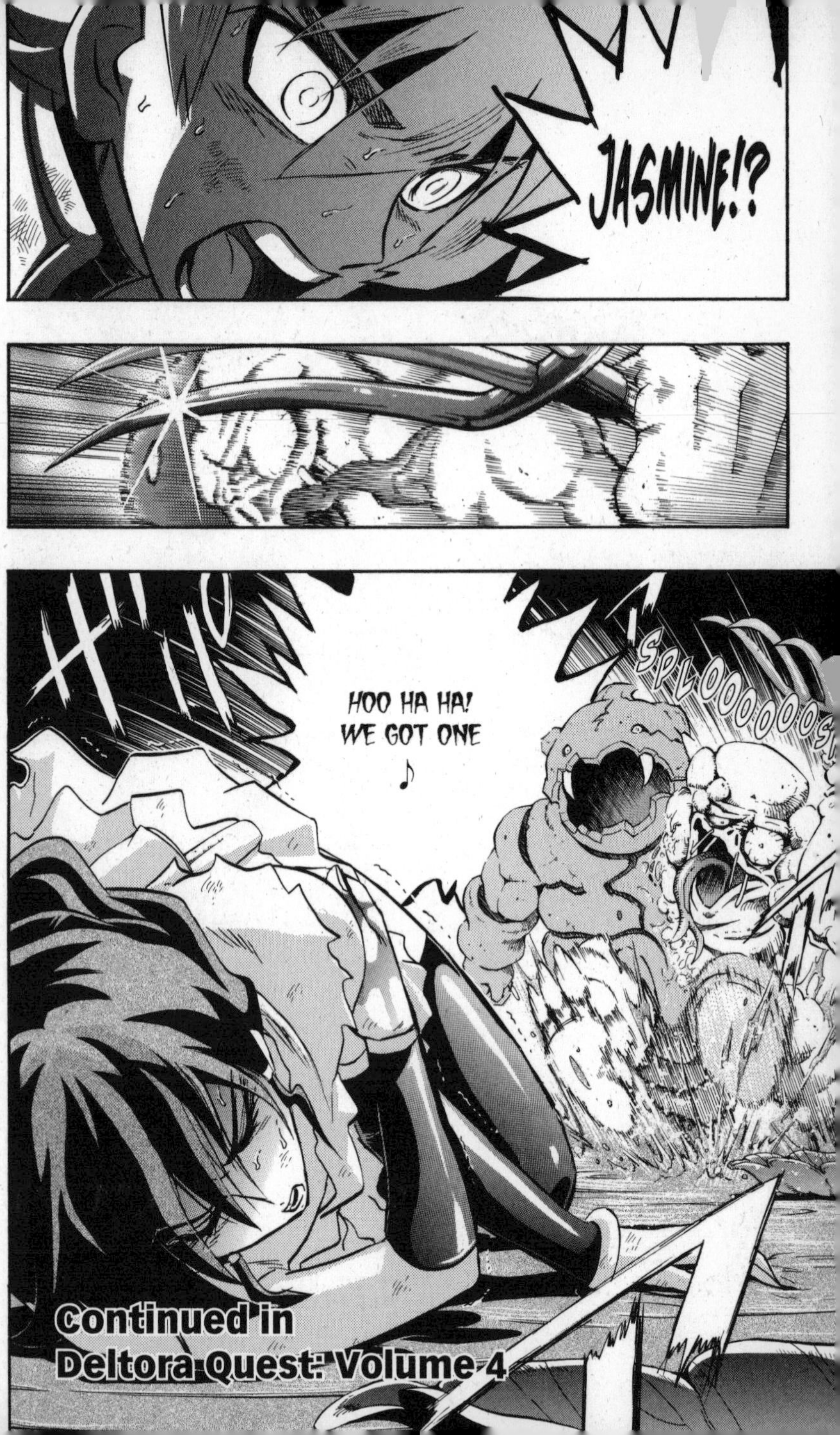
JASMINE!?
HOO HA HA! WE GOT ONE ♪
SPLOOOOOOS
Continued in Deltora Quest: Volume 4

BONUS (TOPAZ)

WE GOT THE TOPAZ!!
IT WILL CLEAR OUR MINDS SO WE'LL KNOW WHEN BAD GUYS ARE LYING TO US!!
I'M THE STRONGEST MAN IN DEL!
ぴかーーっ
FLASH!
I AM GORGEOUS, AREN'T I? ♡
びかびかびかーっ
FLASH! FLASH!
REMEMBER OUR QUEST!!

~AFTERWORD~

Thank you for buying Deltora Quest volume 3!! Wow, volume three already! And the anime starts early in 2007, so I'd better work hard if I don't want to be outdone♪

Please let me know what you think, everyone!

See you again in volume four♪

Makoto Niwano

Translation Notes

Japanese is a tricky language for most Westerners, and translation is often more art than science. For your edification and reading pleasure, here are notes on some of the places where we could have gone in a different direction with our translation of the work, or where a Japanese cultural reference is used.

No soup for you!, page 74

The guard here is doing a joke made popular by the Japanese comedian Junichi Kōmoto. In impersonating a character from the Jackie Chan movie *Drunken Master*, he would pose as shown, and add the line, "*No tanmen for you!*" (*Tanmen* is a kind of ramen.) To make the joke more easily recognizable as a joke, we changed it to the famous Soup Nazi (*Seinfeld*) line, "No soup for you!"

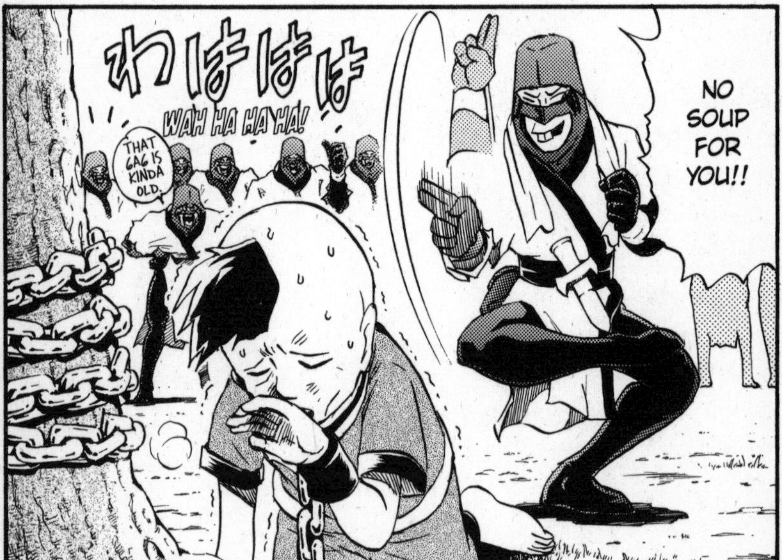
NO SOUP FOR YOU!!
わははは
WAH HA HA HA!
THAT GAG IS KINDA OLD.

PREVIEW OF *DELTORA QUEST 4*

We're pleased to present you a preview from *Deltora Quest 4*. Please check our website (www.kodanshacomics.com) to see when this volume will be available in English. For now you'll have to make do with Japanese!

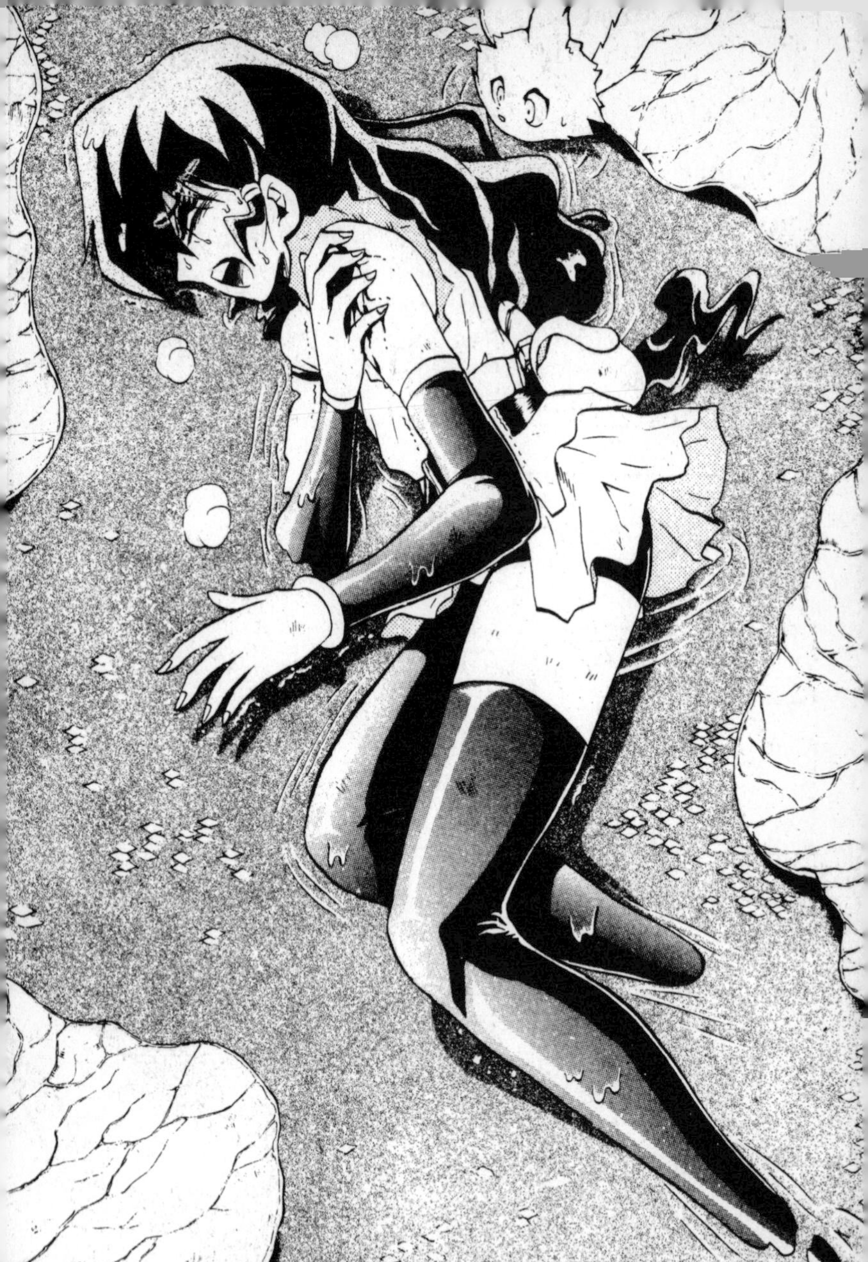

第16話　戦いの終焉

や‥‥

串刺(くしざ)し
だあ
娘(むすめ)〜〜!!

――!!
やめろぉ

カア!!

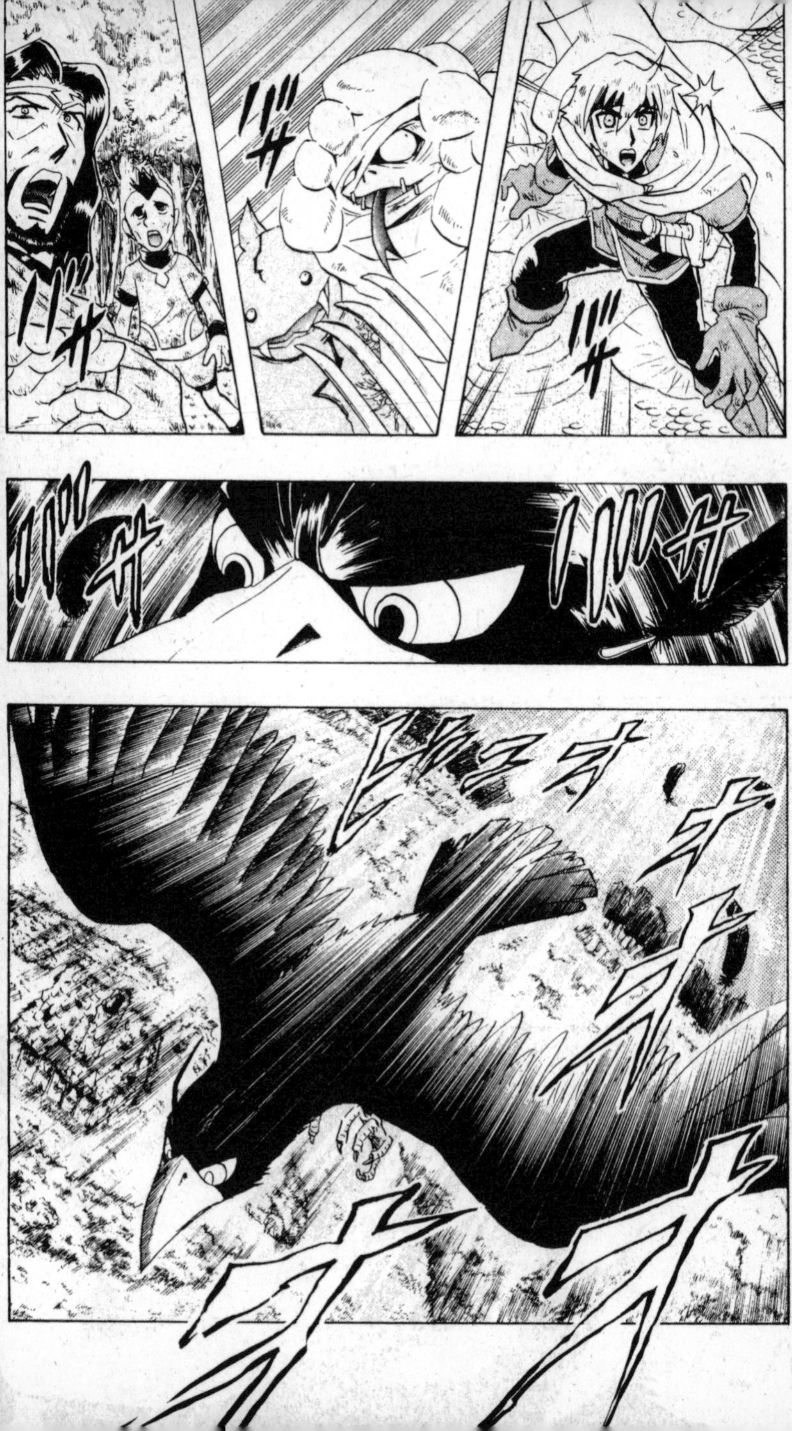

ザ
ザ
ザ
バサ
バサ
ビュオオオオオ

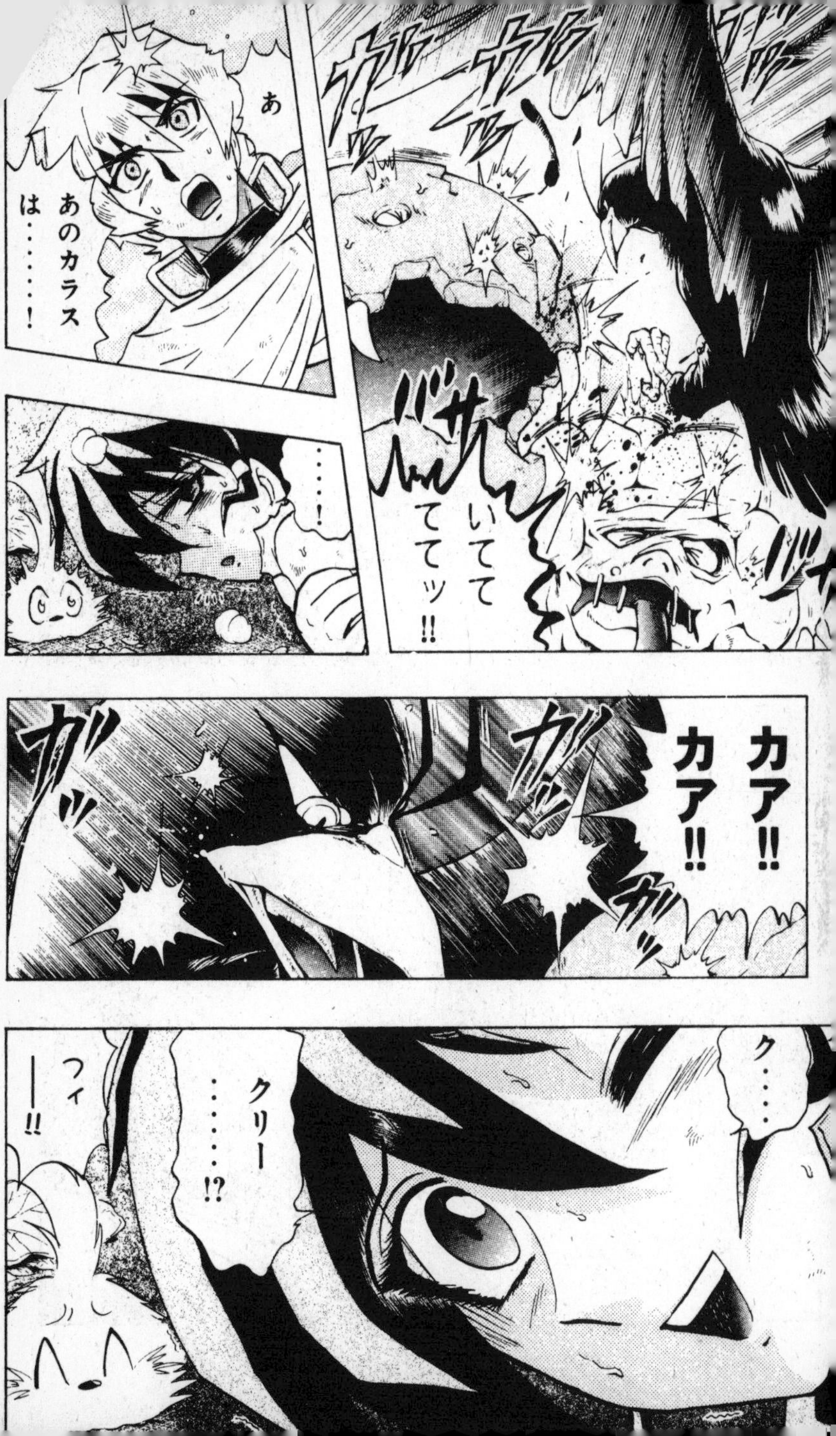

バサ
いててててッ!!
あ
あのカラスは……!
……!
カア!!
カア!!
ガッ
ク……
クリー……!?
フィ――!!

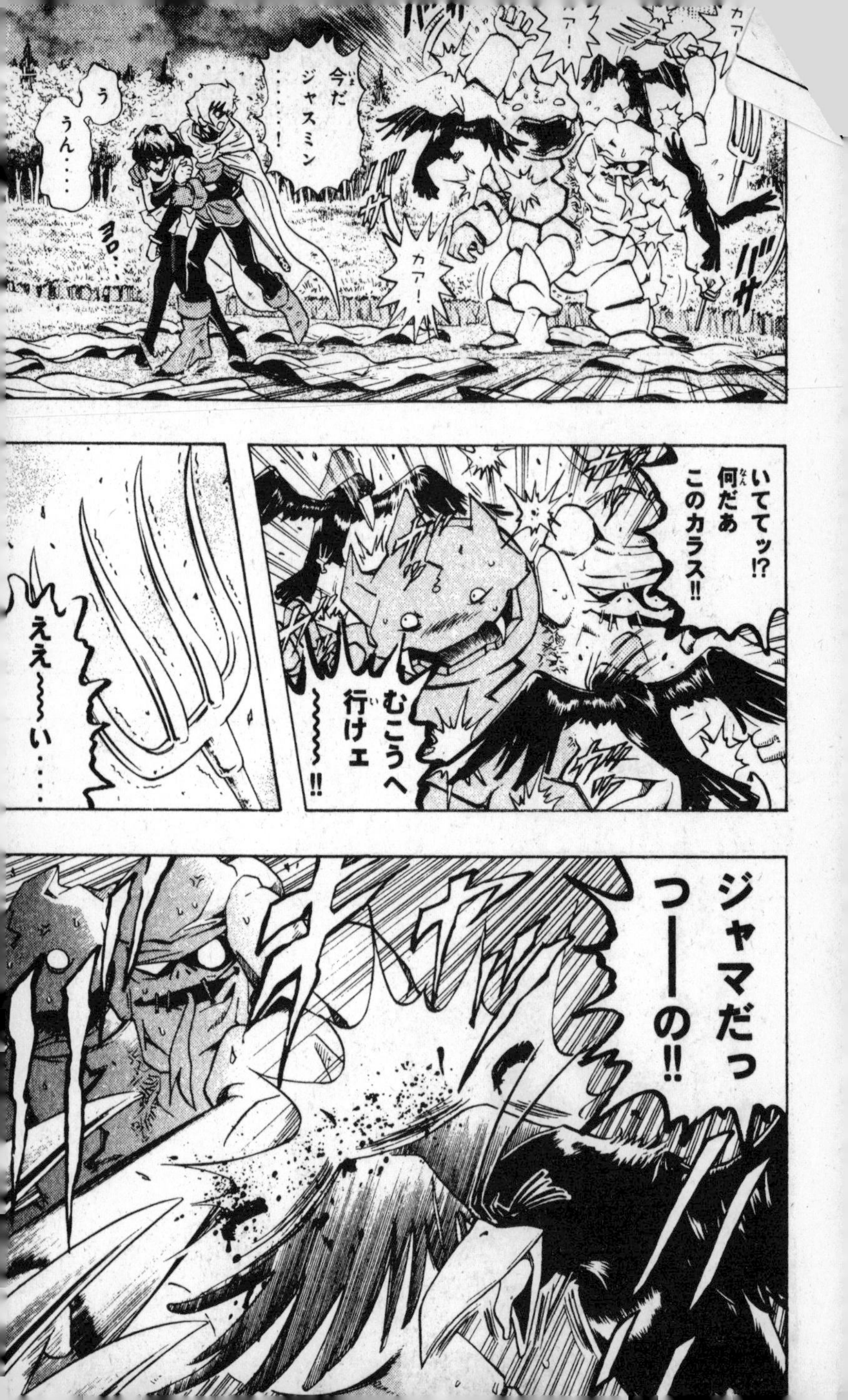
カアー!
カアー!
バサ
今だ
ジャスミン
……!
うん……
ヨロ…
カアー!
いててッ!?
何だあ
このカラス!!
むこうへ
行けエ~~~!!
ええ~~い……
ジャマだっ
つーの!!

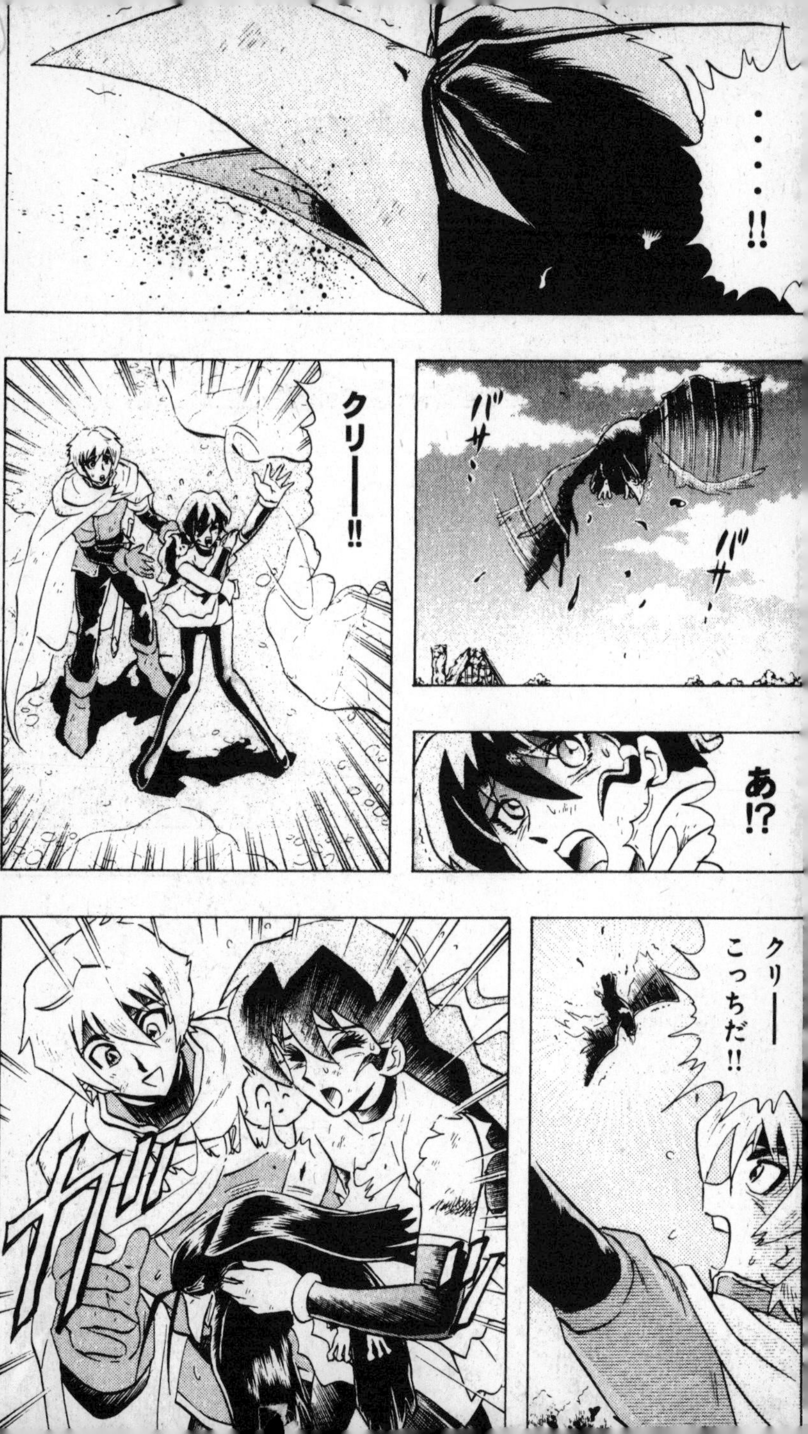
・・・・!!
バサ・・
バサ・・
あ!?
クリーー!!
クリーー
こっちだ!!

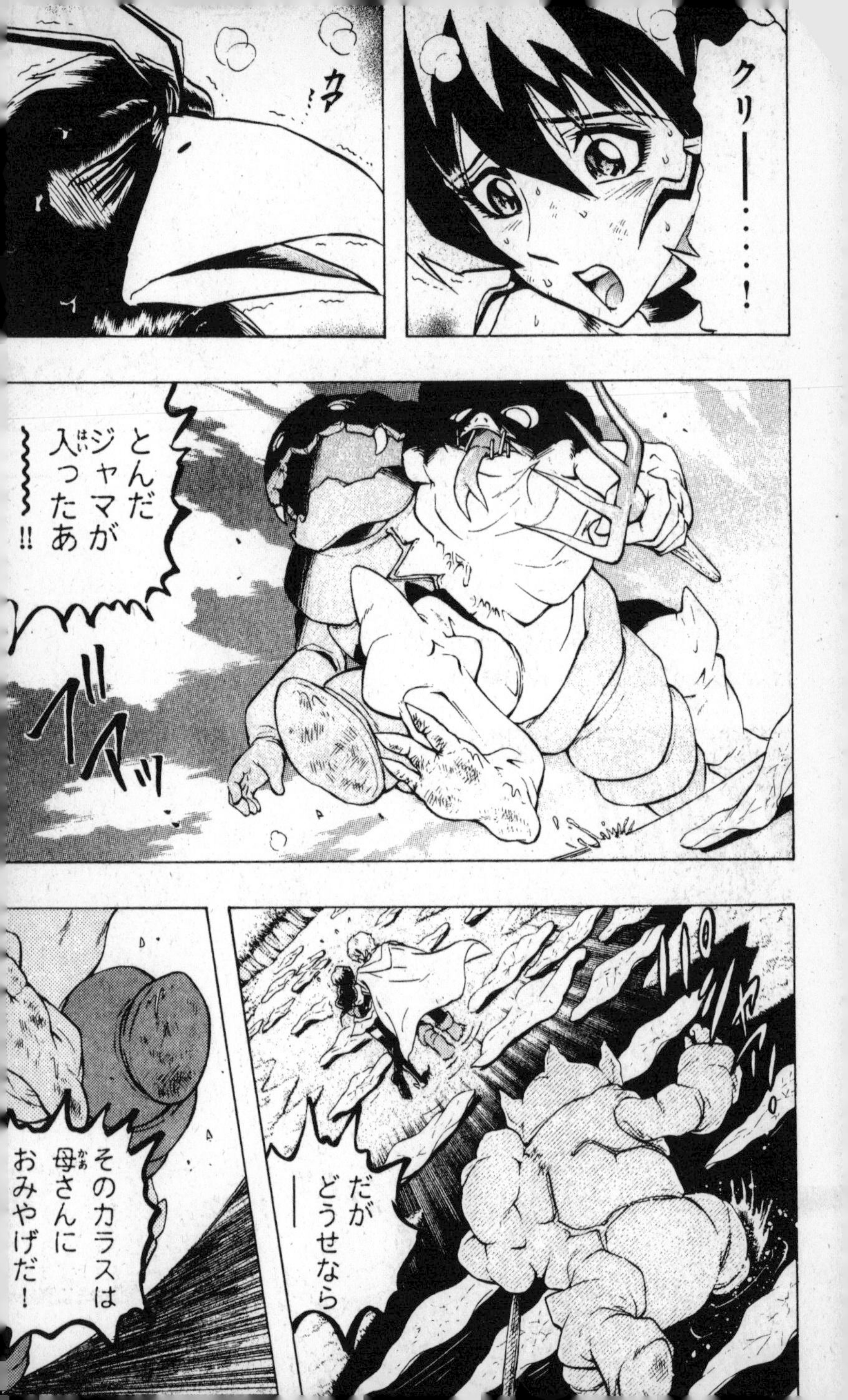
クリー……!
カ……
とんだジャマが入ったあ〜〜〜!!
だがどうせなら——
そのカラスは母さんにおみやげだ!

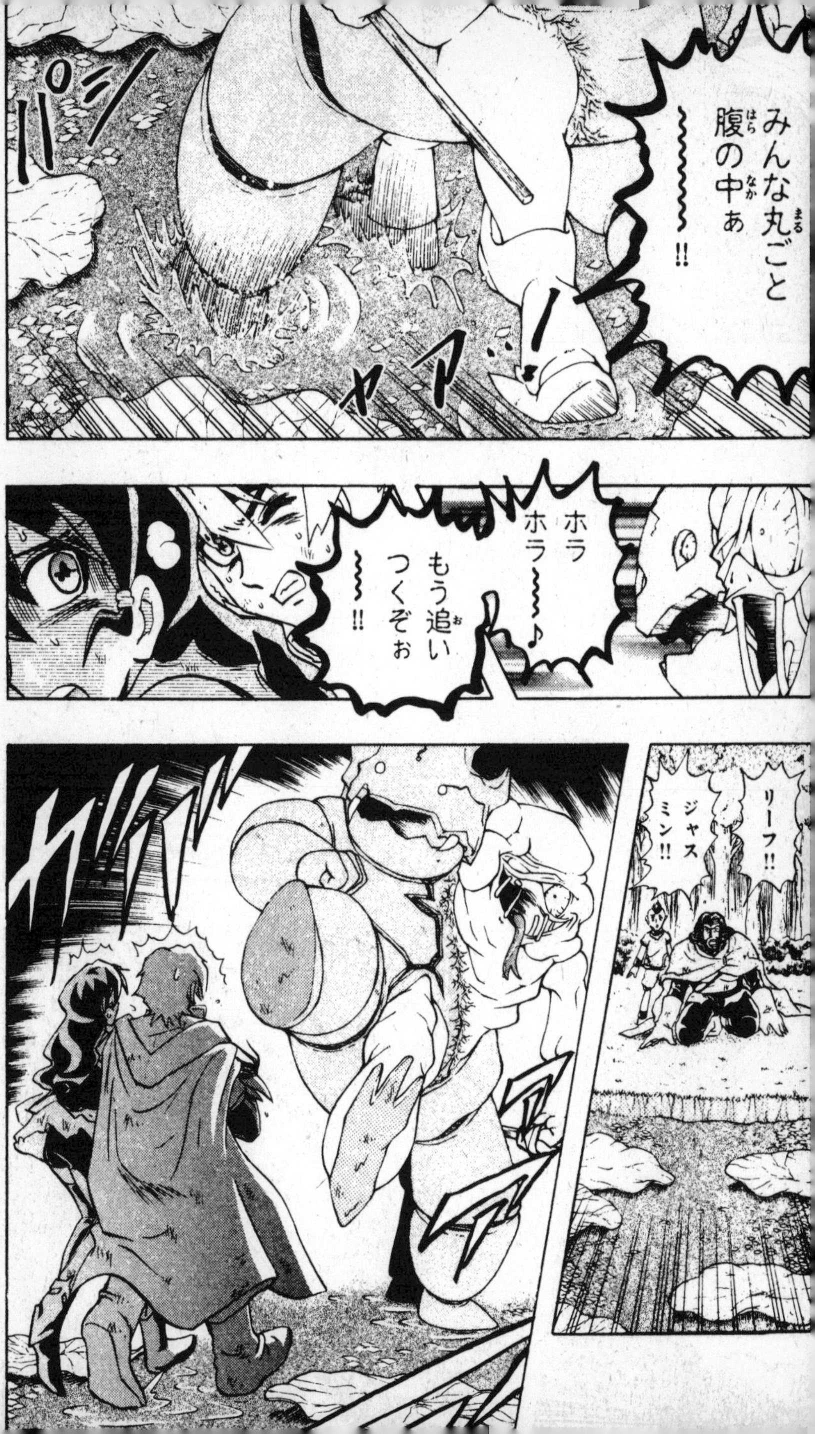
みんな丸ごと腹の中ぁ〜〜〜!!
ホラホラ〜〜〜♪
もう追いつくぞぉ〜〜〜!!
リーフ!!
ジャスミン!!

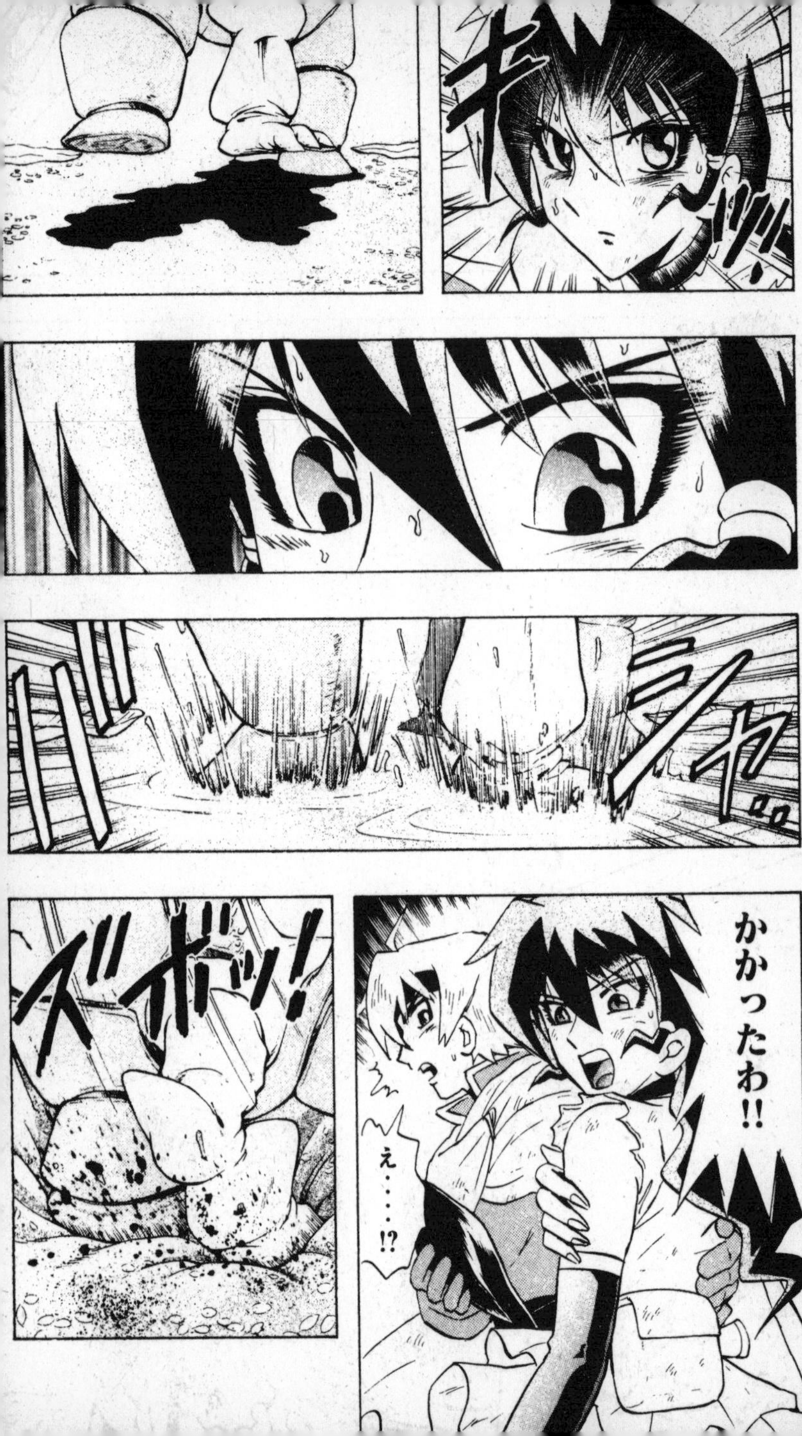
キッ!!
シャ。。
かかったわ!!
え・・・・!?
ズボッ!

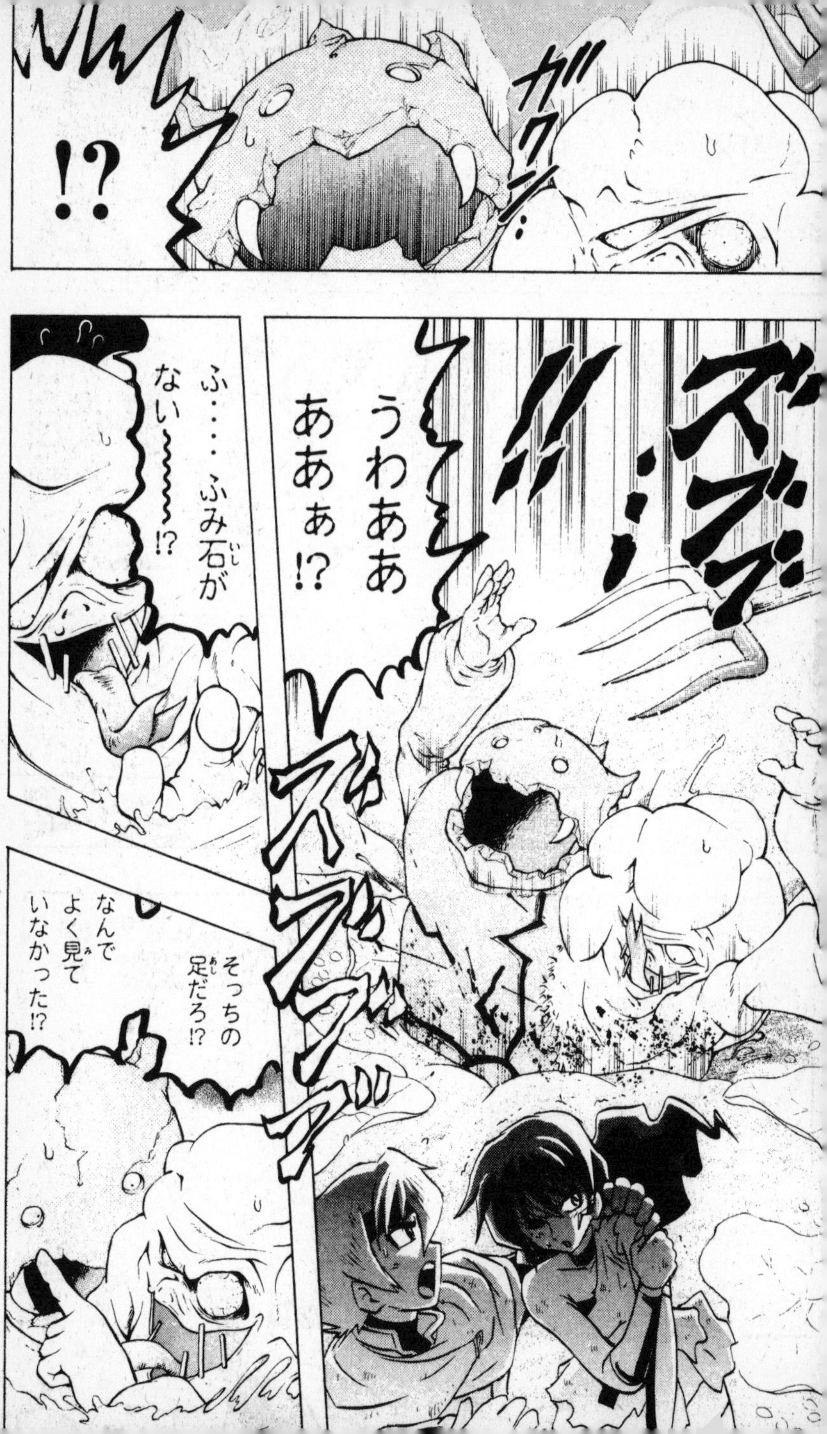
ガクン…
!?
ズブブ…!!
うわああああぁぁ!?
ふ…ふみ石がない〜〜!?
そっちの足だろ!?
なんでよく見ていなかった!?

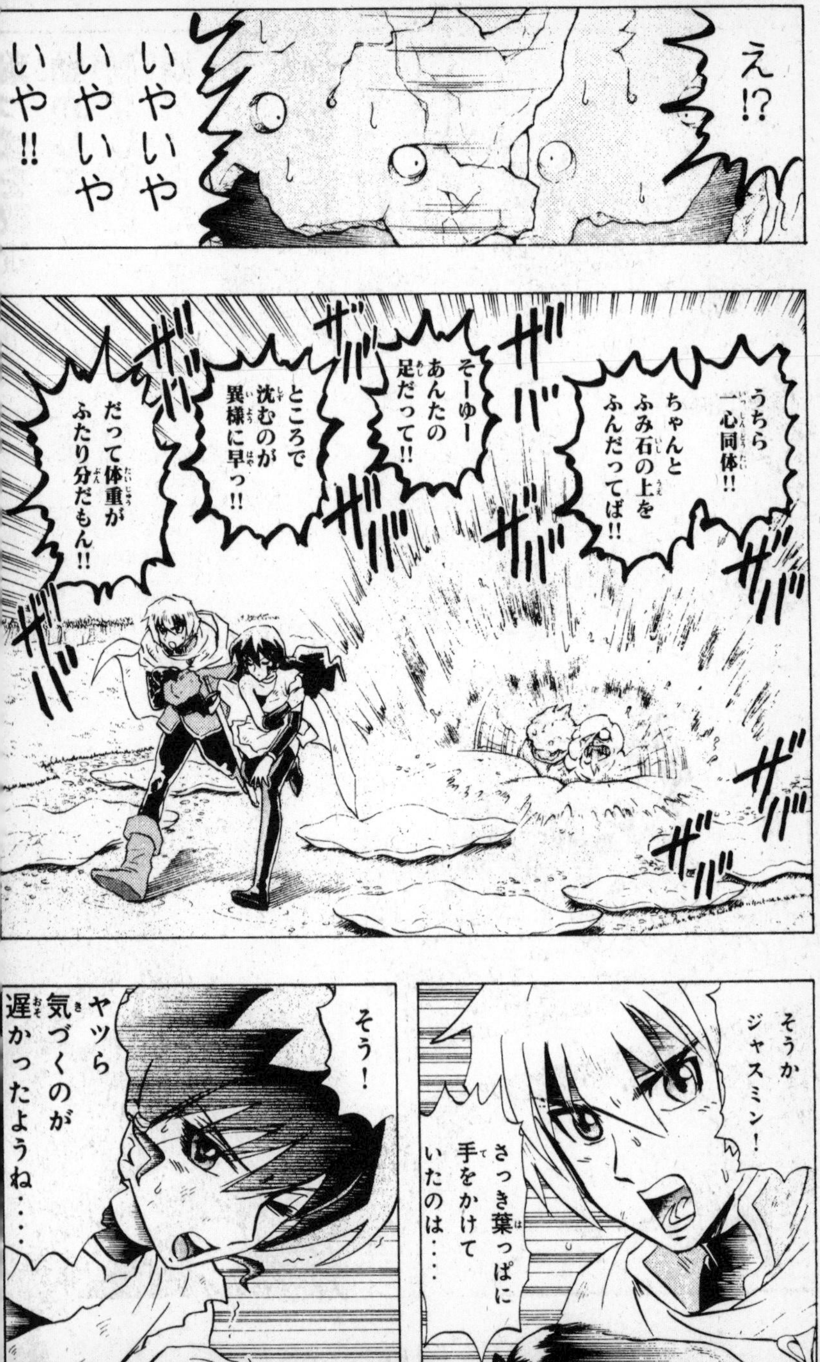
え!?
いやいやいやいやいや!!
うちら一心同体!!
ちゃんとふみ石の上をふんだってば!!
そーゆーあんたの足だって!!
ところで沈むのが異様に早っ!!
だって体重がふたり分だもん!!
そうかジャスミン!
さっき葉っぱに手をかけていたのは・・・
そう!
ヤツら気づくのが遅かったようね・・・・

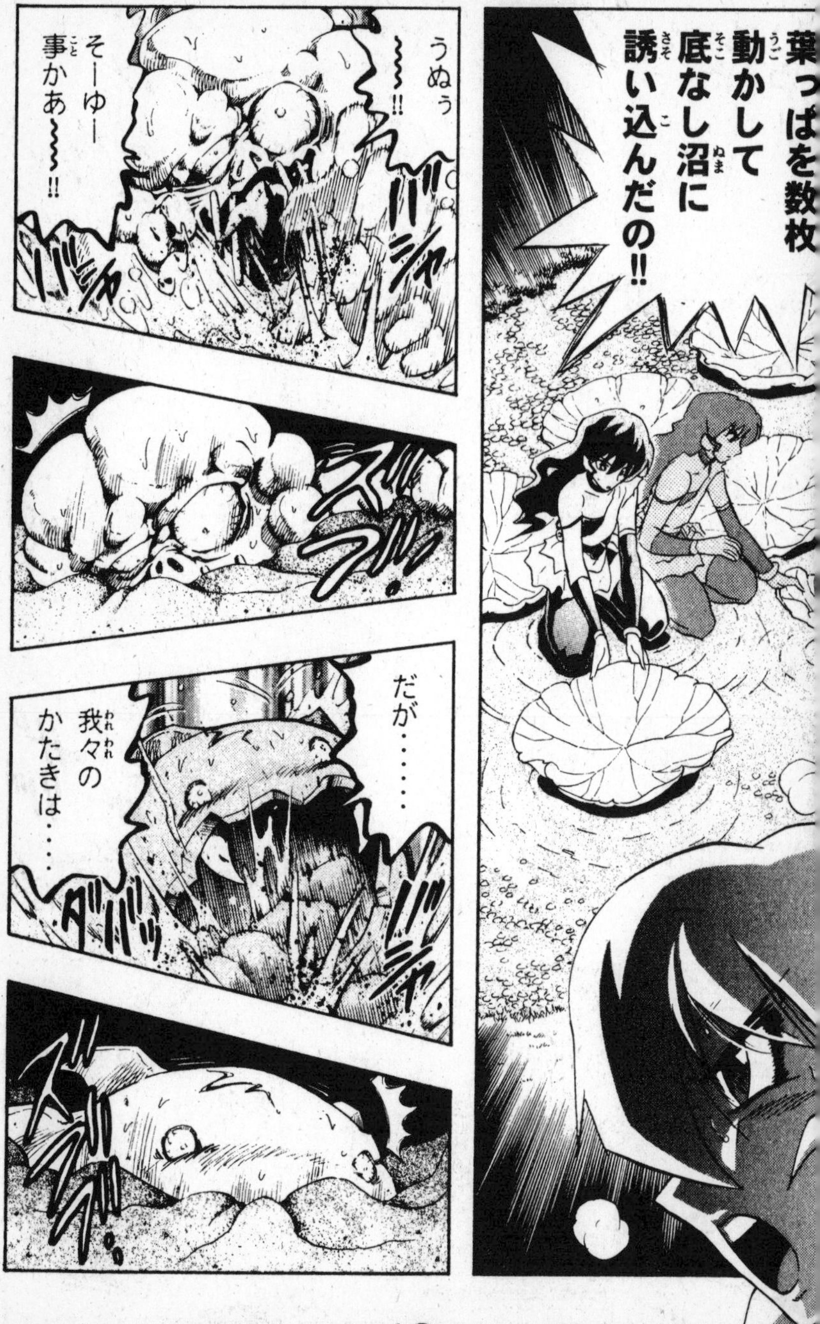

葉っぱを数枚動かして底なし沼に誘い込んだの!!
うぬう〜〜〜!!
そーゆー事かあ〜〜〜!!
バシャ
バシャ
だが……
我々のかたきは……
ダバッ
バシャ

ANIMAL LAND

BY MAKOTO RAIKU

In a world of animals, where the strong eat the weak, Monoko the tanuki stumbles across a strange creature the likes of which has never been seen before–a human baby! While the newborn has no claws or teeth to protect itself, it does have the special ability to speak to and understand all different animals. Can the gift of speech between species change the balance of power in a land where the weak must always fear the strong?

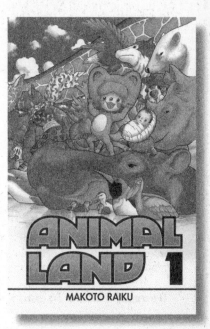

ANIMAL LAND 1

MAKOTO RAIKU

Ages 13+

VISIT KODANSHACOMICS.COM TO:

- View release date calendars for upcoming volumes
- Find out the latest about upcoming Kodansha Comics series

© Makoto Raiku / KODANSHA LTD. All rights reserved.

FROM HIRO MASHIMA, CREATOR OF **RAVE MASTER**

Lucy has always dreamed of joining the Fairy Tail, a club for the most powerful sorcerers in the land. But once she becomes a member, the fun really starts!

Special extras in each volume! Read them all!

RATING T AGES 13+

VISIT WWW.KODANSHACOMICS.COM TO:
• View release date calendars for upcoming volumes
• Find out the latest about new Kodansha Comics series

Fairy Tail © Hiro Mashima / KODANSHA LTD. All rights reserved.

TOMARE!

[STOP!]

You are going the wrong way!

Manga is a completely different type of reading experience.

To start at the *beginning*, go to the *end*!

That's right! Authentic manga is read the traditional Japanese way—from right to left, exactly the opposite of how American books are read. It's easy to follow: Just go to the other end of the book, and read each page—and each panel—from the right side to the left side, starting at the top right. Now you're experiencing manga as it was meant to be.